Beyond the Subtitle

Beyond the Subtitle

Remapping European Art Cinema

MARK BETZ

University of Minnesota Press

Minneapolis

London

An earlier version of chapter 2 was published as "The Name of the (Sub)title: Internationalism, Coproduction, and Polyglot European Art Cinema," *Camera Obscura* 46, vol. 16, no. 1 (2001); reprinted with permission from Duke University Press. Parts of chapter 4 were published as "Film History, Film Genre, and Their Discontents: The Case of the Omnibus Film," *The Moving Image* 1, no. 2 (2001): 57–87.

Published by the University of Minnesota Press
111 Third Avenue South, Suite 290
Minneapolis, MN 55401-2520
http://www.upress.umn.edu

Library of Congress Cataloging-in-Publication Data

Betz, Mark.
    Beyond the subtitle : remapping European art cinema / Mark Betz.
        p. cm.
    Includes bibliographical references and index.
    ISBN 978-0-8166-4035-5 (hc : alk. paper) — ISBN 978-0-8166-4036-2 (pb : alk. paper)
    1. Motion pictures—Europe—History—20th century. I. Title.
    PN1993.5.E8B48 2009
    791.43′0940904—dc22

                                                    2008046571

Printed in the United States of America on acid-free paper

The University of Minnesota is an equal-opportunity educator and employer.

18 17 16 15 14 13 12 11 10 09   10 9 8 7 6 5 4 3 2 1

Contents

Acknowledgments

As with many first books, the history of this one is entwined with my own personal and intellectual development. More people than can be named have contributed to it, and acknowledging them all would be impossible. But tracing a bit of that history and noting those who have played significant roles are important, as this book would not be what it is without them.

While my interest in cinema long preceded any scholarly study of it, my years spent at the University of Manitoba were foundational as they introduced new ways of experiencing and thinking and writing about films—in fact, new ways to be fascinated by them, and so needing to think and write about them. Much of the spirit of this book owes a debt to my first teachers of film: Frank Burke, Steve Snyder, Gene Walz, and especially George Toles, on whom nothing is lost.

A ten-year stint in Rochester, New York, proved the cauldron for many of the ideas and their original drafting into a large-scale study of European art cinema. My graduate education at the University of Rochester, as guided by Kaja Silverman, Constance Penley, John Michael, Thomas DiPiero, Sharon Willis, Jan-Christopher Horak, and Lisa Cartwright, has directed this work in untold ways, as have the convivial discussions and countless generosities of the friendships forged during my time there, particularly with Mark Lynn Anderson, Michele Balze, Mark Berrettini, Matthew Brown, Robert Cagle, Ed Chan, Lalitha Gopalan, Kelly Hankin, Dave Headlam, Amy Herzog, Bethany Hicok, Amanda Howell, Grant Kester, Jonathan Miller, Tina Takemoto, Swen Voekel, Anna Williams, and Daniela Zanzotto. A George Eastman House Graduate Fellowship opened wide the portals to an archive and a world I would encourage all to visit. The practically unlimited access I was granted to the Eastman House's collections, library, and people over a period of more than three years has left its stamp on this book in ways both indelible and unfathomable; I am thankful to Chris Horak, Paolo Cherchi Usai, and Ed Stratmann, among many others, for showing me an archivist's understanding of the medium and its history, as well as for supporting my own research activities (whether or not they were in strict accord with my programming duties).

Other archives and individuals have benefited this book over the years. Charles Silver and Ron Magliozzi have been great resources, as has the Museum of Modern Art's Film Study Center. Untold hours were spent poring through the files and collections of the Performing Arts Research Library and the Billy Rose Theatre Collection of the New York Public Library (both at Lincoln Center); the Margaret Herrick Library and the Academy Film Archive, Beverly Hills; the Harvard Film Archive; and the Special Collections and National Film Library of the British Film Institute. My appreciation and thanks go to the staffs of these collections.

Conversations with and good humor provided by associates at the University of Alberta, especially Bill Beard, Aniko Bodroghkozy, Chris Gittings, Gamal Abdel-Shehid, Maria Ng, Paul Robberecht, and Anne Whitelaw, were helpful during a transition phase of this work. I am grateful to several colleagues at King's College London for their support as I finished research and writing, particularly Stephanie Green, Sarah Cooper, Michele Pierson, Richard Dyer, and Ginette Vincendeau. King's College provided me with two small research grants for overseas research, as well as a one-term sabbatical leave. Students at both institutions were constantly inspirational, and I especially thank those who challenged my positions on art cinema—I can only hope they found our classes and discussions as engaging as I have.

The same holds true for the many audiences at conferences and public lectures to whom I have presented portions of this research. Conferences include the Ohio University Film Conference, the Screen Studies Conference in Glasgow, and several annual meetings of the Film Studies Association of Canada and the Society for Cinema and Media Studies. Lectures were given at the University of Kent Canterbury, the University of Nottingham, University College London, the University of Sussex, Shih Hsin University in Taipei, and National Chiao Tung University, Hsinchu, Taiwan. I am grateful to Kien Ket Lim for inviting me to Taiwan and for making that unforgettable trip possible.

I would like to recognize other colleagues and friends who have contributed valuable advice, feedback, or assistance at different moments of this project: Dominique Bluher, Jonathan Buchsbaum, Liz Czach, Kay Dickinson, Rosalind Galt, Mark Jancovich, Ernest Mathijs, Laura Mulvey, Geoffrey Nowell-Smith, John David Rhodes, Sara Ross, Christel Schmidt, and Haidee Wasson. Dana Polan's critical comments on the manuscript were very helpful, as were the reports prepared by Peter Brunette, whose suggestions and advocacy for the book proved invaluable in the revision process. Lee Grieveson has been a playful and serious critic of my work for the past several years, and his camaraderie through some hard graft warrants special mention. Three close personal friends, along with my family, have lived with this book hovering over me for too many years, and I treasure their warmth and understanding: Derek Brueckner, Bruce McCulloch, and Derrick Larsen, my siblings Michele, Vaughn, Patrick, and Grant, and my parents Isabel and Bill.

I appreciate the confidence and support of the good people at the University of Minnesota Press who patiently prodded me through the editing and production processes of the book, especially copy editor Nancy Sauro and my editor Jason Weidemann. The glorious cover still was generously furnished by Ginette Vincendeau from her own collection. Markos Hadjioannou provided valuable and considerable help with the index.

Four individuals in my life and my work have loomed large during the book's origins and completion. David Rodowick was a mentor, a friend, and a tireless supporter of this project, never failing to encourage me through the valleys and devoting much time and energy to reading and discussing its various guises; his influence and guidance are immeasurable. My cherished friendships with Heather Hendershot and John Palattella date back nearly twenty years and are abiding; their boundless acumen, bonhomie, and generosity have been instrumental. Finally, I would never have been able to see the book through without the careful reading of the manuscript given by Rosemary Barrow, whose example, patience, and belief ensured its completion and continue to sustain me beyond.

Recovering European Art Cinema

To articulate the past historically does not mean to recognize it
"the way it really was" (Ranke). It means to seize hold of a memory
as it flashes up at a moment of danger.

—WALTER BENJAMIN, "Theses on the Philosophy of History"

Whither Art Cinema?

IN FEBRUARY 1996, following a year of celebrations marking the centenary of cinema, a two-page article in the *New York Times Magazine*
mourned the passing of a particular era in the first one hundred years
of the medium's history. Penned by Susan Sontag, "The Decay of Cinema" recalls with bittersweet melancholy an age of cinephilia "born
of the conviction that cinema was an art unlike any other: quintes-
sentially modern; distinctively accessible; poetic and mysterious and
erotic and moral—all at the same time. For cinephiles, the movies
encapsulated everything. Cinema was both the book of art and the
book of life."[1] The cinephilia Sontag describes "became a passion
among university students and other young people" who shared "not
simply love of but a certain *taste* in films," most particularly those
that succeeded in resolving the "conflict between cinema as an industry and cinema as an art, cinema as routine and cinema as experiment." As a contrast to this era of practically unbridled worship at the
altar of cinematic art—the religious metaphor is explicitly woven into
the prose—Sontag juxtaposes the present, wherein films are no longer
watched on theater screens but televisual ones, conditions that "are
radically disrespectful to film"; wherein "the unprincipled manipulation of images . . . has produced a disincarnated, lightweight cinema"
lost in a sea of moving images that "has steadily undermined the standards people once had both for cinema as art and cinema as popular
entertainment"; wherein "the lowering of expectations for quality and
the inflation of expectations for profit" have made it all but impossible

for "artistically ambitious" directors "to work at their best level" and rendered "the idea of the film as, first of all, a poetic object" as "something quaint, outmoded, snobbish." Her elegy concludes with a muted call for "the birth of a new kind of cine-love" at the close of the twentieth century to revivify what has become "a decadent art."

Sontag's *New York Times Magazine* piece, subsequently expanded in a journal article and a short book chapter,[2] is a cogent evocation of a certain version of film culture's investments as well as its take on the history of the cinema: one suffused with wonder, mystery, pleasure, and now nostalgia for a declining art form; one rooted in an almost exclusively aesthetic regard for its love object; one concerned with the exceptional rather than the usual, with the rare rather than the ordinary, with "masterpieces"—even if there were new ones every month. It is also a history that is of central interest to this book, concerning as it does the international profile once enjoyed by European art cinema. Indeed, when Sontag refers to the third quarter of the twentieth century as "the feverish age of moviegoing," especially the fifteen-year period from the late 1950s to the early 1970s, she is making a qualitative rather than quantitative statement for the United States in particular, for during this time the total number of American cinemagoers was continuing a steady decline that began after its peak year of 1946, a decline that the national film industries of Europe would also soon encounter. Moviegoing during this period was not "feverish" for mass audiences but for a specialized one for whom attending the cinema was not a recreational but a cultural, even intellectual activity; films directed by Roberto Rossellini, Bernardo Bertolucci, and Jean-Luc Godard, the three European directors Sontag names, were considered by this audience as works "of the highest seriousness." For the most part, it is this audience that formed the parameters upon which such films and their meanings were and continue largely to be based. In other words, a certain kind of film culture was fostered in the first three postwar decades (and reached its apogee in European art cinema of the 1960s) that has shaped our understanding of cinema ever since. For during this decade the idea that filmmaking was a personal form of artistic expression combined with the international marketing of European films in ways that distinguished the latter as more than mere commercial entertainments—and in ways that have indelibly stamped both the history of the cinema and the practices of Anglo-American academic film studies.

This film culture, as Sontag so succinctly summarized in 1996 and thirty years earlier had participated in as an advocate and exegete of several European art films and directors, would seem to be in its final death throes.[3] The recent publication of three books on cinephilia, however, is one indication that this is not the case; rather, the particular type of cinephilia Sontag mourns has been transformed by new technologies at the same time as its initial impulses have been maintained.[4] In the contemporary film festival world it is largely the cinemas of Asia and Eastern Central Europe that continue to produce art cinema, now denoted as "world cinema," with filmmakers like Hou Hsiao-hsien, Tsai Ming-liang, Zhang Ke-jia, Abbas Kiarostami, Jafar Panahi, Andrei Sokurov, Béla Tarr, and Nuri Bilge Ceylan continuing to make challenging films based on the long-take aesthetic favored by Sontag.

As well, the picture changes considerably if the focus of inquiry is expanded to include objects other than films or their auteurs. In the true spirit of the cinephile, Sontag pits cinema as an art against cinema as an industry and bemoans the "melancholy fate of some of the greatest directors of the last decades" as profit margins have eclipsed more noble aesthetic aspirations. In Sontag's estimation, "original, passionate films," their artistically ambitious makers, and knowledgeable, tasteful spectators were the prime ingredients constituting the rise of cinephilia, and they are still now the only hope for halting its decay. But it is possible to offer a different history of film culture in this era, one that might regard films and their directors as something less than the most important components in a network of forces contributing to film culture in its broadest sense. For to examine the historical status of European art cinema and film culture, one must consider what most determines the ways in which its films and filmmakers are received by audiences: written and spoken discourses on or about cinema, including academic scholarship and teaching. In this sense, I understand the institutions devoted to the study, the *appreciation* of the cinema in both meanings of the word, as being very much alive. What is dead, however, is the particular object of Sontag's age of cinephilia: European art cinema as an intellectual, even viably commercial force on contemporary American and British screens.

To understand why this is so, it is necessary first to examine briefly what appeal art cinema held for its audiences, the preferred ways in which its formal experiment and difficulty were interpreted, what it was about these European films of the 1960s that so excited "university students and other young people." Anglo-American academic interest in art cinema never reached a groundswell approaching the level of cinephilia that Sontag has described, and the reasons for this require explication as well. But before turning to the academic side of things, I want to stay for the moment close to the languages of art cinema's time, for it is in these that the framework for its understanding was established and continues to inhere. I want, in other words, to keep an eye on what Sontag so passionately loved. In doing so I will indicate some long-standing interrelations between film culture and academic film studies, both during and after the great age of European art cinema and cinephilia—interrelations that have yet to be adequately explored.

What did art cinema mean for its audiences? The answers to this question are as varied as the approaches and agendas of the film spectators, critics, scholars, and historians who have asked it—and in this they are perfectly in line with the quality of "open" textuality so often invoked in discussions of art films and art cinema. In the context of the modern Italian cinema of the 1960s, the film historian Pierre Sorlin reports: "Contemporary audiences were interested and puzzled, they wondered what these works were about. There was no answer to their query. However, it could have been argued that the films were about time, about cinema and about spectators."[5] Time, cinema, spectatorship: to these must be added authorship, in my estimation a crucial fourth term and in fact the anchor that holds the others from swirling off into undecidability. If art cinema is about itself—the variable spatial and temporal organizations of its design (form), the aesthetic heritage that serves as its animus and to which it so frequently refers (cinema), the space and experience of viewing (spectatorship)—this circuit of potential meanings nonetheless achieves ultimate resonance through the signature of its director/creator (authorship). To understand an art film, at least on its own terms, is to recognize its status as a self-referential aesthetic production, a system of motifs, allusions, and devices that the director combines to create a complex world of signs.

Time in modern European cinema is frequently held as the hallmark of its particular formal innovations in narration and storytelling. Unlike classical cinema—with its rather strict and elaborate set of rules that presuppose and reinforce a stable viewing position through a steady flow of differing views of time, space, and character in accordance with conventions of linear causality, continuity, and narrative—art cinema works the extremes of the temporal-spatial-narrative continuum, testing the boundaries among foregrounded aesthetic construction, spectatorial engagement, and narrative intelligibility. The filmic registration and manipulation of time is in fact, as Gilles Deleuze has famously proposed, the key factor in the operation of modern cinema.[6] In certain films time is compressed through editing so as to evoke a world of abrupt change, shock, and speed, as in the famous jump cuts that punctuate the driving sequences in Jean-Luc Godard's *A bout de souffle* (*Breathless,* 1960), most particularly the solo ride Jean-Paul Belmondo/ Michel takes in a newly stolen car at the beginning of the film that results in his unplanned murder of a motorcycle cop and sets the tempo for the remainder of the drama, with Michel contradictorily on the lam by openly traversing the daylit streets of Paris, waiting for love and money as the ineffectual forces of law and order nevertheless close in. Assembled in an intensely present tense, Alain Resnais's *Muriel ou le temps d'un retour* (*Muriel,* 1963) concentrates time in its second and fourth acts through the extraordinarily tight sequencing of brief shots whose juxtaposition suggests simultaneity of action and spatial separation. The narrative line is thus advanced in fits and starts, evoking the pulsions and flashes of memory through a rigorous strategy of presentation that shows spaces marked by and characters obsessed with the past, but only in snatches of an incessantly retreating present.

More often, however, the sum produced by adding the variables "time" and "art film" is "slow." In the languid, seemingly directionless trajectories of much of European art cinema, the question of meaning is even more achingly evoked. As plot winds down and character motivation becomes null, the so-called dead time *(temps mort)* and apparently empty narrative spaces of art cinema may create discomfort for viewers who, accustomed to clearly motivated action or dialogue or movement, feel pressured to fill the image with their own thoughts or mental images. The noisy reception that greeted Michelangelo Antonioni's *L'avventura* when it was screened publicly in 1960 at the Cannes Film Festival demonstrated, through the chorus of shouting and whistling and the cries of "Cut!" punctuating the film's long takes and silences, the festival audience's impatience with the film's unhurried tempo.[7] It also marked the arrival on the international film scene of a figure who has since served as an archetype for the cerebral and contemplative (as opposed to instinctual and dynamic) art film director.

But such films were not without their viewing pleasures for those willing to take the time. The moments of spatial or temporal excess, unjustified by the narrative requirements of the story, could become justified and rendered meaningful through the active engagement of the spectator. And in the heyday of art cinema there were plenty of viewers up for the challenge, not just a small coterie of cinema specialists; *L'avventura* went on to successful runs in major cities internationally. Even at Cannes, Antonioni was not without his defenders. Many of the influential critics and industry personnel present rallied to his defense by drafting and presenting him with a collective statement of admiration and support.[8] Six years later, Christian Metz would write that Antonioni's cinema was

> a new—and a profoundly original—appreciation of what is or is not a "dull moment" in life, and it is not based on a mere aesthetics of space that is filmically "dead." Innovation is an ideological rather than a cinematographic matter, and Antonioni is "modern" far more because of the human substance of his films than because of their "language." He excels in showing us the diffuse significance of those moments of everyday life that are considered insignificant; integrated within the film, the dull moment is reborn to our perception.[9]

As the examples of the Cannes screening and the preceding quote demonstrate, separating time, cinematic knowledge, and spectatorship is difficult when considering the conventions of meaning evoked and addressed by art cinema. The durational time of the films of Antonioni, Resnais, and Robert Bresson is, as John Orr describes it, "mesmeric, hypnotic, a magnet to the gaze even when its narrative appears endless, directionless, indeterminate."[10] But it is also a time that, by its very elongation, draws attention to cinematic mise-en-scène and the tacit contract that exists between the narrative film and its spectator. What is modern about this cinema is its renegotiation of that contract, its formal mimicry of the subjective experience of time—as flying, as dragging—the cinematic representation of which invites, compels the viewer to reflect on the time of the film itself and, by association, cinema itself.

Dudley Andrew has tendered a claim for the French New Wave as "the first movement in the history of cinema to take its inspiration quite openly from the history of cinema itself—rather than from the world or the broader culture." For Andrew, who singles out a scene inside a movie theater showing re-creations of early Lumière actualities in Godard's *Les Carabiniers* (1963), the French New Wave, indeed French cinema more generally, is preoccupied "more with the experience of cinema than with the world the cinema exhibits" and interested more "with the space of the movie theater and what can happen within it than with the magnificent and varied landscapes of France itself."[11] In a similar vein, Robert Phillip Kolker states the following of Resnais's *L'Année dernière à Marienbad* (1961): "What *Last Year at Marienbad* is 'about' is the way we look at film and the way film regards its subjects, the characters in it and the characters who watch it. It is about the creation of cinematic narrative and the conventions that have developed through the history of that creation."[12] To watch these films is to do more than appreciate their reflexivity toward the history of the cinema, toward themselves as aesthetic artifacts, and toward the theatrical space of their viewing; it is also to participate in their production of meaning.

This consensus in fact takes it cues from the critical writings of the period and often from the filmmakers themselves. Resnais's *Muriel,* for example, set in the aftermath of the long Algerian war, appears to be only marginally about Algeria and more centrally concerned with the French perception of Algeria as an imperfectly repressed memory. In this respect it is not so difficult to see why an analysis of the film might take the following steps: *Muriel* is not about Algeria, nor even about France; it is about Resnais, and as such, about cinema. In a critical roundtable published in *Cahiers du cinéma* in late 1963, the movement toward this position is an illuminating demonstration of what may be characterized as a preferred reading of modern cinema. Claude Ollier speaks at length near the beginning of the discussion as he extends the idea that *Muriel* is an "'expanded' sequel" to Resnais's previous film, "a *Marienbad* suddenly plunged into history. . . . In *Marienbad* you could tell yourself ultimately—it's a nightmare, it's all very beautiful, but that's it. While in *Muriel* you have Boulogne-sur-Mer, the France of lower middle-class Europe in all the colours of today's world, and it's the same nightmare."[13] The conversation quickly turns, however, toward a "purer" form of meaning interpretation, one centered not simply on the previous work of the film's director but quite literally inside the director himself, as in the following exchange between Jean-Louis Comolli and André S. Labarthe:

> [COMOLLI:] It would be a mistake to imagine that Resnais is trying to present a picture of the outside world, in whatever style, or even that he is interested in the outside world or in extrapolating some new logical system from it. . . . An investigation is under way all right, but it's turned on himself and what he ends up by discovering is himself. He is executing a self-portrait using the characters he interposes and disguised situations. So the pointers he gives, which are simply traces of Resnais himself, serve a purpose for him as much for us.
>
> LABARTHE: That's right. Because these characters are in the end all to some extent Resnais's fantasy of himself.
>
> COMOLLI: All the characters in the film are Resnais.[14]

For the rest of the conversation, any efforts to analyze the film in relation to France (let alone Algeria) or the particularities of its images, its narrative, or its historical moment and place are tabled in favor of more generalized musings about Resnais's worldview or about the collective totality of new European cinema. The roundtable thus enacts precisely the repression that is at least one of the film's levels of address. More important, it represents a dominant reading strategy for art cinema, one that retreats "from the world or the broader culture" in favor of authorship and critical biography.

In effect, this interpretive line limits the outcomes for active viewing that modern European cinema provokes and enables. Within an economy that regards the director as both generator and locus of meaning, viewers of the art film are encouraged to reflect any enlightenment they might receive back onto the director in a closed circuit of mutual yet hierarchical exchange.[15] In its most extreme manifestations of unbridled evaluative enthusiasm, the brilliance of the director is magnified with every critical reflection, and the spectator/reader illuminated in the pale light of the afterglow. Writing on *Last Year at Marienbad* for *Cahiers du cinéma* in 1961, Labarthe places it next to Orson Welles's *Citizen Kane* (1941) and Rossellini's *Paisà* (1946) as examples of modern films that no longer offer "predigested material ready for absorption. On the contrary, they present the spectator with raw material (even if it has in fact been heavily worked on) from which he may extract his *own* film. . . . The true successor of the traditional film-maker is not Resnais or Robbe-Grillet, but the spectator of *Marienbad.*"[16] The line between film criticism and filmmaking—a line already literally crossed by several of Labarthe's colleagues at *Cahiers*— is here presented as one that the act of film viewing itself can collapse. In short, the critical aim is to become one with the film's creator.

While recognizing a certain elegance in this particular analytical line, I must also point out that it is bound by a closed circuit of exchange between text, spectatorship, and director. Apart from their Ouroboros-like qualities, such readings must be seen from a historical perspective as having by and large exhausted their critical usefulness as concerns postwar European art cinema, given not only their destination but also their ubiquity—it is difficult to conceive of any new knowledges to be advanced by them. I am therefore not in this book taking the position that art cinema's meaning is ultimately or even predominantly a thematic or an aesthetic one limited to individual films, to their makers, or to the moments in the history of cinema to which they might refer, nor even to the individual national cinemas with which most art films and directors are associated and understood to represent. These are nonetheless powerful discursive positions subtending critical and historical work on European art cinema in Anglo-American academic film studies today.

In what ways has film studies analyzed and/or historicized art cinema? Before answering this question, one must address why art cinema is more or less synonymous in the field with a particular outpouring of narrative films from Europe in the postwar era. Haidee Wasson has noted how the phrase "film art" can invoke

very different assumptions about aesthetics, practice, and politics. Terms such as *foreign cinema, experimental film, avant-garde cinema, art cinema, modernist cinema,* and *classical Hollywood cinema* can all be considered subcategories of the more general category of film art. Each refers to a very different configuration of what film art might be. A term might identify a film as art based on a particular mode of production, a national origin, or a specialized mode of exhibition. The idea of art cinema might be underpinned by formal principles based on modernist theories of disruption. It might describe a group of films, made and seen at a particular point in history, circumscribed by common formal features and points of origin (German expressionism, French New Wave). Some scholars have suggested

that film art is best understood as a generic strategy designed to counter
Hollywood's reign or American international dominance. Some people use
the term to indicate films they like a lot.[17]

While the variables "film" and "art" yield a panoply of responses, tastes,
and specialized terms, those of "art" and "cinema" present a more circumscribed terrain: a distinct set of formal properties or a style of narration linked to modernist aesthetics; a body of films that cohere by
period and national origin and are designed to distinguish themselves
from or compete with Hollywood cinema by being different from it.
In Anglo-American film culture, these two possibilities have congealed
so that art cinema overwhelmingly refers to a volume of narrative
films produced in Europe from the late 1950s through the mid-1970s
that share modernist formal traits, distinguishable in terms of their
respective national movements and designed to counter Hollywood
dominance on screens in Europe and abroad, including the United
States itself. In other words, art cinema is both a formal–aesthetic category and a national–institutional one, historically and geographically
locatable to postwar Europe, especially the 1960s.

How film studies has analyzed and/or historicized art cinema is inseparable from these overlapping categories, which have been ampli-
fied by two influential articles published within two years of one
another at the turn of the 1980s: David Bordwell's "The Art Cinema
as a Mode of Film Practice" (1979) and Steve Neale's "Art Cinema as
Institution" (1981).[18] While neither article contains the word "European" in its title, the examples they use concentrate largely (Bordwell)
or entirely (Neale) on the films or cinemas of Europe, France and Italy
in particular. They have become the two touchstone texts on art cinema as a discursive field in Anglo-American film studies, the evidence
of which can be seen in two key collections: *The Oxford History of
World Cinema,* which contains an essay titled "Art Cinema" in its final
section that concentrates on European cinemas of the 1960s; and *The
European Cinema Reader,* which includes a subsection on art cinema
in its third part, "European Films and Theory," comprising only Bordwell's and Neale's articles.[19] Indeed, my own understanding of European art cinema and deployment of that term derives in many ways
from the positions articulated in these pieces.[20]

In "The Art Cinema as a Mode of Film Practice," Bordwell distinguishes art cinema from "classical narrative cinema" and "modernist

cinema."[21] If classical Hollywood cinema motivates itself on the cause-effect linkage of events to tell a coherent story, art cinema motivates its narrative by two principles: realism and authorial expressivity. For Bordwell, art cinema "softened modernism's attack of narrative causality by creating mediating structures," such as objective and subjective verisimilitude and character subjectivity, neither of which are requirements for modernism.[22] Importantly, art cinema presents itself as a realist cinema. Classical cinema does not depend on realism per se but verisimilitude, "the appearance of being true or real," with this appearance being tied not to the "real world" that its spectators live in and themselves live but to a plausible fictional world whose conventions depend largely on the genre of the film and not natural laws. By contrast, art cinema shows us real locations and real problems and "uses realistic—that is, psychologically complex—characters." Like classical cinema, art cinema is centrally concerned with characters and their effects on one another. But unlike classical cinema, art cinema presents characters without clearly defined goals or desires. As a result, the art film's "attempt to pronounce judgement on 'modern life' as a whole thus proceeds from its formal needs: had the characters a goal, life would no longer seem so meaningless."[23]

The psychological emphasis of much art cinema means that its causation is equally psychological rather than story-driven: "art cinema is less concerned with action than reaction"; cause-effect logic is attenuated in favor of slow, reflective causation.[24] This adds to the realism of art cinema in terms of its salient stylistic traits: long takes, real-time exposition with *temps mort,* a characteristic slowness of pace; or jump cuts, montage that mixes up story order, fast motion, freeze frames, or other violations of "real time" to express the psychological experience of characters and their actions or reactions. But art cinema also foregrounds the author—the director—"as a structure in the film's system" of operations, a "formal component" of the film, "the overriding intelligence organizing the film for our comprehension." The art film thus "uses a concept of authorship to unify the text." The viewer of an art film is expected then to be at least familiar with the general principle of the director as auteur and preferably with the particular stylistic signatures of the director in question, as every film "offers itself as a chapter in an *ouvre [sic],*" an ongoing artistic project.[25] What these two contrary impulses—realism, authorial expressivity—lead to ultimately is *ambiguity,* for Bordwell the key attribute of art cinema. Breaks in classical narration can be interpreted as a move on the part of the film toward greater realism or overt authorial commentary or both. The open textual quality of art films, their extending of themselves as something to be read, is a function of such ambiguity.

Two years after Bordwell, Steve Neale provided the most detailed explication that Anglo-American film studies has to date of European art cinema as a set of institutional forces. In "Art Cinema as Institution" he defines art cinema as a series of historically and nationally situated attempts by "a number of European countries both to counter American domination of their indigenous markets in film and also to foster a film industry and a film culture of their own."[26] Certain nations of Europe deliberately aimed to put into circulation films that were distinct from those produced and distributed by the Hollywood studios so as to compete with them for their own audiences. This aim was activated on two complementary fronts: one ideological, the other economic/industrial. Following on from Bordwell, Neale observes that the formal features connoting realism in art cinema "function as the positive marks of Art" and that those that emphasize the hand of the director "engage the other primary ideology of Art, the Romantic view that Art is subjective expression."[27] The discourses of art and culture are thus woven into the formal operations of art cinema itself through its variety of expressive possibilities, but these are also "contained both by the economic infrastructure of Art Cinema, its basis in commodity-dominated modes of production, distribution, and exhibition, and by repetitions that tend to mark cultural discourses in general and the discourses of high art and culture in particular."[28] In other words, art films depend on long-standing ideas regarding art as individual and creative-expressive as well as the specific market for trading such ideas as artisanal objects. Here is where the economic/industrial front is key, particularly in the postwar era: the production and dissemination of art films depend on infrastructures provided by national institutions, both unofficial (ciné-clubs, magazines, journals) and official (quota legislation, taxes on foreign film receipts, subsidies, and other forms of state financial support). Interventions by industries and governments and the incentives for native productions of artistic value they provided were thus generative forces in the institutionalization of art cinema.

By way of concretization, Neale traces the instances of art cinema institutionalization in France, Germany, and Italy. The historical moments and movements range from the first French avant-garde and German expressionism in the 1920s to Italian neorealism in the late 1940s through early 1950s, to the French New Wave and the Italian film renaissance from the late 1950s through mid-1960s, to the New German cinema from the mid-1960s through mid-1970s. Neale establishes a pattern across this history, one that moves from early proletarian appeal to the development of a bourgeois audience in the 1910s, to the first protective legislations in the 1920s, to the postwar era, when "state support became firmly linked to the promotion and development of national Art Cinemas under the aegis of liberal-democratic and social democratic governments and under the pressure of the presence of America and Hollywood in Europe. The result was an efflorescence of Art Cinema, the production of the films and the figures and the movements with which Art Cinema tends massively to be associated today."[29] This efflorescence involved a balance "between a national aspect on the one hand and an international aspect on the other." The incursion of Hollywood films in Europe was perceived "as a specifically *national problem*," and art films bore the marks of their nationalities—language being the most important—in ways that served "further to differentiate them from the films produced in Hollywood."[30] At the same time, art cinema circulates internationally as a specialized or niche sector; it functions as "a mechanism of discrimination" for a particular class of audience existing across nations.[31] It is in this sense that art cinema itself can be understood as an institution.

Bordwell and Neale present two different approaches to art cinema as a distinct category of film style and production, one aesthetic and one economic/institutional. But it is their similarities rather than their differences that have proven the most abiding: that art cinema is fundamentally opposed to Hollywood cinema; that it constitutes a European response to Hollywood; and that its richest vein appeared in the postwar era, especially in the 1960s. While both authors consider art cinema as a broad category, these specificities are the ones that have been pursued in Anglo-American film studies in their wake. But other aspects of these articles have been even more influential. In the case of Bordwell's, the emphasis on formal textual structures and the importance of the director within those structures has yielded countless thematic/mise-en-scène analyses of individual (European) films and auteurs that constitute one of the main lines of art cinema scholarship. This course is a continuation of that practiced by critics at the time of art cinema's efflorescence, at home and abroad.[32] Indeed, Neale ends his piece with a plea to displace "two conceptions central to the institution of art cinema ... those of authorship on the one hand, and of the individual, self-contained work on the other," a plea that has gone largely unheeded.[33] The other main trajectory for art cinema scholarship proceeds from Neale, though here through the organization of his argument more so than the argument itself: he structures the historical instances of art cinema institutionalization in Europe not as a chronology but in three separate sections, each devoted to one national example—France, Italy, and Germany. Art cinema as cases of national productions exemplified by specific movements thus constitutes another huge body of scholarship, particularly historical/critical, in Anglo-American film studies. Again, the studies in this research line are countless.

What *is* countable is the number of book-length works published since the 1980s that analyze art cinema as a mode of film practice or as an institution, of which there are four: John Orr's *Cinema and Modernity* and Peter Lev's *The Euro-American Cinema* (both 1993), Barbara Wilinsky's *Sure Seaters: The Emergence of Art House Cinema* (2001), and Haidee Wasson's *Museum Movies: The Museum of Modern Art and the Birth of Art Cinema* (2005).[34] Orr's work takes the formal-aesthetic approach, offering largely explicative criticism of individual films and directors within the contexts of broad postwar social and thematic categories, though it also includes some American films and filmmakers and so does not limit itself to Europe. Lev's too includes American filmmaking, but in a more integrated way: he examines the phenomenon of the Euro-American art film coproduction, though mainly through case studies of individual films. While his work does address Euro-American art cinema as a mode of film practice to a certain extent, it favors an institutional line of analysis more. Wilinsky and Wasson follow this line as well, though in historical terms and increasingly in the American context. *Sure Seaters* discusses the growth of the art house exhibition circuit for foreign films in the United States as an alternative cultural formation, especially in the 1950s.[35] And *Museum Movies* undertakes an analysis of the transformation of cinema from an entertainment to an art form in America through close historical study of the central role played by New York's Museum of Modern Art Film Library in the development of nontheatrical exhibition.[36]

As these four books attest, the institutional approach has proven the more productive for in-depth analysis of art cinema as a category as opposed to more localized instances of it, whether a national film movement, a director's oeuvre, or individual films. At the same time, none of these books could be described as theoretical, and the latter three are unquestionably works of film history (and, in Wasson's case, of historiography). These three too increasingly align art cinema with American cinema and/or culture. This is a refreshing change from the overwhelmingly European focus of most studies of art cinema; but it also points to a certain consensus that European art cinema is now "done," in both the market and scholarly senses of the word. Art cinema is thus both present and absent in academic film studies, and this presence and absence has developed historically through a schism between theory and history. To understand how this split developed and why it is important to address it, one needs to return to the period of academic film studies' formation and examine the roles that political, cultural, industrial, intellectual, and institutional forces played in producing this outcome. At its root is the alignment of art cinema with modernism.

The Break of 1968

The post–World War II era in Europe is understood in the history of the medium as a period of formation both for modern cinema and for the growth of an informed, critical, and intellectually ambitious film culture extending beyond mere popular moviegoing.[37] The standard historical account of this development centers on art cinema, especially as produced in Italy and France, in order to demonstrate the challenges it made to national commercial practices as well as to the incursions of American film culture and capital via aesthetic innovation and personal authorial vision.[38] Roberto Rossellini, Vittorio De Sica, Luchino Visconti, Federico Fellini, Michelangelo Antonioni, Pier Paolo Pasolini, Robert Bresson, Jacques Tati, Alain Resnais, Agnès Varda, François Truffaut, Jean-Luc Godard: these and other Italian and French filmmakers of the 1950s and 1960s, along with occasional nods in the direction of Japan, Sweden, Eastern Central Europe, and India, hold prominent and imposing positions within the histories of postwar film culture. It was during these decades, in short, that narrative film came broadly to be accepted as an art and the film director as an artist.

It is in this period too that official institutions dedicated to show-casing, promoting, preserving, or disseminating filmic materials and knowledge about film settled or expanded into a compass of cultural organs: festivals, museums, institutes, and archives, what are now gen-erally referred to as the culture industries.[39] Given the ferment that led to such institutionalizations of film culture, it is not surprising that higher educational mandates would follow suit. Indeed, riding on the slipstream of this transformation in cinema culture was academic film studies itself, which developed in the 1960s in America (and would a few years later in Britain) into a field that would lead to rapid growth over the next decade.[40] The translation and migration of auteurism and mise-en-scène analysis of the sort exemplified by *Cahiers du cinéma* to Britain (through the film magazine *Movie* as well as the various activities of the British Film Institute's Education Department, among others) and to the United States (largely through Andrew Sarris in his capacity as a critic for the journal *Film Culture* and later as editor of the short-lived *Cahiers du Cinema in English*), alongside the increasingly widespread international exhibition of European art cinema, contrib-uted enormously not only to the age of cinephilia identified by Sontag but also to academic posts in film studies in the colleges and univer-sities of Britain and America. The creation in 1960 of a lectureship in film at London's Slade School of Art is a marker for the academic legitimization of cinema in the United Kingdom. Across the Atlantic, film studies courses began appearing in ever greater numbers in the American arts and humanities curriculum throughout the 1960s, and by the end of the decade many postsecondary institutions were offer-ing fully fledged film study degree programs. As Robert C. Allen and Douglas Gomery have described it, film studies was quite probably "the fastest growing academic discipline in American universities between 1965 and 1975."[41]

The year 1968 has come to be understood as a nodal point in twentieth-century political and intellectual history, as a moment when the new world system established by the postwar settlement was re-vealed as not simply out of step but in open conflict with the values and politics of the young, the working class, students, women, and peoples of color, resulting in state-sanctioned repression of dissent to maintain power and control.[42] Vietnam: the United States launches the Tet offensive. Japan: students lock Nihon University administrators in their offices and shut down classes. Czechoslovakia: a Soviet-led invasion reverses the liberal reforms of the "Prague Spring." Spain: after students close the University of Madrid, more than one thousand are sent to military service. Britain: a peace march in London's Grosvenor Square sparks a battle between police and twenty thousand demonstrators. West Germany: socialist student leader Rudi Dutschke is shot in the head by a young unskilled worker, and police kill two and arrest one thousand in the insurrection that follows. Italy: student seizures of universities are supported by strikes among workers and high school students. France: filmmakers and intellectuals protest and then petition the government following the removal of Henri Langlois, the head of the Paris Cinémathèque, by French Minister of Cultural Affairs André Malraux; a series of violent clashes between police and students takes place in early May in Paris's Latin Quarter after the arrest of students at the Sorbonne; on 24 May nearly ten million French workers go on strike, with more battles at night with riot police after a fire is started in the Paris stock exchange.[43] Mexico: on 2 October five thousand students and workers rally at the Plaza de Las Tres Culturas in the Tlatelolco section of Mexico City, demanding democratic reforms; a combined military and police assault leaves hundreds dead. United States: Martin Luther King Jr. and Robert F. Kennedy are assassinated, the former event sparking riots and arson waves in urban ghettos across the country; campus sit-ins and revolts spread to more than two hundred campuses, notably Columbia, San Francisco State, Berkeley, Wisconsin, Michigan, and Cornell, where armed black students occupy university buildings; women stage a protest at the Miss America pageant in Atlantic City; demonstrations against President Lyndon B. Johnson's escalation of the war in Vietnam lead to mayhem and a "police riot" at the Chicago Democratic Convention.

The year 1968 also functioned as an unofficial "end of innocence" for European art cinema. The vibrant burst of aesthetic experimentation epitomized in the early 1960s by this cinema was influential in terms of other nations' film practices, especially in America in the latter half of that decade and into the 1970s in the form of the New Hollywood cinema.[44] But while it enjoyed throughout this period some notable successes internationally, European art cinema can be seen in retrospect to have been marking time—particularly in terms of U.S. exhibition where, from the establishment of the Code and Rating Administration system in 1968, it would proceed into irreversible decline.[45] As well, film culture more generally became politicized; in France, the Langlois Affair in February and the forced closure of the Cannes Film Festival by filmmakers and jury members in May are two examples. Additionally, artists, journalists, and film/television/radio workers were particularly sympathetic with the students' protests and their violent treatment at the hands of the riot police. They organized the Estates Générale du Cinéma to discuss the role of filmmakers, technicians, and critics as well as screenings at factories and sit-ins and documentation of the protests.[46] The failure of the events of May '68 to effect lasting change in the ruling party's dominance over all aspects of public and private life did not dull the import of these concerns. Rather, it produced an intellectual milieu that increasingly called for the need for political intervention on the theoretical as well as the practical/activist fronts.

It is important to place Anglo-American academic film studies within this nexus of historical forces. For despite some obvious differences that would develop between the newly formed film cultural and academic sectors—manifested, for example, in the levels of specialization in the critical languages common to each, as well as in the size and thickness of their journals and the circulations of their readerships—both are nonetheless bound to a common period of formation and continue to share a number of traits as regards cinematic taste, value, and community. Importantly, 1968 also demarcates the point from which academic film studies, still only in its formative stages, began to grapple with "the political" in its own way.[47] In this sense, the 1960s was the time for both academic film studies' formation and its first great "break." European art cinema was to suffer in this, as it came to be regarded by a burgeoning, politicized academic film studies from 1968 on as a compromised form of cultural production, one whose figuration of the individual's relation to modern society—particularly the alienated, bourgeois individual—had been called into question by the collective social and political events of the late 1960s.

A second outcome of this break was a scholarly division that still resonates as a not incommensurable yet lingering schism between film theory and film history.

The political upheavals of the late 1960s precipitated a reevaluation on the part of many intellectuals of their assumptions, priorities, and practices. For example, throughout the 1950s and 1960s editorial policy at *Cahiers du cinéma* was marked by a commitment to auteur and mise-en-scène criticism that manifested itself in an almost unqualified celebration of Italian neorealism, the French New Wave, and American cinema.[48] Concomitant with this policy was distaste for (and often outright rejection of) explicitly partisan films and filmmakers: cinema was decidedly the realm of "the individual," "beauty," "sensitivity," "morality"—not politics. Statements of militancy fell well within the boundaries of a liberal humanism tempered with existentialism.[49] A change in editorial policy at *Cahiers* in summer 1968, and a year later the publication of Jean Narboni and Jean-Louis Comolli's editorial drafted for the October–November 1969 issue titled "Cinéma/idéologie/critique," sealed *Cahiers'* commitment to political criticism and initiated a crisis within the magazine that led to a change in its ownership.[50] *Cahiers'* abandonment of its former evaluative approach in favor of analysis of cinema's role in the perpetuation of the social formation called for a more rigorously theoretical examination of how cinema functioned ideologically, how meaning was produced, and how it addressed the spectator.[51]

A similar shift in 1971 in the editorial policy of *Screen*—initially an organ of the British Film Institute's educational initiatives—as well as the inauguration in and around the 1970s of journals like *Cinéthique* in France, *Afterimage* and *Framework* in Britain, *Jump Cut* and *Camera Obscura* in the United States, and *Ciné-Tracts* in Canada, launched and sustained an intellectual program for the nascent discipline of academic film studies.[52] It was a program that combined in exciting and often untenable ways a variety of structuralist and later poststructuralist discourses. It was also a program that made the terms "political" and "theoretical" synonymous, at least for those writing and making films within the main currents of its concerns. The pages of these journals promoted subsequent developments in film theory: neo-Marxism and semiotics, psychoanalysis and feminism, queer theory and postcolonial and cultural studies. It is through these terms and discourses that most scholars would recognize the main political trajectory of post-1968 Anglo-American film studies through the late 1980s.

This trajectory has not been matched by a corollary one for film history, particularly as far as art cinema is concerned. Unlike film theory, which can claim a legacy dating at least to the 1910s, film history as a distinct field of inquiry appeared much later. Before the institutionalization of academic film studies in Britain and America, film history was written by archivists, independent scholars, and buffs. Film theory too was largely the province of artists, independent scholars, and buffs throughout the first half of the twentieth century, but it went through a much more visible process of academic development before 1968 and politicization quickly afterward. As a result of the break of 1968, art cinema was left largely to critics and historians to concern themselves about.[53] And while the discourses one might group under film theory are of a wide variety and span a number of disciplines, the approaches to film historical writing have remained remarkably few. Robert C. Allen and Douglas Gomery described in 1985 four historiographic categories—aesthetic, technological, economic, and social—to which we can now add institutional, exhibition, and reception.[54] Of these, however, the aesthetic and the social dominate the historiography of European art cinema, which engages largely with the history of its object's formal experiments and innovations and noteworthy exemplars (films and directors) within the contexts of specific national cinemas.

One of the root causes for the relative lack of theoretical interest in European art cinema—whether deconstruction, feminism, psychoanalysis, postcolonialism, queer theory, or cognitivism—was due to its designation as modernist, and modernist of a certain strain. A determining critical mechanism for this designation derives from a tendency to distinguish two strands of modern and modernist cinema. In the case of the French New Wave, these strands are articulated as two waves: the New Wave proper of 1958–62 and a second wave in 1966–68. According to this sequencing, the first wave is modernist and apolitical, the second militant and political. Susan Hayward, for example, considers a myth "the belief that because this cinema was controversial or different in style it was also radical and political cinema. This is predominantly not true: the New Wave film-makers were largely non-politicized."[55] Such a bipartition rests then on a general consensus about what a "political" film is, based on either the politics of its maker or the historical context in which it is embedded. Thus the first New Wave coincides with a growing youth culture, the rise of the *jeune cadre,* modernization, unprecedented industrial growth, economic prosperity and consumer power, the reformation of national institutions through the advent of the Fifth Republic and its new constitution, and decolonization. (The only way to regard this period as "non-political," however, is to ignore the last two items in this series and consign the first four to cultural or economic spheres.) The second New Wave, on the other hand, corresponds with "the progressive disenchantment with [Charles] de Gaulle's authoritarian presidential style, unrest on social and educational levels due to a lack of resources to accommodate the expanding urban society and student university numbers, workers' concern at their conditions, and lastly concern with the rise in unemployment, all of which culminated in the events of May 1968."[56] In other words, the latter half of the 1960s was in France a more properly "political" time in the nation's history.

The force of politics in the late 1960s has underscored academic film studies in ways no less telling than, and in many ways parallel to, its effects on cultural life in general. The politicization of film culture in the wake of 1968 is conceded to have been short-lived and of limited success in altering the dominant modes of film production and reception. But by taking on the econopolitical bases of cinematic production as it did, by splintering modern cinema into two different camps, it threw into theoretical disfavor European art cinema. For film studies, it was precisely a conception of "the political" that placed two categories or branches of the field at odds with one another: theory versus history. The call for countercinematic practices by proponents of the former in the pages of *Cahiers du cinéma, Cinéthique,* and *Positif* in 1969 and *Screen, Jump Cut, Camera Obscura,* and others in the 1970s should not be underestimated as a generative factor in the decline of European art cinema in this period. The cinematic movements that grew out of the political foment of the late 1960s in Western and Eastern Central Europe, in Asia, and in Cuba and Latin America more readily provided examples of filmmakers who represented, both for the film culture of the 1970s and the burgeoning discipline of film studies alike, a certain type of politically committed and engaged auteur preferable to those who merely made art films.[57] Pier Paolo Pasolini, Jean-Luc Godard and Jean-Pierre Gorin, Jean-Marie Straub and Danièle Huillet, Alexander Kluge, Hans-Jürgen Syberberg, Rainer Werner Fassbinder, Miklós Jancsó, Dušan Makavejev, Nagisa Oshima, Fernando Solanas and Octavio Getino, Glauber Rocha—these filmmakers collectively practiced a form of political cinema that contested and went beyond the domesticated modernism of art cinema, drawing instead from a political avant-garde tradition of aesthetics including dialecticism, distantiation, and unpleasure.[58] They were, in the parlance of the period, good object choices.

Rather than a simple bipartite division between cinema as art or as popular entertainment, political discourse led academic film studies to make more finite distinctions, though terminology proved confusing. The avant-garde, modernism, militant cinema, countercinema, and political modernism all were deployed at various (and often overlapping) times to describe the preferred political course for film practice and, in the latter two cases, film theory. Published in 1975, Peter Wollen's "The Two Avant-Gardes" drew a distinction between two currents of contemporary film practice, one merely aesthetic and the other political/radical, both developing from two strands of modernism of the 1920s.[59] A further elaboration of this position by Paul Willemen distinguished between modernism and the avant-garde, aligning the former with aestheticism and the latter with political engagement.[60] A decade after Wollen, in the final chapter of *The Classical Hollywood Cinema,* David Bordwell and Janet Staiger posited that, in relation to their title subject's style/mode of production, "only a few other general modes of film practice have existed. Three significant ones would be 'art cinema,' the avant-garde cinema, and the 'modernist' cinema"; for the authors, *none* of these was de facto political.[61] In the same year Bordwell elaborated on these modes in his *Narration in the Fiction Film,* though here the modernist mode is confusingly called "parametric" and a special note is added about "the problem of modernism."[62] Finally, D. N. Rodowick, following Sylvia Harvey, deployed the term "political modernism" to describe a "specific formation of theoretical discourse" that aligned with the practices Wollen considered one type of avant-garde and Willemen modernism tout court.[63]

Another consensus was reached without altercation: classical cinema meant Hollywood cinema. Film theory thus concentrated on two forms of textual analysis, and for similar political ends: "against the grain" readings of mainstream cinema as epitomized by classical Hollywood, either to demythologize, using Marxist, psychoanalytic, and/or feminist frameworks, its hegemonic workings or to tease out potentially progressive genres (melodrama, film noir, the B film, the horror film) and occasionally auteurs (Dorothy Arzner and Douglas Sirk, preeminently); and "with the grain" readings (though never termed as such) of more identifiably progressive films, especially those deriving from independent and counterhegemonic practices such as countercinema, Third Cinema, and the feminist avant-garde. These latter practices further splintered from the 1980s through the work of a range of gay, lesbian, postcolonial, diasporic, exilic, and accented filmmakers, now encompassed broadly by the term "postmodern" and including the likes of Derek Jarman, Trinh T. Minh-ha, Isaac Julien, Julie Dash, and Atom Egoyan. "Political" thus expanded to take in the politics of difference and identity as enacted by postmodern film and video practices.[64]

Through all this, art cinema remained aligned with the high arts and relegated wholly to the aesthetic—and so of little theoretical concern.[65] It occupied a middle ground between popular American cinema (democratic) and the independent avant-garde (progressive), an official, bourgeois cultural position. Steve Neale notes that art cinema in this period "was often defined as the 'enemy': as a bastion of 'high art' ideologies, as the kind of cinema supported by *Sight and Sound* and the critical establishment, therefore, as the kind of cinema to be fought. To parody the debate somewhat, it was a question of Siegel, Fuller, Hitchcock, Hawks and Corman versus Antonioni, Bergman and Fellini, of genre versus personal expression, of (in some extreme cases) trash versus taste, hysteria versus restraint, energy versus decorum and quality."[66] And John Caughie has recalled: "The films of Godard and Straub-Huillet provided the stick with which to beat bourgeois realism, and the films of Duras and Chantal Akerman began to open up the question of a feminine discourse in cinema. The rest was silence: classified as European 'art cinema' in which the word 'art' couldn't be spoken without an involuntary curl of the lips."[67] European art cinema was thus from almost the start of Anglo-American academic film studies deemed outmoded and elitist, with Bergman, Truffaut, and others of their ilk reviled by a politicized film culture located in the left wing of the academy in America and soon to be so in Britain.[68] Poststructuralist and postmodern theorists labeled European art cinema irredeemably modernist, with consequently appropriate reading strategies: nonpoliticized, humanist, formal/aesthetic ones for the modernist cinemas of the French New Wave and the new Italian cinema; politicized, antihumanist, ideological ones for the militant cinemas of the late 1960s and beyond. This was no radical break from the past. David Forgacs has traced left political antipathy to modernism to 1940s Italy as a consequence of the Communist Party's support for the discourse of realism: "Modernist works are only valued positively when they can be interpreted in a realist or a socially committed key: the work of avant-garde artists belonging to or aligned with the Left, for instance Aragon or Picasso, is interpreted and defended in this way. Otherwise Modernist works are consigned to cultural waste-paper baskets variously labelled 'formalist', 'decadent', 'abstract', 'irrational', 'sterile', 'snobbish' and 'bourgeois'."[69]

Remarkably, these critical protocols have changed very little. A great deal of this has to do with a continuing designation of European art cinema of the late 1950s through the 1960s as modernist in the wake of theories of the postmodern. But the issue of terminology is actually a sticky one when one considers the cinema's place among other arts and cultural discourses. Fredric Jameson, for example, famously identified the three fundamental stages in secular bourgeois or capitalist culture as realism, modernism, and postmodernism, each of which accords with Ernest Mandel's (after Marx's) three historical stages of capital: classical or market capitalism; monopoly capitalism, or what Lenin called "the age of imperialism"; and late capitalism.[70] For Jameson, the confluence of the last term/stage—postmodernism/late capitalism—is crucial as a means for designating a new social positioning of art within a new multinational organization of capital.[71] The chronological mappings of aesthetic forms according to these stages of development have for the most part proceeded through hindsight, with the emergence of the postmodern determining the end of modernism and so on. But these mappings have produced a highly contradictory array of historical periodizations. The philosopher of history Arnold Toynbee first used the term *postmodernism* in the late 1940s to refer, negatively, to an age that begins in the late nineteenth century in the second stage of capital. It was not until the late 1970s, with the publication of Charles Jencks's *The Language of Post-Modern Architecture* and Jean-François Lyotard's *La Condition postmoderne,* that the territorial lines really began to be drawn.[72] Scholars of English literature coalesced around the year 1939 as heralding the "birth" of postmodern literature, using the outbreak of World War II and the publication of James Joyce's *Finnegans Wake* as markers. American literary critics and writers decided to set the advent of postmodernism in the postwar period. The visual arts community has more or less settled on the transition from the Abstract Expressionism of the New York School to Pop around 1960. And from a Habermasian perspective the rise of postmodernism would have to be associated with the emergence of numerous poststructuralist writings in the late sixties.[73]

And film? On the one hand, most of its history coincides at one level or another with modernism in the other arts. On the other hand, the cinema is a product of sophisticated forms of cultural production, impossible to understand outside of the development of the latest stage of capitalism, and one may be tempted to proclaim it as always already postmodern and leave it at that. Few have made either of these moves, however, and the historiography of the medium has, following an art history model, produced a set of periodizations that look roughly as follows: pre- and early cinema (1880s–1914), silent cinema (1913–1929), classical sound cinema (1927–1955), modern cinema (1955–1975), and contemporary or postmodern cinema (1975–present). The more elegant tripartite periodization of cinema history into silent cinema (1895–1930), classical sound cinema (1930–60), and modern cinema (1960–present) would seem to carry with it the benefit of coinciding with Jameson's three stages, but the coincidence is a false one.[74] According to Colin MacCabe, "One has to reckon with the historical paradox that this post-modern medium recapitulates the basic realism/modernism/post-modernism aesthetic development, with the classic Hollywood cinema representing realism . . . , the European cinema of the 50s and 60s reliving all the paradoxes of modernism . . . and a fully post-modern cinema having to wait until the early 70s."[75] In the accepted idiom of Jameson's three-stage socioeconomic-aesthetic development, film "signally fails to coincide with any of the rhythms or coordinates of development in the other arts or media."[76]

Much of the confusion that surrounds efforts to map the concept is due to a conflation of postmodernism as an epoch, involving a shift of societal and economic paradigms, and postmodernism as a period style in the arts visibly and/or aurally distinct from modernism. This is nowhere more evident than in Susan Hayward's periodizing of French cinema according to the three stages of Mandelian/Jamesonian development so that silent French cinema, "the classical age," is realist, sound cinema from 1930 to the French New Wave is "the age of modernism," and 1958 to the present is French cinema's "age of the postmodern." Her alignment of the New Wave with postmodernism relies on a privileging of historical time over aesthetic transformation:

> The postmodern does not . . . refer to a style; rather, it refers to a periodising concept "whose function is to correlate the emergence of new formal features in culture with the emergence of a new type of social life and a new economic order". . . . In other words, it is a conjunctural term at the interface between artefact and the new moment of capitalism. In the case of France this moment dates from the birth of the Fifth Republic, again justifying the nomenclature for this age of cinema as postmodern.[77]

But how can this square up with the long-standing consensus that the films of the New Wave—with the exception perhaps of Truffaut's *Tirez sur le pianiste* (*Shoot the Piano Player,* 1960) and of those Godard films that playfully incorporate references across a range of high and low culture—conform to the high seriousness and self-referential formal tendencies of modernism in general and of other European art films of this period in particular?

The issue of whether the French New Wave (and, by extension, the European art cinemas of the same era) is postmodern or modern is more than simply a terminological quibble. It carves out a space for how one should read this cinema, how one should understand its relation to the history of the medium and to the cultures of its time. D. N. Rodowick has observed how

> the protagonists of New Wave films . . . define a nomadism where the characters of the time-image wander errantly and observe in emptied and disconnected spaces; linear actions dissolve into aleatory strolls that organize elliptical narratives guided predominantly by chance. . . . In so doing they represent a kind of postmodern historical subjectivity—the faltering belief in totality, either from the point of view of the great organic ideologies or from a belief in the image as anything other than a partial and contingent description of reality.[78]

I would extend this observation to contend that, although the characters may indeed "represent a kind of postmodern historical subjectivity," their place and function within the narratives of these films are nevertheless to register the loss of a certain totality and to secure the boundaries of a new kind of totality in which they might find a space to circulate. In this respect, one could say that the European art cinemas of the late 1950s and early 1960s are not postmodern but a form of modernism that populates its formal aspirations, which accord with those of modernism in its high phase, with proto-postmodern subjects who do not fully embrace the new because they are incapable of making the successful transition.

A reconsideration of European art cinema in relation to the discursive formations of modernism and postmodernism complicates our understanding of the ways in which it responded to the social, economic, industrial, and political shifts that provided the context for its emergence. Indeed, these shifts may be seen as the generative mechanisms for that emergence. The nomadism of the characters that Rodowick identifies is one example, especially in terms of their gendering in this cinema. The trope of the modern wandering woman or female flâneur in art cinema foregrounds the uncomfortable position she occupies vis-à-vis private and public space, narrative and spectacle, director and performer, subject and object—and modernism and postmodernism. In the classical accounts of flanerie provided by Walter Benjamin through the writings of Baudelaire, the flâneur's existence was built upon a sustained disavowal of a social, utilitarian ordering of space, favoring instead a self-defined, self-centered aesthetic spacing. Indeed, Benjamin's description of the petit bourgeoisie as the privileged class of the flâneur circa 1859 could just as easily stand as a description of the filmmakers of European art cinema circa 1959: "Inevitably, one day many of its members had to become aware of the commodity nature of their labour power. But this day had not as yet come; until that day they were permitted, if one may put it that way, to pass their time. The very fact that their share could at best be enjoyment, but never power, made the period which history gave them a space for passing time."[79] This is the high modernist sensibility in a nutshell: a retreat from the complexity, indeed unrepresentability, of social relations in modernity into the aesthetic. Both the flâneur's existence in the labyrinthine, disorienting, turbulent space of the modern city and Benjamin's assessment of it is riven through with a melancholic nostalgia for a lost world. Is this not also the age of cinephilia that Sontag so fondly, so wistfully recalled?

Mapping the Subject

Given the complex interplay among the political, industrial, intellectual, and institutional forces that coalesced around and have extended beyond 1968, it is imperative to examine how film culture, academic film studies, film theory, and film history are mutually implicated in the discourses of European art cinema. For even though most contemporary accounts of aesthetic, historical, and political development would agree that we are now, and have been for some time, in the age of the postmodern, the ideologies of modernism, of which European art cinema is so much a part, continue to underscore the disciplinary practices of film studies leveled at this mode of film practice. In fact, analyzing European art cinema as part of a cultural and historical milieu that gave rise to postmodernism reveals that its modernism is not so much an aesthetic phase or an epoch that has now been exhausted as it is a set of historical and theoretical reading protocols that have held art cinema in a holding pattern for Anglo-American film studies. In this respect, ostensibly outmoded concepts like the auteur, nationalism, Eurocentrism, art versus commerce, high versus low culture, and modernism and the modern continue to manifest themselves in disciplinary thought and practice with respect to this particular object.

In this book I will be mapping the practices and paradigms of film history and of film studies alongside postwar European art cinema to propose remappings that are at the same time institutional and geopolitical. The cinemas of the French New Wave and the new Italian cinema of the late 1950s through the late 1960s are central to this analysis for a number of reasons. The countries are comparable in size and population and share similar economic, social, and political developments in the decade before, during, and after the period in focus. Italian and French film culture played key roles in establishing the discourses of European art cinema internationally through respective national film movements (Italian neorealism, the French New Wave, the new Italian cinema), specialized journals, high-profile film festivals

(Venice and Cannes, the first two to be instituted), and a proportionately high number of directors and films constituting a large percentage of the art cinema pantheon and canon. There is considerable overlap among the film cultures and film industries of France and Italy in this period as well, in terms of both the sizes of their respective native audiences and their frequent coproduction of films. The French New Wave and the new Italian cinema thus concentrate a historical period, an accepted body of important figures and texts, a set of cultural discourses, and an economic/industrial/institutional infrastructure that are imbricated on a number of levels.

In "Re-Framing the Fingerprints: A Short Survey of European Film," Wendy Everett groups European cinema into three main categories: the long-established industries of Britain, France, Germany, Italy, and Spain; smaller national cinemas such as Austria, Belgium, Luxembourg, Portugal, and Switzerland; and the Scandinavian countries—Denmark, Finland, Iceland, Norway, and Sweden. (Interestingly, the cinemas of Eastern Central Europe are not grouped but considered as separate cases.)[80] Everett's first category includes France and Italy, and I should explain further why I am focusing on these two nations and not the others in the group. Britain has historically shared closer ties and allegiances with America than with its continental neighbors in both general and cinema-specific terms, the latter at the levels of language and production finance especially: during the 1960s, the focus of this study, American financial investment in British production reached unprecedented levels, peaking at 90 percent in 1967.[81] Britain's postwar economic growth rate through the 1960s was also far behind that of France, Italy, and other Western European countries.[82] Apart from coproduction agreements, the film cultures of Spain and West Germany existed in relative isolation from those of other Western European nations, neither of them enjoying international success on the art house exhibition or film festival circuits anything like France and Italy did between 1945 and 1975, when they dominated all others. It was not until the 1970s that film culture in West Germany and Spain became recognized internationally within the context of art cinema discourse.

The West German case, however, requires further comments. On the econopolitical front, West Germany was an original member of the European Economic Community, one of "the Six" who signed the Treaty of Rome in early 1958, the others being France, Italy, and Benelux. But West Germany's postwar economic development was inextricable from its immediate division into occupation zones and later Cold War partitions in a way that was not the case for Italy or France. On the cinematic front, the New German cinema of the late 1960s through late 1970s is often grouped with other new wave cinemas in Europe and as such is considered a continuing manifestation of European art cinema. But in fact its status in this regard is very different from that of its predecessors in important ways, especially as concerns production and reception. The financial structure of the New German cinema was dependent on television funding to an extremely high degree, one not shared by France or Italy (or any other European country) in the 1960s. In fact, television funding in these nations in the 1970s is a conspicuous reason for the decline in coproductions, a key feature of European art cinema in my estimation.[83] As for reception, many of the directors of the New German cinema were embraced by academic film studies as fulfilling countercinema requirements in a way that the art film directors of Italy and France (Pasolini and Godard excepted) were not. As Thomas Elsaesser describes, "Compared to other European New Waves, it was striking how many militant platforms but also how many committees the directors felt obliged to sit on, and how few admitted to a simple passion for cinema. . . . They had to be spokespersons on social issues, since the new cinema rarely filled the cinemas; but it found compensation by occupying a public sphere, where it stood for solidarity, the class struggle, and sexual emancipation, rather than for *mise-en-scène,* deep focus, the long take, or montage."[84] At both the industrial and discursive levels, New German cinema is of a different order and era than European art cinema as I am examining it here.

The rest of this book is organized in three chapters, each of which addresses matters of film form or representation that have been previously marked in film scholarship as peripheral to postwar French and Italian art cinema. Throughout I will be arguing the converse: that the issues at stake are central to the discourse of art cinema, and that their repression in film historical writing is due to a preferred form of analysis that has considered as extratextual what are in fact deeply structuring historical and political tensions of the period that everywhere leave their textual traces. In the case of coproductions, international casting, and the polyglot sound track of French and Italian art films, the trace is both the unsynced speech of the international performers who have been dubbed and the subtitles at the bottom of the screen that anchor to individual national cinemas what are in fact trans-European cooperative efforts. The nomadic female protagonist of art cinema is another trace as well, though of a different sort of geopolitical realignment Europe was undergoing at the time: the economic and cultural modernizations of the postwar boom alongside colonial war, decolonization, and loss of Empire. Finally, the omnibus film is a trace too, both within the history of art cinema and of an even broader institution: the protocols of film historical writing, which derive from the structuring paradigms of academic film studies and construct a horizon of intelligibility for historicizing not only the omnibus film but also European art cinema as a whole. In examining these peripheries I endeavor to draw attention to their unstable centers.

In my second chapter, "The Name above the Subtitle: Language, Coproduction, Transnationalism," I foreground the filmed body in art cinema as a locus for crisis and contestation. Here I argue that film sound, particularly the embodied voice/body of the actor, functions within European art cinema in complex and contradictory ways. Writing on film sound has tended toward three analytical approaches: the technological/historical (scholarship on the late 1920s transition to sound, for example); the aesthetic/formalist (which focuses on either film music or the particular *uses* of sound by directors, cultures, et cetera); and the theoretical/ideological (suture, the cinematic apparatus, the gendered voice, et cetera).[85] What has not received much attention is the matter of language translation/transformation in the production, distribution, and exhibition of art films made in one language community and exported or imported into another—in other words, the issue of subtitling and dubbing in its economic/institutional and theoretical dimensions.[86] A focus for fierce debate in the United States in the 1960s, when film art was synonymous with European art cinema, dubbing and subtitling have been integral features of the national and transnational film industries of Europe since the introduction of sound to the cinema. They are also fascinating sites of inquiry for any study of modern European cinema, tied as they are to the political, economic, and ideological dimensions of that cinema, dimensions that remain largely unexplored in Anglo-American academic film studies given the aesthetic purview of so much of the historiography of European art cinema.

What are the political and economic bases of the international art film? How do institutional developments within Europe aimed at economic and political cooperation and integration align with concepts like the nation and national identity in the 1960s and after? How does the history of coproduction agreements and mandates between and among European nations impinge on the reception of European art films with their transnational casts and crews? There is much at stake in these questions; I focus on the ideologies surrounding the subtitling and/or dubbing of Italian and French cinema of the late 1950s through the early 1970s. During this period the stability of the concept of nation generally, and that of Italy and France specifically, was placed in crisis by modernization and neocapitalism on the one hand and an increasingly integrating Europe on the other. The voice/celebrity (of the actor, but also of the director) emerges in the coproduced European art film as a means toward imaginary nation building. The film actor, whose language and country of origin combine with her or his star power to determine the voice in which she or he speaks, is a register of and means for conflicted constructions of national identity in a new and developing Europe, constructions that the identity of the auteur shores up.

Following the 1993 Uruguay round of the General Agreement on Tariffs and Trade (GATT), during which film and audiovisual material were excluded from its terms, there has been a burst of scholarship on the economic and industrial intersections between European cinema and Hollywood. Much of this writing proceeds from European anxieties concerning American domination and fears about the disappearance of distinct national cultures as an effect of globalization. Certainly, the prominence of international coproductions and of the adoption of English as the lingua franca of global cinema in the 1990s has increased awareness of recent strategies taken by national cinema industries in the European Union. But such strategies are by no means a recent phenomenon. Indeed, they have been employed, in varying degrees, throughout the history of European sound cinema. Anxieties about the autonomy of the nation and national cultures in the face of the American threat and of Europeanization are well documented in the histories of the pan-European initiatives of the "Film Europe" movement in the 1920s and the spate of studio "multiple language versions" in Europe in the early 1930s. But such tensions and anxieties are also evident as traces in the heavily coproduced Italian and French art cinemas of the 1950s and 1960s, a period that, not coincidentally, witnessed the growth of the European Economic Community among other cultural and economic partnerships.

While economic/institutional histories of Hollywood cinema are common in Anglo-American academic film studies, only recently has this approach been taken for European or transnational cinemas. This scholarship either centers on contemporary international coproductions and cinemas or describes the economic and cultural encroachment of American film interests in Europe. I am interested in this chapter in placing European art cinema squarely within this network, not only to suggest the importance of an economic and industrial analysis of it but also to question the nationalist emphasis of art cinema scholarship. I consider the establishment and support of various national new waves circa 1958–68 as nation-building responses at the cultural level to transnational cooperation and European unification at the economic and industrial levels.

For the casts, the production, and the distribution of the canonical postwar French and Italian cinema are prominently transnational, and as such may be read in terms of discourses concerning national authenticity during the first years of the European Economic Community. The late 1950s marked a crucial point for European film production: it was during these years that the major European film-producing nations (France, Italy, Britain, Spain, West Germany) turned increasingly to coproduction agreements with themselves and other nations as a necessary economic strategy. These agreements carried with them detailed and specific requirements regarding film locations, the nationalities of prominent members of the cast and crew, and the necessary financial commitments nations needed to make to qualify for national subsidies. Such requirements bespeak the extent to which the concept of nationhood is a consistent and explicit concern in the economic history of postwar European film production, a concern that conflicted with simultaneous pan-European strategies. The textual terrain upon which this conflict was staged is the actor's body in (or out of) sync with her or his voice. By mapping this terrain, I wish to exert pressure on the national cinemas model for the historical writing of European art cinema.

"Wandering Women: Decolonization, Modernity, Recolonization" is the title of my third chapter. There is within Anglo-American film studies a strong operational tendency to read postwar European art cinema as "modern" and "alienated" rather than as "engaged" and "motivated." One of the means for this operation is to separate and explain the historical and ideological undercurrents of the various new waves of the 1960s according to a conception of a divided, Cold War Europe. Such a separation produces constitutively different forms of historical analysis. The history of numerous Eastern Central European new waves is thus grounded in the historical and political context of the Soviet bloc: the ideological thaw following the death of Stalin provides a space for freer filmic practices that critique the totalitarianism of the Communist Party. Western European new waves, on the other hand, are considered according to a different set of criteria. Here, "new" refers to philosophical questions and aesthetic innovations that have less to do with politics or ideology than with the aesthetics of filmic style and meaning. The jump cut, the long take, intertextual referencing, and other narrative destructions are thus characteristic of the broader intellectual and philosophical (as opposed to political) concerns of Western European culture, ranging from moral decadence (Buñuel, Visconti) to metaphysical doubt (Bresson, Bergman) to existential questioning (Resnais, Antonioni) to technological dehumanization (Tati, Godard) to humanist understanding (Fellini, Truffaut).

Against these retrograde modernist sensibilities are often held progressive postmodern ones. Appropriation, misappropriation, collage, heterogeneity, hybridization, a mixing up of visual and verbal texts and discourses—postmodern style plays freely with these, and with little of the nostalgia or angst that characterizes modernism. The linking of postmodern thought and practice to the discourses of feminism— which Craig Owens presented in 1983 as an intersection between the "feminist critique of patriarchy and the postmodernist critique of representation"—adds another comparative level: modernism as an expression of an exhausted culture steeped in nostalgia for not only a lost center but also the logic of a patriarchal system that, with the rise of feminist movements since the late nineteenth century, has ever since scrambled to maintain its own grand narrative.[87] If one of the few widely agreed-upon features of postmodernism is its attempt to negotiate high art with the forms of mass culture and the culture of everyday life, European art cinema, with its elevation of the film director to artist status, can certainly be seen as a similar effort on the part of the nations of Europe to quell the tide of the massive influx of American mass culture and commodities. But how are we to consider female representation in this period and this cultural form? A primary object of address and fascination for European modernization and commodity culture, the modern woman is also a primary *subject* of art cinema. Might the political effects or meanings of this figure be read in terms not of this cinema's immanence—its modernism—but through a postmodern interpretive framework? In other words, the contradictory female representations in modern cinema may be understood as signifying aesthetic, spatial, and national-historical crises particular to Western Europe.

In the contemporary discourses of European art cinema there is a notable critical line on the matter of women. They are treated as positive agents of their own desire, central to the narrative, a liberated image of modern European womanhood. They are also insular, isolated, alienated beings, out of touch with the social world around them, unable to communicate freely or fully with men, unlikely to achieve happiness by narrative's end. In short, they are like the films for which they iconically stand: representative not of the broader culture but of themselves, singular subjects in the same way that modern films are singular objets d'art. For example, the British critic Penelope Houston would state in 1963 that "*Hiroshima mon Amour* is not about peace or the Bomb, as much it is about a woman trying to live with her past.... *À Bout de Souffle [sic]* is not about crime, but about Jean-Paul Belmondo and Jean Seberg; *La Notte* is not a tract on modern marriage."[88] In the same year, the American critic Andrew Sarris wrote, "Monica Vitti is an intellectual actress, the visible flowering of what has come to be known as the modern cinema. As Greta Garbo and Emmanuelle Riva have been the pin-up girls of the soul, and Marlene Dietrich and Jeanne Moreau the pin-up girls of the senses, perhaps Monica Vitti will go down in film history as the first pin-up girl of the intellect."[89]

The tone of such pronouncements was largely set by *Cahiers du cinéma,* which from the beginning of the New Wave demonstrated a stake in modern French cinema that was inseparable from a notion of the modern woman. The *Cahiers* roundtable discussion on *Hiroshima mon amour,* published in summer 1959, is notable for its participants' fascination with "adult women in the cinema" and for the connections they make between the work of Simone de Beauvoir—whose critique of the formidable dilemmas facing independent and professional women in a postwar male-dominated world, *The Second Sex,* had been published a decade earlier—and the modern cinema of Alain Resnais and Michelangelo Antonioni.[90] With all credit for *Hiroshima mon amour* going to the male director and none to the female screenwriter or performer, Jacques Doniol-Valcroze declares that "Emmanuelle Riva is a modern adult woman because she is not an adult woman. Quite the contrary, she is very childish, motivated solely by her impulses and not by her ideas. Antonioni was the first to show us this kind of woman." Jacques Rivette sees her as "a woman who is starting all over again, going right back to the beginning, trying to define herself in existential terms before the world and before her past, as if she were once more unformed matter in the process of being born." And Jean-Luc Godard and Jean Domarchi pronounce *Hiroshima mon amour* to be "Simone de Beauvoir that works" and "a documentary on Emmanuelle Riva," respectively.[91] For these critics, as for the British and American ones over whom they exerted influence, the portrayals of modern women by Riva, Moreau, and Vitti are vital signs of the arrival of a modern cinema whose creation is attributable not to their abilities as performers nor to a general societal trend but to the vision of the male auteurs these critics champion and in some cases would become.

For many film historians, the seeds of this modern cinema were sown by Italian neorealism, and what links neorealism to the French New Wave and to the new Italian cinema is a similar set of production practices: low to mid budgets, location shooting in natural light, editing strategies alien to the seamlessness of the continuity system, and (to a debatable degree) nonprofessional actors and/or a no-star system. But the links between the two may also be traced through the ways in which these cinemas frame, narrativize, and explore transforming urban spaces. In his cinema books Gilles Deleuze has presented a fascinating philosophical account of the transition from classical to modern cinema, or in his terms from the movement-image to the time-image, and he gestures toward the historical and spatial determinants of this transition. Deleuze suggests that

> after the war, a proliferation of . . . [deconnected or emptied] spaces could be seen both in film sets [décors] and in exteriors, under various influences. The first, independent of the cinema, was the post-war situation with its towns demolished or being reconstructed, its waste grounds, its shanty towns, and even in places where the war had not penetrated, its undifferentiated urban tissue, its vast unused places, docks, warehouses, heaps of girders and scrap iron.[92]

The ruins, derelict buildings, and deserted streets of postwar European cityscapes created what Deleuze calls "any-space-whatevers," a milieu that lent itself to disruption of the organic unities of narrative and setting, sound and vision that characterize classical cinema. The wasted and empty spaces wrought by World War II and undergoing reconstruction are not for Deleuze simply the settings for Italian neorealist cinema. Rather, they are sites of physical and psychological crises that produce a radically new approach to storytelling and filming, one that "broke with spatial co-ordinates, with the old realism of places, and mixed up the references which gave the film movement (as in the marshes or the fortress in Rossellini's *Païsa*) or constituted visual 'abstracts' (the factory of *Europa '51*) in the indefinite lunar spaces."[93] Italian neorealism was the first of a number of postwar cinemas to effect a break with the motivated sensory situations of the cinematic movement-image and open the way toward the "pure" optical and sound situations of the time-image. For Deleuze, the sequencing of those breaks is Italy in 1948, France in 1958, and Germany in 1968.[94]

The relationship between history and aesthetics here is interesting and, as it turns out, attenuated: Deleuze does not explore the connection between the two, nor does he account for precisely how historical contexts act as determining influences on national image cultures.[95] Nevertheless, his work points toward another way in which one might read aesthetic change via historical crisis: through detailed analysis of cinematic movements and figures in their constructions of time, space, and visuality. One of the striking features of modern European cinema is precisely the circuit it sets up between the spaces it frames, the time in which it sequences them, the placement of its characters as viewing subjects, and the spectator, who is not so much a recipient of a unified spatial/temporal text as a participant in a disunified one.

These spaces are not generalized but very specific—and, by the time of European art cinemas proper, very urban. They are spaces of collision between the old and the new, the traditional and the modern. They signify a burst of infrastructural modernization that radically reoriented how the modern subject works, lives, and perceives her positioning in the metropole of the new Europe.

In my third chapter I map the modern subject in European art cinema through a trope common to many of the canonical examples of this cinema: the wandering woman. The films of the French New Wave and the new Italian cinema are replete with female characters who function as both main protagonists and spectacles of alienated flanerie. Films such as *Hiroshima mon amour, Cléo de 5 à 7* (*Cleo from 5 to 7,* 1961), and *Last Year at Marienbad,* along with the numerous Jean-Luc Godard/Anna Karina, Louis Malle/Jeanne Moreau, and Michelangelo Antonioni/Monica Vitti collaborations, all feature women as the central movers of narratives that do not really move anywhere. The main female characters of these films traverse changing cities and landscapes in varying states of crisis and abjection. I align the production of the flâneuse in this period of European art cinema with the Continent's postwar economic recovery, modernization, and, most important, decolonization. These female protagonists are in my readings emblematic of recolonizations of various sorts; their circulation in and around the changing faces of city and country, coupled with their romantic longing and/or despair, may be read as symptoms of broader European anxieties concerning colonial war, decolonization, and modernization. The discourse of recolonization works its way through the canon of European art cinema in a variety of forms, sometimes overtly as female masquerade of the racialized Other but also and more important covertly, and always anchored on the spectacle of white European women engaged in some form of physical movement, usually of an aleatory and aimless sort. My goal in chapter 3 is to historicize the modern woman of European art cinema so as to demonstrate how the discourse of postcolonialism may be applied and extended to texts not generally considered to engage with such issues. European art cinema emerges in this chapter as a highly contested form that rebuilds national identity in the wake of decolonization through an interior form of recolonization, the locus of which is the modern, white European woman and the register of which is her flanerie.

The alienation that is so much a part of her characterization is a key sensibility of the flâneur as celebrated by Baudelaire in Paris of the Second Empire and eulogized by Benjamin in Berlin of the Weimar era. The flâneur emerges in these and in more recent feminist interventions as a rich site of registration for the temporal, spatial, and gendered transformations and discontinuities wrought by modernity. The rise of the modern woman as a major player in the European art cinemas of the economic miracle raises for me deeply political and historical questions that, because these cinemas have been designated irredeemably modernist, have yet to be answered. The loss of and nostalgia for Empire embodied in the figure of the female flâneur in these cinemas gets to the marrow of contemporary calls for a less Eurocentric, more global approach to the study of media cultures. To approach high modern European art cinema with this agenda in mind is not so much a contradiction as it is a remapping of coordinates. In 1984 Giuliana Bruno sounded a general note of concern when she called for a film history of "suppressed knowledges" that

> may be located in the recent uncovering of "other" histories of film or modes of production. However, . . . in order to achieve a history of suppressed knowledges, it is neither essential nor sufficient simply to write a history of third world film or independent cinemas. . . . If, on the one hand, the history of a suppressed knowledge is not to be automatically equated with the mere choice of the suppressed other as the object of research, conversely, the history of a dominant mode of production may also assume a connotation of suppressed knowledge.[96]

While I do not in this chapter undertake a full history of European cinema in its age of modernization and decolonization, I would suggest that the suppressed knowledge of the racialized, colonial Other that is projected through the wandering women of the French New Wave and the new Italian cinema is present in these cinemas in other disguised forms. My analysis of the female colonial masquerade thus points to a new historiographic direction for European art cinema.

In my fourth and final chapter, "Exquisite Corpses: Art Cinema, Film Studies, and the Omnibus Film," I combine various aesthetic and theoretical discourses to examine the protocols of film historical writing and the structuring paradigms of Anglo-American film studies to uncover the problems they present for the historicizing of certain filmic forms, including art cinema. The Surrealist game of the exquisite corpse produced visual figures of unexpected combinations that serve here as graphic illustrations for both the omnibus film and academic film studies as a discursive field. The omnibus or multidirector episode film barely registers on film studies' radar: most histories of film all but ignore it as a particular form warranting mention, with references to only a dozen or so of them scattered across a small body of scholarship pell-mell—and of this dozen, fully half were made in Italy and France (usually as coproductions between them) in the 1960s. On the rare occasions that they do make an appearance in the literature on European art cinema, omnibus films are either dismissed as a spurt of commercially oriented film ventures, the products of producers more than directors and therefore of no aesthetic interest, or read selectively and exclusively under an auteurist umbrella: specific episodes directed by major European directors are isolated as minor contributions to their bodies of work and evaluated on those terms only. Omnibus films are thus not considered readable units in and of themselves but instead as assemblages of segments to be excised for analysis within the context of a contributing famous director's oeuvre. Yet the prevalence of these films across the history of sound cinema—and especially between 1960 and 1970, the period in which film culture was legitimated by various national new waves—positions them as a potentially rich object of analysis not only for European art cinema but also for film studies as a whole.

As part of my research for this book I have compiled a filmography of 747 omnibus films, extending from 1930 to 2007 and across many film-producing countries of the world, seventy-two in all. After the United States, whose output of omnibus films is consistent only since the 1990s, Italy and France account for the highest levels of production, most notably in the 1960s when a startling number of art film auteurs made one or, more usually, two or more. The habitual institutional response to a case such as this would be to recognize that these films constitute an interesting group for study, that they are evidence of a gap in knowledge for the field, and that a few essays or perhaps a short book on them will serve to fill that gap. But how should one proceed to analyze and historicize such a data set? While there are occasional temporal patterns that emerge from it—a spike of production in the 1960s, an increasing incidence from the 1990s through the 2000s—omnibus films nonetheless cut across every decade since the 1930s. A national cinemas model is equally problematic, not simply because of its inability to deal with the one-sixth of the total that are coproduced and hence transnational but also because of the sheer extent of the form's geographic breadth, a different kind of transnationalism. I have come to the conclusion that these films are important not as discrete texts or as a genre or type of film but as a heterogeneous body through which can be traced the structures of film history and film studies into which it is incapable of being slotted— which is precisely why it has remained so hidden to the discipline.

In my fourth chapter I argue that the omnibus film's peripheral status in the field is a product of an inertia that is a structuring principle of both the Surrealist exquisite corpse and academic film studies as a form of practice. By deploying the omnibus film as a heuristic device, I map the paradigms that underscore film historical writing— and, indeed, academic film studies from its inception—to demonstrate the reasons why they do not serve adequately for this form as well as more generally for the range of discourses it embodies. These paradigms include periods, nations, film movements, genres, authorship, and the film text itself. The omnibus film is an unsettling presence when placed in any and all of these categories, and as such is of interest beyond the immediate issue of its marginalization within the literature on European art cinema.

The additive tendency that characterizes academic film studies vis-à-vis new research programs and their objects has done very little to redraw the borders of the discipline that have been in place since the 1960s. In fact, this tendency firms up these borders through the very idea of gaps themselves, which when exposed are simply incorporated as supplements to a main body of knowledge that is organized precisely on the logic of center/periphery. This is true more so of film history than film theory, as the latter undergoes notable paradigm shifts in the way the former does not. Theories are contested, rendered epistemologically or practically unsound, displaced or otherwise compromised in their explanatory power. History, however, is ostensibly more accommodating, especially since the "piecemeal histories" agenda has assumed dominance in the field—though its innocence must be regarded as compromised by the manner in which it has through its more vocal proponents actively sought to displace theory itself from the discipline.

As the omnibus film is a fragmented unity of periods, nations, styles, genres, and creative personnel, I have chosen in the end to write its body in the spirit of the game that gives the chapter its name. But such game playing is more than a means to passing time. It is a collaborative act, a recognition of and a taking of pleasure in community —in my case, a community of scholarship to which I hope my playing in this chapter will contribute. It is also, in the case of the exquisite corpse certainly, if not for all such instances, a game that produces unexpected results.

One of the results of my game playing is a set of routes for remapping European art cinema and academic film studies by tracing through the omnibus film its own passages across its history. This history encompasses a series of ongoing responses—to political events, cultural and societal trends, audiences and the differing markets they comprise, formats and platforms for their production and consumption—that I understand European art cinema to have made as well. For the cleaving off of European art cinema from the countercinemas of the 1970s as a product of the discipline's politicization has led to a critical consensus that misrecognizes how art cinema has commented upon, in both implicit and explicit ways, the geopolitical shifts and crises of its time. European art cinema was in the 1960s a form of political engagement, and its designation as modernist has limited our understanding of both the degrees to and the manners in which this might be read textually and historically. A second level of that engagement was cultural, particularly as concerns the categories of high versus low culture. Art cinema's alignment with the former has obfuscated the degree to which it participated actively in the latter, especially in terms of sexual and erotic display. Here the historiographic tendency has been to locate these as effects—of production requirements, of marketing strategies—rather than as constitutive parts of art cinema discourse itself. In this sense, European art cinema's modernist textuality needs to be remapped across the high/low divide that postmodernism is often understood as having usurped. A final alternative historiography places the art film within the context of the audiovisual technologies and forms of consumption that have proliferated since the 1960s and that by dint of this history have been largely considered separately from the art film. Television, video, and DVD, alongside the repackaging of art films by distributors of these technologies, as well as the international film festival, have been inadequately addressed in the study and history of European art cinema. It is through the omnibus film that such remappings are envisioned in this book.

So, three more chapters, three different approaches to a range of objects. Chapter 2 undertakes a historiographic survey of coproduction in Europe and a mapping of the visual and sonic terrain of the European art film so as to examine how the stubborn discourses of the nation and of national cinemas in film culture and film studies depend upon the ideology of the auteur for their support. Chapter 3 analyzes the discourses of colonialism, flanerie, and the romantically linked auteur/actress star couple, the implicit remapping being of the tradition of close textual reading of art films and directors' oeuvres, here deployed toward historical enquiry extending beyond the geographic and political borders of France and Italy. And chapter 4 moves beyond European art cinema discourse itself to engage the broader institutional contexts that subtend it: the paradigms of film historical writing and of academic film studies as a whole. Across each, finally, there is a fading of the individual importance of the auteur for understanding the meanings of European art cinema, from an absent, "authorizing" force for tenuous national stability to being part of a heterosexual couple and a group of couples working through the national divorce undergone by Europe and its colonial empire, to a member of a collective and hence a participant in, rather than the sole generator of, filmic meaning.

I opened this chapter with an epigraph from Walter Benjamin's "Theses on the Philosophy of History."[97] The memory I am seizing hold of in this book is of the significance that European art cinema could have, should have held for academic film studies. The danger is not that this significance has become entirely lost but that its potential for the future will. In the pages that follow, I hope to remap this potential as well as imagine its future.

2

The Name above the Subtitle

Language, Coproduction, Transnationalism

Dubbing is not only a technique, it's also an ideology. In a dubbed film, there is not the least rapport between what you see and what you hear. The dubbed cinema is the cinema of lies, mental laziness, and violence, because it gives no space to the viewer and makes him still more deaf and insensitive. In Italy, every day the people are becoming more deaf at an alarming rate.

> —JEAN-MARIE STRAUB, "Direct Sound: An Interview with
> Jean-Marie Straub and Danièle Huillet"

By 1982 . . . French, Italian, German, and even Greek directors felt that it could not conceivably be in the interest of a united Europe to destroy nationally specific cultural or cinematic traditions by the stroke of a bureaucrat's pen in favour of more harmonisation. "Every film must declare its nationality and its own cultural identity," pronounced Bertrand Tavernier, who condemned the multinational cinema of coproductions and poured scorn on the prospect of "Sophia Loren playing a Berlin housewife, and Catherine Deneuve a Sicilian peasant." The Eurofilm of the future could join the Golden Delicious Euro-apple: tasteless and bland.

> —THOMAS ELSAESSER, *New German Cinema: A History*

Sounding Off

FOR MORE THAN THREE YEARS in the late 1990s I worked as the film programmer at George Eastman House / International Museum of Photography and Film, one of the largest film archives in the United States. As programmer I was responsible for conceptualizing film series and programming approximately 270 evening screenings per year in the museum's on-site Dryden Theatre. One of the series I put together, "Soon To Be a Major Motion Picture," comprised eight feature films on the subject of filmmaking and was scheduled in the early summer of 1998. The choices were eclectic and based on various factors, including relevance to the subject, print availability and condition, and frequency of exhibition: *The Big Knife* (United States, 1955); *8½* (Italy/France, 1963); *Le Mépris* (*Contempt,* France/Italy/United States, 1963); *For Ever Mozart* (Switzerland/France, 1997); *La Nuit américaine* (*Day for Night,* France/Italy/United Kingdom, 1973); *Stardust Memories* (United States, 1980); *Venice/Venice* (United States, 1992); *Irma Vep* (France, 1996). The series leaned toward European art cinema, which has not only produced a high proportion of such metafilms but has proven a mainstay of contemporary international film archive exhibition. As one might expect, the clientele for this and other similar series at the Dryden Theatre was a mix of film buffs and aficionados, professors and students, and local residents, all of whom possessed relatively high amounts of cultural capital.[1]

Early into the series, the museum received and passed on to me for response the following e-mail from a member who lived in another state and had perused the calendar in both a hard copy and on the Internet:

> Please tell me it's a typo in your calendar. You can't seriously plan on a DUBBED version of "Day for Night"!! Especially not as a 25th Anniversary special. I saw a lovely new subtitled print in NYC last summer; surely you can get your hands on that.
>
> I had planned to tell my parents and brother to attend, as "Day for Night" is one of my favorite films. But I would tell everyone I can to avoid at all costs a dubbed version.
>
> I grew up in Rochester, and spent more time at the Dryden than I can guess. For a real movie fan, the Eastman House is a treasure.
>
> How can a film archive, dedicating [*sic*] to preserving films as originally produced, fall to such a level as this? If this is the real policy, I'll have to consider my membership and support of the Eastman House.
>
> Please advise ASAP. (And, if it is merely a typo (though I checked your on-line calendar for corrections)), please accept my apologies for this rant.

The person who wrote this message clearly had a deep investment in film culture and felt strongly about the matter of a dubbed print, so I was careful in preparing my response regarding film dubbing in general and *Day for Night* in particular. I explained, for example, that the (indeed) dubbed print of *Day for Night* we were screening was not from the Eastman House's archive but a neighboring one, that the only other prints in current distribution were also dubbed, that we chose the best quality print we could find (a beautifully conserved 35mm IB Technicolor print from the film's original U.S. release run), and that the subtitled print shown in New York City the year previous was one made available through the French consulate and at that time unavailable for screening in the country. I pointed out that *Day for Night* was shot in France by a French director with a largely French cast and crew save for the key exceptions of the Italian Valentina Cortese and the British actors David Markham and Jacqueline Bisset; their presence registers the fact that *Day for Night* is not a French film but an international coproduction between France and Italy and Great Britain. In fact, the film was coproduced by Warner Bros. through its London subsidiary, and one of the stipulations of the agreement was that Warner Bros. would have worldwide distribution rights for the film, excluding France and Italy.[2] This meant that, in its first-run release in North America and Great Britain in late 1973, *Day for Night* was shown widely in a version dubbed into English, as one would expect of a major studio whose business is to reach as large an audience as possible. And the director of the film, François Truffaut, entered into production with full knowledge of this outcome.

Like so many other postwar European films that won an Academy Award of some kind, the critical and popular success of *Day for Night* in the United States was due in no small part to the fact that it was generally distributed in English-dubbed prints (other examples, from France and Italy alone, include *Jeux interdits* [*Forbidden Games,* 1952], *La strada* [1956], *Mon oncle* [1958], *Ieri oggi domani* [*Yesterday, Today, and Tomorrow,* 1964], *Un homme et une femme* [1966], and *Amarcord* [1974]). From a historical/exhibition standpoint, showing a dubbed print of *Day for Night* for a twenty-fifth-anniversary screening was entirely in keeping with how the film was seen in the United States in 1973 except for occasional prestigious festival and art house screenings in major cities. From an archival standpoint, there really is no version of a film "as originally produced" to preserve or, as is more often the case, conserve, except perhaps for the unviewable in-camera negative—the only use for which is to strike positive prints, all of which are, in effect, copies that constitute the bulk of every film archive's holdings. (In fact, the newly struck and subtitled print this person had seen would be rather far removed, historically and generationally, from the "original" source and, according to the slippery logic of origins, would have less business being in a film archive than a vintage dubbed print.) Our presentation of a dubbed print of *Day for Night* was thus archivally sound as a practice.

A related issue, and one that warrants future research in the form of reception studies, is how high/low distinctions determine one's expectations and reactions concerning dubbed versus subtitled films. Of the ten features not produced in English that were presented at the Eastman House that early summer, only two were shown in dubbed prints: *Day for Night* and *Fuego* (1968), the latter an erotic melodrama from Argentina screened as part of a series on exploitation films. I expected no complaints regarding the aural status of *Fuego,* nor did I receive any. Further, I was never questioned about other dubbed prints we had shown recently from similarly low genres: spaghetti westerns like *Il buono il brutto il cattivo* (*The Good, the Bad, and the Ugly,* 1966), gialli like *L'uccello dalle piume di cristallo* (*The Bird with the Crystal Plumage,* 1970), Hong Kong kung fu comedies like *Drunken Master* (1978), and anime like *Hadashi no gen* (*Barefoot Gen,* 1983). One of the unwritten rules of art cinema culture is not simply a preference but the exigency for the subtitled print. The name of the auteur and the purity of his or her intentions, the need to hear the "original" sound track in its "original" language—both of these mutually determining notions are ritually invoked as proof of the superiority of subtitling over dubbing, yet the same standards do not apply to popular cinemas. One of the ironies here is that many low-genre films are distributed and exhibited, cheek-by-jowl with art films, in subtitled versions in several countries (the Nordic states, for example) where the matter is one not of aesthetic distinction, as it is in the Anglo-American context, but of size, wealth, and tradition. The national preferences for subtitled or dubbed films thus stem from several factors, including historical and political circumstances, traditions and industries, costs, and the form to which audiences are accustomed. When it comes to the distribution and exhibition of non-English-language films in Britain or North America, however, other factors determine which are subtitled and which dubbed. And when a European art film is shown (and heard) in the latter format, cinephiles are the first to object.

The 1968 Academy Award winner for Best Foreign Film, Sergei Bondarchuk's mammoth adaptation of *Voina i mir (War and Peace)* was, like almost all of the non–English-language Oscar winners of its time, distributed in the United States in a dubbed version, a fact that every reviewer of the film mentioned with varying degrees of disparagement. Writing for *Commonweal,* Philip Hartung admits that the American version prepared by the Walter Reade Organization has the best dubbing he has heard (and seen), but that "dubbing still leaves much to be desired—the synchronization is never perfect; and the voices themselves, while good, have a certain sameness and flatness." *New Republic* reviewer Stanley Kauffmann complains that "there is a dead studio sound to the process, an absence of liveness and of planes, and we can never quite forget that all the speech *is* dubbed. Obviously we can never forget the subtitles in a subtitled film, but we know we are watching an attempt to bring us an unimpaired original, which is considerable compensation." Richard Schickel of *Life* magazine is most vociferous in his opinions on the subject, and in this he is in fact more representative than his peers of the general high/low tenor of American art film culture in the late 1960s:

> [The film's American distributors] have treated *War and Peace* with a lack of respect usually accorded sleazy Italian sex-and-sandal epics designed for short runs at the bottom of the bill. They have cut it and dubbed it and thereby ruined whatever merit it may have had. Both of these practices are painfully common among movie businessmen, and since they betray a fundamental lack of respect for the artist and the uniqueness of his vision, they are reprehensible at any level; the worst B picture is entitled to fail on its own terms. . . . As for the dubbing, it has the familiar effect of alienating audience from characters. You get fixed on those lips so obviously not speaking the lines you are hearing, you get to brooding about those radio-station voices *reading* instead of *acting* their parts, and it becomes impossible to sustain identification with the figures on the screen. Subtitling is not a perfect solution to the language barrier, but it is relatively unobtrusive, does not deny actors the use of their voices, the basic tools of their art, does not tamper with an intrinsic part of the film's design.[3]

Poor synchronicity between voice and body, flatness of performance and acoustics, alteration or truncation of the wholeness of the "original" film—all of these are sources of distress and distraction for these American reviewers. On the one hand, these complaints seem perfectly reasonable even if they tend to be leveled only at art films. On the other hand, as I will explore at greater length in the pages to come, many classics of European art cinema (*8½,* for example, one of the films in the Eastman House series) have no original sound track at all in the most generous of senses—or have a sound track so thoroughly compromised by linguistic and performative instabilities that to speak of subtitling over dubbing is a moot point, or at least one that fails to recognize the historical, economic, industrial, and cultural complexities of the matter.

In fact, it is only by tabling these complexities and concentrating almost wholly on aesthetic considerations that one can argue for the inferiority of dubbed prints compared to subtitled ones. Such debates raged in the entertainment and op-ed pages of the *New York Times* and in film culture journals and little magazines in the early to mid-1960s; their outcomes effectively determined common knowledge that to this day permeates Anglo-American academic film studies, which was forged equally as much by the cosmopolitan British and American film magazine cultures bolstered by European art cinema in the 1960s as by forces within the academy.[4] The case against dubbing includes imperfect lip and audio synchronicity between voice and body, flatness of performances and acoustics, and alteration or elimination of the original film's sound track and design. The quality of the acting is frequently noted as suffering in dubbed films as the vocal qualities, tones, and rhythms of specific languages, combined with the gestures and facial expressions that mark national characters and acting styles, are lost in translation. Most critics of dubbing thus see it as less authentic than subtitling because of the alterations it makes to the filmed performances and the destruction it enacts to the film's sound track.

A survey of introductory film texts published in North America and Britain reveals that many contain at least a paragraph on the matter of subtitling versus dubbing. While some admit that subtitles have their deficiencies (they are distracting and make it difficult to concentrate on the visuals, they often leave significant portions of the dialogue untranslated, they divide viewer attention between reading text and watching images), subtitling is nevertheless considered as altering the source text the least and thus enables the audience to experience the authentic "foreignness" of the film.[5] In *Film Art: An Introduction,* one of the most widely used introductory film texts, David Bordwell and Kristin Thompson recite their version in a special "Notes and Queries" section, and their answer to the question "Why do most people who study movies prefer subtitles?" is representative:

Dubbed voices usually have a bland studio sound. Elimination of the original actors' voices wipes out an important component of their performance. (Partisans of dubbing ought to look at dubbed versions of English-language films to see how a performance by Katharine Hepburn, Orson Welles, or John Wayne can be hurt by a voice that does not fit the body.) With dubbing, all of the usual problems of translation are multiplied by the need to synchronize specific words with specific lip movements. Most important, with subtitling viewers still have access to the original soundtrack. By eliminating the original voice track, dubbing simply destroys part of the film.[6]

Strong support for this position is provided by many a European auteur working within national industries that postsynchronize domestic films and dub imports, especially Italy and Germany. In *Cahiers du cinéma* in the mid-1950s, Roberto Rossellini pronounced the "dubbing of Italian films in English and attempting to distribute them in America" a "mad idea. . . . Failure is assured." This aside was less than prescient of the distribution and commercial success of Italian cinema abroad, and Rossellini would later recant and accuse critics who objected to dubbing of being "cinematic fetishists."[7] But it was prescient indeed of the objections that would begin to be expressed by other Italian filmmakers and would result in a manifesto, presented in February 1967 in Amalfi at a conference on film language and the sound film and signed by some of Italy's most renowned auteurs, which called for the "abolition of the indiscriminate use of dubbing, whose existence compromises the very possibility of an Italian sound cinema."[8] A most extreme protest was voiced in a 1970 *Cahiers du cinéma* interview with Jean-Marie Straub and Danièle Huillet, who are noted for filming in direct sound and one of whose statements appears as an epigraph at the beginning of this chapter. While it is difficult to take seriously Straub's claim that Italian people were literally becoming deaf due to their exposure to postsynchronized films, he and his partner do offer other provocative comments that broaden the scope of the matter and in many ways set the terms for my exploration of the soundscape of European art cinema in this chapter: that postsynchronization is not only a technique but also an ideology; that "only by accepting the dictatorship of dubbing can you use two or three stars from different countries in the same film"; that it is part and parcel of an "international aesthetic" that "is like Esperanto."[9] The tensions here, ones that dubbing ostensibly magnifies or produces and that direct sound or subtitling apparently solves, exist between the industrial and economic determinants of European art cinema casting and the personal vision of the director, between language as a root national signifier and nation builder, and between conflicting national and international ideologies. The dialogue tracks of art films are thus a rich site of contestation and are symptomatic of larger economic, political, and cultural forces in Europe in the 1960s and 1970s.

Indeed, the same critics who were engaged in debates over the dubbing and/or subtitling of foreign films into English also recognized that the issue was related to the transformation of Europe's national cinemas into an international film industry in the postwar era. In his response to a questionnaire circulated among members of the National Society of Film Critics in 1968, Philip Hartung noted that "so many films are international with director, writer, technicians, actors, and perhaps even the producer and bankroll coming from different countries for a single picture, it is often impossible to put a nationality label on a movie." Two years earlier, Peter Cowie opened his *International Film Guide* with the following observation: "During the past year the differences between one country's cinema and another's have become blurred: we are in an age of co-productions." And Penelope Houston, writing in 1963, pointed out that a key aspect of France's contemporary film industry is

> co-production, mainly between France and Italy but on more exotic occasions involving tie-ups between three or four nations. A British or American film will usually be promoted by one company, or perhaps a couple: a Franco-Italian film may be backed by as many as half a dozen firms, with a key impresario who has set up the deal. All this was becoming standard form even before the Common Market; and as the film industries of Western Europe gradually come closer together there are obvious economic benefits all round. The Western European market, viewed as a single identity, is a great deal more enticing than the French, Italian, or West German markets, seen as separate units divided from each other by language barriers. . . . International casting, international financing, fit the whole European pattern. Europe is moving towards a Common Market cinema.[10]

At the time of these writings, the stability of the concept of nationhood in France, Italy, and other Western European countries was becoming increasingly compromised by American-style modernization and capitalism on the one hand and increasing European economic and political cooperation and integration on the other. In film industrial terms, one of the results of this ferment was a huge increase in bi-, tri-, and multilateral coproductions with transnational, polyglot casts.

Although the outcomes of the critical debates about dubbing versus subtitling in the 1960s have become received wisdom in Anglo-American academic film studies, the facts of pan-European coproduction during the same period have only sporadically been addressed in film historical writing, and even here they tend to be confined to other periods or narrativized in ways that continue to place European cinema as a victim of Hollywood. Examples of these include the Film Europe movement of the 1920s, the coming of sound to Europe and the failed experiments with multilanguage film versions in 1930–31, and the cross-cultural initiatives of the European Community (EC) since the early 1980s. Work in the 2000s on postwar European coproduction by Tim Bergfelder and Marc Silberman are exceptions to a standard line of film historical writing that continues to fall comfortably under the rubric of the nation as a stable category and geopolitical entity in Europe.[11] The subject of European coproductions in the 1950s through the 1970s remains largely unacknowledged in most macrohistory or national survey history texts, as the stubborn paradigm of national cinema has tended to preclude extensive scholarly discussion on the subject. And most of that discussion focuses on the menace American moving-image culture and commerce presented to Europe's national film industries, which were forced to compete on Hollywood's terms by increasing film budgets and opting for high-production values, popular stars, elaborate and expensive costumes and sets, and so on. European coproduction, especially between France and Italy, emerges in this narrative as a purely industrial and economic response that holds little interest for stylistic or aesthetic national studies. Thus, Robin Buss considers postwar film initiatives toward internationalization to be "disastrous for Italian cinema," and Susan Hayward, who documents some of the more interesting and detailed things on the matter, nevertheless refers to coproductions as a "thorny problem" and a "murky area."[12]

Peter Lev has coined the term "Euro-American Cinema" to describe an aesthetically higher form of American industrial influence on European film production, "the big budget English-language film made by a European art film director."[13] Lev's study stands at time of writing as one of only two sustained English-language studies of post-war European film coproduction presently in circulation.[14] Another important one, Thomas Guback's *The International Film Industry: Western Europe and America since 1945,* published in 1969, has been out of print for several years.[15] I will be drawing upon Guback's work later. What is most significant about these works for the present discussion is that they situate their analyses of European coproduction in a clear and constant relationship to Hollywood. The result is that the ubiquitous coproductions of European art cinema are, in the case of their backing by American coin, read as rather unnatural hybrids, as compromises of the auteur's vision or as cautionary examples of the damage brought upon Western European cinematic traditions by the commercialism and manifest destiny inherent in Hollywood's colonizing interests in Europe.

European coproductions, particularly those that fall within the category of art cinema, have thus been all but eliminated from the equation, and so left free to carry on as signifiers of stable national cinemas and identities or as gleaming expressions of their auteur's vision, which has somehow not been blurred by the determinants of cross-national cooperation that leave their marks everywhere on art films, from their budgets to their shooting locations to their casts to their sound tracks. Here is an interesting passage, penned by Geoffrey Nowell-Smith in 1996, in a sidebar on Michelangelo Antonioni in the context of a piece titled "Art Cinema": "The success of *L'avventura* gave Antonioni access to larger budgets and the opportunity to work with international stars: a languid Marcello Mastroianni and morose Jeanne Moreau in *La notte,* a wonderfully dynamic Alain Delon in *The Eclipse,* and a rather doltish Richard Harris in *Red Desert.* He was then engaged by producer Carlo Ponti to make a series of international co-productions."[16] Those films are, of course, *Blow-Up* (1966), *Zabriskie Point* (1969), and *Professione: Reporter* (*The Passenger,* 1975), English-language coproductions initiated by Ponti and financed through a three-picture deal with the American studio Metro-Goldwyn-Mayer. They are indeed "international co-productions," all made with largely Italian crews and non-Italian casts in London, Southern California, and in the case of *The Passenger,* Algeria, London, Munich, Barcelona, and coastal Spain. But what of Antonioni's three previous films, all Italo-French coproductions? Are not these "international co-productions" as well?

When I watch and listen to these films in English-subtitled versions with their "original" Italian sound tracks, I notice something that gives me pause: the "morose Jeanne Moreau" in *La notte* (1961) is mouthing Italian, but the sync between her lips and her voice is off. In fact, it is not her distinctive voice at all: her vocal part has been dubbed into Italian by someone else. The "wonderfully dynamic Alain Delon" in *The Eclipse* (*L'eclisse*, 1962) is out of sync as well: at times he appears to be voicing Italian as his labials lag behind the speed of the speech on the dialogue track, at others his lip movements seem to have no correspondence at all to the Italian and he may very well be speaking French. In any case his vocal part, like Moreau's, has been dubbed into Italian by a voice actor. As for the "rather doltish Richard Harris" in *Red Desert* (*Il deserto rosso*, 1964), he clearly

Jeanne Moreau, Bernhard Wicki, and Marcello Mastroianni in *La notte* (1961). Courtesy of the Museum of Modern Art Film Stills Archive.

enunciates his lines in English, so infrequently do they correspond with the Italian dialogue postsynchronized onto the sound track by yet another voice actor.

Other non-Italian actors in these films with speaking parts are noticeably out of sync and similarly looped or dubbed: Bernhard Wicki in *La notte,* Francisco Rabal and Louis Seigner in *The Eclipse,* Rita Renoir in *Red Desert.* In fact, the sync is frequently off at times for even the Italian actors. All three of these films were undoubtedly shot without sound and postsynchronized later, sometimes with the performers looping their own dialogue (Monica Vitti, for example, who met Antonioni in her capacity as a voice actress dubbing the Italian vocal part for one of the three non-Italian female performers in the Italo-American coproduction *Il grido* [1957]), at others—especially when they involved international stars—with the dialogue dubbed into Italian by uncredited Italian voice actors. There is no "original" sound track to speak of for any of these films: they are always already dubbed in any release print one can see and hear. And it is this very instability—a historical and economic fact of the Italian sound film industry on the one hand, a variable syncing of bodies to voices in the case of non-Italian performers in prominent roles in coproductions on the other—that offers a fascinating site of incoherence in European art cinema.

There has in the past two decades been a revival of interest in the issue of a contemporary European audiovisual production arising through coproduction, of much-maligned Euro-films whose policy-driven mixing of performers from various countries and cultural traditions yields a so-called "Euro-pudding" that collectively bespeaks contemporary fears of American cultural and economic imperialism and predicts the erosion of national cultures in the wake of globalization. "Every film must declare its nationality and its own cultural identity," stated Bertrand Tavernier in 1982. The persistent need to retain the notion of national cinemas in Europe is rendered by Tavernier in terms of film stars as secure embodiments of nationhood. And it is more than fortuitous that the stars he chooses for his negative prediction of Euro-film casting, Sophia Loren and Catherine Deneuve, rose to prominence in the 1950s and 1960s and themselves participated in numerous European coproductions during the very period when they became national icons. "It has to be possible to think of a

European film. To think of film in European terms. Without the consequence of a thoroughly watered-down Euro-film," wrote the German filmmaker Alfred Behrens in 1986. That possibility was realized, I contend, through the new European cinemas of the 1960s.

In this chapter I am claiming that anxieties in Europe about economic and cultural cooperation on the one hand and nationalism and national identity on the other are present and readable through the coproduced art cinemas of Italy and France from the late 1950s through the mid-1970s, which was fully a part of the complicated establishment of the European Economic Community (EEC), not to mention numerous other economic and cultural alliances in the period. From the late 1940s on, the Western European landscape was permeated by intercontinental development as the area moved protractedly but consistently toward the institution of a European Union (EU) based on mutual economic and political (preeminently) but also cultural benefit. And the soundscape of the European art film, particularly the coproduced one, is a terrain upon which such trans/national growth and tension may be mapped. Rick Altman acknowledged some of the limitations of film-sound scholarship and criticism by concluding his collection *Sound Theory, Sound Practice* with a section titled "Neglected Domains," and his introductory essay to that section identifies several "Dark Corners" that call most urgently for investigation: Third World cinema, local and regional productions, documentary, music in/on film, animation, short forms, media shifts, silent cinema, idiosyncratic auteurs, and technicians.[17] Absent from Altman's list is the question of language translation/transformation in the production, distribution, and exhibition of films made in one language community and exported/imported into another—in other words, the issue of subtitling or dubbing in all its historical, economic/industrial, and cultural dimensions. It is on this "dark corner" that I hope to shed a little light.

The aims of this chapter are more speculative than definitive in that they intend to bring into relation varying sets of discourses—historiographic, aesthetic, industrial, and geopolitical—to propose their ubiquitous and necessary intersection. While I do not come to a firm conclusion about precisely how European art films are functioning in this network of conditions, I do want to stress the importance of reading these films closely through the discourses of transnationalism, auteurism, subtitling/dubbing, polyglot filmmaking, and star textuality.

For it is through such readings that one might concretize some of the tensions and contradictions I understand as essential to explore in a remapping of European art cinema. And to see—and hear—the historiographic significance of these discourses, it is necessary to read critically Anglo-American historical writing concerning European cooperative responses to the American film industry.

Hollywood and Coproduction in Europe: A Historiographic Survey

The issues I am juxtaposing as generative of modern European cinema are ones that circulate throughout the historiography of world cinema, but their deployment tends to remain limited to certain periods. One important historical moment in the historiography of the cooperative strategies of national film industries of Europe is located in the early 1920s, when American competition became too great for any one country to counter.[18] "What if European film industries could cooperate by guaranteeing to import each other's films? European films might make as much money as Hollywood films did. Then their budgets could be raised, their production values would improve, and they might even be able to compete with American films in other world markets. The idea was gradually formulated as the 'pan-European' cinema, or 'Film Europe.'"[19] German producer Erich Pommer was at the forefront of the Film Europe movement, and it is through a complex chain of industrial and economic events that he rose to that position and implicitly answered these questions.[20] The founder of Decla (Deutsche Eclair), Pommer advanced through a series of mergers, first with Bioscop, then Ufa (Universum Film Aktien Gessellschaft), to be head of production for most of the German film industry by early 1923. It was in this capacity that he encouraged the production of big-budget films as an investor strategy to protect profits, but Germany's market was too limited to recoup the high production costs. His negotiations with France's Establissement Aubert in 1924 yielded the first bilateral film import deal between two European countries, and with him as its leader the German film industry moved toward increasingly cooperative pan-European efforts.

One of the interesting things about how these efforts are documented is the lack of consensus about the national status of the films produced in Germany under their auspices. On the one hand, Pommer is characterized as a nationalist, compromising in his internationalist initiatives "neither his belief in 'nationally specific' films nor his desire to remove national boundaries through the cinema. Just as *Der letzte Mann* (1924) was recognized in France as 'thoroughly German,' it was celebrated in Germany as a 'world film.'"[21] On the other hand, he is quoted as advocating an international aesthetic for the European film: "I think that European producers must at last think of establishing a certain cooperation among themselves. . . . It is necessary to create 'European' films, which will no longer be French, English, Italian, or German films, but entirely 'continental' films."[22] In the mid-1920s, the European film industries, with Germany, France, and Great Britain at the forefront, built the base for a cooperative continental market that slowly reduced the number of American imports and replaced them with European product. But the ideological price of such cooperation was considered by some to herald a loss of national character, often an Americanization of national moving-image culture. Paul Rotha wrote in 1930 that German film production in the late 1920s "was rapidly becoming like that of Hollywood in external appearances. Many of the big pictures of 1928, for example, might have been the product of American studios. They were made for an international market, and little of the old German feeling for psychology and simplicity of treatment remained." In his canonical 1947 study of interwar German cinema, *From Caligari to Hitler,* Siegfried Kracauer begins his chapter "The Stabilized Period (1924–1929)" with a section tellingly titled "Decline." Fifty years after Kracauer, Ursula Hardt used two Fritz Lang films to chart the decadence of the German film between 1924 and 1927, the era of Film Europe: "*Die Nibelungen* became the epitome of German filmmaking in its national specificity; the utopian city of *Metropolis* constituted a betrayal in its departure from Pommer's and Lang's vision of a 'German' film. . . . Ufa's Hans Traub justifiably interpreted *Metropolis* as Ufa's desire to create a film style equal to America's and therefore capable of winning in the American market."[23] In even its earliest cinematic incarnation, European cooperation is represented as cultural loss for economic and industrial gain, as a kind of Americanization.

In this respect these historians reproduce what Richard Maltby and Ruth Vasey have characterized as "a pervasive, pan-European discourse of Anti-Americanism among European cultural élites" in the interwar period and what André Visson called in 1948 "the fundamental prejudice of the European intellectual elite toward American conceptions of the 'Common Man.'"[24] The cultural elites of England, for example, were worried less about American films themselves than about the working classes who saw them and were becoming affected by what Paul Swann states was "their supposed homogenizing effect," by which the "external differences in dress, speech and demeanor, which had previously been clear demarcators of class and background," were becoming increasingly ambiguous.[25] Fear of American mass culture in Europe in the 1920s and 1930s was also thus a fear of the loss of privilege on the part of European elites.[26] The establishment of, first, nationally specific art film movements (French Impressionism, German Expressionism), then an international art film aesthetic, together with the concomitant rise of an art film culture across Europe in the 1920s in the form of ciné-clubs, art shows, and exhibitions, may thus be considered a reaction formation to the perceived leveling effects of American visual culture and a shoring up of cultural capital wherein national and European identities intersect and blur in common cause to maintain class boundaries. Already then, in its first incarnation, European art cinema was counterposed to American culture, and it entailed transnational cooperative initiatives that placed class and national distinctions in sometimes precarious relation.

The coming of sound to Europe in 1929 cut the Film Europe movement short through the introduction of language to the European sphere, an introduction that produced a fragmentation of a forced unity: "Dialogue created language barriers, and each country's producers began to hope that they could succeed locally because English-language imports would decline" (Thompson and Bordwell); "The effect of talking pictures was to splinter any incipient European unity into its component language groups. Any sense of cohesion that had arisen from the shared determination to resist the American industry was undermined by the local cultural imperative of hearing the accents of one's own language" (Maltby and Vasey); "A silent picture could be exhibited in all countries of the world. A talking picture, however, became the prisoner of its language" (Karel Dibbets).[27] The national isolationism that is the natural preserve of language thus crested in 1927–31 as a wave of quota legislations that were established, pending, or newly created on the part of Europe's national film industries: the "Kontingent" quota legislation of 1925, which provided (in substance though not in practice) that only as many films could be imported as were produced in Germany; the 1927 Cinematograph Films Act in Great Britain, which similarly instituted a quota on foreign film imports; the Herriot decree of 1929 in France, establishing an import-export ratio of seven foreign films to one French one.[28] National bans on foreign-language films in Italy, France, Germany, Czechoslovakia, and Hungary marked foreign-language sound films from the beginning as a threat to national identity and a seemingly insurmountable problem for European coproduction.

But America, with its sights set on the European market, entered the fray with a production method to overcome the language barrier: multilinguals, foreign-language versions, or as they are most frequently called, multiple-language versions (MLVs).[29] The basic strategy was to shoot, either scene by scene, in timed shifts, or one after another, a number of different language versions of the same film using the same sets and costumes and, in the case of multilingual personnel, the same directors, actors, and crews. In 1930 American studios thus began to invest heavily in the European film industry to make MLVs for the international market, either by importing European personnel (or in the case of the Central and South American markets, Central and South American personnel) to Hollywood "to do the hasty rewriting, acting, and directing needed to turn a $300,000 English language film into four $100,000 European versions," or by establishing studios in Europe and to produce MLVs much closer to the national language communities for which they were intended. The building by Paramount of a giant studio complex equipped with Western Electric sound equipment in Joinville outside Paris is by the far the most famous of these, a "Babel sur la Seine" that between March 1930 and March 1931 "turned out an incredible 100 features and 50 shorts in as many as 14 languages."[30] Films that were shot simultaneously in two or three languages usually had just one director, but for a higher number of MLVs each could have a different one, corresponding to the languages used. Polyglot actors might perform in more than one language version, but the norm was different casts for different versions. Sets and costumes were reused, entailing the shooting of versions in shifts according to a twenty-four-hour schedule. Production time was short, often less than two weeks per feature. By September 1931, all of the American studio majors had established MLV production facilities in Europe: Paramount, United Artists, and Fox in Paris; Warner Bros., Universal, RKO, Paramount, United Artists, and MGM in London; and Fox and United Artists in Berlin.[31]

The other famous MLV studio—in Epinay, France—was bought by the German company Tobis, and after equipping it with a Tri-Ergon sound system Tobis began a more cautious pace than Paramount of "quality" MLVs and leased the studio to all takers. The German presence in France, like the American one, was not without precedent at the level of distribution. As a result of its expansionist export strategies, Germany had a large portion of the European market share by the coming of sound, much larger than any of its cooperative European partners; out of the 437 feature films shown in France in 1929, for example, 211 were American and 130 German (and only 52 French).[32] It is here that the historicization of MLV production is strikingly parallel to that of the Film Europe movement: America and Germany are placed at the forefront of a type of international filmmaking that threatened national filmmaking traditions. Despite the participation of some canonized auteurs (Marcel Pagnol, René Clair, G. W. Pabst) and several other directors of note (Claude Autant-Lara, Alberto Cavalcanti, Julien Duvivier, Jacques Feyder, Anatole Litvak) in the making of MLVs, the products of this second attempt at an international style or aesthetic are generally denigrated by Anglo-American historians of European cinema, particularly French cinema. Dudley Andrew, for example, reports that "scarcely a film of lasting interest was made" by Paramount at Joinville, with the only ones directed by its flagship director, Marcel Pagnol. The same holds true for Epinay: the few films of note produced there were made by another great French director, René Clair. Thus, although the MLVs were, from an aesthetic and a commercial standpoint, a failure, in "the context of foreign capital and pressures . . . the native French genius developed two radical and radically opposed approaches to sound (Pagnol at Paramount, Clair at Tobis) which contributed far more to the history of film practice than the standard products, which, because of their very size, the studios were bound to continue to produce."[33]

Ginette Vincendeau has challenged the idea that MLVs must be situated "along a rather blurred line of division between . . . two types of discourse . . . : that of a European resistance (however ephemeral, disorganised or doomed to failure) to US hegemony, and that of a continued expansion by Hollywood in the face of a sudden increase in foreign competition."[34] She also explains convincingly the reasons for their failure. Despite rationalization of production, MLVs meant an enormous increase in costs, and their standardization of plots worked against satisfying the cultural diversity of their target audiences. Their lack of profitability, combined with their perception as purely commercial products and their inability to meet generic requirements across cultures, led to a precipitous decline in MLVs in 1932, with Hollywood ceasing multilingual production in 1933 and Germany and France soon thereafter. Vincendeau points out as well that the first MLV was not a Hollywood production but an Anglo-German one: *Atlantic,* shot simultaneously by E. A. Dupont in English and German for British International Pictures at Elstree studios in November 1929 (a third French version was shot immediately afterward).[35] In doing so, Vincendeau indicates a need for further reevaluation of MLVs as an ostensibly American production-line practice, apparently incompatible with a less mechanized and more artistic European sensibility, which actually originated in London and Berlin.

An economic historical narrative of European domination by Hollywood in the immediate postwar era was forcefully proposed in 1969 by Thomas Guback. His study was constructed from published statistics and unattributed interviews by necessity, for it was undertaken before government files began to be opened and when no studio files were yet made available. As Robert C. Allen and Douglas Gomery have noted, "Guback proceeds from an analysis of the economic base of European-American trade in motion pictures to one of the ideological effects on the motion pictures produced. First looking at the economic base, he finds that, with the direct assistance of the U.S. government, the giant Hollywood corporations . . . formed a cartel after World War II to coordinate economic action in Western Europe."[36] That cartel was the Motion Picture Export Association of America (MPEAA), formed in September 1945 out of the former Foreign Department as an exploiting arm of the Motion Picture Producers and Distributors of America (MPPDA) to expand markets and to lobby for international free trade of U.S. films. Dubbed by Jack Valenti as "the little State Department," the MPEAA undertook, with the added ballast of a quid pro quo for Marshall Plan Aid and the establishment of the General Agreement on Tariffs and Trade in October 1947, the ambitious dismantling of the cumbersome structure of quotas, visas, exchange controls, and bilateral trade agreements that had been in effect in Europe since the 1920s and had gained force throughout the 1930s and the war years, particularly for the nationalized film industries of Italy, Germany, and the USSR. Thus began a protracted series of new agreements between the United States and the devastated European nations that at first allowed for the almost unchecked flow of American films onto the screens of a reconstructing Europe. The protests on the part of many national film industries and filmmakers to this development set in motion a new wave of protectionism in the form of revised quota and subsidy systems, reactive MPEAA boycotts, and eventual compromises that bespeak a consistent pressure from the late 1940s through the late 1950s on the European film industry to accommodate American visual culture and capital investment. Postwar Europe emerges in Guback's account as an economic, political, and cultural battleground upon which is waged a war of many fronts between a newly emergent superpower and the disunified nations of Europe.[37]

Perhaps the most insidious aspect of U.S. economic and cultural imperialism in this context was the establishment of studio subsidiaries in almost every Western European country to take advantage of state subsidies intended to aid indigenous production. After an initial wave of so-called "runaway productions"—Hollywood films shot abroad and financed by the large amounts of unremittable revenue earned by American exports but blocked from removal—American companies learned that certain types of films for the European (and indeed the domestic) market could be made more cheaply and with fewer union problems there than in the United States.[38] "Having introduced themselves to shooting films abroad, American companies saw the next logical step as having these films declared 'national' by European countries so they could have access to subsidization. The turning point was around 1950, the year in which a subsidy was initiated in Britain and two years after inauguration of subsidization in France and Italy."[39] The bulk of American overseas participation in the European film industry in the 1960s was centered in Great Britain, Italy, and France, and Guback offers extensive documentation of purportedly European productions or coproductions that are, in fact, American studio productions or Euro-American coproductions. He follows this analysis with a penultimate chapter on European coproduction proper, which he appears to consider a positive development to counter Hollywood imperialism insofar as it allows for a more elaborate kind of film with bigger stars and thus appeals to more markets than a single European country could make financing and producing alone. In a Europe-versus-America conception of the international film industry, whatever pooling of resources it takes, with however many European national industries and with whatever kinds of filmic results, is a necessary and useful armament.

The information Guback provides on the details of French, Italian, and other European countries' coproduction agreements in the 1950s and 1960s is extensive. But importantly, Guback himself did not continue to explore the centrality of European coproductions—economically, ideologically—to postwar European art cinema and film history. He concludes *The International Film Industry* with a warning against internationally coproduced aesthetics, Anglo-European or pan-European, and the kinds of films they effect:

> So many of the new international films border on dehumanization by brutalizing sensitivity, often deflecting attention from reality. They count on developing audience response with synthetic, machine-made images. Their shallowness and cardboard characters are camouflaged with dazzling colors, wide screens, and directorial slickness. Of course, undistinguished pictures have always been made, but now the context in which they are produced and marketed is substantially different. Films of this genre are not a form of cultural exchange. In reality, they are anti-culture, the antithesis of human culture.[40]

This is a familiar diatribe against American mass culture, one that has a legacy in Europe dating to the 1920s. And in taking this tack Guback both forecloses in his own work on a certain avenue of research and sets the terms for subsequent Anglo-American economic analyses of international filmmaking in Europe: economics in the European film industry equals Hollywood imperialism; the true realm of European cinema is not commercial but artistic, cultural—and national. Thus, writing in 1971, Guback argues on the one hand for "pan-European cooperation because the problem is multi-national in character and bigger than the resources any one nation could devote to it," and on the other for "a program which would safeguard and strengthen the existence of an autonomous national film production while encouraging a vigorous multi-national exchange of motion pictures." And by 1974 he has pretty much abandoned the idea of European Community filmmaking as a viable defense against U.S. imperialism: "One must guard against the danger of unwittingly submerging the great variety of spirits in the headlong administrative rush toward creation of a 'Europe.' The aim must be to preserve the mosaic of cultures and to resist the temptation to rely upon bigness itself as a solution— even in the face of seemingly overwhelming political and economic trends."[41] Around this time, a character in Wim Wenders's *Im Lauf der Zeit* (*Kings of the Road,* 1976) would crystallize the set of discourses underpinning this position with the line "The Yanks have colonized our subconscious."

While subsequent histories of the French and Italian cinemas of the 1950s through the 1970s have, then, acknowledged transnational cooperative developments as important factors of each country's cinema culture—the signings and the terms of the Blum-Byrnes Agreement of 1946 and the Franco-American Film Agreement of 1948 for France, or of the Andreotti Law of 1949 and the MPEAA–ANICA Agreement of 1951 for Italy, for example—these developments are couched in terms of national protectionism against or compromises with the American film industry and not in terms of pan-European film industrial initiatives proceeding in parallel with the economic and governmental establishment of a European Community.[42] In short, coproductions are a problem for national cinema, and that problem is connected up with Americanization and cultural imperialism. When coproductions are dealt with, they are characterized as Euro-American and/or summarily relegated to the zone of European popular cinema, wherein "popular" often designates a commercial betrayal of national traditions: *pepla,* spaghetti westerns, horror and sex films in Italy or the Tradition of Quality in France[43]—the latter of which Roy Armes, as an example, links up to "the whole machinery of the expensive international co-production, designed for an anonymous international audience and with pretensions which were commercial rather than artistic."[44]

The French New Wave, the new Italian cinema, and other European art cinemas of the late 1950s through early 1970s thus continue largely to escape the taint of coproduction and internationalization. Whereas coproduction and European international filmmaking represent the attempt to fight Hollywood cinema on its own terms (big budgets, star-studded casts, elaborate sets and costumes, and so on), art cinema proceeds from the opposite direction, one connected to long-standing anti-American discourses: the strength of European culture lies in its specific national artistic cultures. Art films are the products of individuals rather than institutions, authors rather than producers, limitation rather than excess, labors of love rather than money.[45] They thus represent a truer, more genuinely European attempt to counter Hollywood domination through the establishment of indigenous, alternative modes of film practice. Writing on art cinema in 1981, Steve Neale stated that "in competing with Hollywood for a share of the market, or in seeking a space of its own within it, the films produced by a specific national film industry will have in any case to differentiate themselves from those produced by Hollywood. The way of doing so is to turn to high art and to cultural traditions specific to the country involved."[46] Although, then, some of the forms of state legislation—quotas, subsidies—backfired insofar as they produced inferior, inexportable films ("quota quickies") or homogeneous big-budget international films, or they left a loophole by which American subsidiaries in Europe could legally qualify for and receive financial backing from Europe for Hollywood films, other forms of legislation—advances on receipts, prizes, and awards—could apply across a national territory only and thereby aided in the production of national art cinema forms.[47] Thus, as Neale states, art films "participate actively and systematically in the construction and reconstruction of particular national identities while the marks of nationality with which they are inscribed serve further to differentiate them from films produced in Hollywood."[48] There is occasionally in this discourse an acknowledgment of art cinema's transnational dimension, but at the levels of their production and their local and international consumption they almost always remain pure signifiers of their national cinemas and of nationhood in general.

Peter Lev's *The Euro-American Cinema* in some respects challenges entrenched positions about the nationalist base of the European art film. First, he considers how the new wave filmmakers of the late 1950s and on have been involved in their criticism and film practice with a reevaluation of Hollywood cinema rather than an outright rejection of it: the *Cahiers* group, for example, sifted through the lower echelons of Hollywood genres and budgets to find directors—auteurs—as models of individual personalities working within a highly institutionalized system yet able to make personal films. Second, he takes Neale's statement that art cinema "always tends to involve a balance between a national aspect on the one hand and an international aspect on the other"[49] and pushes it in the direction of the international, emphasizing that the art film does not just happen on occasion to find an international audience but is *intended* for such an audience with shared class and cultural backgrounds or pretensions. Third, Lev argues that the art film proceeded after the European new waves of 1958–63 in three directions: a continued flourishing of low-cost, high-prestige, non-English-language art cinema by established auteurs (Fellini, Resnais, Bergman, Godard, et cetera); a move toward American auteurs and art films, beginning with *Bonnie and Clyde* (1967) and extending through the mid-1980s; and a move toward "European-American hybrids, combinations of American and European approaches to filmmaking" in terms of film form, budgeting, finance, and language.[50]

It is the third direction that Lev pursues in his study, and he establishes a set of eight criteria for what he labels "Euro-American art films." Of these, the first two are of particular interest to the present discussion: "1. The film makes prominent, but not always exclusive, use of the English language. 2. One of the film's key collaborators is a European film director."[51] In establishing these criteria, Lev tips the scales toward a certain type of European art film that bears at the level of its aural inscription the markers of American capital investment. But the name of the auteur serves in these Euro-American art films as the ultimate stabilizer of identity in the face of the international aspects of the enterprise. Thus, the films that Lev chooses for his case studies— *Le Mépris (Contempt), Blow-Up, I racconti di Canterbury* (*The Canterbury Tales,* 1972), *Paris, Texas* (1984), and *The Last Emperor* (1987)—are, in film historical writing, Godard, Antonioni, Pasolini, Wenders, and Bertolucci films first and foremost. Few would consider these to be purely French, British, American, or Chinese films, so clearly transnational are they in their casting and use of language (except, perhaps, for *Le Mépris,* which is why the dubbed version of this film is so infamous).[52] But neither would many consider them to be American films, even though the bulk of the funding for most came from the United States and the primary language in each is English (except, again, for Le Mépris). When confronted with the evidence of multinational investment in an art film, authorship picks up the slack.

What this means, ultimately, for the historiographic lineage of the European art film is that it is a national *and* a personal product when it is made in the language of the director, and more simply a personal product when it is made in English. In both cases, the issue of national stability remains relatively unchallenged, although the name of the auteur above the title anchors the European art film to its nation in a way that the same name above an English title does not. Art film coproductions among European nations, with no American investment, thus continue not to be recognized as such because the inscription of national language at the level of the sound track and of national character in the person of the director combine to form an almost inviolable bond—a bond that is broken, I would argue, only by the travesty of the dubbed print. And this is why dubbed prints are perfectly acceptable for coproduced low-genre films rather than high ones. In the former there is no auteur's vision nor national tradition to be thrown into question by a signifier of another language, another culture.

A considerable amount of attention has been focused since the 1990s on the contemporary state of the European film industry and of Common Market or EU filmmaking. The 1993 Uruguay round of the General Agreement on Tariffs and Trade functioned as a catalyst for much of this attention, as it once again brought to a head embattled and entrenched positions regarding the film industry and film culture in Europe.[53] Founded in 1947 with the ambition of liberalizing world trade, GATT began a round of new talks in 1987 that had to be agreed upon by a deadline of 15 December 1994.[54] The audiovisual sector (alongside agriculture) was an issue that threatened this deadline, as American objections to European film subsidies and other protectionist measures were countered by the efforts of the Europeans—defined and articulated largely by the French film and television industry and supported by both a socialist president and a conservative government—to have audiovisual products removed entirely from the negotiations. The French cum European contingent held that, since free trade invariably favors the most powerful producers, to include audiovisual materials within GATT's terms would mean the end of the

European film industry as it would inevitably be swallowed up by the Americans.[55] Further, the Europeans took the position that "audio-visual industries did not belong in the GATT agreement at all, because, as culturally-driven businesses crucial to national identity, they were not comparable to other import/export industries."[56] This issue of "cultural exception" threatened to scuttle the entire GATT agreement, of which film and other audiovisual materials were really only a small part, and "at the eleventh hour this principle was effectively acknowledged in a piece of EU/US political legerdemain: in order to save the GATT treaty, it was agreed simply to exclude film and audiovisual material from its terms."[57]

Two things about these events are noteworthy here. One is that Europe, so intent on its "cultural exception" when faced yet again at the GATT negotiations table with the prospect of American domination of its film industries, pitched the European Community in terms of industry and commerce rather than culture, turning to the latter only as an afterthought. The complex history of the EEC bespeaks an emphasis from the start on economic cooperation, and although the Council of Europe was founded in 1949 and the European Community in its first incarnation in 1957, directives on the cinema came into action only in the mid-1980s, when the issue was catalyzed by a 1984 proposal by then president François Mitterrand of France to establish a pan-European coproduction fund for work in cinema and television. Although Mitterrand's plan was rejected it started the ball rolling, and a panoply of initiatives were put into place that finally addressed cooperation on the part of the European media industries in terms of the Community rather than bilaterally: the Mesures pour Encourager le Développement de l'Industrie de Production Audio-Visuelle (MEDIA), which had a pilot phase from 1987 to 1990 and was adopted by the Council of Ministers of the European Community in December 1990; Eurimages, a coproduction fund in the mold of that proposed by Mitterrand and set up in 1988; the Audiovisual EUREKA programme (AVE), which exists to encourage the development and application of advanced audiovisual technologies; and, most notably for my interest in this chapter, Broadcasting across the Barriers of European Language (BABEL), designed to give support in the area of subtitling and dubbing.[58] To generate popular support and to push through some of these initiatives, particularly MEDIA, 1988 was designated European Cinema and Television Year, and the European Film Awards (FELIX) were inaugurated that year in Berlin as a rival to the Academy Awards and as an attempt to put the European film industry on par with Hollywood in the popular imagination. This flurry of pan-European activity was only partially successful on the industrial level and much less so on the ideological one, however, and in some ways it merely served to point out how little film and other audiovisual media had to do with the by then three-decade history and policies of the EEC.

Related to the belatedness of EC cultural initiatives is something that Angus Finney has pointed out: "Far from inspiring a united European front, GATT served to expose how fragmented Europe's nation states are in their film policies. Although commentators at the time thought that GATT brought the British closer to the French, that was far from the truth. The final months of the negotiation also highlighted the tendency for French politicos, culturecrats and in-dustryites to assume that what is best for France is also best for the rest of Europe."[59] Although the European contingent needed to provide a united front to face down the Americans, in actuality the Commu-nity's film policies were, with the exceptions noted above, relatively unchanged from what they had been since the early 1950s: bilateral treaties, protectionist quotas, advances on receipts, et cetera. The state of European cinema in 1993 was a complicated paradox of coopera-tion and isolationism, of the need to maintain national autonomy and identity alongside the need to present, at times, a united front. Indeed, not every pan-European initiative since the mid-1980s has made it through to legislation. And fears of such coproduced homogenization are expressed through terms like the Euro-film and especially "Euro-pudding," wherein the kaleidoscopic or patchwork or mosaic aspect of European cultures is reduced to a melting pot á la the United States.

The publication in the mid-1990s of a number of EU-sponsored studies on the economic and industrial problems of contemporary European cinema suggests that such outcry was both premature and damaging to the prospect of future health for the industry.[60] In *Bud-gets and Markets: A Study of the Budgeting of European Film,* Terry Ilott documents the complexities, problems, and potential rewards of pan-European filmmaking. His study stresses the practical compromises that must be made (in budget, in language, in casting) to ensure the future of Europe's national film industries. And although he praises Lars von Trier's *Europa* (*Zentropa* in the United States, 1992)—a film made and financed by Swedish, Danish, German, and French partners, filmed in English and German, and shot in Poland—as "that rare thing, a genuinely European film," he ultimately concludes that, despite "the rhetorical desires of some European legislators, the European film does not yet exist."[61] Published the same year, Angus Finney's *The State of European Cinema: A New Dose of Reality* is of similar size and organization as Ilott's study (and, interestingly, as Lev's *The Euro-American Cinema*): a two-part structure comprising a survey of coproduction initiatives and analysis of general data on markets and audiences, then a follow-up section of case studies of individual films and projects. Finney is very critical of the entrenched resistance of Europe's national film industries to European integration, and he even goes so far as to point to 1960s European art cinema's simultaneous elevation of the director and denigration of the scriptwriter and producer as one of the sources for "the undoing of European cinema in the past three decades. . . . In an *auteur*-dominated environment, feature-film development was an idea in a director's head, rather than a team-driven process involving the producer's input, let alone a script editor or co-writer."[62]

The linkage between auteur cinema and national cinema in the context of postwar European cooperation and unification is explicit and telling: both feed into a system that prevents full acknowledgment of the reality of European collaborative filmmaking. While Finney recognizes the problems and dangers of the Euro-film, his criticisms of it are not aesthetic/cultural/national but practical, and he cites Eur-images as a model for a more forward-looking approach to tackling the complexities of an EU film industry.[63] By opting for a cofinancing model over a coproducing one, Finney pinpoints a particular site of both stability and anxiety concerning European coproduction since World War II that is germane to this discussion: personnel. With cofinancing, a film appears at the level of its cast, its crew, and its language to be a national/cultural product and is thus marketable as such internationally; in this way it benefits from (and itself benefits) multinational partnerships but avoids the "Euro-pudding" label. Although, then, these films would be at the financial level multinational European products, they could be consumed both domestically by the host country and internationally (within the EU primarily) as national products.

Still, resistance to either the recognition of past European coproduction or proposals for new forms of multinational cooperation among Europe's national film industries has since the 1990s remained high on the agendas of many art filmmakers, critics, and scholars, and the equation of coproduction in Europe with Hollywoodization and American economic and cultural imperialism is ubiquitous. In June 1992, Spanish filmmakers held a three-day conference in Madrid, Audiovisual Español 93, during which participants "urged the government and, more specifically, the current minister of culture, Jordi Solé Tura, to introduce a new audiovisual law to protect it from the total domination of Spanish screens by Hollywood movies and by North American multinational distributors and from the 'europuding' [sic] coproductions of the new European community that threaten to erase the cultural specificity of Spain and its diverse autonomous regions."[64] One year earlier at Stirling University in Britain, the British Film Institute organized and held a conference titled "Borderlines: Films in Europe," one of the results of which was the publication *Screening Europe: Image and Identity in Contemporary European Cinema.*[65] Reading through the papers presented by the established British film and media scholars at this conference, one soon realizes that they all are reacting, and not positively, to the bustle of EC media program initiatives that since the late 1980s were attempting to construct a notion of "Europeanness." Thus Duncan Petrie writes in his introduction that the "major cultural crisis facing Europe is precisely the manner in which the idea of 'European identity' has been maintained in opposition to the underlying diversity and heterogeneity. . . . Such a conception overlooks both the diverse reality of cultural forms and cultural differences within Europe (both past and present), and the fact that it was this very European tradition which in the twentieth century generated both Fascism and totalitarianism." Ien Ang is one of the several participants who reiterates anxiety over the current Europe-building cultural movements: "European power and authority, however benign and in the spirit of whatever 'new world order', can never be reasserted innocently, given the legacy of European colonialism and imperialism which inaugurated the emergence of today's thoroughly interdependent but unequal world system in the first place."[66]

While I agree with the veracity and tenor of these statements, one of their effects is that they provide an easy retreat to a position of high cultural nationalism that prevents full recognition of the degree to which the cinemas of Europe, not only since the mid-1980s but since the 1920s and especially the 1950s and 1960s, have always maintained an uneasy relation between national isolationism and transnational cooperation. In the context of the historiographic tradition I have outlined here, it comes as no surprise that the filmmakers these scholars point to as representing a positive future direction for European cinema—Jean-Luc Godard, Chantal Akerman, Derek Jarman, Isaac Julien—are, characteristically, art film directors or their preferred replacement, countercinema imagemakers. Despite the fact that all of them have been involved in European coproductions, their auteur status excuses them from complicity with the new imperialism of European integration. It is for me a poignant moment in this publication when, in the discussion after a final panel of final respondents, a member of the audience put forward the following question, in fact the final one of the conference:

> I want to ask a question which hasn't come up. It's about European
> co-production, a trend of co-production between different nationalities
> and different sources of funding which has been accelerating as we
> approach 1992. Does the panel consider that this will vitiate or destroy
> the national tradition of film-making (if there is such a thing), or do
> they think that it's the key to the future and to a unification of European
> film-making?[67]

While European coproduction is no recent trend but extends far into European film history, the question is nonetheless to the point and clearly expressed. And it is symptomatic of all I have been arguing in this section that the question is not answered, not even addressed, by the two respondents who speak after it and wrap up the conference. The matter of European coproduction, at least in terms of European art cinema and its heirs, produces silence.

What all of this means, ultimately, is that the international dimensions of European art cinema, not only in its consumption but also in its production, require more attention in film historical writing.[68] The conceptual boundaries that have been mapped for this cinema—the film text, the director as generator of meaning, the nation as contextual limit—form a set of concentric circles for a synchronic analysis that, with the exception of occasional forays into the diachronic realm of aesthetic cinema history, essentially confine it to the borders of its own nations. The issues of internationalization, European cooperation and integration, and industrial coproduction are anathema to such a historiography, despite the fact that such issues have been a very visible part of European film discourses since the 1920s and were put into place in the form of the European Economic Community at the moment the French New Wave and Italian auteur cinema, among others, were coming to fruition. But the strain of the effort necessary to maintain nationalist positions remains inscribed at the very levels that have served as guarantor of any given art film's national identity: auteurs, stars, and language.[69] The relay among all three is rarely unbroken, and in this respect the art film bears in its very textuality all of the contradictions, tensions, and anxieties of both its time and its historicization.

Speaking of European Art Cinema

Table 1 represents production and coproduction figures for French cinema and Italian cinema between 1941 and 1975, as referenced in the back pages of the two Cassell/British Film Institute *Companion to French/Italian Cinema* guides and in two standard national filmographies. The table reveals that available statistics on the proportions of national productions to coproductions are widely at variance. But the numbers also indicate, despite their disparities, that coproduction has been a consistent feature of both French and Italian cinema since World War II. In fact, in the heyday of each nation's art cinema production, coproductions at times equaled and, in the case of France most definitely, surpassed national productions.

Clearly, the French and Italian film industries were engaged in coproductions in the postwar era. But coproductions with whom? First and foremost, these films were not predominantly Euro-American but intra-European, and the majority of them were Franco-Italian. The signing of the Franco-Italian coproduction agreement in Rome in October 1949 marks the beginning of a consistent trend in French and Italian coproduction that developed slowly until 1953 but then began to take off, hitting its stride in the late 1950s, peaking in the early to mid-1960s, and tapering off somewhat in the late 1960s to

TABLE 1. Film production and coproduction figures for France and Italy, 1941–75

	France		Italy	
Year	Vincendeau	Bessy et al.	Nowell-Smith	Bernardini
1941	—	60	—	72
1942	—	77	—	118
1943	—	60	—	72 + 3
1944	—	21	—	27 + 2
1945	72	73	—	50
1946	94	91 + 2	62	53 + 1
1947	72	78 + 1	60	58 + 1
1948	91	91 + 4	54	54 + 6
1949	99 + 8	104 + 3	76	65 + 4
1950	99 + 18	103 + 3	92	91 + 4
1951	94 + 18	87 + 8	104	105 + 3
1952	88 + 21	85 + 15	119 + 13	131 + 10
1953	64 + 47	67 + 26	125 + 21	133 + 18
1954	52 + 46	49 + 28	144 + 46	178 + 28
1955	76 + 34	70 + 21	74 + 52	124 + 19
1956	90 + 39	85 + 22	68 + 23	75 + 23
1957	81 + 61	80 + 28	66 + 71	105 + 32
1958	75 + 51	69 + 26	76 + 65	97 + 35
1959	68 + 65	70 + 39	83 + 81	131 + 36
1960	79 + 79	83 + 39	94 + 66	139 + 31
1961	98 + 98	65 + 38	117 + 88	167 + 44
1962	43 + 82	47 + 41	139 + 106	178 + 50
1963	36 + 105	40 + 47	135 + 95	187 + 60
1964	45 + 103	42 + 47	135 + 155	217 + 76
1965	34 + 108	33 + 55	94 + 109	143 + 69
1966	45 + 85	46 + 45	89 + 143	176 + 53
1967	47 + 73	56 + 32	130 + 117	195 + 64
1968	49 + 68	49 + 30	130 + 116	204 + 64
1969	70 + 84	74 + 29	146 + 103	200 + 69
1970	66 + 72	60 + 35	132 + 99	185 + 65
1971	67 + 60	—	128 + 88	175 + 67
1972	71 + 98	—	169 + 111	224 + 65
1973	97 + 103	—	171 + 81	196 + 56
1974	137 + 97	—	176 + 55	192 + 55
1975	160 + 62	—	177 + 53	191 + 31

Note: Figures are for feature film production only. Two numerals separated by a plus sign indicate national films + coproductions. The sources are Ginette Vincendeau, *The Companion to French Cinema* (London: Cassell, 1996); Maurice Bessy and Raymond Chirat, *Histoire du cinéma français: Encyclopédie des films 1929–1934, 1935–1939,* and *1940–1950,* 3 vols. (Paris: Pygmalion/Gérard Watelet, 1986–88), and Maurice Bessy, Raymond Chirat, and André Bernard, *Encyclopédie des films, 1951–1955, 1956–1960, 1961–1965,* and *1966–1970,* 4 vols. (Paris: Pygmalion/Gérard Watelet, 1989–92); Geoffrey Nowell-Smith, with James Hay and Gianni Volpi, *The Companion to Italian Cinema* (London: Cassell/British Film Institute, 1996); Aldo Bernardini, ed., *Il Cinema Sonoro 1930–1969* (Rome: ANICA, 1992); and Bernardini, ed., *Il Cinema Sonoro 1970–1990* (Rome: ANICA, 1993).

early 1970s. According to Maurice Bessy et al., in 1959 thirty of France's thirty-nine coproductions were with Italy; in 1963, forty-three of forty-seven; and in 1968, twenty-one of thirty. Aldo Bernardini documents similar ratios for Italy: in 1959 twenty-seven coproductions with France of a total of thirty-six; in 1963 forty-two of sixty; and in 1968 twenty-five of sixty-four. Another trend for both cinemas through the 1950s and 1960s is the proliferation of bi- and trilateral coproductions with more and more national partners. By 1950, for example, Italy had established bilateral agreements and was actively co-producing films with France, Spain, Great Britain, the United States, and Austria. By 1960 Italy's partners included all of the above plus West Germany, Yugoslavia, Turkey, Japan, Argentina, and Venezuela, and trilateral coproductions between Italy, France, Spain, and West Germany were on the upswing. And by 1970 Italy's roster of bilateral partners had expanded to include Bulgaria, the USSR, Algeria, Tunisia, and Egypt; trilateral coproductions were prominent as well, in a dizzying array of combinations among an ever-widening group of participants. Two trends are thus notable: a high incidence of French-Italian coproduction since 1950 and a proliferation of bi- and trilateral coproduction agreements since the late 1950s among the film-producing nations of Europe, along with several from North Africa and South America.[70]

What kinds of films are these coproductions? Their impetus was to allow for a broadening of their financial base and at the same time to ensure their status as "national" products in their respective countries to qualify for state subsidization. This means that coproductions generally cost more than purely national productions; indeed, the qualifications for state subsidies and the rules for the coproduction agreements established strict guidelines for minimum and maximum financial outlay on the parts of the coproducing partners according to broad definitions of film types. As Steve Lipkin has pointed out, from

> 1950 to 1965, the average cost of Italian/French coproductions was $465,000 with Italy supplying 52 percent of the total investment. These coproductions were at least one-and-a-half, and often three times as expensive as normal national productions.... A 1966 treaty between Italy and France recognized three classes of coproductions: "normal coproductions," "coproductions of artistic value," and "coproductions of

exceptional entertainment value." Normal coproductions cost at least
$285,000 with the minority partner's financial contribution amounting
to at least 30 percent of the total cost. Films of artistic value cost somewhat
less, and lowered the minority partner's contribution to no less than
20 percent of the production cost. Coproductions of exceptional
entertainment value, however, had a minimum budget of $509,000, with
similarly lowered requirements for the minority partner's contributions.[71]

For historians of French cinema, it is the third category, "coproductions of exceptional entertainment value," that has been deemed the
most salient of France's coproductions, and in this way coproduction
has become one of the sticks with which to beat the aesthetically mori-
bund and internationally oriented Tradition of Quality and other big-
budget costumers of the 1950s and early 1960s.[72] And for Italian film
historians, the first category, "normal coproductions," is most characteristic of Italy's multinational films of the 1960s, purely commercial
ventures that tend toward the popular/low end of the genre scale.[73]

But there is no doubt: a high proportion of French and Italian
art films from the late 1950s through the early 1960s were transna-
tional—European—coproductions. Indeed, some of the prototypically
"French" and "Italian" art films of the period directed by the most
celebrated auteurs were in fact the products of French and Italian (and
West German and British and Swedish and Spanish) partnerships:
Louis Malle's *Zazie dans le métro* (1960) and *Le Feu follet* (*The Fire
Within,* 1963); Alain Resnais's *L'Année dernière à Marienbad* (*Last Year
at Marienbad,* 1961), *Muriel ou le temps d'un retour* (*Muriel,* 1963), and
La Guerre est finie (1966); Truffaut's *Jules et Jim* (1961), *La Mariée était
en noir* (*The Bride Wore Black,* 1968), and *La Sirène du Mississippi* (*Mississippi Mermaid,* 1969); all of the films of Antonioni's tetralogy starring Monica Vitti (1960–1964); all of Luchino Visconti's films from *Lo
straniero* (*The Stranger,* 1967) through *L'innocente* (*The Innocent,* 1976),
and several before; all of Fellini's films from *La strada* (1954) through
Satyricon (1969); most of the 1960s films directed by Jean-Luc Godard,
Claude Chabrol, Vittorio De Sica, and Bernardo Bertolucci. This is
just the tip of the iceberg. Without having conducted a systematic
study of the proportion of art film coproductions to wholly national
productions, I would nevertheless venture that the ratios for wholly
national to transnational French and Italian art films in the 1960s are
the same as for each nation's annual output.[74]

Such art film coproductions at times acknowledge their status as such through allegory or indirection. Godard is particularly noteworthy in this respect: of the thirteen features and five shorts for omnibus films he made during the Anna Karina years, eight of the features and four of the shorts were coproductions, and of those, three have been noted for their critiques of such international filmmaking. One is *Le Mépris,* of course, whose subject is precisely the making of an American-Italian-French coproduction, which it itself is. And Susan Hayward has put forward an intriguing take on *Pierrot le fou* (1965) as a coproduction allegory:

> Near the beginning of the film Ferdinand (alias Pierrot), who is in the advertising business, is obliged by his Italian wife to attend a cocktail party. He turns up with her, as an unwilling guest. This seemingly "innocent" beginning is in fact a reference to the state of the French film industry which, in order to compete against Hollywood products, has found itself since the mid-1950s obliged to make co-productions with Italy. At the party, the entire shooting of which is through a pink filter, women and men talk to each other in advertising-speak. . . . At the end of this sequence, Ferdinand picks up a huge piece of angel cake and throws it at a woman's face. He then runs out of the party and dashes home only to elope with his former lover of five years past. . . . Marianne, the symbolic name of France, might just rescue Ferdinand/Pierrot from the "hell" in which he finds himself. In other words, the French film industry might just be able to avoid going under as an indigenous industry in its own right not only by foregoing co-productions with Italy but also by refusing to follow the candy-floss practices of Hollywood.[75]

This is an ingenious reading of the opening of *Pierrot le fou,* though the Italian coproduction critique appears rather a force fit. Not so in Godard's next film, *Masculin féminin* (1965), at the center of which is a scene in which the four young Parisian protagonists watch a rather lumbering foreign film in a not very chic movie house. When the lights dim and the credit titles appear on the screen, 4X: EIN SENSITIV UND RAPID FILM, Madeleine (Chantal Goya) remarks, "Oh, it's in the original language," to which Elisabeth (Marlène Jobert) replies, "All the better. This way they can't put anything over on you." And neither apparently will Godard: for *Masculin féminin* is a Franco-Swedish coproduction and as such requires the participation of Swedish personnel, including actors, in its making. Rather than arbitrarily cast the requisite performers and have them dubbed into French, the filmmaker has placed them in a Swedish film within the film, where their presence is both contained and draws attention to itself as a fiction and a construction. As well, Godard does not know Swedish and was therefore not in a position to direct their vocal performances, another problem coproductions elicit among their casts and crews. So the film in which they appear is a heavy chamber drama about male-female sexuality (reputedly a parody of Ingmar Bergman's *Tystnaden* [*The Silence*, 1963]), in which a man and a woman (credited only as "He" and "She") meet in an uninviting apartment for an afternoon tryst, grunt and paw at each other clumsily as they undress, and engage in joyless sex. An allegory for the arbitrary and pleasureless conjoining of national cinema traditions and personnel necessary to make a European film in the mid-1960s? Perhaps. At the very least, through this scene the filmmaker fulfills the stipulations of the coproduction agreement without compromising his own film. Or does he? The romantic Paul (Jean-Pierre Léaud), hero of the film, closes the scene with a voice-over: "This wasn't the film we'd dreamed of. This wasn't the

Jean-Pierre Léaud, Chantal Goya, and Marlène Jobert in *Masculin féminin* (1965). Courtesy of the Museum of Modern Art Film Stills Archive.

total film that each of us had carried within himself, the film that we wanted to make, or more secretly, no doubt, that we wanted to live."

It is tempting just to take Godard's critique of European coopera-tive filmmaking in these films at face value, but to do so is to foreclose on a potentially rich avenue of research.[76] What do coproduction agreements actually consist of, for example, and how does that affect the textuality of films made according to their strictures? The bilat-eral film agreements drawn up between European national partners have since 1949 contained clauses that serve to ensure that the nation-ality of a given film is not in any way "endangered," and these clauses circulate around sets of criteria that define a film as national for both coproducing partners, including minimum financial outlay, language, location of shooting, and cast and crew as well as other prominent creative personnel. In the French-Italian Agreement of 1 August 1966, for example, one finds the following stipulations under Article 5:

I The budget of a coproduction can be no less than $285,000.

II The minority participation in each film cannot be inferior to 30 percent of the cost of its production.

III 1. The contribution of the minority coproducer must include an effective technical and artistic participation and at least an assistant director, a writer, an actor in a principle role, and actor in a secondary role.

2. Each film must include employment of an Italian director or a French director corresponding to the conditions cited in Article 2.

IV Exceptions to the conditions of the preceding paragraphs can be granted by the authorities of the two countries to films of obvious artistic value or to special entertainment films.[77]

Regulations such as these go some way toward explaining the wave from the early 1950s through the early 1970s of several prominent film actors who were in migration across national borders to make Euro-pean films—some, famous art films with directors in the pantheon of the art film canon, and others, less than famous entertainment films with directors whose names have been long forgotten. These inter-national performers constitute a casting call of impressive geographic and generational breadth: Mel Ferrer, Burt Lancaster, Rod Steiger, Anthony Perkins, Charles Bronson, Clint Eastwood, Jack Palance, Jean Seberg, Jane Fonda, and Raquel Welch of the United States; Alex-andra Stewart, Genevieve Bujold, and Donald Sutherland of Canada;

Dirk Bogarde, Peter Ustinov, Terence Stamp, Alan Bates, Richard Harris, David Hemmings, Barbara Steele, Jane Birkin, Charlotte Rampling, and Jacqueline Bisset of Great Britain; Anita Ekberg, Ingrid Thulin, and Britt Ekland of Sweden; Curt Jurgens, Hardy Kruger, Klaus Kinski, and Elke Sommer of Germany; Maria Schell, Oskar Werner, Romy Schneider, Senta Berger, and Helmut Berger of Austria; Ursula Andress of Switzerland; Silva Koscina of Yugoslavia; Francisco Rabal and Fernando Rey of Spain; Alida Valli, Gina Lollobrigida, Sophia Loren, Pier Angeli, Lea Massari, Virna Lisi, Elsa Martinelli, Monica Vitti, Raf Vallone, Claudia Cardinale, Franco Nero, Ugo Tognazzi, and Laura Antonelli of Italy; and Brigitte Bardot, Jeanne Moreau, Annie Girardot, Anouk Aimée, Anna Karina, Catherine Deneuve, Dominique Sanda, Delphine Seyrig, Alain Delon, Michel Piccoli, Jean-Louis Trintignant, and Gérard Depardieu of France. Their cross presence in art films from all nations of the burgeoning European Community registers how national and transnational filmmaking structures and practices are in a continual process of negotiation and redefinition in parallel with other economic and political developments of the period. The appearance of an actor from one nation in an art film from another represents more than the fortuitous meeting across national borders of a talented performer and a brilliant director; it is also an indicator of two (or more) nations' capital investments and industrial cooperation in the making of a film misrecognized as a purely national product by dint of its language and the nationality of the director, the name above the subtitle.

It is at the levels of casting, language, and aural translation/transformation that perhaps the most interesting ideological tensions between nationalism and internationalism are inscribed and played out in the European art film. Multilingual productions or multiple language versions have, of course, been made since the introduction of sound in film, and Josephine Dries distinguishes three methods of multilingual production: double shooting, remakes, and double versions.[78] Double shooting refers to the multiple language versions (MLVs) shot predominantly in Hollywood and in Joinville, France, in the early years of sound, whereby the same sets were used for up to fourteen separate groups of casts and crews from different countries and language communities. While the MLVs are generally considered to have been a failed experiment of the early sound period, a look at some art films suggests the degree to which they neither failed nor were an experiment. For MLVs have continued to be made in Europe past the Joinville era and through the postwar period: Jean Renoir's *Le Carosse d'or* (*The Golden Coach,* 1952) was shot MOS at Cinecittà with a largely Italian cast, most of whom, including the star Anna Magnani, played and spoke in three languages in three separately shot English, Italian, and French versions. Another Renoir MLV bears different titles for its French and English versions, *Elena et les hommes* and *Paris Does Strange Things* (1956), respectively. And Werner Herzog's *Nosferatu* (1979), to take an even later example, was shot as well with the same cast performing separate German and English versions.

Related to the MLVs are remakes, which for Dries occur when there is a time lag between the productions of two language versions. Many of these language remakes, especially today, are of popular European films that American companies find less profit in promoting and distributing than in buying the rights for the original story, adapting them to American values, and shooting the whole production in an American context.[79] But the reverse is not unheard of: Renoir's *Diary of a Chambermaid* (United States, 1946) and Luis Buñuel's 1964 French remake of the same title, for example. However, the vast majority of multilingual productions are neither MLVs nor remakes but what Dries calls double versions, of which there are two types: "The first is the production that is shot in one language and afterwards dubbed into other languages. Actors can be of different nationalities, but they must have the ability to act in the shooting language. The second is the so-called 'Babelonian' shooting: the international cast will all act in their mother tongue. Their voices will be dubbed afterwards by dubbing actors from the respective language areas."[80] It is the second of these double versions, the Babelonian or polyglot film, which is of primary concern here.

As an example: *Cronaca di una morte annunciata (Chronicle of a Death Foretold),* coproduced by Italy, Spain, and Great Britain, directed by Francesco Rosi, adapted from a short story by Gabriel García Márquez, starring Rupert Everett, and shot in Colombia. The preview screening of this film in June 1987 at London's National Film Theatre was neither subtitled nor dubbed. Everett delivered his lines in English while other members of the cast spoke in Spanish. Of the film Thomas Elsaesser has written:

> One of the more puzzling things about *Chronicle of a Death Foretold* is no
> doubt the presence of Rupert Everett. As a character in a fictional story,
> he is barely present. Even by the end, we do not know who he is, where he
> is from, or what he wants. With so passive a part, it is difficult to accept
> him as the star of a major international production. . . . The role dissolves
> into poses, narcissistic and non-functional in the narrative. Is this a flaw in
> the acting, the consequence of a production with an eye to the market,
> using up a face while it is still in the news, or is it the sign of a mutation
> in the concept of the European anti-hero who has become the clone-hero
> of jeans ads and beer commercials? In other words, are we watching a
> European art film, a Hollywood movie, or a Third Cinema post-modernist
> co-production?[81]

The categorical confusion caused by Everett's presence can be resolved
in all three directions for the anglophone viewer/listener, depending
on how the polyglot sound track of the film is transformed. If it is
left as a polyglot film, with Everett speaking English and the other
actors speaking Spanish, with everyone in the film understanding
each other perfectly and with only the Spanish subtitled, it is a "Third
Cinema post-modernist co-production." If the entire film is dubbed
into English, it becomes a Hollywood film. And if it is dubbed into
Italian to match the national identity of the director and then subtitled in English, it would be for most cinephiles a European art film.
Simply subtitling the film, preserving all its linguistic polyphony, thus
complicates rather than simplifies its national status. Dubbing it into
English turns it into an entertainment film and would appear, as Neale
suggests, to erase the marks of its more complex national status.[82] But
dubbing it into Italian, *then* subtitling it in English, seemingly clarifies
but actually erases its transnational origins. And this is the case not
simply for this more recent polyglot film but also for some of the
great European art films of the 1960s and 1970s.

Indeed, at the end of his discussion of Rosi's *Chronicle,* Elsaesser
compares it to Luchino Visconti's *Il gattopardo* (*The Leopard,* 1963) and
Bernardo Bertolucci's *1900* (1976) to put a finer point on Rosi's
political understanding of his material. The comparisons are apt in
terms of polyglot casting and Italian auteur cinema. Indeed, both *The
Leopard* and *1900* were transnational coproductions whose lead roles
were played by performers from America speaking in English (Burt
Lancaster, Robert De Niro, Donald Sutherland), from France speaking
in French or voicing Italian (Alain Delon, Dominique Sanda, Gérard

Depardieu), and from Italy speaking Italian (Claudia Cardinale, Stefania Sandrelli). What are the authentic versions of these films sound-wise? There are none: like almost all Italian films of their period, they were shot without sound and dubbed into different language versions (Italian, French, English) for the domestic markets of each coproducing partner. Despite the fact that in both films the English-speaking actors who were actually speaking English during the profilmic event predominate in terms of screen time, and that therefore dubbed-in-English versions would make the most sense for an English-speaking audience, Anglo-American viewers and listeners of European art cinema invariably opt for the dubbed-in-Italian, subtitled-in-English versions as the more authentic ones, the more artistic ones, the ones truer to the intentions of their auteurs.[83] *The Leopard* was first released in the United States by its American coproducer, Twentieth Century Fox, in an English-dubbed version with Burt Lancaster looping his own dialogue, and Andrew Sarris's reactions to this version are telling: "It is necessary to criticize the dubbing into English, if only because Burt Lancaster would probably gain authority and plausibility if his over-enunciated Americanese were dubbed into Italian. After all, Fellini did wonders for Anthony Quinn *(La Strada)* and Broderick Crawford *(Il Bidone)*."[84]

When confronted with the reality of coproduction and the particular problems it produces for a national cinema—an international cast and a polyglot sound track—art film directors tend to take three approaches. The first involves foregrounding the tyranny and/or absurdity of transnational coproduction in the texture of the film's narrative, as Godard does in *Le Mépris* and *Masculin féminin*. A second, more frequent approach is to acknowledge at the level of narrative the copresence of multiple nationalities in the same national space by casting actors as characters of their own nationalities. This approach appears to increase in frequency in France-located coproductions in the late 1960s and early 1970s, and such celebrated films as *Le Souffle au coeur* (*Murmur of the Heart,* France/Italy/West Germany 1971) and *Ultimo tango a Parigi* (*Last Tango in Paris,* Italy/France/United States 1972) employ the model. Perhaps my favorite example, however, is *Mademoiselle* (1964), a Franco-Italo-Anglo coproduction set in France, starring Jeanne Moreau and Ettore Manni, and directed by Tony Richardson. Here Manni is cast as an Italian woodcutter and thus his appearance and language nominally indicated, though not entirely explained. But *Mademoiselle* goes a step further in filming his and Moreau's climactic nocturnal tryst, toward which the entire film has been building and which occupies several minutes of screen time, in silence: the characters cannot and do not communicate with each other except through gesture and their own expectant bodies, eliminating on the one hand the need for Richardson to master French or Italian to direct his two key actors to complete performances and, on the other, the inevitable sync problems their close-ups here would display in both the French- and the Italian-dubbed release versions of the film.

But neither of the preceding forms of open acknowledgment of international casts and polyglot sound/image tracks is practiced in art cinema with anything like the frequency of the third approach, which is to ignore the matter entirely and simply make everyone on the screen French (*Cléo de 5 à 7* [1961]) or Italian (*Teorema* [1968]) or Spanish (*Tristana* [1970]). The result in such cases is the dubbing of much of the polyglot dialogue of the film into one language, a reduction of a film's polyphonic, profilmic event into a univocal sound track that nevertheless leaves as trace of its production context the unsynced images of mouths and voices of an international community of actors. In a passage that draws attention to the unhinging of voice and body in art cinema at the same time as it offers a restabilization of national integrity as regards this issue, Michel Chion states:

> The freedom allotted in Italy for the synching of voices is already enormous, but Fellini in particular breaks all records with his voices that hang on the bodies of actors only in the loosest and freest sense, in space as well as in time. . . . In France the voice is often something people keep to themselves, as if someone might steal it. In Italian cinema, when someone begins to speak, everyone joins in; it's all right to leave behind your own individual vocal contours, then return to them. No one makes a big deal out of it. Fellini takes this convivial side of voices in Italian movies quite far. He plays to the hilt the freedom cinema gives him to mix together voices and actors.[85]

It is certainly the case that every Fellini film from *La strada* through to the end of his career exhibits noticeable and at times considerable evidence of its postsynchronization and casts of multiple nations and languages. Italian-dubbed, English-subtitled prints of these films present something of a limit case of loose play between actor and language,

voice and body, that is everywhere in operation in not only Italian
but also French art cinema of the period. Yet perhaps the real limit
cases are those coproductions by Italian art film directors whose lead
roles are played by performers who speak in a language other than
Italian during the profilmic event: Fellini's *La strada, Il bidone* (1956),
and *Satyricon;* Visconti's *The Leopard, Rocco e i suoi fratelli* (*Rocco and His
Brothers,* 1960) and *Vaghe stelle dell'orsa* (*Sandra,* 1965); Bertolucci's *Il
conformista* (*The Conformist,* 1970) and *1900,* et cetera. In such cases,
to demand a unilingual Italian sound track is to erase the linguistic
polyvocality that registers the political economy of art filmmaking in
that country from the 1950s through the 1970s. As the films were
predominantly shot without sound, there is no "original" sound track
to fret about. Yet art film viewers invariably prefer to listen to the
dialogue dubbed into Italian and watch an image track with not one
but two added idiosyncracies—subtitles, of course, but also the major
characters' lips out of sync with the language quite evidently not
emerging from their body. Why?

One reason is that these are Fellini and Visconti and Bertolucci films,
thereby art films, and therefore they should be seen in subtitled prints.
While this seems self-evident enough, it does not sufficiently explain
the process by which the image/sound and actor/language disunities
are bridged. Ella Shohat and Robert Stam have offered one theory:

> In the case of the subtitled film, we hear the more-or-less alien sounds of
> another tongue. If the language neighbours are our own, we may recognise
> a substantial proportion of the words and phrases. If more distant, we may
> find ourselves adrift on an alien sea of undecipherable phonic substance.
> Specific sound combinations might remind us of locutions in our own
> language, but we cannot be certain they are not phonetic *faux amis.* The
> intertitles and subtitles of foreign films, meanwhile, trigger a process of
> what linguists call "endophony," i.e., the soundless mental enunciation of
> words, the calling to mind of the phonetic signifier. But the interlingual
> film experience is perceptually bifurcated: we hear another's language
> while we read our own. As spectators, we forge a synthetic unity which
> transcends the heteroglot source material.[86]

The "synthetic unity" forged by the spectator of a subtitled film is
twofold. On the one hand, the interlingual film experience synthesizes
the discoordination between the mouths and words of those in the
film's diegesis who are either voicing their lines or speaking a different

source language than the one on the sound track. This is a rather remarkable achievement given the traditional impatience British and American viewers demonstrate when confronted with poor sync, the product of both lack of exposure to dubbed films (as they live in an English-language culture and cultural marketplace) and a fetishistic attachment to the idea of the "authentic" cut of film, an attachment dubbing disturbs. In the art film, the achievement is related to the issue of an imagined nationhood as it pertains to language and director more than to a cognitive process. The "synthetic unity" forged at the meeting of hearing another's language while reading one's own is one in which the spectator imagines him or herself to be actually understanding, speaking, another's language as he or she reads and calls "to mind the phonetic signifier." But it is also a unity that extends across the sound/image and international actor/national film divide that dubbed and subtitled coproductions like *The Leopard* produce. In the Italian-dubbed, English-subtitled version of this film Burt Lancaster and Alain Delon become, *are* Italian as an effect of the spectator's own desire for imagined nationhood through his or her interlingual relation to the film. This is why, as linguist Thomas Rowe noted in 1960, "audience consciousness of lip synchronization is confined to films in its own language. Even film critics are blithely indifferent to the fact that most of the foreign films shown in original version with subtitles are egregiously out of synch by American standards, although their criticism invariably notes such defects in the [English-]dubbed version."[87]

In "Moving Lips: Cinema as Ventriloquism," Rick Altman leveled a different yet germane critique of auteurism as it pertains to a repression of sound analysis in film theory: "As the thirties progressed . . . it became increasingly clear all over the world that language, far from being anathema to the cinema experience, lay at its very heart. Unable to suppress language, cinema theory transferred its resentment to the source of that language, banning the screenwriter eternally from serious consideration. With the *auteur* 'theory' the screenwriter was finally done away with all together, and the scandal of language's dominance over and independence from the image was further repressed."[88] This development leads to an interesting paradox when it is thought in concert with the translation of art films into other tongues. For if art cinema is even more a cinema of the image than others by dint of its auteurist mode of production, it would seem to be the case that the image should take priority over sound; an art film, then, should be dubbed into other languages to preserve the purity of its mise-en-scène. And yet the opposite is the case, in America and Britain at least: the image track of the subtitled art film is transgressed by the sound track in the form of text and punctuation. In effect, language in a subtitled art film is present at the level of both sound *and* text, and is thus privileged over image. While the nationality of the coproduced art film is thus fixed by that of its director, the auteur's vision is simultaneously usurped by the very signifier of his/her nationhood: language.

Nonetheless, in the art film as it is received in Britain and America, non-English language and subtitles are perceived as markers of authentic nationhood. Even at other levels, however, it is evident that subtitles afford *more* opportunity than dubbing for cross-cultural translation and transformation, for the effacement of the marks of national differences. Indeed, part of the means effecting the silent cinema as a "universal language" was precisely the malleability of the film's cultural signifiers as relayed by dialogue. As Richard Maltby and Ruth Vasey have pointed out, "Silent movies were peculiarly well-suited to consumption in a wide range of different cultural contexts, but this was probably due less to their capacity to impart a single universal message than to the fact that they were amenable to a wide range of different interpretations."[89] Intertitles were not simply translated from source to target languages but creatively adapted to cater to diverse national and language groups: the names of characters, settings and plot developments, and other cultural references were altered as necessary to make the films internationally understandable through their domestication for different national audiences. By 1927 the intertitles of Hollywood films were routinely translated into as many as thirty-six languages. With the sound film it was no longer possible simply to replace intertitles. Both subtitling and dubbing had been in use since 1929, when the first American sound films reached Europe. But they did not become the preferred solutions to sound-film translation until the early 1930s, with many countries opting for subtitling not only because it was much cheaper but also because it "managed to ameliorate some of the problems produced by the cultural specificity that characterised sound production, re-introducing some of the advantages of semantic flexibility provided by silent intertitles. Although audiences could hear the action being played out in a foreign tongue, the meaning of the dialogue was less specifically located through being in-dicated, in condensed form, in the local language. Specific cultural sen-sibilities could be accommodated by adjustments and naturalisations in the titles themselves."[90] Thus, the "original" language of another on the sound track would seem to bind the film to its nation of origin, but the subtitles the spectator reads may equally become that language, take it over, colonize it, make it into their own.

By the same token, the dubbing of films both intra- and interna-tionally in France, Italy, Germany, and Spain (sometimes referred to as the FIGS group) functions variably as the effacement of the national signifier and the very building block of it. In France, where the Join-ville studio was converted into a dubbing center, the reasons for the supremacy of dubbing derive from the nation's cultural mission to preserve and protect the French language in the face of foreign (espe-cially American) influence, and the ubiquity of French as the lingua franca for a populace accustomed to hearing it both on television and in cinemas due to a significant number of domestic productions. For the other countries of the FIGS group, culture and political ideology were determining causes. Italy, Germany, and Spain, all of which faced cultural boycotts in the mid-1930s and were ruled by fascist govern-ments that were culturally defensive, allowed only dubbed versions of foreign films. The dictators of these countries were fully aware of how hearing one's language served to confirm its importance and reinforce a sense of national identity and autonomy. In Italy especially, where most people, including the filmmakers themselves, spoke dialect rather than the official Tuscan, dubbing forged a synthetic unity of a shared national language. Intranational dialects and the specificities of social and cultural differences were ironed out in the process. At the in-ternational level, then, dubbing may be regarded not as a leveler of national difference but as a form of national protectionism, a differ-ent kind of nation building. As early as 1929, Mussolini's government had decreed that all films projected on Italian screens must have an Italian-language sound track regardless of where it was produced. Both Franco's Spain and Hitler's Germany established strict quotas regard-ing imports, almost all of which were dubbed.

Through the quickly established and standardized dubbing indus-tries that were built up in these countries to fulfill these directives and that are still active today, dubbed movies might be considered as more local productions than subtitled ones. For the subtitling industry is not nationalized to the same degree as the dubbing one, as the translators are the key personnel and need not reside in the target country. Indeed, Dries notes that, from an industrial perspective, "national borders are of less importance in the operation of the subtitling industry than for dubbing. A dubbing company is dependent on the availability of actors for the recording of voices and therefore needs to be situated in an environment with good infrastructure, studios and a lot of actors. For subtitling, these factors are not an issue at all. Translators are used to working at home with their own subtitling equipment. Competition in the subtitling business crosses national borders much more easily than it does for dubbing."[91] In all of these senses, subtitling is more international, more "American" (free market capitalist, competitive) than is dubbing (national-protectionist, union controlled), which is more "European."

In terms of aesthetics, it is also arguable that subtitling involves the least interference with the original film. A primary issue for subtitling lies in the translation, which entails enormous cuts to the source dialogue—as much as half. While the ideal in subtitling is to translate each utterance in full, the limitation of screen space is a major obstacle. The average viewer's reading speed is 150 to 180 words per minute, with necessary intervals; this severely limits the duration and hence completeness of the subtitles, which means that source-language dialogue must often be translated in a condensed form. Subtitles also obstruct the integrity of composition and mise-en-scène by leading the viewer's look to the bottom of the frame. They focus audience attention on the translated words and the actors speaking them, excluding peripheral or background dialogue, sound, or characters. And they do not provide as full a translation as does dubbing. As well, audiences of subtitled films do not experience the words and the expressions of the performers simultaneously. Subtitling may thus be regarded as undoing synergy of performance and script as well as of elevating selectively translated verbal messages and downgrading the impact and importance of visual expression.

But where does all this leave the polyglot transnational art film in terms of nationhood and identity? Certainly, the rise of European coproductions, particularly between France and Italy from the 1950s through the early 1970s, had visibly and aurally inscribed effects on the textuality of the European art film in this period. The proliferating internationalism of the casting of these films in accordance with the growing concatenation of cooperative production agreements among the nations of the burgeoning EEC, combined with the polyphony of the languages being spoken during the filmmaking process and the complex ideological, historical, and industrial issues surrounding dubbing and subtitling in these countries, makes the European art film's visual and sonic terrain an extremely rich network of signifiers to map. The tension between national identity and international policy is borne out in the ultimate untranslatability of its specific confluences of sound and image, voice and body, language and performer. More than a set of historically isolated moments or the latest development of the European film industries to the geopolitics of the postmodern era, transnational coproduction has been a consistent feature of European cinemas—quality, entertainment, and art—since the beginnings of European cooperation and integration in the immediate postwar period, and in this sense its elision from Anglo-American film history and film studies must be read as a symptom of the power that discourses of nationalism continue to hold over the discipline. Stephen Heath once wrote, "Language is a site of struggle, and a site of struggle in film: imagine a cinema that would show what was at stake in its language and make heard what was invisible in its images."[92] Without denying the potential validity of Heath's examples of such a cinema—Straub and Huillet's *Othon* (1971), Godard's *Ici et ailleurs* (1977)—I would nevertheless suggest that the coproduced art films I have been dealing with in this chapter offer the critical imagination an equally complex and shifting set of horizons of intelligibility. The stable nationalist base of European art cinema, when unanchored from the name of the author above the subtitle, becomes immediately swept away by a sea of crosscurrents whose new waves may very well be the aftershocks of a rapid continental drift. If the remappings I have undertaken of the postwar cinemas of France and Italy throughout this chapter have clustered around a particular set of coordinates more than others, that set would have to include entanglements of the social, the aesthetic, the economic, and the geopolitical. For it is through the historical and the theoretical examination of these global and local forces, and in the fluctuating space between the illusive boundaries that divide them, that a new historiography of European art cinema may be envisaged.

3

Wandering Women

Decolonization, Modernity, Recolonization

The processes of imperialism express, in representation, white identities. These are forged from the roles and functions of white people in imperialism and the qualities of character that performing them is held to require and call forth. When a text is one of celebration, it is the manly white qualities of expansiveness, enterprise, courage, and control . . . that are in the foreground; but when doubt and uncertainty creep in, women begin to take centre stage. The white male spirit achieves and maintains empire; the white female soul is associated with its demise.

—RICHARD DYER, *White*

Siting the Modern European Woman

AT THE MIDPOINT of *L'avventura* (1960) is a curious scene that seems to serve little narrative function. Sandro, whose lover Anna has recently disappeared during a sailing excursion among the Aeolian Islands, arrives by train in the Sicilian city of Messina to find a journalist who may have information as to her whereabouts. It is midday, and there's a riot going on. A large, boisterous crowd of men swarms the street. Sirens blaring, four jeeps heaving with police cut through the throng, trailed by a string of photographers and reporters. Shouldering his way through the scrum, Sandro discovers the source of the disturbance: a tall, glamorous young woman with dark hair and eyes whose tight-fitting dress has split a seam at the thigh. The glimpse of garter exposed by the tear has attracted the mob of male Sicilians. The woman identifies herself as an English writer named Gloria Perkins (she is clearly dubbed) on her way to Capri to write an article about tourism. She also confesses interest in a film career. As the police escort her from the scene and the onlookers leer, cheer, and jeer, the journalist tells Sandro that she is a prostitute with a price of 50,000 lire who moves from town to town and performs her sexuality in this manner so as to attract customers.

She will return near the end of *L'avventura* to enable Sandro's betrayal of Claudia (Monica Vitti), Anna's best friend, who since Anna's disappearance has begun a love affair with Sandro. The doubling of betrayals—Claudia's and Sandro's of Anna, Sandro's of Anna and Claudia—is brought full circle through Gloria Perkins, who in coloring and complexion bears an uncanny resemblance to the vanished Anna. Not just a flâneuse but a streetwalker, Perkins bridges the movement from the barren island of the film's first half to the populated one of the second. Claudia—who is blonde and fair, "northern" in appearance—from this point forward assumes the role of the wandering woman, a role that is the product of Anna's disappearance and whose most tangible outcome is the beginning of her affair with Sandro. Their first scene of lovemaking in a field near the town of Noto is immediately followed by one in which Claudia slowly walks the town's streets and is tailed by a drove of local men as she makes her way, idly yet improvised, through the square of the town. The implication is clear to Claudia, and by her expression we sense her shame for her betrayal of Anna. She is seen by the men, and sees herself here, as a streetwalker.

Out of sight, out of frame, Anna is made present through Gloria Perkins, whose night with Sandro near the end of the film is an imaginary revenge, the real act of betrayal. In a film that epitomizes the modern, one that itself caused a riot at Cannes for its scandalously slow pace, the relations between female flanerie and prostitution, betrayal and revenge, are ones that the female characters seem doomed to repeat. The ultimate point of connection is the black garter on the white thigh of the streetwalking Gloria Perkins in Messina: the seam split open, the dark prop upon which modern female sexuality rests glimpsed, the tenuous balance between old and new social orders exposed.

Women in the new Italian cinema and the French New Wave are often active participants in the film fiction, frequently the main protagonists. In this respect they were considered in the discourses of the time to reflect the modern woman of France and Italy, unburdened of the restrictive roles of daughter, sister, wife, or mother on the one hand, prostitute, kept woman, or femme fatale on the other, which had previously demarcated her range of possibilities. No longer constrained by the yoke of biology as destiny, the heroines of modern European cinema moved forward to forge more egalitarian relations between men and women—or at least relations unencumbered by the inevitability of marriage, family, and domestication.[1] The female body of 1960s art cinema is one characterized by poise and freedom of movement, a flâneuse exploring the public architectures of the modern city and traversing its spaces with relative ease.

The imaging of women in European art cinema is much more fraught than the one I have too optimistically described above. Indeed, such films usually connote atmospherics not of buoyancy but of depression, narratives not brimming with life and action but dragged out in dull dead time, characters not in touch with the world that surrounds them but alienated from it. In this respect modern European cinema, as Robert Phillip Kolker has put it, "shares with the neo-realist tradition an observation of physical barrenness and a concern about disenfranchised people in a forbidding landscape. Unlike neo-realism, the poverty portrayed is not economic or even social, but emotional, spiritual."[2] And David Bordwell argues that "the characters of art cinema lack defined desires and goals. . . . Choices are vague or nonexistent. Hence a certain drifting episodic quality to the art film's narrative. . . . Slow to act, these characters tell all. The art cinema is less concerned with action than with reaction; it is a cinema of psychological effects in search of causes."[3]

True enough. But the emotional and spiritual isolation represented in the young French and Italian auteur films of the early 1960s, with their fuzzy narrative motivations and frustrated quests for psychological truth, tends as often as not to be embodied in feminine form. The female characters of modern European cinema collectively present the image of a flâneuse engaged in a quest for meaning as she wanders the terrain of a changing Europe. The spaces she encounters in her strolls are by turns ancient and modern, transparent and opaque, threatening and benign, populated and empty. The pace of her flanerie is the pace of the art film itself; the visual shocks she encounters are the shock cuts punctuating and structuring narrative sequences, she is the visualizing subject. But she is also an object *in* the narrative and *in* the landscapes and architectures she traverses. How might one read her functions and placements in the cinema for which she is so clearly a trope?

One claim for art cinema's inclusion in revisionist film historical writing is to consider it as an alternative or resistant mode of film practice to that of Hollywood in the global media marketplace. The new European cinemas thus arose in the postwar era as an almost simultaneous series of national responses to U.S. cultural imperialism in Europe during a period of reconstruction, economic recovery, and modernization. Frequently in French New Wave films, European film culture's fraught association with Hollywood is allegorized at the level of character and plot. Jean-Luc Godard's films of the 1960s offer particularly rich encounters with what he himself has called "a two-way fascination and a one-way exploitation": the relationship between the French Jean-Paul Belmondo/Michel Poiccard and the American Jean Seberg/Patricia Franchini in *A bout de souffle* (*Breathless,* 1960), or the cowardly screenwriter Michel Piccoli/Paul's pimping of his wife, Brigitte Bardot/Camille, to the heinous Hollywood producer Jack Palance/Jerry in *Le Mépris* (1963). Tellingly, both narratives achieve closure through the deaths of the French protagonists at the hands of the Americans. In such an economy art cinema plays out the tragedy of its own inevitable colonization by the forces of American capital and culture.

As chapter 2 makes clear, there is more to be done with European art cinema than reiterate this position. In this chapter I turn the imperial allegory around so as to demonstrate how the modern cinemas of France and Italy are embedded and engaged in colonial projects of their own. The figure of the wandering woman is central to this project, for she is placed within art cinema in the mobile, contradictory position of both self and Other: the self in national terms, the Other in both gendered *and* racial terms. A case can surely be made to read through the female characters of the new Italian cinema and the French New Wave the tumultuous transformations into modern nations that France and Italy were in the late 1950s and early 1960s undergoing, with all of the questions and crises of national and individual identity such changes produced in their national and social spheres. I will be making such a case. But I will also be making a case to read the female flâneur as a highly charged site of national recolonization. For the liberated young woman of modernizing Europe emerges as a figure in French and Italian art cinema at precisely a period in history when the imperial powers and colonial empires of

Europe are not simply waning but clearly defunct, when the resistances of the peoples of colonial Africa and Asia to their subjugation by Europe are at their peak. The years 1958–60 mark the moment of Europe's national cinematic regeneration and rebirth, of the French New Wave and the new Italian cinema, of *Hiroshima mon amour* and *Les Quatre cents coups (The 400 Blows)* and *Breathless*, of *La dolce vita* and *Rocco e i suoi fratelli (Rocco and His Brothers)* and *L'avventura*—of, in short, modern European cinema. But these years also mark the great moment of African decolonization, of the achievement of the right to self-determination for Algeria and the full independence of Guinea, Italian Somalia, Madagascar, Dahomey, Niger, Upper Volta, Chad, the Central African Republic, Gabon, the Congo, Ivory Coast, Senegal, Mali, and Mauritania. What to make of the simultaneous birth of modern European cinema and death of European colonialism?

A link between the two is located in the figure of the wandering woman of the modern French and Italian films of this period, particularly in the textual functions (and extratextual circumstances) of the characters played by iconic art film stars like Anna Karina, Jeanne Moreau, and Monica Vitti in films directed by Jean-Luc Godard, Louis Malle, and Michelangelo Antonioni, among others. For if, as Richard Dyer avers in the epigraph that opens this chapter, the white female soul is associated with Empire's demise, in art cinema the white female *body* is the linchpin of that association.[4] In the sections to come, then, I will focus on the site/sight of the female body, trace its movement through many of the canonized texts of the French New Wave and the new Italian cinema, and align it with current critical discourses concerned with the narratival and visual representations of history, nation, space, and modernity.

The first flickerings of the thoroughly modern female flâneur may be glimpsed in the women performers of the popular cinemas of France and Italy in the 1950s. The rise of well-endowed young female stars like Gina Lollobrigida and Sophia Loren in the melodramas and "pink" neorealist films of the period linked the Italian economic boom of the early 1950s to the female body in explicit and important ways. At the same time, France was undergoing its own program of industrial reorganization and modernization, and equally popular female stars of the so-called Tradition of Quality such as Martine Carol embodied many of the cultural contradictions wrought by the reorientation of the French nation in the throes of economic and cultural transformation. In both of these national-popular cinema traditions, women are addressed by and poised for modernity but have yet to become fully active participants in it. The key transitional figure between these popular cinemas of the 1950s and the new art cinemas of the 1960s was Brigitte Bardot. In all of her films, but particularly in the one that made her an international superstar, *Et Dieu . . . créa la femme (And God Created Woman,* 1956), the Bardot characterization and star text is riven with paradoxes: she is simultaneously subject and object, mobile and immobile, new and old, modernity and its other.

By the decade's turn the figure of the flâneuse would be pervasive in the new cinemas of France and Italy, and the national allegories she incarnates are complicated. In films such as *Ascenseur pour l'échafaud* (1957), *Cléo de 5 à 7 (Cleo from 5 to 7,* 1961), *La notte* (1961), *Vivre sa vie* (1962), and *The Eclipse (L'eclisse,* 1962) the female protagonist's flanerie itself structures modern filmic narrative, her looks designate her as the agent of the visible. But the privileged place she occupies is contradictory: she pays a price for the insights she makes and quite literally embodies as the existential bourgeois subject of modern, modernizing Europe. That price may be the ultimate one: death (Anna Karina's fate in some of her husband's films). More frequently, it is a profound dislocation from the people who once were or could be close to her, signified spatially by an ultimately uninhabitable view of the modern European city. She is, in a word, "alienated."

In this chapter I unpack the valences of that word in both gendered and racial terms. I argue that European national crises produced by the loss of their colonial empires, inter- and intranational migration, and xenophobia serve collectively as absent causes or suppressed knowledges of modern French and Italian cinema. Through readings of the trope of the flâneuse in some key texts of the cinematic renaissances of Italy and France, I wish to reveal the flip side of art cinema's much-vaunted existentialism and involution: the alienation of not simply "the modern subject" but of the quite specifically modern national European subject. New wave cinemas are most certainly embedded in larger projects of nation building, but to explain the need for reconstruction and reaffirmation of European national identities in relation primarily to Hollywood economic and cultural imperialism is to buy into a unidirectional model of historical competition-as-inscription—

one filmic tradition versus another, one Western culture versus another. Rather than continuing to consider Hollywood as the generative source of art cinema, it is time to look elsewhere. That elsewhere is here the nostalgia produced by the loss of imperial power and unified national identity that the nation states of France and Italy encountered in their similar yet distinct relations to decolonization and modernization. The period of decolonization would produce a modern art cinema of recolonization, one locus for which is the wandering woman.

Colonial Cinematic Representation

The rapidity with which European countries established their colonial empires in the late nineteenth century was more than matched by the rapidity with which they relinquished their colonies after World War II. In 1945 Europe ruled the world; two decades later, virtually all the former European colonies had become independent states. Indigenous nationalisms and independence movements in the colonies gained strength in the interwar years, as education provided by missionaries and colonial administrations, though grossly inadequate, proved that the native peoples were capable of self-determination, undermined the case for paternalistic European control, and created small but influential native elites. The strain placed on the colonies by their "home" countries during World War II and the period of the reconstruction— increasing demands for exports of food, industrial raw materials, and manufactured goods, the breaking down of traditional local social structures attending the massive uprooting of colonized people to expanding urban centers to meet the demands of the inflationary industrial boom—created a broader audience for nationalist movements. Britain, the Netherlands, Germany, Belgium, Spain, and Portugal, as well as Italy and France, were either stripped of former colonies by Allied forces during World War II or were not equipped, financially or ideologically, to deal with colonial resistance movements that pressed the European powers into expensive military repression and domestically unpopular conscription policies.

Between 1945 and 1955, India, Indonesia, Egypt, Ethiopia, and Libya all had become independent states; the eight-year war in Indochina had ended in the defeat of French forces at Dien Bien Phu and the establishment of independence for Cambodia, Laos, and a partitioned Vietnam; uprisings in Madagascar and Algeria were either violently repressed or forcing France into another drawn-out colonial war; and the Conference of the Afro-Asiatic Nations at Bandung declared its support for the desired independence of Algeria, Tunisia, and Morocco. The year 1956 was crucial in the history of decolonization. The escalating war in Algeria was provoking on the part of French troops, whose numbers were now 500,000, systematic torture and summary executions of National Liberation Front (FLN) insurrectionists, practices that would lead to the fading of French support for war in Algeria. In March of that year, Morocco and Tunisia achieved independence. And in the autumn, a failed Franco-British campaign for control of the Suez Canal confirmed in the eyes of the world the inability of the major European powers to effect the course of events in their colonies, former or otherwise. At the close of 1956, it was clear that the finale of the European empires was near.

The degree to which the waning and end of Empire had an impact on cinematic representation and film culture in France and Italy has yet to be explored in depth. Certainly, Italian cinema would seem by dint of its much smaller colonial interests to be less affected than its French counterpart.[5] But both nations' cinema industries and cultures had up to World War II been invested in colonialism both ideologically and economically. The alignment of colonialism, nation building, and the Italian film industry is an acknowledged and consistent feature of media culture in Italy up to World War II.[6] And France's colonial empire was throughout the first half of the twentieth century much more extensive than that of Italy's. Like its British counterpart, the French Empire was wide-ranging, extending from French Indochina to French West, Equatorial, and Central Africa to Somaliland and Madagascar. An aggressive program of colonial conquest and expansion of the young Third Republic between 1880 and 1919 consolidated the French Empire, which began to fall away beginning in World War II with the Japanese occupation of Indochina. By 1962 it would be all but gone. As with Italy, imperialism and nation building in France proceeded in parallel with cinematic representation and spectacle from the beginnings of cinema at the fin de siècle through the early 1900s, World War I, and the interwar period to produce a field of audiovisual textuality one might generally refer to as "colonial."[7]

In the historiography of French cinema the colonial film resists precise definition. Nonetheless, for Pierre Sorlin it is "the geographical and political context within which the plot, or at least some sequences, occur, that constitutes the significant variable in determining the colonial characteristic of a film."[8] Listing some sixty-two colonial films produced in/by France between 1930 and 1939, the bottom-line criterion for Sorlin, as for other film historians, is that a colonial film be set in the colonies, whether or not "the natives" serve any plot function. With such a definition in hand, the peak period of French colonial cinema is undoubtedly the 1930s, when such films as *Le Grand Jeu* (1934), *La Bandera* (1935), *Princesse Tam Tam* (1935), *L'Appel du silence* (1936), *Pépé le Moko* (1937), and a remake of *La Maison du Maltais* (1938) celebrated France as a civilizing force in Africa and won critical and commercial acclaim.

But what of colonial cinematic representation in France during the years of decolonization? French film historical writing has tended toward two consenses. On the one hand, the great phase of Asian and African decolonization that might effectively be bracketed as occurring between 1946 (the beginning of France's eight-year war in Indochina) and 1962 (the end of France's eight-year war in Algeria), and which reached a peak of national liberationist activity in the years 1958–62, is invariably referenced through the critical ethnographic film practices of Jean Rouch and Chris Marker.[9] Many of Rouch's films—*Les Maîtres fous* (1955) *Moi, un noir* (1957), *La Pyramide humaine* (*The Human Pyramid,* 1959), and *Jaguar* (1954–67)—are reflexive documentaries in which the African subjects become increasingly active participants in the construction of their own filmic representations. Chris Marker too is an important figure in this respect for historians of French cinema as a more "poetic" documentarist of other cultures. His first film, *Les Statues meureunt aussi* (*Statues Also Die,* 1953, co-d. Alain Resnais), presented a scathing critique of the destruction of colonized cultures that attends the appropriation and display of African art in Western museums, and it was banned from release in France until 1965. But what really links Rouch and Marker is less their global concerns than their turning of reflexive ethnographic practice back onto the French themselves in two Parisian documentaries of the early 1960s: Rouch's *Chronique d'un été* (1961, co-d. Edgar Morin) and Marker's *Le Joli mai* (1963).[10] As critics of colonialism in general and of France's war in Algeria in particular, Rouch and Marker share the distinction of being the only well-known French filmmakers active in the late 1950s and early 1960s to be firmly linked to a film culture of decolonization in this period.

For on the other hand, there seems to be little else. Here, for example, is Dina Sherzer: "There is a strange silence of French cinema on the subject of decolonization and colonial wars, because viewers preferred to close their eyes; they wanted the past behind them as France was busy entering the consumer society and enjoying an economic boom. . . . Colonial wars were doomed topics *(sujets maudits)*." And here, Martine Astier Loutfi: "The complex and powerful state system that protected and supported the development of the French film industry exerted enormous economic, artistic, and political influence. The weight of the political control is obvious in the fact that during the 1950s, when anticolonial movements dominated national life, French films totally avoided the subject." Finally, Susan Hayward:

> The 1950s and 1960s were periods of tight censorship equal to that of the Occupation. The explanation lies . . . with the issues of war and political instability. These years were initially marked by France's impotence in dealing with the problems of her declining empire, first in Indo-China, then in Algeria. . . . The two peak years for proscribing films were 1952 (with fourteen films) and 1960 (ten films). . . . During the eight-year war with Algeria (1954–62), not a single film on the Algerian question was granted a visa. . . . In the 1960s, films that tried to address this conflict, or the role of the army in any context, were again effectively blocked.[11]

The matter seems clear: colonial films had their heyday during the glory days of the French Empire. In sociological terms, by the 1950s Empire "had lost something of its pre-war glamour," and the economic boom directed everyone's attention toward the future; the past was the past and well rid of.[12] But the literary adaptations and costume films of the Tradition of Quality, which quite obviously reveled in the glories of a French past, could be seen to contradict this explanation. As for filmic representations of the colonies themselves and the degree to which the French film industry, like that of Italy, often supported statist colonial policy, it seems reasonable to assume that the waning of Empire would yield a commensurate waning of colonial film production. While this is true enough as a general principle, Loutfi's statement that French films in the 1950s "totally avoided the subject" is not the case. On the crisis in Indochina alone, both Roy Armes and Alan Williams cite two examples: Claude Bernard-Aubert's *Patrouille de choc* (1956) and Marcel Camus's *Mort en fraude* (*Fugitive in Saigon,* 1957).[13] More convincing is the fact of political and industrial censorship, and Loutfi notes the censoring of several French films from the mid-1950s to the early 1960s that dealt with Indochina or more often Africa (Godard's *Le Petit soldat* [1960], Jacques Rozier's *Adieu Philippine* [1961], Robert Enrico's *La Belle vie* [1962]).[14] But in considering Hayward's statement that "not a single film on the Algerian question was granted a visa," I have two questions: Is the granting of a visa—an industrial, economic, statist seal of approval—a prerequisite for historical consideration? And what exactly *is* a "film on the Algerian question"?

In answering the first question, Hayward goes on to mention a clutch of censored films that demonstrate the persistence of certain directors to register on film their disgust for French colonial policy and the Algerian war—René Vautier most notably, whose *Afrique 50* (1955) and *L'Algerie en flammes* (1958) were both banned, with the former resulting in a one-year prison sentence for the director.[15] Philip Dine has expanded on the issue of the French film establishment's self-imposed silence on Algeria in the period by pointing to a "parallel cinema" that clandestinely produced and projected short antiwar documentaries on the premises of trade unions and leftist ciné-clubs. Vautier is again a conspicuous presence, although Pierre Clément, Guy Chalon and Philippe Durand, and the Vérité-Liberté collective receive mentions as well.[16] In this sense, a small yet militant anti-entertainment, anti-imperialist film practice emerged in the late 1950s to give cinematic voice to an intellectual print culture that had since the turn of the decade criticized French colonial policy and argued for the nationalist independence of the overseas departments, territories, and protectorates of the French Union.[17] Significantly, none of the participants of this group was a member of the French New Wave, whose narrative feature films tend to garner the lion's share of critical attention on the subject, despite their more muted anticolonialism. In the case of French narrative films made between 1957 and 1963 and dealing either acutely or obliquely with decolonization, two titles are noteworthy for their relative frequency in the historiography of French cinema: *Le Petit soldat* and *Muriel ou le temps d'un retour* (*Muriel,* 1963).[18]

Shot on location in Switzerland in 1959, Jean-Luc Godard's second feature film *Le Petit soldat* centers on the implausible adventures and self-absorption of Michel Subor/Bruno Forestier, a deserter who becomes caught up in the secret terrorist war being fought in Geneva by the FLN and the forerunners of the right-wing Organisation de l'Armée Secrète (OAS), a group of military and civilian defenders of French Algeria that engaged in terrorist campaings in both Algeria and France in 1961–62 in a failed attempt to sabotage peace efforts. *Le Petit soldat* was banned in France and would not be released until 1963, whereupon it was violently denounced by the left as politically insensitive and obsolete, "an insult to all the victims whose sufferings have not been purely intellectual."[19] Watching the film now and reading Godard's own ideas about it from interviews before the ban was lifted, one can see why the left would not welcome *Le Petit soldat;* in it the FLN are visualized as agents of torture, and the film assumes an unpartisan, amoral position toward war that is intended to justify the solipsism of the main character. For Bruno, politics have become meaningless; he resists torture and kills for personal rather than political reasons and without conviction; the right and the left are indistinguishable in their methods. Both Subor/Bruno and his love interest Anna Karina/Véronica Dreyer are tortured—he by the FLN, she by the OAS—but only his torture is shown. She suffers and dies offscreen, elsewhere.

Before its ban, Godard said the following about *Le Petit soldat:*

> · The film should bear witness to the period. Politics are talked about in it, but it has no political bias. My way of engaging myself was to say: the Nouvelle Vague is accused of showing nothing but people in bed; my characters will be active in politics and have no time for bed. Well, politics meant Algeria. But I had to deal with my own experience and my own feelings. If Kyrou or the people from *L'Observateur* wanted it treated differently, that's fine, and they should have visited the F.L.N. in Tripoli or somewhere with a camera. If Dupont wanted a different angle, he should have filmed Algiers from the point of view of the "paras." Nothing like that was done—more's the pity. I spoke of what concerned me, a Parisian in 1960, belonging to no party. And what concerned me was the problem of war and its moral repercussions.[20]

Like other films of the New Wave banned for their perceived criticisms of France's role in Algeria, *Le Petit soldat* is set in metropolitan

Europe and evokes the war at a distance. Part of the confusion the antihero faces is played out as the unfortunate condition of youth in modern Europe, the inevitable consequence of the historical absurdity of a time when one's beliefs no longer have meaning outside of the self. Hence, Bruno (and, as the quotation below indicates, Godard) hankers for the revolutionary past of the Spanish Civil War: "Today, we live in a less lyrical period. One is more compelled to find truth inside oneself than outside. The little soldier is searching for truth, he is searching for what is most important: that is to say not to be defeated, not to be bitter, to continue being active, to feel free."[21] *Le Petit soldat* is more about youth culture than about Algeria—the latter serves merely as a pretext. The reinsertion of a former member of the *contingent* into a rapidly modernizing society provides the film with a focus for existential reflections on a subject out of time and out of place in a hazy present.

Nonetheless, Algeria is "there" in this and other films, enough at least for them to have been considered a threat to the official government line and thus necessitating their censorship. Other films that addressed Algeria in a timely manner were not banned because they were released after the war was over: Marker's *Le Joli mai,* Jacques Demy's *Les Parapluies de Cherbourg* (*The Umbrellas of Cherbourg,* 1964), and most famously Alain Resnais's *Muriel.* This film is constructed as a highly fragmented circulation among four characters in Boulogne over the course of a fortnight, from Saturday, 29 September, to Sunday, 14 October 1962. The title character is everywhere and nowhere in the film: it is the name given to an Arab woman raped, tortured, and murdered in Algeria before the film begins. The war is thus encapsulated, here as in *Le Petit soldat,* in the absent figure of a dead woman. "Muriel" refers less to a person than an event haunting the traumatized conscript survivor Bernard Aughain, who lives with his stepmother Hélène, an antiques dealer whose shop is her apartment. Combining the tale of Hélène's World War II lover's return with that of Bernard's guilt, *Muriel* juxtaposes "the individual and collective will to forgetfulness as regards events in Algeria, with its characters' and the French nation's obsessive remembering of the Second World War: by hinting at convenient omissions in the memory of that earlier devastation, it serves to emphasize, if not quite to define, the officially encouraged silence surrounding events on the other side of the Mediterranean."[22]

Muriel is an intensely physical film, rooted in the specificity of its time and place. It was also the first French feature film granted a visa to lift the taboo on the French military's use of torture in Algeria (Godard's *Le Petit soldat* and Chris Marker's *La Jetée* [1962] were made before but released after *Muriel*). Yet it also demonstrates the extent to which France, with its "let's forget about Algeria" zeitgeist, has no present, is caught between a misremembered past and a questionable future. The jarring, rapid cutting in *Muriel* suggests not merely a fragmented reality but also a confrontation between two pasts, each of which is capable of being present only in relation to the next. As Gilles Deleuze puts it, "This is a memory world, for several people, and at several levels, who contradict, accuse, and grab each other."[23] The Boulogne of *Muriel* is a modern metropole that is nonetheless inscribed with the suffering it endured between 1940 and 1944. Early on, the viewer is confronted with a series of images of the Channel port's high-rise buildings and modern shops that alternate with shots of street signs commemorating the local Resistance to the Occupation. Like its characters the city is centerless; it has no present. Hélène's flat with its provisional furniture (her surroundings are for sale or already sold) suggests the extent to which the past may be selected and purchased to facilitate the memory or construction of a family history that is not inherent but the product of an object's juxtaposition to a space.[24]

Perhaps the central image/metaphor of the film is the local attraction of the "sliding house," a Le Corbusier–style apartment building on stilts erected on the steep pitch of a hill. Prior to its architecture, the site and building plans are subject to all of the necessary geographical and engineering studies, tests, and safeguards. Its construction is carried out without incident, according to plan and on schedule. Finally the building is complete, but on the eve of its occupancy "it slips and the cliff slides back," rendering it unstable and uninhabitable. And yet it does not fall down: it remains standing on the hill and from all exterior appearances is perfectly sound. Everyone simply watches and waits for it to collapse of its own volition, which it shows no indication of doing. This building, like the characters of *Muriel,* like Boulogne, like France, is defined in relation to its past and its future: it has no present, it is modern and obsolete at the same time. Like the grainy documentary footage of soldiers in Algeria that Bernard projects at the center point of the film and over which he narrates the events leading to "Muriel's" death, like the effect of the war on modern France, it is an event both complete and unfinished, an empty center, a hollow monument, a structuring absence.

But to return to my second question: What exactly *is* a "film on the Algerian question"? Certainly the ones I have just briefly examined, as well as others made and released in the years following the end of the war that continued the project of the leftist "parallel cinema" of the late 1950s; Philip Dine describes them as sharing "an all-too-obvious desire to make up for lost time, which is reflected in a bludgeoning emphasis on the horrors of war and the impossibility of avoiding contamination once exposed to its brutal and brutalizing logic."[25] The most famous film on the subject is undoubtedly the Italian-Algerian coproduction *La battaglia di Algeri* (*The Battle of Algiers*, 1966), a brilliant docudrama of the French paratroopers' 1957 campaign against the FLN's bomb networks. When *The Battle of Algiers* was awarded the Golden Lion at the 1966 Venice Film Festival the French delegation walked out in protest, and the film was not granted certification in France until 1970. While neither the first nor the last word on the Algerian war, this film stands in Anglo-American film studies as the key reference text.

The Battle of Algiers inverts the colonial adventure film through a deployment of identificatory mechanisms on behalf of the colonized. Its reversals of European colonial cinematic representation have been unpacked by others, and I will not duplicate their arguments here.[26] Germane to the present discussion is the critical importance of one of the film's set pieces: the sequence in which three Algerian women masquerade as Europeans to make it through the French-guarded checkpoints and place bombs in a milk bar, a cafeteria, and the Air France terminal, three crowded settler spaces in the European sector of the city. As Ella Shohat and Robert Stam have pointed out in *Unthinking Eurocentrism,* the film turns Western iconography and looking relations into a revolutionary tool:

> The lighting highlights the women's faces as they remove their veils, cut and dye their hair, and apply makeup so as to look more European. They look at themselves as they put on an enemy identity, ready to perform their national task but with no apparent vindictiveness toward their future victims. . . . The French soldiers treat the Algerians with discriminatory

scorn and suspicion, but greet the Europeans with amiable "bonjours.". . .
As Algerians, the women are objects of a military as well as a sexual gaze;
they are publicly desirable for the soldiers, however, only when they
masquerade as French. They use their knowledge of European codes to
trick the Europeans, putting their own "looks" and the soldiers' "looking"
(and failure to see) to revolutionary purpose.[27]

In this sequence, as in the film as a whole, femininity and the female
body are figured as mutable and motile in a way that masculinity and
the male body is not. The object of both "a military and a sexual gaze,"
the Algerian women are able to subvert their surveillance through a
particular form of masquerade that plays into one form of colonization
(sexual) to work against another (national-racial). The checkpoint
through which they must pass is not an imaginary border but a very
real one that separates one part of the city from another, one culture
from another, one nation from another. In permeating that border they
simultaneously assume the position of desirable object and desiring
subject, both doubly inscribed as masquerade: they present themselves
as desirable objects to the French soldiers by assuming the trappings
of modern European femininity, including the reciprocation of the
desiring soldiers' looks; their real desires are not sexual-personal but
national-collective.

The Battle of Algiers is a touchstone in the history of cinematic
representations of the Algerian war and of colonialism. Directed and
scripted by the Italian political filmmakers Gillo Pontecorvo and
Franco Solinas, the film also figures prominently in the historiography of the Italian cinema in particular and European art cinema in
general. At all levels The Battle of Algiers presents itself as a hybrid
geopolitical text: scripted, directed, and scored by Italian personnel;
shot in Algeria with Algerian financing and by an Algerian producer,
Yacef Saadi, who also stars in the film with a cast of largely nonprofessional actors from Europe and North Africa; complicating in its
narrative the idea of—and, at the level of spectacle, the visual perception of—stable national identity. Shohat and Stam place their discussion of the film in a chapter titled "The Third Worldist Film," and in
doing so they locate it in the context of Third Cinema rather than
European cinema. Unthinking Eurocentrism is a work whose examples
and analyses of film practices span a range from First to Fourth World,
short subject to feature, documentary to fiction, militant to popular,

progressive to regressive, and silent to contemporary. But a conspicuous absence in *Unthinking Eurocentrism* is the very cinema that dominates survey histories of world cinema in the period of decolonization:
European art cinema.

In the chapter that precedes "The Third Worldist Film," the authors
of this important book argue that issues of race and ethnicity are often
filmically "submerged" in "non-ethnic" texts so that "many epidermi-
cally 'White' films bear the traces of an erased multicultural presence."
If the challenge is "to render visible, or at least audible, the repressed
multiculturalism even of dominant texts," that challenge is answered
in *Unthinking Eurocentrism* through examinations of Hollywood rather
than European cinema.[28] The latter appears only as occasional references to ten films, six in an endnote that warrants quotation:

> One could easily perform parallel analyses of European cinema in terms
> of a submerged colonial presence. Witness for example the coded
> references to the war in Algeria in the films of the French New Wave: a
> brief radio mention of Algeria in *Cléo de 5 à 7* (1962), whose protagonist
> is frightened by African masks, the presumably North African cellmate of
> Jean-Pierre Leaud [sic] in *400 Coups* (1959), the unspecified war for which
> the protagonist embarks in *Adieu Phillipine [sic]* (1962), the fragmented
> references to Algeria in *Muriel* (1956) *[sic]*. (Only Jean Rouch and Chris
> Marker brought the War center stage in such films as *Chronique d'un Eté
> [sic]*, 1961, and *Le Joli Mai,* 1962).[29]

Another question arises here. If "parallel analyses of European cinema
in terms of a submerged colonial presence" are so easily performed,
why are there so few analyses in film historical writing on the French
New Wave or other European film movements? Perhaps their performance is neither easy nor limited to scattered moments in a few films
but must also address the extratextual discourses of European art cinema of the 1950s and 1960s. Perhaps they need to be contextualized
in terms of the traditions of European colonial cinematic representation, as a continuation and transformation of those traditions in the
light of postwar decolonization and modernization. Perhaps they are
inextricable from ideologies of gender and regimes of vision, as in the
three women/three bombs sequence of *The Battle of Algiers.*

Rather than take Shohat and Stam to task for eliding European
art cinema, I wish to take seriously their challenge to explore the ethnic and racial traces that "haunt" the French New Wave and the new

Italian cinema. Those traces are embedded, embodied, in the figure of
the wandering woman whose modernity and liberated sexuality enable
a mobility that takes her through the liminal spaces of the modern
European city in much the same way as the women in *The Battle of
Algiers* cross the boundary separating European and Arab in Algiers
through a sexual and racial masquerade. But what motivates the female
flâneurs of European art cinema is rendered on the surface of the text
not as revolutionary but as bourgeois, psychological, individualistic.
Through their movement another form of colonial cinematic representation may be traced that is equally as much a part of projects of
nation building as are the more obvious colonial cinemas of France
and Italy in the first half of the century. To understand how the flâneuse
is deployed geographically and historically, one must first attend to the
cinematic imaging of women in the popular cinemas of France and
Italy in the period that marked the end of the classical and the beginnings of the modern European cinema: the early to mid-1950s.

Boom, Bust, Bardot

In the periodizations of Italian and French culture and cinema, the
immediate postwar periods of the reconstruction (1945–52) and of the
so-called economic miracle (1958–63) are ones of exciting change
and "newness." During the reconstruction, Italy and France began a
process of economic and industrial organization and development
that effectively started with the establishment of the Fourth French
Republic in France in 1946 and the landslide victory of the Christian Democrats in Italy in 1948, the respective policies of which led
both countries toward modernization and the construction of a competitive industrial economy that would reach its apogee of activity a
decade later.[30] These changes are mirrored to a certain degree at the
levels of cinematic culture, with Italian neorealism functioning for the
critics (though not the popular publics) of both nations as a cinema
and an aesthetics of reconstruction—a volley of unprettified images
showing the realities faced by the working class and the unemployed
poor during war and occupation. The French New Wave and the new
Italian cinema appear in the early 1960s as true representations of
the economic miracle and of modern nationhood and identity. The
period in between is by contrast generally regarded as out of step. For

the young critics of the time, and by and large for film scholars and historians since, the national cinema cultures that Pier Paolo Pasolini called the "grim, gloomy 1950s" and that François Truffaut dubbed the "Tradition of Quality" were thankfully superseded by the new cinemas of 1958–63. The economic miracle was paralleled by an aesthetic one.

Histories of postwar Italy have tended to support the view that the watershed years of modernization were those of the economic miracle, 1958–63, for it was during this five-year period that massive changes in industrial production, population distribution, standard and style of living, and consumption were greatly in evidence. The statistics are impressive: Italy's domestic product maintained an average annual growth of 6.3 percent as industrial production more than doubled over that of previous years. More than 1.3 million persons moved from the south to other regions of Italy, mostly to the cities of the industrialized north. At the same time wages, kept low for most of the 1950s, started to rise, with the effect that "per capita income grew more rapidly in Italy than in any other European country: from a base of 100 in 1950 to 234.1 in 1970. By 1970 Italian per-capita income, which had lagged far behind that of the Northern European countries, had reached 60 per cent of that in France and 82 per cent of that in Britain."[31]

But concentration on the years of the Italian economic miracle has tended to obscure the extent to which industry, infrastructure, and patterns of consumption were already changing in the decade that preceded it. By the end of the 1940s a set of interrelated conditions— left parties in opposition, weak unions, a surplus of labor, low wages, confidence among investors—made possible the long so-called boom of the next decade.[32] Industry grew at an unprecedented rate, and the combined market health of the state petrochemicals company ENI (Ente Nazionale Idrocarburi), of the major automobile company (Fiat), and of the Italian steel industry (Finsider) led to ambitious building and road construction projects that literally paved the way for private automobile ownership. In terms of cultural consumption, the 1950s saw "the renewal and expansion of the operations of many of the cultural industries, including the RAI [Radio Audizioni Italia], the major book and magazine publishers and the record companies," as well as "the expansion or advent of modern popular cultural forms, notably illustrated magazines (rotocalchi) and television, which began regular transmissions in 1954."[33] There was a marked increase in the popularity of spectator sports (Rome was the site for the 1960 summer Olympic Games). And radio listening and moviegoing reached all-time peaks in 1955; for the latter, the annual attendance figures of 819.4 million were double what they were one decade before.[34]

France's postwar recovery and modernization was a process that extended from the end of the war until the mid-1970s, a boom of sustained economic growth known as *les trente glorieuses,* "the thirty glorious years." A series of four- and five-year plans—begun in 1947 when General Charles de Gaulle, then president of the provisional government of the Fourth Republic, instructed former businessman Jean Monnet to prepare "un premier plan d'ensemble pour la modernisation et l'équipement économique" (First Plan of Economic and Social Development)—were the foundations of postwar growth, and the initial emphases were on coal, electricity, steel, cement, tractors, automobiles, and transport. Production grew by 41 percent between 1950 and 1958, exceeding the targets of the Second Plan.[35] Nationalization and modernization of the Régie Renault factory at Billancourt, the largest factory in the most powerful French industry and, until the mid-1970s, the very symbol for the French working class, quickly led in 1947 to the introduction of the Renault 4 CV, the first French car produced to be affordable on a mass scale. As in Italy, however, it was not until the 1960s that individual car ownership really took off (in 1961 one of every eight French people owned a car, compared to one of every three Americans).[36] Also as with Italy, wages did not grow significantly in the 1950s, and the standard of living did not keep pace with the rapid advances in the industrial economy, which meant that the payoff for the people in terms of purchasing power was delayed for a decade or so.[37] Nevertheless, the economic boom of the 1950s thrust France into the age of the commodity: the Salon des Arts Ménagers, launched in Paris in 1953, became the annual showcase for the latest domestic appliances.[38]

In 1950s Italy, the rural exodus and the rise in personal income led to an orientation toward consumption and home-centered living. The emergence of new forms of deferred payment, the availability of ready-made clothes, and the increased mobility within urban areas brought about by the introduction of Vespa and Lambretta motor scooters profoundly altered people's conceptions of personal expenditure and spatial exchange. Many working-class families were now able to afford meat in their daily diet, domestic appliances like washing machines and refrigerators, cars, and holidays in the mountains or at the seaside. During the 1960s a large number of Italian homes were internally modernized: the kitchen was reduced from a large eating/living area to a much smaller functional space, as was seen in American television programs; the wooden furniture of the old *tinello* (kitchen diner) was replaced by plastic chairs in a living/dining area based (again) on the model of the American living room; and the shared lavatory on the balcony or at the end of the tenement hall was replaced with modern tiled bathrooms with mirror and toilet.[39] More Italian women than ever before became full-time housewives, and television programs and women's magazines "exalted this new figure of the modern Italian woman, *tutta casa e famiglia,* smartly dressed, with well turned-out children and a sparkling home full of consumer durables."[40] The transformations of the Italian economic miracle led to increased atomization of civil society, and women were the principal targets of new consumerism and domestication.

Cultural discourses in 1950s France also essayed life in increasingly atomized ways, breaking up traditional class and family structures and encouraging privatization,

> a movement echoed on the level of everyday life by the withdrawal of the new middle classes to their newly comfortable domestic interiors, to the electric kitchens, to the enclosure of private automobiles, to the interior of a new vision of conjugality and an ideology of happiness built around the new unit of middle-class consumption, the couple, and to depoliticization as a response to the increase in bureaucratic control of daily life.[41]

The immediate postwar period saw a surge in the number and circulation of French magazines—*Marie-France, Elle, Femmes d'aujourd'hui, Marie-Claire*—targeting a female readership of housewives, domestic engineers who could do their part to help modernize and clean up France by investing in domestic appliances and beauty culture. But the predominant images of women in 1950s French cinema were less role models for young French women than embodiments of a nation in the process of modernizing, poised between the past and the future. Not quite modern themselves, the female stars of this period functioned as fixed sites of narration for the goals and discourses of French modernity.

Susan Hayward has noted that women performers gained in the 1950s "a relative ascendancy over their male counterparts for the first time in France's film history. In terms of performance, the 1930s was dominated by male actors (*the* star being Gabin)."[42] Gabin remained throughout the 1940s and 1950s the symbol of French proletarian masculinity, though there were new male performers too whose star power was considerable: Jean Marais, Gérard Philipe, Georges Marchal, the singer turned actor Yves Montand. But, for the first time in French film history, a higher proportion of the major stars were women. The majority of the actresses who were prominent in the late 1940s and early 1950s had either got their start or were already established before World War II—Gaby Morlay, Arletty, Simone Simon, Edwige Feuillère, Danielle Darrieux, Michèle Morgan—and all were in their thirties or older. There were those as well who gained renown during the Occupation or the reconstruction—Micheline Presle, Simone Signoret, Martine Carol—and, though they were slightly younger than their more established counterparts and achieved stardom a bit later, the continuities in character types, roles, and overall visual look among them is apparent.

All of these women starred in, and through their star power sold, high-end commercial films of the Tradition of Quality. Actively promoted to project a "quality" image of French cinema, these studio-produced works combined expert craftsmanship with high production values (many were Franco-Italian coproductions), lavish sets, and star power to burn. Collectively, they projected an image of "Frenchness" that was tied to good taste and high culture. These award-winning, commercially successful films ranged over four genres: films noir such as *Dédée d'Anvers* (1948) and *Les Diaboliques* (1954); psychological (melo)dramas such as *Le Diable au corps* (*Devil in the Flesh,* 1946) and *Olivia* (*Pit of Loneliness,* 1951); costume dramas such as *Caroline chérie* (1951) and *Destinées* (*Daughters of Destiny,* 1953); and literary adaptations of works by Maupassant (*Le Plaisir* [1952]), Stendhal (*Le Rouge et le noir* [*The Red and the Black,* 1954]), Zola (*Nana* [1955]), and other greats of the French literary pantheon. Wry comedic elements were often prominent in the costume dramas, particularly the ones that circulated around sexuality and female desire. Many of the costumers were also omnibus or episode films that stacked a star cast appearing across a number of sketches about infidelity (*La Ronde* [1950], *Le Plaisir, Secrets d'alcôve* [*The Bed*, 1954]) or the notion of woman, imaginary or historical (*Adorable Créatures* [1952], *Daughters of Destiny*). Across all genres, a certain image of femininity and female stardom was at the center of the production.[43]

The Tradition of Quality extends from the early sound era to the French New Wave, and there are continuities throughout in its depiction of women and female sexuality. Thus women in the 1930s and 1940s are frequently marked as unattainable yet eager to give themselves to the hero, often Gabin (Michèle Morgan and Danielle Darrieux epitomize this strain). Or they are quite down to earth, whores with hearts of gold or vamps looking out for number one (Arletty, Simone Simon). In the immediate postwar period as well, women in French cinema are adulterous, duplicitous, fallen or in the process of falling, and they are punished accordingly.[44] But they are also repeatedly shown as agents of their own desire rather than that of the male characters/spectators of the narrative. Women in postwar French cinema take on more central roles as narrative agents, albeit agents in a limited realm of female desire. The succès de scandale of *Devil in the Flesh* was due not to its story, which is quite conventional, but to the national and international viewing public's perception of it as amoral and an open endorsement of adultery (even though the older married woman, Micheline Presle, dies in childbirth as a result of her affair with the cynical young Gérard Philipe). Set during World War I but clearly speaking to the malaise of post–World War II French youth, *Devil in the Flesh* presages the particular form of scapegoating of women that psychological melodramas and films noir would increasingly take in the era of French reconstruction and into the boom. Simone Signoret, whose woman-in-her-own-right eroticism is coupled with an inability to effect change over her own circumstances, is emblematic of this type of female representation.[45]

In Italy, women's magazines and movies functioned synergistically to present a more uniform conception of new womanhood to their overwhelmingly female audience. It is nonetheless a conception built on paradox. Launched just after the war, illustrated weekly women's magazines like *Epoca, Oggi,* and *Tempo* reached by 1952 total circulation figures of 12.6 million, more than three times that of the daily press.[46] In an interesting content analysis of newsreels, women's magazines, and movies in Italy in the 1950s, Luisa Cicognetti and Lorenza

Servetti show that these magazines devoted space to the supposed problems and concerns of their female readers and that each published several issues about, interviews with, and case studies on "Today's girls" (*Ragazze d'oggi,* also the title of a 1955 film directed by Luigi Zampa). The modern young women who populated the pages of these magazines were self-confident, intelligent, and ambitious, entering professions heretofore barred to them (as in France, women in Italy did not achieve suffrage until after World War II). But they were also characterized as potential or already excellent mothers, eager to lead a married life and have children.[47]

The images women saw of themselves on Italian movie screens, however, were contradictory. Giuliana Bruno has noted that "it was not until the 1950s that going to the cinema gained definite acceptance as a group activity for women unaccompanied by men," and by all indications women made full use of their new rights and privileges as moviegoers.[48] Next to American blockbusters, melodramas were the most popular films. Abiding by the narrative codes of the genre, Italian melodramas of the 1950s centered on women who were either betrayed or adulterous wives, always involved in extraordinary, torrid affairs. One innovation, however, is noteworthy: rather than dealing with the aristocratic or working-class patriarchal families of their predecessors, Italian melodramas of the 1950s tended to deal with middle-class families with no more than two children and to situate their characters in contemporary surroundings. As Pierre Sorlin puts it, "Protagonists are purposely represented slightly above their actual condition; they are neither princes nor gypsies but middle-class people."[49] Like the women's magazines, Italian melodrama associated women with beauty, elegance, marriage, children, and family life.

And the stars? Anna Magnani, the neorealist emblem of partisan womanhood, actually portrayed a wide range of archetypes in postwar Italian cinema, including the *popolana* (woman of the people), the mistress, the chanteuse, the prostitute, the Italo-American immigrant, and the (often bad) mother. While Magnani is undoubtedly a unique figure in Italian cinema, she was not particularly popular with the domestic audience: *L'onorevole Angelina* (*Angelina,* 1947) was the only financially successful film she made in Italy.[50] More representative of Italian film culture in the 1950s are the actresses who achieved stardom through a hybrid cycle of films often dealing with the working or peasant classes and combining melodrama, eroticism, and comedy. Dubbed *neorealismo rosa* by leftist critics, the color of the qualifier is instructive. For the world these films image is a rosy one, materially poor but full of optimism and hope, as indicated by the title of the film generally considered as initiating the cycle, *Due soldi de speranza* (*Two Cents Worth of Hope,* 1952). And the protagonists who operate in this picturesque world are, unlike those in its neorealist predecessors or the more critically acceptable *commedia all'italiana* to come, women.

For most scholars and historians of Italian cinema, the demise of neorealism is signaled by the Silvana Mangano vehicle *Riso amaro* (*Bitter Rice,* 1948), one of the few neorealist films that appealed to the domestic audience (fifth-highest box office earner of 1949–50) and the second Italian postwar film (after *Roma, città aperta* [*Rome, Open City,* 1945]) to achieve international commercial success. Mangano's appearance in *Bitter Rice* brought glamour and earthy sensuality to the neorealist heroine previously represented by Magnani.[51] Sylvana Pampanini, like Mangano, was associated more with the melodramatic than the comic end of the rosy neorealist continuum. She played vamps and elegant women of irrepressible sensuality whose erotic appetites defined and undid her; in her "honor" the beloved comic actor Totò wrote one of his most memorable songs, "Malafemmina" ("Wicked Woman").[52] But the two most enduring female stars of Italian cinema who debuted and achieved phenomenal international success in the 1950s were Gina Lollobrigida and Sophia Loren. Their starring roles in a series of both melodramatic and comic *neorealismo rosa* made them the symbols of Italian womanhood in the 1950s. The rosy neorealist cycle was, as Mira Liehm has suggested, "unthinkable without the glamour of its main protagonists and the so-called 'pink vamp' as the leading lady. Dressed in sexy rags, with carefully unkempt hair and made up to look like a true poor peasant girl, the pink vamp was the Italian version of the American pin-up."[53]

The relationships between the star images of Mangano, Lollobrigida, and Loren, the boom years of the mid-1950s, the rebuilding of Italian national identity, and landscape are complex, but they coalesce in the composite image of the voluptuous female body these actresses project.[54] At the end of *Il processo di Frine,* the final segment in Alessandro Blasetti's 1952 episode film *Altri tempi (Infidelity),* Lollobrigida is standing trial for having poisoned a sister-in-law who objected to her many adulteries. The summation of the defense attorney (Vittorio De Sica) relied on a pun that not only convinces the jury to acquit Lollobrigida but that also came to signify the wave of busty stars of which she was representative: "If we absolve the *minorati psichici* (psychically underendowed), why not the *maggiorate fisiche* (physically amply endowed)?" Millicent Marcus has suggested that Mangano, Pampanini, Lollobrigida, and Loren "represented a *divismo* (stardom) of a totally physical sort. The discourse of the *maggiorate fisiche* has, as its sole sign and referent, the body itself—eloquent testimony to Italy's emergence from the devastations of war and entrance into the well-nourished arena of advanced consumer society."[55] That nourishment is signified by the large breasts of the *maggiorate fisiche,* whose bustlines have come to shape as well the contours of an entire nation's cinema culture.

The voluptuous female forms of the *maggiorate fisiche* represent a concerted program of nation building that may be traced through the interrelated discourses of beauty, nationhood, nature, and bounty. The establishment and popularity of beauty contests in postwar Italy enabled the rise to film stardom of all the female actresses of the statuesque school, their bodyscapes "discovered" by the filmmakers and producers who presided on the contest juries and fashioned the nation's postwar cinematic culture: Cesare Zavattini, Luchino Visconti, Vittorio De Sica, Giuseppe De Santis, Dino De Laurentiis, Carlo Ponti, Franco Cristaldi. The titles conferred upon the winners speak toward a homology between young womanhood and geographical and national identity: Pampanini, runner-up in the first Miss Italy competition of 1946; Mangano, Miss Rome; Lollobrigida, finalist for both Miss Italy and Miss Rome; Loren, at fourteen a contestant in several beauty contests in Naples, recipient of the consolation title Miss Princess of the Sea.[56] Postwar rites of "Italianness," these contests celebrated and staged young women as embodiments of a burgeoning new national identity rooted in landscape.

In an analysis of female identity in Italian cinema of the 1950s, Giovanna Grignaffini argues that the rebirth of Italian popular cinema

> relied on the "rediscovery" of two complementary centralities: landscape and the human presence in it. . . . Human beings are represented as *operators* of the landscape, in the sense that they both receive and regulate its modulations, the geographical as well as the anthropological; human beings

and the landscape are then, in turn, represented as *operators* of a new
national identity and physical characteristics, bodies, and gestures, restored
to an immediately legible *transparency,* also become landscape. . . . And a
film like *Bitter Rice,* and more generally the cinema of the 1950s, refers
precisely to a femininity understood as *naturalness,* body "of the earth",
in harmony with the landscape.[57]

Not operators *in* but *of* the spatialities of a nation in the throes of an
infrastructural boom connecting urban to rural, culture to nature, the
buxom bodies of Mangano, Pampanini, Lollobrigida, and Loren are
poised between past and future. The step from beauty contest stage to
film screen was one of degree rather than kind, as both institutions
celebrated "the female body, intact and uncontaminated by the look
of Fascist ideology, a creature of the earth, rich with joyous sensuality,
generous in its proportions, warm, and familiar: a body-landscape,
along whose outline you could read the future of a nation that had
to start again from scratch."[58] The Italian stars of the 1950s presented
an image of modern womanhood rooted in the past but ready for
the future.

The iconic female stars of 1950s French popular cinema also
embody contradictions between the old and the new, tradition and
modernity, limitation and freedom. But there are differences as well
between the representations of women in these two cinemas. Eroticism and nudity had been features of female representation in French
cinema dating to at least the 1920s, and in the 1930s and 1940s they
tended to be affixed to familiar female types: the vamp, the whore,
the femme fatale.[59] In the postwar costume films of the Tradition of
Quality, historical period and emphasis on the desires of the female
protagonists became a paradoxical means toward more open display
and fetishization of their bodies, with the portals to the sumptuously
appointed bathrooms, boudoirs, and bedrooms of courtesans and ladies-
in-waiting thrown open in the interest of exploring women's time
and space. Such domestic spaces are not in and of themselves modern,
especially when decorated to the historical demands of films set during the Revolution, the Second Empire, or the fin de siècle. But the
Tradition of Quality's persistent plotting within them dovetails with the
concerted attention to beauty culture, commodity consumption, and
domestic engineering in the popular culture of the postwar boom.
The heroines of French cinema in the early 1950s are thus figured not

as fallow body landscapes of a bounteous future à la the *maggiorate fisiche,* but as cultivated bodies narcissistically dedicated to their own beautification within the houses of French culture.

In this respect, the return and popularity of the costume film in the late 1940s and early 1950s may be read alongside the "new look" of French fashion set by a group of mostly male designers including Pierre Balmain, Hubert de Givenchy, Jacques Fath, and especially Christian Dior. Highlighting womanly curves through full, swinging skirts, breast-emphasizing but concealing tops implying rigid bras, tailored jackets pinched at a wasplike waist achieved through tight corsetry, stiletto heels, gloves, and broad hats, the French designers privileged constricting and conformist clothes. The "new look" sharply contrasted the utilitarian appearance and limited range of fabrics of wartime fashions and sought to be both beautiful and impractical despite the continuing rationing and shortages of the late 1940s. In this it is tied to both the national and international interests of the French economy of the reconstruction: nationally as a response to wartime deprivation and the developing female consumer market, encouraging women to return to a more traditional feminine ornamentation; and internationally as an attempt to reestablish French fashion's world hegemony, an initiative enabled by the Franco-American Blum-Byrnes treaty of 1946–48, which exchanged French luxury goods against the almost unchecked entry of American films to the French market. The interplay between the new fashion and French cinema is thus very complex. On the one hand the interaction is direct and modern: Ginette Vincendeau has noted the frequency of films in the early 1950s that were set in the contemporary French fashion world.[60] On the other hand it is indirect and traditional, the Tradition of Quality as a means toward rebuilding and maintaining French national cinema and identity in the face of an influx of Hollywood visual culture. The two discourses meet in the costume film, which dresses its female stars in fitted gowns that accentuate breasts and hips and promises, through its settings in the "woman's arena" of bathroom, boudoir, or bedroom and through its narratives focusing on female desire and infidelity, to undress them as well.

The staging of female bodies and desires in postwar French costumers is coterminous with the nation's drive toward modernization, urbanization, and consumer power: in both cases women are restricted sites of display and narration. Martine Carol may be singled out as French cinema's first true sex symbol, but her performance style and costuming codes are clearly in line with dominant trends of the period.[61] These trends coalesce into a visual fetishization of the image of the bound/unbound shapely female form and a narrative fixation of that form in the space and time of her story. Represented in her flashbacks as the agent of her own desire, Martine Carol/Lola in *Lola Montès* (1955) is imprisoned in the present public narrative within the cage of her past personal history. She is a tragic figure, but one whose tragedy lies in the contradictory space between public and private by which young women generally, and female film stars specifically, were in the early 1950s so insistently interpellated. Indeed, director Max Ophüls said at the time of the film's release that he "was struck by a series of news items which, directly or indirectly, took me back to Lola: Judy Garland's nervous breakdown, the sentimental adventures of Zsa Zsa Gabor . . . the questions asked by the audience in *Lola* were inspired by certain radio programs."[62] Like their Hollywood counterparts with whom they were designed to compete, the female stars of the Tradition of Quality were simultaneously subjects of desire and glamorous objects of visual and narrative investigation, and their place was most definitely in the home.

And then there was Brigitte Bardot. She made her film debut in 1952 and played a variety of secondary roles in Tradition of Quality films, causing a sensation with her outrageous behavior at the 1953 Cannes Film Festival and graduating to leads in 1955. But it was her performance in *Et Dieu . . . créa la femme* (*And God Created Woman*, 1956), directed by her then husband Roger Vadim, that turned Bardot overnight into an icon of rebellious youth, unapologetic sexuality, and French womanhood, both in and out of France. *And God Created Woman* was received in its time as the very emblem of French modernity, which meant it was sharply criticized in the mainstream press for its licentiousness and nudity and praised by the young critics of the *Cahiers du cinéma* group—particularly François Truffaut, who wrote in *Arts* in late 1956, "It is a film typical of our generation [. . .] despite the vast audience that *Et Dieu* will certainly find, only young spectators will be on Vadim's side, because he shares their vision."[63] One week later Truffaut published in the same magazine a rousing defense of the film, but here his emphasis shifted to defending Bardot herself.

While there are elements of *And God Created Woman* besides Bardot that signified for the *Cahiers* critics that modern French cinema had finally come of age—low budget, location shooting, attention to small, everyday details—the figuration of Bardot in the film was undeniably the main draw for both the international viewing public and the future filmmakers of the French New Wave, and in this she set the stage for a type of female representation ubiquitous in the films of Truffaut, Godard, et al.[64]

Bardot is shown throughout *And God Created Woman* (and her career) in figure-hugging clothes as well as in various stages of undress, including total nudity: the first imaging of her in the film (cut by American censors) is a low-angle full shot that displays her uncovered body horizontally as she lies sunbathing on her stomach across the entirety of the CinemaScope frame. In her conspicuous nudity Bardot is clearly in a line of development with other eroticized French stars of the early 1950s whose attired/unattired bodies were integral to their image and popularity: Martine Carol, the reigning sex goddess, or the younger Françoise Arnoul, publicized in France from her debut in 1950 as a "sex kitten," a moniker Bardot would quickly assume. What *is* different about the clothing and unclothing of Bardot's body is that they are marked explicitly in the context of the film as self-motivated acts of rebellion against conventional values and decorum. The viewer is no longer a fly on the wall in the bedroom, bathroom, or boudoir of the Tradition of Quality but out in the sun, sand, and sea of Saint-Tropez. Bardot's *déshabillé* is in part motivated by setting (nude sunbathing, soaked dresses clinging to her body as she frolics in the surf, et cetera), but it is always represented narratively as a conscious, frequently rebellious act on her part rather than a mere function of place. And it is an act that shocks and scandalizes the older, "old maid-ish" women who play the foil within the narrative to Bardot's coquette.

But it does not shock the older men within the narrative of *And God Created Woman* and the films that followed, and in this one can see how at another level, that of vision and the look, Bardot is similarly poised between old and new. Her physical features, particularly her face, have been read by Edgar Morin among others as a text that

> simultaneously expresses the infantile and the feline: the long hair falling down her back is the very symbol of lascivious undress, the proferred [*sic*] nudity, yet a deceptively disordered row of bangs across the forehead

reminds us of the little high-school girl. Her tiny roguish nose accentuates both her *gaminerie* and her animality; her fleshy lower lip is pursed into a baby's pout as often as into a provocation to be kissed. The little cleft in her chin adds the final touch to the charming *gaminerie* of this face, of which it would be libelous to say it has only one expression—it has two: eroticism and childishness.[65]

Bardot is thus not simply a modern young woman but a child-woman, as her nickname connoted: B. B., or *bébé* (baby). Again, in this she is not a singular figure, as the mid-1950s and early 1960s witnessed the rising appeal, in France and the United States especially, of narratives centered on older men's fascination with young tomboys, gamines, or nymphettes, a fascination represented either as entirely sexual and therefore perverse (*Baby Doll* [1956], *Lolita* [1962]) or as ambiguously paternal and therefore charming (Audrey Hepburn in *Sabrina* [1954] and *Funny Face* [1957], Leslie Caron in *An American in Paris* [1951] and *Gigi* [1958], a slew of movies starring Marina Vlady, Michèle Mercier, Debbie Reynolds, Sandra Dee, Tuesday Weld, et cetera). The hallmark of Bardot is that she combined the attributes of the gamine (*Cette sacrée gamine,* a comedy she made in 1956) with that of the mature sexual woman, the international ideals of which, whether blonde (Marilyn Monroe, Diana Dors, Jayne Mansfield, Anita Ekberg) or brunette (Jane Russell, Elizabeth Taylor, Lollobrigida, Loren), leaned toward exaggerated female forms, particularly large breasts. Bardot shared the latter feature, but she also had a small waist and hips and a slim silhouette. If screen models of the female body in the 1950s may be considered as the dualism boyish/full figure, Bardot was both/and.

The exhibitionism and narcissism of the Bardot persona, the evident pleasure she takes in her own body, is what prevents her from being a passive icon: whether she displays her body for herself or for men, she is the operator of her own sexuality—and in this she was considered a progressive figure by none other than Simone de Beauvoir, who saw in Bardot a representation of woman who for the first time is "as much a hunter as she is a prey."[66] Yet the contradiction of Bardot's positionality is such that narrative is frequently fused to spectacle. Her searches for erotic fulfillment are thus inseparable from her erotic display, emphasized in *And God Created Woman* by her revealing attire, "her walk (that of a model and a dancer) and, oddly enough, the absence of accessories: the fact that she has no handbag, and often walks barefoot and barehanded (with the exception of her bicycle), highlights the fact that her walking has no narrative function, but is designed to display herself and her clothes."[67] Bardot is a figure of mobility rather than stasis, a development that links her to the New Wave heroines to come.

A final attribute that distinguishes Bardot's transitional place between the fixed popular Tradition of Quality heroines and the more mobile ones of the New Wave, and one that links her to the contemporaneous *maggiorate fisiche* of Italian cinema, is her "naturalness," which is inscribed in the codes of her films through the setting, her clothes, and her sexuality and reiterated in the extrafilmic discourses of the time: "'she doesn't act, she exists' (Vadim), 'in front of the camera, I am myself' (Bardot), 'what did Bardot bring to the 1950s? The natural, very simply, the natural they needed so much' (Pierre Murat)."[68] A child of nature, Bardot follows her instincts, she is pleasure-seeking. The Saint-Tropez that is the setting of *And God Created Woman,* and to which Bardot has so stubbornly remained attached (she is a particularly insular and xenophobic star), is a far cry in terms of both time and space from the ornate rooms in which the stars of the Tradition of Quality circulated. But it is also a far cry from the city. If urbanization is a key feature of French (and Italian) modernity, Bardot is regressive in this respect; or rather, she encapsulates a particular relation between the culture of the workaday city and the nature of the holiday beach or mountains. A central fact of French cultural existence, the paid summer holiday dates back, like the forty-hour workweek, to the worker reforms of Léon Blum's Popular Front government. The fortnight's holiday with pay that went into effect in July 1936 was an instant success, and half a million French people took advantage of the reduced ticket price on the special "Lagrange trains" (60 percent of those who went to the Riviera that summer admitted that they had never before seen the sea). By the time of *And God Created Woman* two decades later, little more had been achieved in the way of worker reforms except for an added third week of holidays with pay in February 1956.[69] Bardot's intimate relation to the paradisaical space of the paid holiday, the beach, in the fall of that year thus connects her to what was (and still is) a "natural" fact of French life, but a fact whose meaning derives from its difference from the space of work and everyday life.

Michael Kelly, Tony Jones, and Jill Forbes have argued the following:

> One of the most characteristic aspects of modernization is that, in
> marginalizing all of the social and cultural elements which do not
> correspond to its modernizing project, it constructs an image of those
> elements as its Other. While this Other may be despised or excluded, it
> may also become a focus for the loss and mourning which accompany
> any process of change, and for any opposition to the direction of change.
> Invested with the nostalgia of lost innocence or the power of a radical
> alternative, the primitive and the exotic are the atavistic shadow of the
> modern.[70]

In what ways can Bardot be considered to signify both modernity and
its Other? One could certainly read the contradictions between narrative and spectacle in her films through this relation. The spectacle of
her body, while pleasurable, is in psychoanalytic terms also supposed
to evoke male fear of castration. As a freely roaming woman who
initiates sex she most definitely blurs the boundary between subject
and object, self and Other, which is the determining fiction of male
subjectivity. But the threat she presents is ultimately diffused through
her childishness and searching for approval from father figures. Bardot
also connotes nature, even animality: she is a "sex kitten," and her irrepressible sexuality, while acceptable because "natural," must nevertheless be tamed in her film narratives. In this she may be seen as Other
to French modernity, which so insistently interpellated young women
as housewives and, through popular audiovisual culture, undertook to
train them in the rules and consumption of beauty applications, of the
new "miracle" materials of modern science (nylon, plastic), of ratio-
nal planning and domestic engineering. To such a project Bardot is
an intolerable figure, which may go some way toward explaining why
she provoked the hostility of the French female public—why, for a
surefire box-office draw, she was not very well liked in France. What
makes Bardot so importantly of her time, and what makes her the key
transitional figure between the stars of 1950s French and Italian popular cinema and the new and modern cinemas of those two countries
to come, is how her persona and image are "invested with the nostalgia of lost innocence" *and* with "the power of a radical alternative."

In a preamble to the climactic scene of *And God Created Woman,*
Bardot/Juliette Tardieu wanders the streets of Saint-Tropez barefoot,
clad in a short black bodysuit and a knee-length blue skirt. Full of guilt

and self-loathing for having cuckolded (in nature, by the beach) her newlywed husband, Jean-Louis Trintignant/Michel, with his more virile and sexually experienced older brother, Christian Marquand/ Antoine, while Michel was away on a trip, she ends up at François's bar, a dive by the docks, slinging back brandy. Unbeknownst to Juliette, her mother-in-law has just informed Michel of her indiscretion, and he has raced from the house to find her. When Michel arrives at the office of the family shipyard business he confronts his brother, who informs him of Juliette's whereabouts but prevents him from seeing her by locking the door to the street. Michel takes a gun from a desk drawer, threatens Antoine with it, and they fight each other clumsily, Michel emerging the victor and running to his wife. Meanwhile, back at the bar, a female friend of Juliette's discreetly telephones Curt Jurgens/Eric, an urbane businessman who wants to turn the brothers' shipyard into a casino and is a father figure to all, and informs him that Juliette is in a bad way. As she hangs up the phone, music emanates from downstairs, where an "orchestra from Paris" is rehearsing. Juliette descends the stairs to the basement.

The climactic scene that ensues is a complex interplay of sights and sounds. The band, with the exceptions of the bass and saxophone players, comprises black musicians on a variety of percussion instruments, and the two groupings are spatially separated—the white players on the stage, the black ones on the floor. The bandleader, his back to the stage, plays the maracas and speaks directions first to the black band members, then to Juliette as she enters the space and situates

And God Created Woman (1956)

herself on the floor among the band (in the English-dubbed version of the film, he is the only character who is not dubbed but left speaking French). As Juliette becomes more and more rhythmically receptive to the beat, thumping her hands on a table and swaying her hips, the music and her body begin to play off one another, alternately leading and following the tempo.

She moves back and forth between dancing by herself and with the black bandleader, who along with the group encourages her to ever more provocative displays and movements. After a slower passage, during which Juliette has popped open all but the top button of her skirt, refused to leave with Eric (who has arrived to witness the scene), and undulated sensuously with her own image in a full-length mirror, the band begins a fast-paced mambo that inspires her into a frenzied dance. Juliette jumps to the center of the black-and-white-checkered tile dance floor and is flanked by two black male dancers on either side. The camera cuts to a midshot at a low height and angle that frames her in the center from the waist down; the visual emphasis is on her skirt, which she splays open with her hands, her frenetically moving legs, her crotch, her gyrating hips. She is a whirl of bare feet and syncopated movements, an autoerotic spectacle.

When Michel arrives we see the white musicians for only the second time; they are no longer playing but conversing on the stage, the music now dominated by the percussive drumbeat. Michel implores her to stop. Juliette refuses, but not defiantly: the expression on her face is pained, and as she shakes her head wildly from side to side, she

is at the same time saying no to her husband, saying no to the music that has control over her body, and salaciously jouncing her long, unruly hair. She is unable to extricate herself from the rhythms of the music or her own body, both of which now seem fully to "possess" her.

The relay of onscreen looks alternates between the powerless Michel and Eric looking at Juliette, the dancing bandleader looking at (and dancing with) Juliette, the musicians looking at Juliette or at nothing (one conga player is repeatedly shown with eyes closed and head inclined rapturously), and Juliette looking at Michel or at herself. As the music and her movements once again accelerate to a fever pitch and Michel draws his gun and points it at his flagrantly disobedient wife, the cutting accelerates to a series of medium close-ups that establish eyeline matches among the principal onlookers and that isolate the body parts of Juliette and of the band members, a flurry of dark hands beating on light drum skins, bare (Juliette's) and moccasin-clad (the bandleader's) feet alternately touching black and white tiles, and tousled blonde hair, all contrasted with the stiff immobility of the French male onlookers. At a peak moment Eric makes a grab for the gun Michel brandishes and it goes off, wounding Eric slightly in the side; he hides the injury and makes a quick retreat with Antoine. The sound of the shot abruptly stops both the music and Juliette, who receives from Michel four slaps across the face that discompose her hair even more. She initially cries out but is soon sighing approvingly and peering provocatively through her tangled tresses at her now masculinized husband.

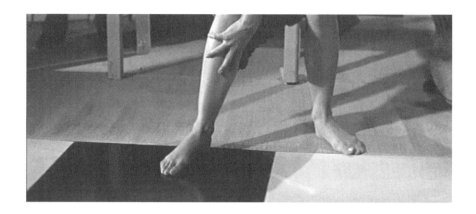

The oedipal dynamics of this six-minute-long scene are obvious and not of primary interest to me here.[71] Rather, I want to pursue the degree to which the scopophilic and fetishistic aspects of the climax of *And God Created Woman* are ones that inextricably link sexual difference with race. Ginette Vincendeau reports that "Curt Jurgens's description of Bardot as 'une négresse blonde'—a blonde negress—at the time of the making of *Et Dieu* is, despite but also because of, its racism, revealing, in that its linking of Bardot with 'the primitive' also acknowledges the constructed aspect of her image (the bleached hair)."[72] The connection between Bardot and "the primitive" is evoked in the film's climactic mambo scene on a number of levels, and it is a connection that produces a great deal of tension dramatically, visually, and aurally. Dramatically, the tension involves incestual family relations, Juliette's "uncontrollable" free spirit and sexuality, and the need for her taming by an assumption on Michel's part of patriarchal power and control: the instinctual laws of nature (primitive femininity) have run wild and must be brought back into check through a reassertion of the kinship codes of culture. Visually, the tension is between two races, two worlds—the black world of physical movement and abandon, the white world of stasis and order, with Juliette's body threatening instinctually to "go native" despite her conscious attempts to remain true to the domestic life she has chosen for herself (her head says no to the music but her body says yes, her body says no to Michel but her eyes say yes). Her split subjectivity is reinforced through cutting, which not only isolates her head from parts of her body that move as if they had a will of their own, but also through a Manichaean system of light and dark: the black band versus the white onlookers, the black hands and broad grins of the musicians beating their drums versus the white legs and blonde distress of Bardot in dynamic frenzy, her dark clothing revealing underneath her light skin (though not as light as the other white women's—she sunbathes), the black and white tiles of the dance floor. Aurally, the tension is between melody and rhythm as blasts of trumpet burst through the incessant beat of the drums to cue not only the cutting but also the spectators to peak moments in Bardot's dance and the domestic crisis it is bringing to a head. But look: we never see a trumpet player among the band members; the horn sounds are extradiegetic, interjections from outside the scene that a battle is being fought for possession of the body and soul of Bardot, of white womanhood, of French nationhood.[73]

Bardot is both modernity and its Other, a contradictory position-ality encapsulated by all of the above tensions. An emblem of youth, she is associated here as elsewhere with modern music that mixes "for-eign" sounds with French ones, Afro-Caribbean rhythms (the mambo) with American forms (jazz). Freed from the stasis that characterized the desiring subjects/desired objects of the Tradition of Quality, the modern mobile woman as embodied by Bardot is not free of that paradox but reorients it to a terrain where the status of the nation in relation to its colonial heritage is not just in jeopardy but clearly declining. If there is much about Bardot that is "new," equally she evokes "the primitive and the exotic . . . the atavistic shadow of the modern." It is a shadow cast by the body of the woman/star/wife as illuminated by the nervous controlling gaze of the man/director/hus-band (the story of Juliette and Michel would be replayed by Bardot and Vadim soon after the former deified the latter in *And God Created Woman*). And it is also a shadow cast by a modernizing national body politic bathed in the fading light of a colonial empire in declension. The full force of that equation was felt most strongly in the city.

The Place of Flanerie

The figure of the flâneur appears in the work of many commentators on the phenomenon of modernity, but it is in the writings of Walter Benjamin that he is first celebrated as a positionality bearing a certain subversive potential. Written in the 1930s, Benjamin's pieces on Charles Baudelaire represent a detailed and at times cryptic elaboration of the poet and occasional essayist's reflections on "the modern." Like the turn-of-the-century sociologist Georg Simmel and his contempo-rary critic of mass culture, Siegfried Kracauer, Benjamin considered the flâneur an expression of the decidedly different character urban existence took in the mid-nineteenth century, a period of accelerated industrial-capitalist development that quickly and utterly transformed the conditions of housing, work, and social relations—in a word, mod-ernity. But unlike Simmel and Kracauer, Benjamin saw in the flâneur of Baudelaire's Paris a figure through whom the experience of moder-nity could not only be extrapolated but also resisted.[74]

For Benjamin, the flâneur's importance as a pivotal figure and dis-position of modern life lies partly in his status as outsider, one whose existence and practice is marginal to the main currents of industrial capitalism. In the relative tranquillity of the Arcades, the flâneur is not bound by economic direction or social function: an overall lack of purpose characterizes his activity and his gaze. The speed of modernity is something for which the flâneur is particularly suited as a site of registration. Within the space of urban perception, a panoramic panoply of views and details transmits itself with dizzying swiftness, and the flâneur, who defines and distinguishes himself by his leisurely pace, contradicts the speed of modern life at the same time as he constitutes its focal point through his attentive watching. His slowness is also what enables him to absorb and filter, to render meaningful, the myriad shocks that the city in its very newness emits. In the same way that these shocks disturb the tranquil equilibrium of the city-as-well-oiled-machine they also disturb the flâneur, who functions as a kind of a lightning rod for those moments when modernity reveals its underside. Insofar as the experience of the modern city is one of accelerating change—in social and economic relations, in living arrangements, in spatiality—the flâneur puts himself in a position to perceive these phenomena in dialectical terms, to slow the speed of modern life so as to witness it not as a blur but as discrete developments within history. In this way the flâneur is "the true subject of modernity."[75]

That said, the Baudelairean/Benjaminian flâneur is not immune to the commodifying effects of the ceaseless march of capital; rather, he is inscribed by it. The price to be paid for the insights he reaches regarding his place in the system of capitalist production, a system the flâneur resists through his own purposelessness, is the fact that his share of the wealth is perceptual rather than material. The space that history gives to the class of the flâneur, the petit bourgeoisie, is not one of agency but of passing time. Enjoyment within such a space depends upon embracing rather than spurning the transitoriness of commodity culture—in fact empathizing with it, becoming one with it.[76] Flanerie thus functions as a kind of "walking cure" against the prevailing melancholy in capitalist modernity—the melancholy to which the modern subject is subjected in his periods of waiting, transit, and transition, certainly, but also the melancholy that is the very condition of modern life. The flâneur's disposition develops out of what Kracauer describes as the disorienting "loneliness of big cities [and] the emptiness of spiritual space" that all occupants of the modern metropolis share, "a deep sadness which grows from the knowledge of their being inscribed in a certain spiritual situation."[77] Since there is no escape from the melancholy that attends modern urban existence, the flâneur focuses his attention on the precise perception of its environs and spaces. He goes through life with eyes open.

The preponderance of male pronouns in the above consideration of the literature of flanerie is indicative of the priority given to the male flâneur as a modern figure of importance and resistance, a priority that has since the 1990s been challenged by a number of feminist writers. Janet Wolff was one of the first to search through the literature and culture of nineteenth-century modernity for the female counterpart to this heroic male subject. While she admits that none of the authors she discusses (Baudelaire and Benjamin, of course, but also more contemporary critics and scholars such as Marshall Berman and Richard Sennett) is unaware of the different experience of women in the modern city, the female flâneur is an invisible figure in the literature of modernity: "There is no question of inventing the *flâneuse:* the essential point is that such a character was rendered impossible by the sexual divisions of the nineteenth century."[78] Although Wolff's conclusion has since been revealed as overstated—if not for mid-nineteenth-century London than for Paris, where the atmosphere provided more opportunity for women to participate in the public life of concerts and spectacles—women who strolled the streets of modernity nonetheless ran the risk of sexualization and of themselves becoming spectacles of male voyeurism. In fact, the pages of Baudelaire's *Les Fleurs du mal* and of Benjamin's unfinished Arcades Project do contain numerous references to a significant female figure inhabiting the Arcades: the prostitute. While prostitution is for male flâneurs a metaphor from which their flanerie permits them the opportunity of escape, for female flâneurs it is a specific condition and occupation to which their flanerie inevitably binds them. If the figure of the (male) flâneur is for Benjamin the embodiment of the "transformation of perception characteristic of modern subjectivity, the figure of the whore is the allegory for the transformation of objects, the world of things."[79]

In the writings of Baudelaire and Benjamin, the demise of the male flâneur is linked with the destruction of the Arcades, which was part of a massive transformation of Paris undertaken by Napoleon III and George Haussmann, appointed prefect of the Seine in 1853. Contemporaneous with this ambitious rebuilding of Paris to make it a modern city is the rise of the department store, which became a central fixture in major cities beginning in the mid-nineteenth century: it is in the department store that women found a paradisaical, respectable space to participate in the pleasures of flanerie heretofore reserved for men.[80] The development of shopping in the late nineteenth century thus presented for bourgeois women a public leisure activity that was socially acceptable, and the department store, like the Arcades before it, offered fantasy worlds for a new breed of itinerant lookers: "The great stores may have been the *flâneur's* last coup, but they were the *flâneuse's* first."[81]

The relations between shopping, consumerism, women, and spectatorship have produced important scholarship, most particularly in the ways in which cinema and visual culture are embedded in some or all of the above at the discursive or practical levels.[82] Although Anke Gleber brooks no quarter with the nineteenth-century female shopper as a symbolic figure for feminism—"the early 'department store flâneuses' who 'roam' the interiors of capitalist consumption represent little more than a bourgeois variant of domesticized 'flanerie'"—she is invested in carving out a space for female flanerie in the streets and on the screens of Weimar Germany.[83] While for Kracauer the cinema was the mass ornament par excellence, for Gleber it is simply another manifestation of the fundamentally visual disposition of modernity: Weimar Germany is one of those places and periods "of reduced clarity or consensus about the social or ideological rationales of their realities . . . [that] seem to inspire flanerie," a time and a space in which the "confrontation of the prevailing status quo with a new and liberated women's movement yielded an open moment of modernity."[84]

In the literature on flanerie, the flâneur, male or female, is a rich register of his or her specific place and time, be it Paris of the mid- or late nineteenth century, Berlin of the Weimar Republic, or the suburban malls of the postmodern era. In all as well, the activity of flanerie—its slow pace, its itinerant manner of looking, its simultaneous detachment from and investment in the objects that cross the field of vision— mark the flâneur both as out of sync with the rhythms of modernity and as a potential model for active female spectatorship. But while these connections between flanerie and film spectatorship have been made, the figure of the female flâneur, especially her particular presences and functions within the space and time of the French New Wave and the new Italian cinema, has yet to be fully examined. Indeed, the period of rapid modernization and urbanization in these two countries, from the mid-1950s to the mid-1960s, has been effectively bypassed in all previous studies of flanerie; it is the gap between the modernity of Weimar Germany and the postmodernity of contemporary American suburbia.[85] The almost iconic figure of the wandering woman in modern European art cinema was a new development in the imaging of women in Western cinema, and it bears analysis within the context of feminist criticism of moving-image culture.

Cléo de 5 à 7 is one film of the French New Wave to have received what might be called a full feminist explication. It is not coincidental that *Cléo* was directed by a woman, Agnès Varda, and Sandy Flitterman-Lewis reads *Cléo* in the context of other works by Varda as "exploring the feminist dialectic of the woman seeing/the woman seen." Flitterman-Lewis argues that many of Varda's films "show us Paris, to be sure, in the best tradition of the early New Wave films, but they show us a very precise view of that city, one constructed by a female point of view and fully determined by feminine subjectivity."[86] As with so many European art films of the period, the central protagonist of the film is a young, beautiful, modern woman literally on the move, a female flâneur who traverses the streets, quarters, and parks of Paris not in quest of a specific goal but as a means toward killing time and exploring space—an errant trajectory that, in this case at least, leads to self-recognition. The title character, Cléo, is distressed about the impending results of a medical examination for what she fears is stomach cancer, and the film charts in a prologue and thirteen episodes the course of her life in the late Parisian afternoon of 21 June 1961 between 5:00 and 6:30 p.m. The feminist reading regards Cléo's flanerie as a process of conversion from a static and traditional feminine object—she's a pop chanteuse and is treated by her handler Angèle, her older lover José, and her songwriters Bob and Plumitif, as a doll and a child—into a self-determining female subject, from "woman-as-spectacle" into "an active social participant."[87]

While such a reading is true to the spirit of the film, to concentrate on the issue of gender stereotyping and role-playing is to push to the margins a great deal of what the main character (and the viewer) sees and hears in the Paris of June 1961. For *Cléo de 5 à 7* is an audiovisual text suffused with the tensions and contradictions of a modern French metropole gripped by anxieties of its own, a malady both external and internal: decolonization and colonial war. When *Cléo* was made in the spring of 1961, die-hard defenders of French Algeria formed the Organisation de l'Armée Secrète and were undertaking terrorist campaigns in Algeria and France in an attempt to sabotage peace efforts. At the turning point of the film in the seventh episode, a rehearsal session in her apartment, Cléo breaks down while singing a song about emptiness and aloneness, explodes in a rage at her songwriters, disappears behind a black curtain, emerges wearing a black dress (as opposed to her former white feathered satin peignoir), tears off her blonde wig, puts on her new black hat, grabs a dark coat, and leaves. Soon after taking to the streets she enters the Café Le Dôme, makes a selection from the jukebox, and dons dark glasses. In the foreground of the same shot are two men seated at a table and conversing. Just as the song kicks in, one of the men remarks, "This Algerian craziness. You don't know where you stand." At this point in the film, neither does Cléo nor the viewer—both are on the move.

This is merely one example of an explicit reference in the film to the war in Algeria. There are others as well: on the radio in the taxi ride Cléo and Angèle take from the Pont Neuf to the rue Huygens in episode III; in the figure of Antoine, the talkative young conscript on leave who Cléo meets in episode XI in the Parc Montsouris and who accompanies her to the Salpêtrière hospital. More important, Cléo's changing vision of the city, and of the people around her and her place in it and among them, is inscribed throughout the film with the sights and sounds of a nation in the throes of modernity and renegotiating its relation to its past and passing empire. From 5:13 to 5:18 p.m., Cléo and Angèle take a ride with a female cabbie who turns on the radio to hear the latest sounds. Cléo realizes that the radio is playing one of her popular songs, but she is not happy with the recording and pleads with the driver to turn it off, huffing and puffing all the while. Finally finding her role, she leans forward from the backseat and says with sweet and false humility, "I said turn the music off! It's me singing," throwing back her head and giggling. Cléo then leans out the window and looks. The camera pans quickly to the right and shock cuts to a medium close-up of two African masks in a shop window.

The effect of Cléo's duplicity, her role-playing, is registered not simply through masks, but African ones. She sinks back in her seat, disturbed. As they drive on and the driver talks with Angèle about her job, Cléo asks, "Aren't you afraid at night?" The car stops, and we see along with Cléo from the inside of the taxi and through her window another storefront display with three African objets d'art, the two darkest ones quickly singled out by separate shots for emphasis before the car moves on. Then the cabbie turns on the radio again and we are inundated with news from Algeria.[88] There is no escape. Colonial reminders are everywhere.[89]

Cléo's progress toward personal and visual liberation as a modern French woman is linked to a certain flight or regress from the (de)colonized and racialized Other, an Other she is figured variously as and as not. When she first takes to the streets, Cléo stops to gaze at her own image in a mirror outside the Restaurant La Pagode painted over with Chinese letters and remarks in an interior monologue, "My unchanging doll's face, this ridiculous hat, I can't see my own fears. I thought everyone looked at me. I only look at myself. It's wearisome." But when she turns away from her reflection to join a crowd that has gathered round the call of a barker, she is disturbed by what she sees: a male street performer who ingests a number of frogs from an aquarium and then, steeling himself to the task, vomits them in a torrent of fluid.

Cléo de 5 à 7 (1961)

Cléo is not purged of her worries by this grotesque reminder of her own potentially fatal stomach ailment and flees the scene to the Café Le Dôme, whereupon begins episode VIII, titled "Some others from 5:45 to 5:52." In this sequence more than any other, the film becomes one with its protagonist in toeing a thin line between self-reflexivity and narcissism, between insight and self-absorption. Flitterman-Lewis describes it well:

> Camera position and Cleo's viewpoint coalesce as the subjective vision of social reality imposes itself.... A Baudelairean flâneur, Cleo glides through the cafe, hearing snatches of conversations ... as she tries to see the impact of her song, her selection on the jukebox.... The anonymity she craves—the better to observe others around her—is facilitated when she puts on dark glasses. Her dark glasses become the instrument of vision, of insight: By becoming anonymous, Cleo thus sees, and in seeing others, she begins to understand herself.[90]

The "others" of this sequence do not exist for themselves; neither Cléo nor the viewer gets to know any of them as characters in this, the only episode of the film not titled with the name of a person. They are just snatches of visual stimuli for the flâneur's directed gaze, reflective surfaces off which may be read the image of her own identity. As she leaves Le Dôme and walks to the Académie de Sculpture, the film

intercuts Cléo's subjective vision of the real, ordinary Parisians she passes on the street and who look back at her (and at the camera/ viewer: this sequence was quite evidently unrehearsed and filmed on the fly) with staged and remembered medium close-ups of faces and objects from a receding, fictionalized past. Cléo's flanerie throughout the rest of the film will be marked by this tension between a flight from the Other and the growing recognition of herself as implicated in the world of "some others" who are not her but who nevertheless enable, through their existence as sights to be seen or as faces populating her personal life, the (re)construction of her own image.

Like most of the lower-budgeted European art films of the early 1960s, *Cléo de 5 à 7* was shot in high-contrast black-and-white, and the visual register of the film consistently works at the extreme ranges of its stock to image its protagonist as never fully at home with herself or her surroundings. Perhaps the whitest of the white New Wave heroines, Cléo is nevertheless throughout the film a Manichaean presence. She begins the film in a white dress with black polka dots and promptly buys a black peaked hat, is smothered in the episodes leading up to her flanerie in the ethereal yet constraining whiteness of her apartment and downy lingerie as compared to the darker Angèle (black skirt, zebra-print top), and wanders through the second half of the film as a visual contrast of light skin and hair and dark dress and (initially) glasses.[91] The entire film may be read as a complex interplay of light and dark, white and black. And Cléo is figured at the crux of those polarities. She reveals to Antoine in the film's final episode that her real name is Florence and that Cléo, short for Cleopatra, is her stage name, to which he responds, "Florence! It conjures thoughts of Italy . . . the Renaissance . . . Botticelli . . . a rose. Cleopatra! Egypt . . . the Sphinx . . . the asp . . . the tigress." The film clearly encourages the viewer here to side with Antoine's predilection for the "real" name over the constructed one ("I prefer flora to fauna"), a forsaking of the distant, the exotic, and the animal for the simpler vegetable comforts of the continent that one is to understand as a step toward a more unified sense of self.

Cléo de 5 à 7 is certainly readable as a colonial allegory, though the allegory is not fixed but as aleatory as the movements of its protagonist, an alternation between past conceptions of self and nationhood and the new potentialities of the modern woman and a modernizing nation.

The final episode of the film is titled "Cléo and Antoine from 6:15 to 6:30," and although it ends with the conventional image of the male/female couple the allegorical implications of their alignment are by no means clear. In the transition scene to "Cléo and Antoine," the two are seated at a bench in the Parc Montsouris. Antoine notices her ring, the setting of which is a small gold toad clutching a large pearl. "A pearl and a frog," remarks Cléo, to which Antoine rejoins dreamily, "You and me."[92] Pearl and frog, object and subject, Cléo and Antoine. A hetero-normative resolution to the dilemma of modern female identity? Certainly. And in this resolution one must seriously question the feminist import of the film. But what about France and Algeria? In a film explicitly constructed as a series of episodes, the occasional and fragmentary references to Algeria are of a piece with the text's formal strategy, and at least one French film historian has remarked that it takes only a brief appearance by a soldier on leave for the whole film to assume an extra dimension alongside its more obvious concerns.[93] The conjoining of Cléo and Antoine at the film's conclusion may thus be seen as both a conventional gendered coupling and a less conventional national coupling of France and Algeria. Even more: if Cléo is the embodiment of French national identity in this film, her body is itself a text riven through with both self and Other: her internal cancer is confirmed at the film's end but so is a program of treatment and, one assumes, full recovery. Like the street performer who ingests frogs to expel them—the first sight she consumes visually as a flâneuse—Cléo's bodily inscription is a mutual incorporation and expulsion of an Other as metaphorical disease, the recognition of which is represented as part of a process of self-definition. The disease may be regarded in the Algerian context as war as a means toward liberation, in the French one as the loss of Empire necessary to become a modern nation. The two are of a piece. Cléo is thus both pearl and frog, France and its colonial Other, an inharmonious yet ultimately irreducible incarnation borne on, in, and through the body of the modern female flâneur.

The Modern Cinematic Couple and Recolonization

Kristin Ross has written at some length about the interdependency of postwar French film culture and national historical change in the 1950s and 1960s.[94] In her book *Fast Cars, Clean Bodies,* she presents a thesis that was generative for my thinking about modern French and Italian cinema. She writes:

> I want to suggest that in the roughly ten-year period of the mid-1950s to the mid-1960s in France—the decade that saw both the end of the empire and the surge in French consumption and modernization—the colonies are in some sense "replaced," and the effort that once went into maintaining and disciplining a colonial people and situation becomes instead concentrated on a particular "level" of metropolitan existence: everyday life. . . . And women, of course, as the primary victims and arbiters of social reproduction, as the subjects of everydayness and as those most subjected to it, as the class of people most responsible for consumption, and those responsible for the complex movement whereby the social existence of human beings is produced and reproduced, *are* the everyday: its managers, its embodiment.[95]

Rather than choose between the two narratives of "French modernization and Americanization on the one hand" and that of "decolonization on the other," Ross undertakes to think the two narratives together and to take seriously "the catchphrase popularized by Lefebvre and the Situationists in the early 1960s: 'the colonization of everyday life.'"[96] Across a range of media cultures, women emerge as the primary objects of figuration and subjects of interpellation for this recolonization.

Of all of the categories Ross deploys in her analysis, the trope of the modern couple is the most germane to my present discussion. *L'Express* co-editors Jean-Jacques Servan-Schreiber and Françoise Giroud, the reigning intellectuals Jean-Paul Sartre and Simone de Beauvoir, the actors Yves Montand and Simone Signoret—the cultural fascination surrounding such career couples emerges in Ross's study as a complicated working through of French modernity and decolonization. For a

> set of popular metaphors and figures of speech suggests that, with the emergence of the nationalist movement in Algeria, the relation between France and Algeria was widely held, by the French at least, to be a kind of marriage: a long and abiding "mixed" marriage, with its history of dirty family secrets that should best remain hidden. . . . What Jacques Soustelle called the great "rupture between the Sahara and France," the national divorce whose violence and tensions defined the entire period, was transpiring in the midst of a massive postwar French affirmation of the couple as standard-bearer of the state-led modernization effort and as bearer of all affective values as well.[97]

While it is commonly held that the young heterosexual couple is the focus of new wave cinema, another type of cinematic couple salient throughout film history became prevalent more generally in postwar European art cinema, that of the (often romantically involved) male director and female star.[98] A list would include:

> Roberto Rossellini / Anna Magnani / Ingrid Bergman
> Ingmar Bergman / Harriet and Bibi Andersson / Ingrid Thulin / Liv Ullmann
> Federico Fellini / Giulietta Masina
> Roger Vadim / Brigitte Bardot / Annette Stroyberg / Jane Fonda
> Louis Malle / Jeanne Moreau
> Jules Dassin / Melina Mercouri
> Vittorio De Sica / Sophia Loren
> Luchino Visconti / Claudia Cardinale
> Michelangelo Antonioni / Monica Vitti
> Jean-Luc Godard / Anna Karina
> François Truffaut / Jeanne Moreau
> John Schlesinger / Julie Christie
> Michael Cacoyannis / Irene Papas
> Claude Chabrol / Stephane Audran
> Luis Buñuel / Catherine Deneuve

In keeping with the prevailing colonial metaphor of France and Algeria as a mixed marriage on the rocks, the director/star couples of the French New Wave (and, in a different but related way, the new Italian cinema) reveal at the level of filmic discourse a predilection toward mourning and nostalgia for a happier past of female subservience and wedded bliss and a simultaneous celebration and punishment of the modern woman emancipated by the colonial divorce. The female flâneur is often the crux of this allegory.

One of the many interesting aspects of Jean-Luc Godard's career as an imagemaker is the ease with which it may be periodized according to his relationships with another woman/actress/collaborator: *des années* Anna Karina for his New Wave period from *Breathless* (1960) through *Anticipation ou l'amour en l'an 2000,* the episode he directed for the omnibus film *Le Plus vieux métier du monde* (*The Oldest Profession,* 1967); *des années* Anne Wiazemsky for his Maoist/Marxist period from *La Chinoise* (1967) through *Lettre à Jane* (1972); and *des années* Anne-Marie Miéville for his video period from *Ici et ailleurs* (1974) to the present, with a renewed interest in feature filmmaking since 1980.

From the start Godard was recognized—and recognized himself—as being particularly invested in the image and imaging of women in modern culture, and he has functioned as a problematic figure in relation to feminist film criticism and theory ever since.[99] Reading the films of Godard's Karina years along the lines of the gender/culture/race/nation conjuncture I have been proposing throughout this chapter demonstrates how even the works of this most singular of the New Wave auteurs remain firmly embedded in the historical and political time and space of their production.

Although she acted in films directed by others throughout and after the 1960s, Karina's stardom was and remains associated with the remarkably constant image of the new French woman she embodied in her husband's films. Undoubtedly modern in her low-maintenance hairstyles yet classic in her beauty, adult in her existential sensibility yet childlike in her unaffected carriage, a model of French femininity yet Danish by birth and nationality (as well as her accented French), Karina distills the contradictions of Godard's imaging of women in the 1960s.[100] Born in Paris in 1930, naturalized as a Swiss citizen during World War II, trained as an anthropologist at the Sorbonne soon after and receiving a certificate in ethnology in 1950, Godard was a passionate proponent of the work of Jean Rouch in his film criticism throughout the 1950s, and although he apparently holds his anthropological training of little account it is appropriate to read his New Wave period as an extended ethnography of modern France. The Other of this culture is in the films of Godard the modern woman, and that woman is Anna Karina—*infame, une femme,* the closing pun of *Une femme est une femme* and the guiding principle of her characterizations.

Vivre sa vie was the first of Godard's so-called prostitution trilogy, the next installments of which were *Une femme mariée* (1964) and *Deux ou trois choses que je sais d'elle* (Two or Three Things I Know about Her, 1967).[101] In *Vivre sa vie* Karina plays Nana Klein, one of several Godardian wandering women who turn to prostitution to live. To consider, however, prostitution as simply a generalized motif in Godard's films is to obfuscate the specifics of a gendered economy that provides male flâneurs with a metaphor from which their flanerie permits them the opportunity of escape but which limits female flâneurs to a specific condition and occupation to which their flanerie binds them. And it is the latter condition and occupation that *Vivre sa vie* so brilliantly, so anthropologically, so ruthlessly depicts.

Like *Cléo de 5 à 7, Vivre sa vie* is structured as a series of episodes in the life of a young Parisian woman. Unlike *Cléo*, however, the passage of time across episodes is not continuous but disjunctive, and Nana's flanerie leads not in the direction of self-awareness and agency but to a literal dead end. For *Vivre sa vie* traces with an almost clinical detachment the way in which modern society presents to a young woman the illusion of freedom and then systematically strips her of it. The first third of *Vivre sa vie* depicts modern subjectivity as a constant need for money, and the rest of the film plays out the tragic commodifying consequences. Those consequences are quite literally embodied as a young Parisian female flâneur strapped for cash. As with her namesake, the titular heroine of Zola's novel, Nana's career as a *fille de joie* ends in death; but unlike Zola's nineteenth-century Nana, Godard's modern woman is not presented with a stark choice between "fallen" or "respectable" womanhood—it is a casual encounter while traversing the city's streets that informs her decision.[102] Episode V begins with a traveling shot of a street lined on both sides with prostitutes. After a fade, the next shot is a reverse track of Nana walking dejectedly, aimlessly through these streets. Looking first right, then left, Nana's point of view and vision are aligned with the camera through eyeline match cuts of the graffiti-laden walls and of the prostitutes who are standing up against them on either side of the street, waiting for customers.

In this, the first sequence of the film that one might consider in line with a cinema of flanerie, women on the streets of modernity appear to have only one role and purpose; when a male customer passes by Nana in the next shot and blurts out a proposition, her agreement comes as little surprise. Nana thus assumes in this sequence the conditions of her environment—via the logic of glance/point cutting, the regimes of which, so long established in classical narrative cinema, supercede her—and wanders quite naturally into a life of prostitution.

The remaining episodes of *Vivre sa vie* document Nana's increasing lack of agency in her new (the oldest) profession and the inevitable death of her subjecthood as she becomes a literal object of commodity exchange among her pimp, Raoul, and his client, another pimp who indifferently shoots her when the transaction goes sour. Again, like *Cléo, Vivre sa vie* links its panoply of views of Paris circa 1961 to

Vivre sa vie (1962)

the body of the female protagonist who traverses its spaces. But unlike *Cléo,* those views are not witnessed through the vision of a flâneuse discovering herself anew through an engagement with "others" she is seeing for the first time, but through the lens of the ethnographer whose object of research and fascination is itself the young woman of modern France, newly emancipated from the yoke of marriage only to become the victim of another form of colonization.[103] Episode VIII is remarkable in this respect, formally and allegorically, as it fragments her experience and her body in time and space, in image and sound. Beginning with a typically Godardian shot of a young male/female couple in conversation in a car as they drive through the streets of Paris, with Nana asking questions about the rules and rituals of her profession and Raoul (who at the end of the preceding episode had engaged her to take a position in his employ) answering them matter-of-factly, the episode quickly moves into a montage sequence that divorces sound from image. Prostitution is relayed as a highly structured socioeconomic institution through the question–and–answer format of Nana's and Raoul's dialogue on the sound track, while the image track is organized as a serial repetition of truncated tricks and transactions, a cutting up of time, space, and bodies. Weeks, perhaps months pass in this episode visually, but the duration is limited aurally to the real time of the pair's question-and-answer session, less than four minutes. The sequence shows the viewer in images Nana's future as a prostitute, her life to live as it is being described in the diegetic present of the sound track. But Nana doesn't see her future: she sees only the concrete present of her life as a prostitute being lived. Her future is the imagined speculation of her body, fragmented spatially and divorced from the temporal present of her inquiring voice. Raoul, on the other hand, is the voice of the expert, and nowhere present in the image, which depicts not his future but hers as he describes it, as he is scripting and predestinating it for her. Raoul thus moves figuratively behind the camera and images the experiences of her life to come. The sequence encapsulates the anthropological tone and project of the film, a mapping out of the tragic future that awaits its unknowing object, the new woman of modernity.

But *Vivre sa vie* is not a study of a modern young French woman, nor even of a fictional character named Nana Klein, but of a specific individual: Anna Karina, the filmmaker's wife. Indeed, Kaja Silverman has suggested that the three heavily shadowed close-up shots of the film's opening credit sequence—Nana's head in left profile, from the front, and in right profile, a premonition of the police mug shots of her arrest scene in the fourth episode—"represent a documentary of a face, [and] they tilt the film in the direction of Karina rather than Nana. It is the mystery of the actress rather than the mystery of the character being plumbed. . . . Nana is an 'other': we are obliged to look for her 'essence' in the face of Anna Karina."[104]

Such a reading is lent support by the famous shots in episode III of Nana crying as she watches another documentary of an actress's face, Maria Falconetti's in Carl Theodor Dreyer's *La Passion de Jeanne d'Arc* (1928),[105] but gains real persuasive power in the first scene of the film's final episode, during which a young man speaks his love for Nana by reading aloud from Edgar Allan Poe's "The Oval Portrait." As in episode VIII, sound and image are split in this scene, which consists of three parts. In the first and the last Nana and the young man, with whom she has apparently fallen in love (he appeared briefly in episode IX, during which Nana flirts with him and he buys her a pack of Gitanes), converse casually about everyday things, but graphically rather than aurally: what they say to each other is communicated by subtitles inscribed over images of them, as they are not visually speaking. In the middle part of the scene, sound and image are split across the figuration of the young man, who voices lines from the text of "The Oval Portrait" but whose mouth remains hidden behind the volume his eyes are clearly scanning. Given this diegetic information, one assumes it is the young man reading aloud. But the extradiegetic world of the real New Wave couple here ruptures the world of the fiction: the voice on the sound track is Godard's, a fact that even a viewer unacquainted with the filmmaker's distinctive timber and cadence should realize when Nana interrupts the young man's reading and he says, offscreen, "It is our story—a painter who paints a portrait of his wife." Godard thus speaks directly to Karina in this scene, and indirectly to the viewer of Nana's fate in the film he is near completing. For as the male voice proceeds to read from "The Oval Portrait," it tells the tale of an artist who in painting his wife's portrait robs her of her life. If Poe's story, then, is Godard's and Karina's, so is *Vivre sa vie*—Nana will, must die at the end of the film. The movement of Raoul from interlocutor to scriptor and photographer of Nana's life to live in the eighth episode is here reversed as Godard the filmmaker places himself in the fiction as Raoul, the one who leads Nana inevitably to her death immediately after this hotel room scene. The film's final episode, then, dramatizes Godard's "attempt to 'speak' or 'paint' Karina—to subordinate her subjectivity to his meaning."[106]

Susan Sontag objected to the fracturing of the fiction in "The Oval Portrait" scene of *Vivre sa vie,* because in it "Godard is clearly making a reference outside the film to the fact that the young actress who plays Nana, Anna Karina, is his wife. He is mocking his own tale, which is unforgivable."[107] But such references from the world outside frequently puncture and punctuate the films of Godard and of the French New Wave. And that outside, which so forcefully intrudes on the fiction of *Vivre sa vie,* is the world of a modern France, a world that itself is painting a mortifying portrait of the new woman. The "great rupture" of the Algerian war, the national divorce, the domestic recolonization of female subjectivity that subtends colonial liberation—these too invade the fiction of *Vivre sa vie.*

The formal ruptures that occur in episodes VIII and XII, the unwedding of sound and image that blurs the line between the filmic fiction, and the shifting political and cultural realities of France circa 1961–62 are in fact presaged in a scene that links all of the variables in circulation throughout the film: marriage, emancipation, prostitution, violence, politics. In episode VI, Nana is streetwalking and bumps into Yvette, an old friend, and the two go for a drink in a café. Yvette tells the sad but common story of her (and Nana's) life: she turned to prostitution after she found herself without a husband and unable to support herself or her children. Soon Yvette leaves Nana at the table to join a man playing pinball. The subsequent shot of Yvette and the man is framed in precisely the same manner as was the shot that ended the first episode of Nana and Paul, the husband she has left, at a pinball machine. Paul's replacement is Raoul, Yvette's present and Nana's future pimp, and he soon "tests" Nana by baiting and trying to humiliate her. Her response is laughter, she passes the test, and Raoul tells her as he gets up and goes to the bar not to leave, he has something to tell her. Nana glances down at something on the table. The next shot is a close-up of a hand opening a spiral-bound notebook to a page titled "Vendredi" and comprising a list of women's names (including Yvette's) with slash marks beside them—Raoul's record of his business's accounts, the tricks his workers have turned for him on Friday. The camera lingers on the page until the loud sound of machinegun fire bursts onto the sound track, prompting a hand to close the book and quickly remove it from view. The next shot is of Nana sitting alone at her table, looking startled at the sudden commotion, but the book is not in her possession. The film has fooled us with a false eyeline match; we have not witnessed Raoul's business through her point of view at the table but his at the bar. As Anna grabs her coat and moves toward the source of the sound, a series of quick, static shots are cut to the staccato tempo of the gunfire and move from left to right across the bar and out the window. On the street a man moves threateningly, gun raised, toward another man surrendering against a wall. A third man covered in blood runs into the café and collapses on the bar. Raoul is gone. Nana flees.

What is this scene doing in the film? Certainly, it is a common enough device in Godard's films of the 1960s—the sudden intrusion of the real world into the reel one. More specifically, however, it connects the institution of prostitution and the inevitability of Nana's occupational alignment in it with her emancipation from marriage (the duplicate shots of the couple at the pinball machine); a record of accounts into which her name and future is to be inscribed; a slippage in filmic enunciation characteristic of New Wave aesthetics; and the violence of colonial war. For although one might at first consider the gun battle in the street as simply a generic nod to the American gangster films so coveted by the *Cahiers du cinéma* group of critics and filmmakers, Raoul informs us in the next episode that the violence in the street "had something to do with politics"—and politics in Paris in 1961–62 means OAS terrorism, the Algerian war brought home. The fate of Nana, the modern woman, is thus bound up in flanerie, prostitution, violence, death—and politics.

The fading of Anna Karina from Godard's filmic practice in the late 1960s is commonly attributed to his own politicization as a filmmaker, which would manifest itself in an increasing disenchantment with the national model for French modernity: America. Molly Haskell has written that "Godard's feelings for women are remarkably similar to his feelings for America—extreme love-hatred. . . . His actresses are American, or Americanized. Karina is non French . . . and is given a persona that is an amalgam of American genre heroines—or rather,

Vendredi

Liliane

Yvette |||||||||| |||| ||| 17

Germaine || || 4

Monique || || |||| | ||||||| 17

                                            38

Dehort | 16 chambres   59

nuit | 38 passes   6

Godard's affectionate interpretation of American genre heroines—she is gangster's moll, hoofer, singer, virgin, and whore."[108] The initial "innocence" of Karina's early genre roles in Godard's cinema gives way to an increasing agency characterized by danger and destruction, a confirmation and embodiment of the director's own view of U.S. culture and foreign policy. By the time of *Pierrot le fou* (1965), which Susan Hayward has referred to as Godard's "first ostensibly political film," Karina has become almost hysterically Other, standing prominently for America and less so for France (even though her character's name is Marianne).[109] In *Pierrot le fou,* Jean-Paul Belmondo/Ferdinand and Anna Karina/Marianne are explicitly referred to as "the last romantic couple," and in the context of Godard's growing anti-Americanism and leftist politicization they allegorize the breakdown of the filmmaker's own love affair with U.S. culture—by 1965, the honeymoon was over. Karina's function in the film is thus to register in a palpable way and to displace onto modern femininity all that her husband finds objectionable about contemporary commodity, media, and political culture. In a sense, *Pierrot le fou* brings full circle the lovers' dialogue Godard initiated between his film practice and American cinema in his first feature film, *Breathless,* which starred the French Belmondo and the American Jean Seberg as quite literal embodiments of their nation states.[110] For Karina/Marianne is figured in *Pierrot le fou* as the very "origin of violence"[111] and imperialism, and her evident Americanness is throughout the film counterposed to Belmondo's/Ferdinand's Frenchness via their sharply diverging preferences in lifestyle and narrative: he for nineteenth-century romanticism, the quiet life of the sea, Jules Verne and Velasquez; she for twentieth-century corporate terrorism, the violent life of cars and guns, Samuel Fuller and pop art.[112] The film demonstrates the incompatibility of both through a frenetic and fragmented visual style and a narrative of doomed heterosexual romance.

And yet there is one scene in this film that startles me. Short of cash, Ferdinand and Marianne perform a theatrical sketch on the boardwalk of a French coastal resort town for some American sailors in uniform in the hopes of fleecing them of some or all of their money. Punch and Judy–style, the two act out a crude version of the U.S./Vietnam conflict, or as it is handwritten in an insert as if from Ferdinand's diary, "Le neveu de l'oncle Sam contre la niéce de l'oncle Ho." His back to a pockmarked wall, Ferdinand addresses the camera sporting an officer's uniform and cap; he gesticulates belligerently, spits out parodic phrases in a terrible American accent, swigs whiskey, and draws his gun. Her back to the sea, Marianne addresses the camera outfitted in a black and white frock and wide-brimmed straw hat, face painted yellow, cheeks rouged, eyebrows drawn in black on her forehead; she chatters and mumbles intermittently in nasal, mock–Vietnamese tones that alternately suggest cowering and defensiveness.

Then Ferdinand is shown seated alone at a low table, pouring himself some whiskey but aware of a presence behind him in the shrubbery. He jumps up aggressively and points his pistol into the bushes, out of which emerges Marianne, who drops a grenade, arms raised in surrender. Next they are seated on the sea wall, he continuing to brandish his gun while shouting "Yeah!" and she yammering back just as

Pierrot le fou (1965)

loudly. The scene ends with Ferdinand and Marianne, now changed back into their French garb, grabbing one of the sailors' (an officer's) money and making a run for it.

In the colonial masquerade they enact as Uncle Ho's niece and Uncle Sam's nephew, Karina is for the only time in the film cast as the victim and Belmondo as her oppressor, a reversal of roles that has nonetheless tended to be read on face value as a broad slam against American culture and foreign policy. And there is no doubt that the scene sends up belligerent and stupid Americanism in a crude and farcical way. But it is nevertheless significant in terms of the present discussion that Karina is marked as a fungible signifier of nationhood and Belmondo is not: she is sometimes French, more often American, but he remains throughout wholly French, here through his heavily accented Americanese. Marianne and Ferdinand's role-playing in this

piece of boardwalk theater is clearly demarcated as masquerade on both of their parts, but her visual and aural costuming is in excess of the performance in a way that his is not. She becomes here in a very physical way a colonized and racial Other, and in that representation enacts the linkage between decolonization and modernization that is, I would argue, the crux of New Wave femininity. Thus, Belmondo/ Ferdinand is colonial France of the very recent past behind the present American facade, and Karina/Marianne is Indochina of the very recent past behind the present Vietnamese facade. But he and she also allegorize in the sketch a modern France that is undergoing its own process of recolonization, the object of which is the modern white woman and/as Other. One can read in this scene, then, a form of modern colonial cinematic representation fully in line with that of France during its age of Empire. To fob off the import of that onto American imperialism in Vietnam is to me a misdirection, an act that the film surely encourages but nonetheless leaves as its trace the literally colored body of the modern female protagonist.

The Godard/Karina pairing is, of course, merely one of a number of New Wave filmmaking couples whose currency depended partly on her marketability as a vision of modern French womanhood. Perhaps the first female star of the New Wave was Jeanne Moreau, and although unlike many of her contemporaries she was never married to any of those who famously directed her, her career throughout the late 1950s and early 1960s was nevertheless crucially (and sometimes romantically) linked to a small coterie of auteurs with whom she worked: Louis Malle (*Ascenseur pour l'échafaud* [1957], *Les Amants* [1958], *Le Feu follet* [*The Fire Within,* 1963], *Viva Maria* [1965]); Orson Welles (*Le Procès* [*The Trial,* 1962], *Chimes at Midnight* [1966], *Histoire immortelle* [*The Immortal Story,* 1968]); Tony Richardson (*Mademoiselle* [1966], *The Sailor from Gibraltar* [1967]); and François Truffaut (*Jules et Jim* [1961], *La Mariée était en noir* [*The Bride Wore Black,* 1968]). Indeed, Moreau may be *the* paragon of the female flâneur in New Wave cinema: her mobility among a set of auteurs and her famous erotic charms (Vanessa Redgrave divorced Tony Richardson in 1967 on the grounds of adultery, naming Moreau as corespondent) made her an authentically modern woman who asserted her desire without apology, but her equally famous wandering, both within her films and without, fixed her identity ultimately to that of a sexual icon. Moreau and her characterizations thus crystallize the recolonizing of femininity in France in the 1960s.

It is not coincidental that the role that first brought Moreau attention as an actress of considerable affect was one of the few of the late 1950s to make visible in both plot and character the specter of colonial conflict haunting France—*Ascenseur pour l'échafaud,* directed by Louis Malle. In it Moreau plays Florence Carala, the young wife of a wealthy Parisian industrialist whose business and profits are linked to colonialism, as he is presently setting up a deal for building an oil pipeline in Algeria. Florence has hatched a plot with her lover, Julien Tavernier (Maurice Ronet), to murder her husband undetected. An employee of the target, Tavernier happens to be an ex-paratrooper who has served in Indochina, Algeria, and the French Foreign Legion, and the murder plot involves the use of his military skills: he descends by rope outside the building from his own office to his boss's, shoots him, arranges the scene accordingly to suggest suicide, and then climbs back up, again to his own office. But the perfect plan is foiled: upon leaving the building Tavernier notices he has left the rope dangling in plain view, so he reenters the building and takes the elevator to retrieve it. When the janitor turns off the building's power, assuming everyone has left on this Saturday night, Tavernier is trapped in the elevator until Monday morning. Meanwhile, Tavernier's Chevrolet convertible is stolen by a teenage couple who take it for a joyride, meet up with a German couple, spend a night in a motel with them drinking, and then murder them in a panic with Tavernier's gun during a failed attempt to steal their car, a new Mercedes. Tavernier is blamed for the Germans' murder, and his alibi will implicate him in Carala's death.

As the above description implies, *Ascenseur pour l'échafaud* is a *policier,* and it meets all of the generic requirements. Within the conventions of the genre, Moreau's role would be that of the femme fatale who seduces the hero into his criminal actions and fate, and to a certain degree she fulfills that role. In an article on the film's colonial subtext, David Nicholls argues that the "rest of the plot, which involves Florence searching for Tavernier, then trying to clear his name and the uncovering of the truth by wily police inspector Lino Ventura, need not concern us except to note that Tavernier and Florence are eventually caught as a result of a photograph showing them together and that the depiction of the forces of law and order is highly un-flattering."[113] Florence thus leads Tavernier to his eventual downfall by implicating him as her lover.

It is an overstatement, however, to say that the "rest of plot need not concern us," for much of the visual fascination and popular and critical success of the film revolves precisely around the image of Moreau/Florence wandering the streets in search of her lover. *Ascenseur pour l'échafaud* is a film largely about modern time and the way it entraps characters who are either past their time (Tavernier, the ex-soldier) or before it (the teenagers), in either case never fully *of* it—except for Florence, whose only time seems to be the time of the film itself, particularly the night of her flanerie. Whereas the teenage couple is defined in relation to their social space with the Germans and Tavernier in relation to a confining technological space (the elevator), Florence is space itself. She is in the film palpably connected to the world of modern Paris, engaging in its cold materialities as she wanders the streets through the evening and rainy night, the click–click–click of her heels echoing among the gleaming urban corridors and late-night bars housing the new *jeune cadre,* looking urgently for the man whose distinctive car she had seen speed past their designated rendezvous (significantly, on Boulevard Haussmann) on the evening of the murders.

Nicholls is right when he suggests that the film offers the audience no comfortable viewing position from which to gauge the events on-screen. But the figure of Moreau/Florence is nonetheless the point of connection for all of the film's positionalities: wayward youth, fading colonial heroism, capital accumulation, inefficient social control. (On the latter count, mistaken for a streetwalker by the police, she ends up in a paddy wagon in the early morning hours only to have her identity and social standing revealed at the station.) Colonial loss and modern culture find their locus in *Ascenseur pour l'échafaud* in the image of Moreau as flâneuse, gazing passionately beyond herself and her surroundings, consumed by romantic longing and doubt.

Moreau's next starring role in a Malle film was as Jeanne Tournier, a bored wife who abandons herself and her life to overpowering de-sire in *Les Amants,* the selling point of which was described in its U.S. press kit as "the miraculous transformation of a woman of the world into a primitive creature of love." A highly civilized woman of thirty with a lovely provincial home in Dijon and well-bred young

Ascenseur pour l'échafaud (1957)

daughter, Jeanne nevertheless is spending at the film's start an increasing amount of time in Paris, playing with her society friends and dallying with Raoul, a handsome but shallow polo player. Her husband, a stern newspaper publisher, resents her lack of enthusiasm for the life he has made for her and, suspecting infidelity, insists in a fit of spleen on inviting to the couple's country house Raoul and Jeanne's friend Maggie, with whom she has been staying every week as a cloak of respectability for her Paris love affair. When Jeanne's Peugot 203 convertible breaks down on the way home from the city for the party, a young philosophy student and budding archaeologist gives her a lift in his rickety Citroën 2 CV (again, cars are central in demarcating boundaries to be crossed). He is invited to join the group and stay the evening, and the stage is set for Jeanne's sexual awakening. It happens that night after she goes downstairs to turn off a record player the young man has rudely left blaring. Gliding around the room in her long, flowing nightgown, she pours herself a stiff drink from a cut-crystal decanter, but does not so much imbibe the liquid as become transported elsewhere through the inexplicable force of tactility—the touch of the cool glass as she rubs it on her forehead leads to the mirror and then the glass doors of the mansion that holds her hostage and then she is outside, a vision in white, a specter haunting the grounds. The young man appears and a nocturnal seduction ensues with her leading the way, the sounds of animals and the shadows of darkness swathing their mutual plunge into the rhythms of nature. We are clearly here in the realm of fantasy, of fairy tales and ghost stories, of the turnings (like the wheel of the mill by which they pass) of primeval desire, of instinct, of destiny. But the inexorable course of their surrender to these forces through forest, over untilled land and, via a stone bridge upon which they release fish from her husband's traps, moonlit water works against the clichés. She: "La nuit est belle." He: "La nuit est femme." She leaves with him the next morning.[114]

It was in *Les Amants* that the paradoxical features of the Moreau star text established in *Ascenseur pour l'échafaud* would congeal and determine her casting for the next decade: worldly yet instinctual, civilized yet carnal, calculating yet spontaneous, needy yet independent, tender yet vengeful. Moreau's roles throughout the 1960s always circulated around these poles of identity and sexuality, so that sometimes she is the evil seductress incarnate (*Les Liaisons dangereuses 1960, Eva* [1962],

Mata Hari, Agent H21 [1965]), at other times willful and capricious and dangerous and therefore fascinating *(Jules et Jim, Mademoiselle, The Sailor from Gibraltar)*, but always a woman in tune with her senses and their connection to the world surrounding her.[115] Unlike Karina, whose persona was keyed to the young daytime Paris of cafés, car rides, and bustling urban life, Moreau was more muted and adult in her modernity, more free-ranging in her travels, more nocturnal. In Moreau's films the viewer senses a personal history—of regret, recalcitrance, repression—preceding the events on the screen, a depth of thought and feeling bubbling beneath the surface of her characters rarely voiced in dialogue but conveyed by her eyes, her mouth, and her face surely, but also by the slow and deliberate movements of her body through space in languorous sequences of her wandering, looking, touching. The visual power and screen duration of these sequences

Les Amants (1958)

of flanerie are often contained by the time of the plot itself, which frequently turns on the climactic events of a single evening, as in *Ascenseur pour l'échafaud, Les Amants*—and, as its title announces, *La notte* (1961).

The credit sequence of *La notte* foregrounds the architectural, minimalist scopic regime of the film, a regime that seems to cue the characters' stilted relations to one another and, at times, excludes them altogether. The film's opening shot is a slow tilt in long shot, from street level up the corner facade of a charming seven-story building from the late-nineteenth to early-twentieth century built in a neo-classical style. The second and third shots are static, shadowed compositions of empty spaces at the top of a high building. The fourth and fifth shots, over which the credits run, are cut as a continuous mechanical descent down the face of the Pirelli building in Milan. The left and right frames of the first of these shots match those of the glassed windowpanes that move past the camera at an even rate; the reflected image of the smaller modern office and apartment buildings below obstructs and dominates our view of the building's interior. In the next shot, the edge of the building bisects the screen to the right of center so that we see another view of a city of uniform concrete structures stretching far into the distance on the left, and an acutely angled close-up image of the reflective glass and steel surface of the structure on the right. One of the most cosmopolitan, international, and fastest-growing European cities of the 1960s, Milan serves here as more than a backdrop upon which to paint the autopsy of a modern bourgeois marriage that is *La notte*'s narrative theme. The city itself, in its arid and dehumanizing modern spaces over which the camera lingers so lovingly, is as much a character in this film as any of the people who are alienated in it and from one another.

La notte's most famous sequence, perhaps the most famous sequence of female flanerie in modern European cinema, traces an aleatory stroll that Moreau's character, Lidia Pontano, makes through central Milan and in a nearby suburb. The film opens with Lidia and her husband, the celebrated novelist Giovanni Pontano (Marcello Mastroianni), visiting their dying friend Tommaso (played by German actor/director Bernhard Wicki) in the hospital. The experience overwhelms Lidia and she excuses herself to go outside for a cry. Giovanni joins her after a brief dalliance with a beautiful young disturbed female patient, and the nearly estranged couple proceed by car to a book launch celebrating Giovanni's latest publication. The two separate upon entry as Giovanni ignores his wife in favor of the clamoring fans who shower him with attention, and Lidia leaves the building. It is early afternoon when she starts a walk that will last a few hours and takes up a screen time of fully ten minutes, broken into two segments of three and seven minutes by a scene of Giovanni returning to their apartment and, seeing she is not there, making a halfhearted attempt to work and then reclining by a window for a nap.

A dense panoply of textures, sounds, architectures, and people confronts Lidia and the viewer during her wandering through the city's center, and space prohibits me from following her passage step by step.[116] What is notable about this sequence is the degree to which the changing cityscape and the people who are scattered among it so readily seem to lend themselves to a psychological reading: the exteriority and surfaces of the spaces Lidia traverses reflect the exigencies of her interior thoughts and emotions. Guido Aristarco, writing at the time of the film's release, summed up his and subsequent generations of film critics' opinions on the matter when he wrote, "The movement of thoughts and mental associations instead of the movement of events, the ebb and flow of consciousness instead of individual heros [sic], the simultaneity of different states of the soul, all these lie at the heart of La notte. How are we to regard Lidia's interminable wandering, first through the chaos of urban life, then through the apparent tranquillity of the suburb, if not as a long, continuous interior monologue, as the kaleidoscopic image of a disintegrating world that looms up within herself?"[117]

To a large degree the Moreau persona encourages such a reading, insofar as her placid demeanor implies rather than belies an interior swirl of thoughts and feelings, memories and desires. But while the tone of the sequence, like so many of its images of modern glass buildings, is undoubtedly reflective, one sacrifices a great deal of material and spatial detail if one reduces everything Moreau/Lidia sees to a projection of her inner world. What is remarkable about this sequence is how the space of urban perception through which she passes, the sights she sees and the sounds she hears, do not so much reflect her psychology as they cue it into existence. Her interior life, or any sense the viewer has of it, is the product of an interchange between modern urban and suburban spaces, textures, and sounds and her delayed apprehension of them. Indeed, shots of her looking at buildings, at objects, or at people are in the sequence motivated less by the flâneuse herself than by the fact of her flanerie, as if her function is that of a cipher moving through time and space so as to allow for a semblance of narrative and character in what is really a visual exploration of a changing urban

La notte (1961)

space. From the beginning of the longer second part of the sequence, Moreau/Lidia enters already framed shots of the cityscape that linger past the point she has exited them. Once her movement has been established, the film often cuts to shots of near-empty streets that bear no explicit relation to her look or her physical presence, are there before her. Rather than yielding a wealth of information about the heroine's interior state, this sequence of flanerie effects the near aphanisis of her being in favor of abstraction and composition for its own sake.[118]

Moreau/Lidia's movement from city center to periphery is in this long sequence equally a visualization of the effects of the economic miracle on the European metropole and a setting up of her introspective personality crucial to a narrative understanding of her paralyzed marriage and of the long night of the film's title to come. For Moreau is most definitely a star who comes out at night, and her daytime flanerie establishes, in terms of the literal spaces through which she passes and her reactions to them, a pervasive sense of loss and nostalgia that is key to the film's ultimate placement of her on the side of tradition rather than modernity. During the day, Lidia wears a rather old-fashioned light and dark flower-print dress, which strikes an ironic note in juxtaposition with Milan's barren streets. After returning home she has a bath, calling Giovanni into the room in an attempt to gain his attention. They decide to go to a party at the villa of Gherardini, an industrialist who is interested in Giovanni; she rises from the bath, he wraps a towel around her and leaves, uninterested. After fixing himself a drink, he spies Lidia at the end of the hall, posing in a new black cocktail dress with a translucent black lace stole. She struts down the hall purposefully, swinging her hips, hoping to elicit a compliment or at least a reaction from her husband, but it is no use: he offers nothing but slightly amused silence. She suggests they go not to the Gherardinis' but elsewhere, just the two of them. He agrees as he hooks up her stole. It is now nighttime, Moreau's time. Or is it?

The next scene takes place in a nightclub. Beyond establishing even further Giovanni's complete lack of interest in his wife and motivating their decision to be alienated among people at a bourgeois soirée rather than simply from each other, it seems to serve no narrative purpose—the previous scene provided plenty of information about their romantic and physical estrangement, and they could have decided to go to the party then just as easily as now.[119] In essence, the nightclub scene has a dual focus that it crosscuts with almost mathematical precision: a contortionist/striptease/balancing act performed on stage by an acrobatic and undulating black woman, and Lidia's realization in the wings that her husband is not only uninterested in her sexually or socially but mentally as well.

The two are marked off from one another graphically, bodily, spatially. The black female performer begins her number fully clothed in a tight-fitting floor-length white gown that a black male helper, naked

but for a glistening white loincloth, removes piece by piece, and by
the end of her performance she is clad in a strapless bra, panties, garter
belt, fishnet stockings, and pumps, all white. Her movements are fluid
yet controlled; she is in constant motion as she transfers, all the while
keeping level, a glass of red wine across various parts of her body to
the act's climax, when she drinks it with no hands in an inverted back-
stand. Lidia, on the other hand, remains seated and is dressed elegantly
in black. In the preceding scene her helper, Giovanni, covered rather

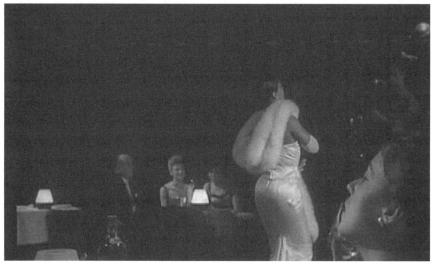

than uncovered her naked body. She is almost motionless as she sits beside her distracted husband, save for a moment when she tugs at his cuff link in recognition of something and asks him if he remembers; he replies that evidently he is to miss the act, and she asks him not to minimize her capabilities—she has thoughts too. But when he asks her what she is thinking, she won't say; she does indicate, however, that her thought is located on the crown of her forehead, the spot on the stage performer's body where, before this interchange, we have

seen her balance the glass of wine. As the act concludes, Lidia abruptly suggests they go to the Gherardinis'.

This scene is a crucial example of how racial and gendered Otherness coalesce in art cinema and represent, not directly but by association, the figure of the modern European woman as a site of anxiety and recolonization—and it is crucial because of rather than despite its marginal narrative relevance. For in its juxtaposition of the performer's black, moving, denuding body that fixes Giovanni's attention and of Lidia's white, placid demeanor and hidden thoughts that hold no interest for him, this scene is a concise mutual staging of Otherness.[120] The black woman is reduced here to pure function: to stage, to render visible through the unclothing of her body and movement in space the affective, practiced, ineffable workings of the mind of the white woman. The open display of the "primitive" performer's body is in this scene equated with the "mystery" of the white modern female's mental and emotional life. Both are for patriarchal Western culture sources of fear and desire, but they have particular relevance within the context and history of European colonial cinematic representation. The contradictory cultural project of the European economic miracle— to address and to celebrate as fully fledged national subjects the modern woman, to explore and contain her sexuality and identity—are writ large in scenes such as this one in *La notte*.

Moreau/Lidia engages in even more flanerie during the long night of the Gherardinis' party, where the decay of her marital relationship with Giovanni is played out to its inevitable, exhausted end. The passage from light to darkness that structures the temporal design of the film and the interplay between white and black clothing and skin in the nightclub scene is rendered in the second half of the film through a visual doubling of the female protagonist in the character of Valentina (Monica Vitti), daughter of the hosts. Like the nightclub performer, Valentina is an object of sexual interest for Giovanni in a way that Lidia is not, and like the performer she exteriorizes Lidia's psychology and inner life. But whereas the black performer is purely functional, Lidia's inverse tonally and physically, Valentina is granted the status of full female characterhood: she is Lidia's visual double as well as mental surrogate. The appearance of Valentina in *La notte* thus fixes Lidia on one side of the tradition/modernity divide she had been traversing in the first half of the film. Like Lidia, Valentina is introspective and attentive to her surroundings; but unlike Lidia, her relation to space is direct and tactile rather than principally of a visual disposition. She is fully on the side of modernity in a way that Lidia is no longer, with the latter's deep sense of loss and the past suffusing her movements and countenance with a kind of somnambulistic pathos. Valentina's is the time of the present, and it is to her present moment and space that she devotes her energies—as in the game she "invents" with a compact on the tiled floor of the veranda, or the poetic monologue she records on a reel-to-reel recorder but erases when Giovanni asks to hear it again. As the embodiment and actant of Lidia's modernity, Valentina in a sense limits and dooms her to the past. In the process, both are rendered Other: Lidia is "invested with the nostalgia for lost innocence," Valentina with "the power of a radical alternative." Both are privileged sites of visual and narrative fascination in *La notte*, but the mobility that their modern femininity ostensibly provides them proves ultimately an illusion. Female flanerie and invention are dead ends at the film's close, with Lidia still stuck in a pointless marriage with an uncomprehending husband and Valentina enclosed in the cold, reflective space of modern domestic design.

The appearance of Vitti/Valentina in *La notte* and her contrapuntal relation to Moreau/Lidia has an extratextual dimension as well. For the film's director, Michelangelo Antonioni, had formed with Vitti in their previous film, *L'avventura,* a professional and personal partnership that made them yet another of the famous modern filmmaking couples so prevalent in European art cinema in the 1960s. Antonioni made four films with Vitti during the heyday of the economic miracle: *L'avventura, La notte, The Eclipse (L'eclisse,* 1962), and *Red Desert (Il deserto rosso,* 1964). In all but the last Vitti was hailed as the paragon for the modern European woman,[121] not the least by Antonioni himself, who explained in interviews that "he found women more in tune with their feelings, more honest, and so more suitable than men as protagonists of films that try to approach the truth about human relations: 'la donna è il filtro più sottile della realtà' ('woman is the more subtle filter of reality')."[122] Along with her peers who were heralded as actresses of a new order and embodiments of modern, emancipated femininity—Bardot, Karina, Moreau—Vitti appears, in retrospect, less than liberated.

But she *is* modern insofar as she embodies the contradictory ideological projects and tensions of modernizing Europe I have been unpacking throughout this chapter. As was true for her peers, Vitti's iconic role is that of the female flâneur, and insofar as the famous films in which she starred are directed by Antonioni, whose work is so characteristically associated with elongated duration, *temps mort*, indirection, and alienation, she is perhaps the archetypal wandering woman of modern European cinema.[123] In the analysis of *The Eclipse* that follows I am less concerned with elucidating her characterization than I am with linking her bodily placement and figuration and her almost homologous alignment with modern urban spatiality to the specificities of race and colonialism in Italian culture. For if in the films of the French New Wave, made during a period of massive ideological fatigue and colonial loss and war, the racial determinants and interpretive context contributing to the riven representations of the modern young French woman seem clear enough, they are less clear for Italy, a nation whose colonial empire was never as extensive as France's and one whose loss of its colonies was swifter and comparatively less bloody. Monica Vitti, the most modern of the modern women of Italian art cinema in the 1960s, embodies these contradictions in all of her Antonioni films, but nowhere more clearly than in *The Eclipse*.

The opening of *The Eclipse* picks up where *La notte* leaves off: it is the cool light of morning just after dawn, and a male/female relationship is ending after a long night of futile argument. Like Moreau's Lidia of *La notte,* Vitti's Vittoria knows it is over, and like Giovanni, Riccardo (Francisco Rabal), her male lover, clings desperately to its last vestiges. After much verbal and physical parrying on his part, Vittoria finally leaves his stifling modern bungalow in the suburbs and takes to the empty streets; Riccardo pointlessly tags along and escorts her to her own modern apartment complex nearby. Later that day, Vittoria visits her mother at the Rome stock exchange, and there follow scenes of nearly incomprehensible shouting, gesticulating, and overwrought emotional expression as a rabble of suited male brokers speculate on the capricious international market in the center, their clamorous clients clinging anxiously to the perimeter. The architectural significance of the stock exchange is important: the magnificent Borsa is the Roman memorial temple of Divus Hadrianeum, built by the son of the deified

Emperor Hadrian in 152 and commuted into a round, high-ceilinged, seventeenth-century customhouse by Pope Innocent XII—the calm grandeur of artistic tradition at odds with the frenetic commercial activity of modern Rome.[124] In this space, Vittoria is introduced briefly to a young and ambitious broker, Piero (Alain Delon), and already there are hints that Vittoria and he may initiate a romantic relationship.

The third sequence of the film contains one of the most shocking examples of colonial/racist representation combined with modern femininity in all of European art cinema. It is night, the first night of the film, and Vittoria is hammering a nail into the wall of her apartment to hang a fossilized flower. She awakens her neighbor, Anita (Rossana Rory), who drops in for a visit. The phone rings. Marta (Mirella Ricciardi), an acquaintance from across the street, has seen the light through Vittoria's window and invites the two of them to come over and keep her company. The first image that greets the viewer of the inside of Marta's apartment is a large, *National Geographic*–style photograph on the wall of an African woman, hand on hip, in native dress. The two women enter and Vittoria makes her way into the main room of the flat, which is decorated with large photographs of Kenyan landscapes and a range of colonial safari paraphernalia (an elephant-foot table, zebra-patterned soft furnishings, hunting rifles and trophy horns on the walls). As Anita and Marta lie on the bed flipping through a picture book, with the hostess describing various facts about the magnificence and sublimity of Africa, Vittoria engages in a bit of interior flanerie, looking intently at the mounted photographs and taking in the textures of the objects scattered about. As she puts on a record of African drum music, the camera pans away from her to the wall and across a panorama of high-contrast photographs of groups of natives in African garb.

Cut to a medium close-up shot of Vittoria in blackface on the left side of the frame, her chin thrust out proudly and her shoulder-length blonde hair sticking up and out and teased into a tangle of tresses. She is wearing a column of shiny neck rings and large hoop earrings and is posing, very still, beside a photograph of a similarly dressed African woman held up for comparison by Anita. At the cut to this shot, the music shifts to a percussive cowbell/drum combination accompanied by call-and-response male vocal parts. The next cut is to a full shot of Vittoria and Anita, the former revealed as wearing full-body makeup that has darkened her skin, a wide metal armband around her left bicep, a light-colored blanket that extends from across her chest to just above the knee, and no shoes. Suddenly, she emerges from her frozen pose and begins dancing energetically, swinging her hips to the beat of the music, waving her arms and hands in circular motions, spreading her fingers in front of her face, interjecting occasionally with high-pitched squawks, wide-eyed and grinning from ear to ear. Her gaze fixed offscreen left (ostensibly at Marta), she moves toward a darkened corner of the room and, striking a pose as if to pounce on something, loses her composure temporarily and laughs, which causes an earring to fall off. Anita, now kneeling off to the side in the same room, looks on approvingly, smiling and slapping her thighs to the infectious beat of the music. As the tempo accelerates, Vittoria bursts into the empty frame from below, reattaches her earring, and begins dancing again with renewed vigor. After exiting the frame below and in the reverse shot emerging with a spear, she holds it aloft and, framed from behind in full shot, makes her way toward the light of the bedroom, jutting her hips and striding jerkily to the beat.

Marta is seated in a wicker chair at the right bottom end of the bed, smiling and nodding to the music. Upon reaching the bed, Vittoria leaps onto it and, with a dramatic turn and a yelp and a smile, points the spear down at Marta. The next shot shows Marta, now turned away and staring offscreen into space, perhaps frightened but certainly and suddenly no longer enjoying the performance. Vittoria jumps off

The Eclipse (1962)

the bed and moves back into the living room, where Anita joins her in her dance, tentatively and at a distance. Marta has now risen from her seat and is in the room as well, but she just stands there, silhouetted in the shadows, staring at the two women who abruptly cease dancing when they notice their hostess's discomfiting presence. Marta then turns on the lights and says to her guests rather sternly, "That's enough. Let's stop playing negroes." Anita appears embarrassed and looks over at a tight-lipped Vittoria, who is slowly removing the neck rings. Vittoria is standing in almost the exact spot from which she began; she has made a complete, 360-degree sweep of the apartment's two visible rooms.

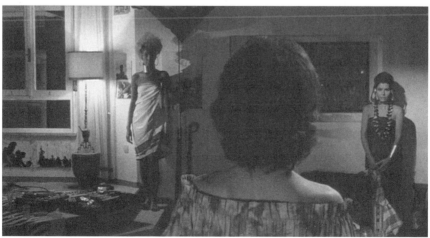

What is this scene doing in a film that otherwise concerns itself with the visual exploration of the urban and suburban spaces of modern Rome?[125] The alignment of ideas of Otherness in this scene with modernity, with white northern European femininity, and with the spectacle of movement of the female body at the periphery of a modern space festooned with the paraphernalia of colonial kitsch, is for me key to understanding the new Italian cinema's relation to the modernization/recolonization project of French national culture of the same period. The differences between the two lie in the details. Marta, a colonist in exile from Kenya, is nostalgic for both the heydays of colonialism and settled male/female marital relationships. On the latter score she is apart from her husband, who to her dismay no longer wants to live in Africa. At the time of *The Eclipse*'s making, Kenya was still a British colony, although the Kikuyu rebellion, the release of Jomo Kenyatta from prison, and the first movements toward colonial reforms suggested a familiar concatenation of anticolonial factors, and by the end of 1963 Kenya would achieve its independence. Marta's sudden change from enjoyment to sullen disapproval of Vittoria's performance occurs when Vittoria wields the spear in her direction, and in the discussion that follows Marta reveals that she took the gesture both literally and personally when she confesses that in Kenya "everybody is again carrying a gun. The six million Negroes want to throw out the 60,000 Whites. Luckily, they're still in trees and have barely lost their tails, otherwise they would have thrown us out. . . . I can only say one thing: There are about ten leaders who have studied at Oxford. The others are all monkeys. Six million monkeys." Marta is clearly delineated in the film as living in self-imposed exile from her own colonial fantasies. But her sentiments could hardly not resonate with some sectors of the Italian populace—those, for example, who had just returned themselves from Somalia, liberated in 1941 from Italy by British forces and to which Italian settlers were allowed to return in 1950 to prepare the country for independence in a ten-year controlled decolonization program under UN trusteeship. At the time of *The Eclipse,* then, the eclipse of the Italian empire in Africa had only just become an inescapable reality.

Other cultural and spatial factors of contemporary Italian modernization, relocation, and xenophobia are pertinent to this discussion as well. The influx of decolonized peoples from Africa, the Middle East,

Asia, and Latin America would not hit its stride until the mid-1970s, but by 1962 a black presence was already beginning to become visible; and although the total number of immigrants to Italy from the south of the world would by the mid-1990s amount to no more than 1.8 percent of the total Italian population, a much smaller percentage than that for Germany, France, or Britain, the degree of "social alarm" among the Italian populace has shown itself to be equally profound and disturbing.[126] The magnitude of this reaction is tied to a range of long-standing ideologies concerning racial and moral difference that continue to separate the country into north and south. Indeed, xenophobic northern Italian perceptions of immigrants tend to be filtered through a small number of symbolic categories that have been used variously to refer to both non-Europeans and southern Italians:"*marocchino, zingaro, meridionale* (Southern Italian), *ebreo, african/negro.* All these 'common-sense' categories suggest exclusion from the moral community rather than serving to identify any particular group, and to this extent they are something more than stereotypes."[127] The moral backwardness and equation of Africa with the south was forcefully taken up in one of the most internationally celebrated Italian films of the economic miracle, *La ciociara* (*Two Women,* 1960), which starred Sophia Loren as the mother of a teenage daughter who, fearing famine, deprivation, and bombardment during the Nazi Occupation, flee Rome for a rugged rural region near Naples, where they are together raped in a church by a roving band of Moroccan troops serving in an auxiliary unit of the French Army as part of the Allied forces liberating Italy.[128] Within the context of contemporary conceptions of the south-as-Africa, this film serves as a reinforcement of racial categories regarding north and south.[129]

At the time of *The Eclipse*'s making, the migration of rural southerners to the richer and more industrialized north was reaching its peak. The newcomers tended to settle in public housing built on the peripheries of cities and were subject to all the racist epithets and regional prejudices I have outlined above.[130] While the "possession" of Vittoria's body by the racial/colonial Other is not in *The Eclipse,* as it is in *Two Women,* narrativized as rape, she nevertheless bears on her body and in her movement through Rome's spaces the prevalent tensions and anxieties of Italian urban spatiality and culture in the early 1960s. In the film's stock-exchange scenes, all of the motion and action occurs on the perimeter of the room: frantic phone calls, hot tips, business partners whispering the rising and falling of stock to get the jump on their competitors. The directional logic of the stock exchange proceeds from the periphery to the center. The wild activities of the brokers and their clients, the distant trading on Wall Street and in Frankfurt, determines the exigencies of centralized capital in the center, and in the film the center does not hold: the market crashes. Similarly, Vittoria lives on the periphery of Rome, and even though she ventures into the city center on several occasions it is her movements from outside to inside and back again that structure the architectural exploration of modern Italian spatiality in the film. As in her sweep of Marta's apartment during her African dance, Vittoria's flanerie circulates on the edges of modern urban development, and it is on those edges that the colonial allegory is played out.

For Vittorio lives, and the film opens and concludes, not just in any Roman suburb but in one of great historical and ideological resonance: Esposizione Universale di Roma (EUR). Both modern and archaic, EUR bears traces that, as Joan Esposito puts it, "reach back through the Italian Renaissance to the days of Roman imperialism and beyond."[131] P. Adams Sitney provides further background information on the cultural politics of the site:

> Initially a grandiose project initiated by Mussolini for a world's fair in 1942, celebrating the twentieth year of Fascism, its construction was suspended during the war. With the consolidation of DC rule in the 1950s it was reactivated, serving the economic and ideological interests of the conservatives and neo-Fascists who urged civic expansion toward the Mediterranean with luxury and middle-class housing, against the Left's pressure for eastward expansion with housing for the increasing poor population emigrating from southern Italy.[132]

Vittoria works as a translator, and she belongs to the new Italian economic/intellectual elite. Her tentative romantic dalliances with Piero, who is clearly marked in the film as embodying the cutthroat mentality and lifestyle of Italy's new young conservative business class, are balanced with her spontaneous wanderings through the deserted yet fascinating modern wasteland of EUR, which she registers as a perpetual amusement ground full of chance occurrences and numinous moments of almost autoerotic spatial and aural pleasure. The drama of *The Eclipse* is one of a sexual topology, with the space of the modern

EUR vying with that of traditional Rome for the body and soul of the modern woman. It is a spatial drama of epic proportions reaching far back into Italy's imperial past, as it is played out in the literal arena of the Seventeenth Olympic Games in 1960, built on the site constructed to celebrate the nation's fascist campaigns through iconic and symbolic recourse to the glorious age of the Roman Empire.[133] Vitti/Vittoria's excision from the narrative in the film's famous final sequence, a five-and-a-half-minute, forty-four-shot montage of almost purely abstracted views of EUR from early evening to twilight, implies either her surrender to or capture by the space of the Other—in either case a narrative sacrifice of modern Italian womanhood at the chiasmus of a traditional Italian empire in declension and a potentional new one in ascension. The most modern of the modern European female flâneurs I have examined in this chapter, Vitti/Vittoria is reduced by film's end to a purely scopic apparatus whose vanishing point is the ultimately unrepresentable moment of a national present equally in awe of its past and its future, its past *in* its future. In closing the circle she becomes it, at once the container and the contained.

4

Exquisite Corpses

Art Cinema, Film Studies, and the Omnibus Film

Before growing indignant, as some have done, at the deconstructive
and destabilizing analysis of certain canons, structures, procedures or
events of canonization, we ought to consider all the devices and
interests presiding over the establishment of "assured values."
Analyzing or reinscribing this history of canonization in a broader,
more diversified, more intelligible field is hardly to argue for amnesia
or the destruction of traditional works. I might be tempted to think
the contrary. From this point of view, deconstruction answers to a
greater desire for memory, intelligibility and responsibility in the face
of tradition.

—JACQUES DERRIDA, "Canons and Metonymies:
An Interview with Jacques Derrida"

The Exquisite Corpse

CONTEMPORANEOUS WITH THE TROPE of the wandering woman in
European art cinema of the early 1960s was a particular film form that
has been all but ignored in film historical writing concerning European
cinema of the period: the omnibus film, a multidirector film constituted
as a combination of episodes, each singly authored yet connected to
others in contiguity to form a whole. Significantly, the figure of woman
serves as a unifying trope for several postwar Italian and French (frequently Italo-French) omnibus films whose segments were directed
by prominent art cinema auteurs. An early instance is *Siamo donne*
(*We, the Women,* 1953), which comprises episodes named after and
featuring the actresses Alida Valli, Ingrid Bergman, Isa Miranda, and
Anna Magnani; although the film's title implies a first-person female
mode of address, the women's signature sketches all were coscripted
by the neorealist critic, screenwriter, and producer Cesare Zavattini
and directed by men (Gianni Franciolini, Roberto Rossellini, Luigi
Zampa, and Luchino Visconti). Others followed in the 1960s: *La*

Française et l'amour (*Love and the Frenchwoman,* 1960), *La mia signora* (1964), *Le fate* (*The Queens/The Fairies,* 1966), *Le streghe* (*The Witches,* 1967), *Quatre d'entre elles* (*Four Women,* 1968). *The Witches,* for example, was conceived by producer Dino De Laurentiis as a tribute to his wife, Silvana Mangano, who stars in all of the film's five episodes, three notably directed by Vittorio De Sica, Pier Paolo Pasolini, and Visconti. Other films of this sort focus on rather less famous female actors for visual examination. And while plenty of omnibus films of the period fixate on the theme of love or sex, none takes the idea of man or men as its unifying theme and disunifying subject (see the appendix for a complete list of omnibus films of the period).

Omnibus films thus participate in an economy—related to but also different from that underscoring European art cinema's updating of the surrealist flâneur, the modern flâneuse—in which women and women's bodies are imaged by men as art.[1] Such imaging reached literal inscription in the artistic practice of the French visual artist Yves Klein, who at a large dinner party in June 1958 at the home of a friend used a woman as a living paintbrush. Soon Klein was staging elaborate public "anthropometry performances" in which nude female models, under the artist's restrained directions, sponged onto themselves his signature ultramarine blue paint and then imprinted their bodies onto paper covering the floor and hanging in long sheets, all to the accompaniment of a small orchestra conducted by Klein himself. The resulting large-scale compositions were then cut into a series of individual *anthropométries* (body paintings) suitable for individual ownership and display.[2] The surrealist elements evident in Klein's practice soon would be made manifest in an infamous Italian episode film, *Mondo Cane* (1962), directed and produced by the journalist turned filmmaker Gualtiero Jacopetti, released to equally great international popular success and moral outrage. Inviting potential viewers to "enter a hundred incredible worlds where the camera has never gone before," *Mondo Cane* comprised thirty-seven episodes showing "bizarre" practices from around the world, most of which emphasize female partial dress or nudity, sex play, animal slaughter, or scenes of human and animal degradation. The thirtieth episode, sandwiched between one detailing America's fatal obsession with the automobile and one mocking elderly American tourists vacationing in Hawaii, documents one of Klein's anthropometric performances, the narrator

Front cover of the Times Film Corporation pressbook for *Mondo Cane* (1962).
Courtesy of George Eastman House.

noting sardonically that the finished work will be sold for a "mere" $8,000. The film's light orchestral theme song, "More," became a Top 40 hit (as well as an Academy Award nominee), and in the next decade some fifty similar "shockumentaries" or mondo films were made, mostly by Italian filmmakers.[3] One of the first was *La donna nel mondo* (*Women of the World,* 1963), assembled by Jacopetti from extra footage shot for *Mondo Cane.*

This is not the place to open a full analysis of either Klein or *Cane.* But I juxtapose them here to suggest two legacies of surrealism as an aesthetic shot through with contradictory sexual and colonial ideologies that can be traced in French and Italian cultural production, high and low, during both cultures' entries into modern, commodity-oriented life in the late 1950s through the 1960s. James Clifford has demonstrated how an important feature of "the ethnographic surrealist attitude [is] a belief that the other (whether accessible in dreams, fetishes, or Lévy-Bruhl's *mentalité primitive*) was a crucial object of modern research."[4] He documents the history of French ethnography between the wars through two museums. Around 1930 the Trocadéro museum "had attained the proportions of what Edward Said has called an 'orientalism'—a knitted together collective representation figuring a geographically and historically vague but symbolically sharp exotic world."[5] To build the museum's collections, a team led by Marcel Griaule undertook in 1931 the "Mission Dakar-Djibouti" to Africa. Although the team brought back considerable quantities of artifacts for display at the Trocadéro, they found their permanent home in the soon-to-be-built Musée de l'Homme, conceived as part of the International Exhibition of 1937. Clifford contends that, although "it shared the scope of surrealism, the ethnographic humanism of the Musée de l'Homme did not adopt an earlier surrealism's corrosive, defamiliarizing attitude toward cultural reality. The aim of science was rather to collect ethnographic artifacts and data and to display them in reconstituted, interpretable contexts."[6]

Clifford's nostalgia for an ethnography "cut with surrealism" is evident, but his advocacy of a theory and practice of juxtaposition as the invention and "interruption of meaningful wholes in works of cultural import-export" is also instructive.[7] Indeed, he might be describing here the Italo-French omnibus or the mondo film of the 1960s. If surrealism's methods of fragmentation, abutment, and collage place the "proper" arrangement of cultural symbols and artifacts in doubt, might not the omnibus film, the mondo film, or other modes of fragmented narrative practices in film history be considered in similar ways? The pre-mondo exploitation/ethnographic film *Congolaise* (*Savage Africa/Wild Rapture,* 1950) was pieced together from footage shot by a group of scientists dispatched into equatorial Africa by the French government and the Musée de l'Homme to make "a lasting record of the different primitive tribes there."[8] Although I have not seen this film, by all reports its divisions of space (Europe/Africa) and time (modern/primitive) are never questioned. The wildly episodic *Mondo Cane,* by comparison, frequently juxtaposes these elements both to blur the distinctions between them and to jar the viewer and auditor from a stable position.

The Surrealists were committed game players, and they found that through tricks, traps, and shocks they could adjoin "apparently unrelated items so as to evoke hidden layers of experience within which the items could be seen as related."[9] The most famous Surrealist technique for exploiting the mystique of accident was the recreational, collective experiment known as the *cadavre exquis* or exquisite corpse. Based on an old parlor game, it was played by several people, each of whom would write a phrase on a sheet of paper, fold the paper to conceal the phrase, and pass it on to the next player for his or her contribution. As many have noted, the technique got its name from results obtained in an initial playing, "Le cadavre exquis boira le vin nouveau" ("The exquisite corpse will drink the new wine").[10] The game was adapted to the possibilities of drawing and collage by assigning a section of a body to each player, with results that usually (though sometimes only vaguely) resembled the human form.

Many of the artists associated with Surrealism participated in the game of the exquisite corpse, the products of which often bear their characteristic icons and artistic signatures. As the accompanying image illustrates, the resultant body may comprise an assortment of objects in an out-of-scale, organic and inorganic animal and machine. But to focus on the parts as discrete and singly authored (which portion is André Breton's, Jacqueline Lamba's, Yves Tanguy's?), to classify the image according to the folds of the paper and segmenting it accordingly, is to ignore the overall shape of the whole as well as the explicitly collective nature of the activity that produced it. It is also to miss

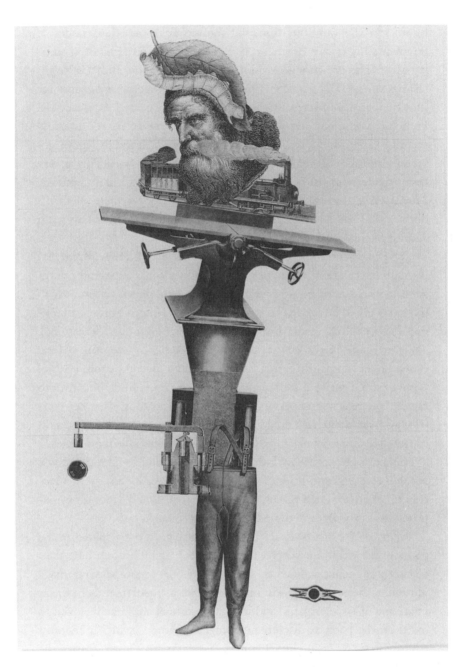

André Breton, Jacqueline Lamba, and Yves Tanguy, *Cadavre exquis (Exquisite Corpse)*, 9 February 1938. Courtesy of the Scottish National Gallery of Modern Art.

the inertia that is at the core of its structure. For the essential characteristic of the exquisite corpse, indeed of all Surrealist games, is that it is both a rule and a transgression. As the art historian Elza Adamowicz has outlined, in both the verbal and visual versions of the game a rigid mechanical principle is strictly adhered to. The verbal version follows the rules of syntax. "In its visual form," writes Adamowicz, "the *cadavre exquis* is based on the 'volonté préexistante de *composition en personnage*' . . . , that is[,] a compositional rule, analogous to the syntactic construction of the sentence, based on the anatomical structure of the body: the first participant drew the equivalent of a head, the second shoulders and arms, and so on."[11] Even when it moved into the medium of visual collage, the exquisite corpse remained committed to basic rules governing the articulation of the body so that "the standard lexicon of the body is partly replaced by random elements which flout the rules of anatomical coherence":

> The segments of the body are in a relationship of contiguity with the other parts of the body, balloon-head on turnip-neck, machine-torso below table-shoulders, etc., establishing metonymical relations, characterized by the copresence of elements within an englobing whole. . . . The limbs of the exquisite corpse remain spare parts, scarcely interlocking; their disparate character is irreducible and they remain allotopic *[sic]*.[12]

Overtly constructed as an assemblage of parts, the collaboratively produced hybrid forms of the exquisite corpse are nevertheless the product of tacitly agreed-upon rules of corporeal coherence.

The exquisite corpse is in several ways an appropriate metaphor for the omnibus film, not the least because the latter makes use of many other poetics of surrealism—an association not lost on former members of the Parisian avant-garde themselves, who as emigrés in America in the 1940s collaborated on a quasisurrealist omnibus film of their own, *Dreams That Money Can Buy* (1944–47). Collage and metaphor were for the Surrealists means toward emphasizing new combinations of shapes and associations. Their preference for fragments—of images, of sentences, of words—displayed a studied avoidance of continuous forms, whether as teleological narrative or as unified image. All of these may be usefully aligned with the omnibus film. But the omnibus film can also be related to the exquisite corpse insofar as it too obeys a rule of coherence: a synchronic principle or theme that determines the diachronic relations of its episodes. And in the case of one omnibus film produced in Canada in 2006, *Cadavre exquis première édition,* that principle is the exquisite corpse itself.

The figure of the exquisite corpse might also be seen as a graphic representation of Anglo-American film studies, a field of metamorphoses and interconnections produced over time whose contributions to the whole have both built upon and swerved away from prior inscriptions. Initially formed as outgrowths from other humanities programs and departments in the academy from the 1960s, academic film studies experienced growth in the next two decades that would establish it as a large-scale academic enterprise, leading to increasing specialization and professionalization.[13] Since the 1990s the field has expanded laterally, establishing connections and alliances with other areas and disciplines, metamorphosing into new shapes dedicated in one fashion or another to the study of visual media. Like the exquisite corpse, Anglo-American academic film studies is a figure of contradiction: its unpredictable accretions have been matched by the inertia of its own interior logic.[14] And it is the inertial side of the field that I find the more fascinating. A diachronic history of the discipline might index the rise, the fall, or the continuing presence of different methodologies, theories, and areas of study that have contributed to the overall shape of the discipline: from the initial influence of the art cinemas of Europe as a form of highbrow legitimation of film as an art, from semiotics and Marxism to psychoanalysis and feminism, from film and television to other forms of popular culture and media, from the developing debates on issues of race and ethnicity to those of national and sexual identity, from theory to history, production to reception. Each successive addition appears at first as a deviation; but its connections to the whole and the rules governing its existence are what make its contraventions readable as such. Transgressions and rules, change and inertia: the tension between these is necessary, productive. The vicissitudes of academic film studies since the 1960s are easy to identify and explicate. But what about the rules?

In beginning this chapter with an epigraph by Jacques Derrida[15] and then an excursus on surrealism, I am invoking two historically situated discourses, one theoretical and the other aesthetic. In linking the Surrealist exquisite corpse and avant-garde aesthetics and practice with poststructuralist theory, especially deconstruction, I am also to a certain degree invoking the transgression/subversion that both, to one degree or another, aim to enact. Derridean deconstruction under-writes a guiding premise of this book: that European art cinema, déclassé in Anglo-American academic film studies almost from its in-ception, is nevertheless inscribed within the discipline as trace, both there and not there at the same time. The omnibus film is a trace too of what the protocols of film historical writing do not accommodate. In this sense the omnibus film poses problems for the historiography of European cinema as well as the structuring paradigms of film studies as an academic discipline. It demonstrates how these paradigms con-dition and limit what is possible to say within the terrain of film his-tory and how they demarcate a disciplinary horizon of intelligibility. A mere fragment in the context of written film history and an always already fragmented text, the omnibus film functions in this chapter as a heuristic device through which to provoke a reading of academic film studies and film historical writing. The omnibus film is thus for me both an object of historical knowledge in itself and a sign of eli-sion—a sign that begs consideration of an alternative historiography.

Its presence is intimated through surrealism, and the spirit of Walter Benjamin, whose Arcades Project was premised on a surrealist historiography, also hangs over this chapter and the book as a whole.[16] As perhaps the fullest elaboration of an avant-garde aesthetic move-ment, Surrealism in its heyday (1924–36) connected up in interesting ways with later avant-gardes in France—the Situationists, the *Tel Quel* group and its allies, New French feminism—many of which looked to Surrealism as a kind of grounding discourse. In considering avant-garde literary production, Susan Rubin Suleiman sees these move-ments as "a collective project (more or less explicitly defined and often shifting over time) that linked artistic experimentation and a critique of outmoded artistic practices with an ideological critique of bour-geois thought and a desire for social change, so that the activity of writing could also be seen as a genuine intervention in the social, cul-tural, and political arena."[17] I am trusting this chapter is received as a similar intervention. But in a less grand way, I am also hoping, by link-ing deconstruction and the game of the exquisite corpse as I am here, to educe the notions of play inhering to each.[18] By way of depar-ture I extend a reading of a famous art film's title, which may serve to demonstrate not only what is at stake in the rules of coherence for academic film studies in general but also the pleasures of play.

Released in 1963, *8½* is one of Federico Fellini's most memorable and original films as well as a key text in the history of European art cinema and the canon of film masterpieces. The *Sight and Sound* "Critics' Top Ten Poll," drawn up every decade since 1952, includes *8½* in all but one poll from 1972 on; its exclusion from the 1992 list is compensated by the fact that it was ranked second (after *Citizen Kane* [1941]) in the first ever "Directors' Top Ten Poll" of that year.[19] Fellini's *8½* was also one of the first art films I saw in the context of my undergraduate education, and I experienced it as difficult, provocative, enigmatic. Comprising some forty major episodes told via stream-of-consciousness narration, *8½* was both exhilarating and baffling, untrained as I was in what David Bordwell calls "the schemata for the 1960s 'art film.'"[20] Such bafflement was crystallized in the film's short, distinctive title: *8½*. What could it mean? The explanation offered at the time by my professor cleared the mystery and set the terms by which the film's value and meaning were made possible. I repeat that explanation now, by way of one of Peter Bondanella's two books on the director:

> The film's strange numerical label . . . underscores the personal nature of *8½* and refers to the total number of films Fellini had produced up to that time. Fellini arrived at this total by considering his first codirected film with [Alberto] Lattuada, *Luci del varietà*, and the two episodes produced with other directors (*Un'agenzia matrimoniale* and *Le tentazioni del dottor Antonio*) each as half of a film for a subtotal of one and one half. This subtotal added to the six previously completed films plus the one in progress came to a total of 8½ films.[21]

This explanation has circulated and functioned as the solution to the enigma of the film's title since its release. Most film scholars and critics are aware of the answer to the question begged by *8½*'s nomenclature—if not in such specific terms, at least in more general ones that acknowledge the film as a self-reflexive, highly authored text about the complexities of being a filmmaker, Federico Fellini in particular.[22] But perhaps, given the distinction that critics and directors have conferred on this film, the value it is accorded as one of the pinnacles of art cinema, and the numerical particularity of its title, the issue of its name might be reopened—to take an accounting, so to speak, of *8½*, film and title.

I will leave aside the question of whether the six feature-length films that Fellini directed before *8½* are indeed equal to one film each (though if this is assumed, what is the value of a film not feature length?). I will leave aside as well the question of whether a codirected film equals half a film for each director—a question that has been asked before, for reasons of authorial authentication and, therefore, aesthetic value. That leaves for my accounting the two short films or episodes that Fellini directed but were released in combination with the work of other directors: *Un'agenzia matrimoniale (A Marriage Agency)* and *Le tentazioni del dottor Antonio (The Temptations of Doctor Antonio)*. Fellini directed *A Marriage Agency* in 1953; it was one episode in the omnibus film *L'amore in città (Love in the City)*, a project conceived by Cesare Zavattini to inaugurate a cinematic form: the *film inchiesta* or film inquiry. *Love in the City* is structured as the first edition of a film magazine, *Lo spettatore (The Spectator)*, and contains six "articles" written by six film "journalists": Michelangelo Antonioni, Federico Fellini, Alberto Lattuada, Carlo Lizzani, Francesco Maselli, and Dino Risi.[23] Fellini and the critics in his wake consider his episode to be half a film—that is, half of *Love in the City*. But to be precise about it, *A Marriage Agency* is not half of the film but only one-sixth (⅙). *The Temptations of Doctor Antonio* is the title of another Fellini-directed short film; it is one of four segments in the 1962-released omnibus film *Boccaccio '70*, which contained other episodes directed by De Sica, Mario Monicelli, and Visconti.[24] Again, it seems imprecise, even unfair, to consider Fellini's episode to be fully half of this film: ¼ is, mathematically at least, the correct value. So, adding to the previous 6½ these filmic quantities of ⅙ and ¼, and adding the figure of 1 for the film yet to be titled, the total is in fact 7¹¹⁄₁₂—by no means 8½, not even an even 8.

But the matter of naming this film is yet more complicated. For the new values determined for the Fellini episodes in the two omnibus films in question tally only for certain *versions* of these films. In North America and elsewhere, *Love in the City* was distributed and seen by audiences as a film composed not of six episodes but of five: Lizzani's contribution, *L'amore che si paga (Paid Love)*, was cut for censorship reasons.[25] And all of the initial release prints of *Boccaccio '70*, except for those screened in Italy and at the Cannes Film Festival of

1962, contained three episodes rather than four; Monicelli's contribution was cut, according to the *Variety* magazine review, "for reasons of length."[26] Taking into account this distribution information, the value of Fellini's yet-to-be-named 1963 film is thus slightly greater in North America than it is in Italy: $6\frac{1}{2} + \frac{1}{5} + \frac{1}{3} + 1 = 8\frac{1}{30}$.

Changing the name of *8½* to *7¹¹/₁₂* or *8¹/₃₀* is not an enterprise I wish seriously to entertain. But the import of this example *is* something I do wish to entertain, and entertain seriously. For bound in these calculations are matters that underpin the practices of film historiography in general and European film historical writing in particular, especially the *value* accorded to certain films and certain types of films as representative, or more particularly *exemplary*, texts upon which a canonical history of cinema is based. So manifestly a personal expression of a single artistic temperament, *8½* may by an inverse operation undertaken on its name be revealed as an exquisite corpse: a fragmented unity, the perilous balance of which depends on the effacement of the collective nature of the film's making, its titular logic, and its reception. For the Surrealists, verbal and linguistic games yielded ambiguous statements. What if we were to subvert the rules of the game and instead ask ambiguous questions?

Mind the Gap

The term *omnibus* is one of the many names given to multidirector episode films in the histories and critical studies of cinema. Some emerge more often than others, but all appear with enough frequency to suggest both the need to call these films something and the relative disinterest in standardizing that term. Variously referred to as anthology, collective, compendium, compilation, composite, episode, omnibus, novella, portmanteau, sketch, or story films, they present a problem case for film studies, one indication of which is the fluidity of the nomenclature used to refer to them.

The rigor many film scholars take in categorizing other aspects of film form and language tends to be relaxed when it comes to these films. Even texts dedicated entirely to terminology reveal inconsistencies. In Kevin Jackson's *The Language of Cinema,* for example, one finds no definition for the term omnibus but overlapping definitions for *composite* and *episode film.* The composite film, according to Jackson, is "a full-length feature containing more than one story, such as the classic Ealing ghost yarn collection *Dead of Night,* directed by Cavalcanti and others, the somewhat less classic *Twilight Zone: The Movie* (Steven Spielberg, Joe Dante and others), Rossellini's *Paisà* (1946), or the various English films based on short stories by Somerset Maugham."[27] The episode film is

> a portmanteau film; a dramatic feature made up of several self-contained or interlocking short stories, either by one director, such as D. W. Griffith's *Intolerance* (1916), Roberto Rossellini's *Paisa* (1946), and Jean Renoir's *Le Petit Théâtre de Jean Renoir,* or by several, as in *RoGoPaG* (1962), by Rossellini, Godard, Pasolini and Gregoretti. They can tend to the uneven, as in Ealing Studios *[sic]* production *Dead of Night* . . . or—to stay within the Gothic field—*Dr Terror's House of Horrors* (Freddie Francis, 1964), *Creepshow* (George A. Romero, 1982), *Twilight Zone—the Movie* (Steven Spielberg, Joe Dante and others, 1983) and *Necronomicon* (1994).[28]

Not only are the same films called three different things here, but the rubrics "composite" and "episode" are equally applicable both to singly and multiply directed films. As well, a certain bias is evident in Jackson's distinction between the episode films directed by one person and those directed by several: the latter tend to be "uneven." Jackson is not alone in this, and for the sake of clarity I will distinguish between the two by referring to the one-director type as the episode film and the multiple-director type as the omnibus film.[29]

Omnibus films occupy a marginal status within Anglo-American academic film studies: most international and national histories all but ignore them as a particular type of filmic product. When I first began researching postwar European art cinema, I was struck by how many of these films I kept coming across, usually via references to individual contributions by certain directors, in the footnotes of various types of film historical texts, in indexes and on databases. Italy and France, either singly or as coproducers (usually with each other), eventually accounted for some 52 omnibus films in the 1960s, nearly half of the total for the decade, and almost all of the most famous directors in European cinema of the era contributed to one or more such films. But that research has since exfoliated beyond its initial geographic and temporal boundaries as interest in the omnibus film became something in and of itself. To date I have established a filmography of some 747 omnibus films, extending from 1930 to 2007 and across a vast number of countries including, in order of prolificity, the United States, Italy, France, Japan, the United Kingdom, postunification Germany, the Soviet Union, Hong Kong, South Korea, Poland, Spain, Canada, West Germany, Argentina, the Philippines, Brazil, Mexico, Austria, and 52 others on every continent (other than Antarctica) that have produced or coproduced ten or fewer (see appendix).

Given this range, it is difficult to find anything beyond the most passing of references to omnibus films in film history texts, international or otherwise. In the world cinema histories—the twenty or so macrohistory texts that have circulated in the field as required reading across every generation of Anglo-American film studies—the same few titles appear again and again: *La Vie est à nous* (France 1936), *Fantasia* (United States 1940), *Dead of Night* (United Kingdom 1945), *Love in the City* (Italy 1953), *L'Amour à vingt ans* (*Love at Twenty*, France/Italy/Japan/Poland/West Germany 1962), *Boccaccio '70* (Italy/France 1962), *RoGoPaG* (France/Italy 1962), *Paris vu par* (*Six in Paris*, France 1964), *Loin du Viêt-nam* (*Far from Vietnam*, France 1967), *Histoires extraordinaires* (*Spirits of the Dead*, France/Italy 1968), and *Deutschland im Herbst* (*Germany in Autumn*, West Germany 1978). Only eleven films—though of these eleven a substantial proportion qualify as examples of postwar European art cinema. Obviously, introductory world cinema histories are only a beginning for film scholarship, the first link of a chain. The next step is to seek out more specialized histories, in this case those pertaining to national cinemas. But the film historical writing on North, Latin, and South America, on Asia, Africa, and Australia, tends toward silence on the matter of omnibus films. A perusal of the histories of British, French, and German cinemas reveals the odd reference to *Dead of Night, La Vie est à nous, Paris vu par,* and *Germany in Autumn,* but certainly not in a way that would link omnibus production with any national or international tradition. The anglophone film scholar must dig rather deeply into the written histories of Italian cinema to find the two or three paragraphs of sustained discussion on omnibus films as a body of related work.[30] ·

Writing in the mid-1960s, an initial peak in omnibus film production, Pierre Leprohon is the first of only two Italian film historians to place the omnibus film in a context. After citing *Boccaccio '70* as "a feeble effort which seems to have been intended as a kind of prototype," Leprohon connects the production of episode films with the rise of pornography, citing *Controsesso (Countersex, 1964)* and *Le bambole (Four Kinds of Love, 1965)* as particularly litigious examples: while the latter "led to Gina Lollobrigida and Virna Lisi appearing in court in Viterbo, along with their directors, Dino Risi and [Mauro] Bolognini, for infringing article 528 of the civil code, which forbids the diffusion of pornographic material," *Countersex* "earned Castellani and the producer, together with the distributor and eight cinema-owners, suspended sentences of two months' prison on the same charge."[31]

The generic permutations do not end there. Leprohon links Italian erotic film production to "another genre in favour in Italy," the postneorealist problem film, "to which Zavattini, in particular, has continued to subscribe." Inspired by *Love in the City,* the episodic problem film moved in the early 1960s toward a more fashionable style, starting "with a problem of the moment (women in society, divorce, the younger generation)" and situating its examination "skilfully *[sic]* around a point midway between fact and fiction."[32] With *I misteri di Roma* (1963), Zavattini apparently

> discarded fiction in favour of the "secret document" type of film (frequently of doubtful authenticity), made popular some years before by Jacopetti's *Mondo Cane.* Here the aim was to collect oddities. . . . These "sexy documentaries", as they are known in Italy, more or less pornographic in spirit, are extremely good business for the producers: *Sexy al Neon* made 400 million lire at the box-office—a very gratifying return for a minimum outlay. In point of fact, insofar as the camera is an eye-witness and striptease has become a modern ritual, the Italian name for the genre is not misplaced, and the sexy documentary, for better or for worse, is a commentary on our times.[33]

One of the interesting aspects of this short yet rich section on episode/omnibus films is how insistently it returns to neorealism as a source and influence. The name of Zavattini is omnipresent and it functions as both an influential center from which issues hybrid imitations and a figure of authority whose critical reputation legitimates a discussion of aesthetically low genres like the secret report, the mondo, the sexy documentary. That said, melodrama—and more generally the quotidian, which includes the sexual—haunts Italian neorealism from its inaugural moment, *Ossessione* (1943), through its "decline" via *neorealismo rosa* to what could be argued is its closing document, the omnibus film *Love in the City.* Despite the disapproving tone of Leprohon's excursus on the episode film, what he indicates about the connections between high (neorealist) and low (mondo) aesthetic practice, about the popular, often prurient basis of much Italo-French episode film production, and about the complex network of generic exchange circulating around this type of film is prescient to what I will be dealing with as integral aspects of European art cinema later in this chapter.

Peter Bondanella has also contributed a paragraph on the phenomenon of the Italian omnibus film; like Leprohon, he refers to it as the episode film and has little positive to say about the form, which "became fashionable with the appearance of *Boccaccio '70* . . . whose express purpose was to exploit recent box-office hits by four different directors and some of their stars. . . . Producers encouraged such works, done in sections by different directors and combining box-office attractions that would normally be employed in three or four

SPECIAL MAT NO. 1

Ad mat for *Boccaccio '70* (1962), from U.S. Exhibitors' Showmanship Manual. Courtesy of George Eastman House.

separate films, because of their relatively low cost and their large short-term profit potential. The vogue of the episode film thus clearly reflects the domination of economic imperatives over artistic ones."[34] Bondanella's comments on the omnibus film appear at the end of a much longer section on the *commedia all'italiana,* which was once "denigrated as merely a commercial genre unworthy of serious critical study . . . [but] has nevertheless provided the film industry with works of undeniable artistic quality that also generated a large percentage of its profits."[35] The same is not said of the omnibus film, however. Taken together, Leprohon's and Bondanella's histories demonstrate a priority of the aesthetic over the economic, and of directors over producers and audiences, which underscores much film scholarship on European art cinema. The only reason omnibus films are included at all is that many of the directors most prized within this discourse have had more than a passing involvement in them. Despite functioning as the repository for much short work by major auteurs, the omnibus film is ultimately relegated to the historical ghetto of popular Italian cinema.[36]

The lack of scholarship on omnibus films provokes a number of responses.[37] One is that they appear so infrequently as objects of study across the range of film historical discourses because they do not constitute a sufficient body, or a sufficiently interesting body, of films in the first place. Anglo-American academic film studies' relative neglect of popular cinemas other than that of Hollywood is instructive here. Writing in 1994, Ella Shohat and Robert Stam argued that, in film studies,

> one name for Eurocentrism is Hollywoodcentrism. "Because of the world-wide imitation of Hollywood's successful mode of production," we are told in a standard text on classical cinema, "oppositional practices have generally not been launched on an industry-wide basis. No absolute, pure alternative to Hollywood exists." The somewhat tautological formulation—since all industries imitate Hollywood, no alternative exists— embeds a sequencing which makes Hollywood the *primum mobile* of film history, when in fact capitalist-based film production appeared roughly simultaneously in many countries, including in what are now called "Third World" countries.[38]

A perusal of the macrohistories of world cinema currently in circulation broadly bears out the claim that Anglo-American film studies is still Hollywoodcentric. Hollywood cinema functions as a central narrative line from which deviate the subplots of other cinemas and their particular national cultures, aesthetics, genres, and auteurs.[39] But a film studies centered on style has a second Eurocentric front: the rare examples of industrywide modes of production that represent alternatives to Hollywood cinema tend to be European.[40] They also tend to be oriented toward specialized, international audiences, as the popular cinemas of these other nations and cultures, in a doubly exclusionary twist of logic, are regarded as attempts to imitate Hollywood films at one remove from the origin.[41] Postwar European cinema, then, becomes equivalent to art cinema. But art cinema is a cinema of auteurs. And most major auteurs of postwar European art cinema engaged at some level with omnibus production. Omnibus films thus warrant attention in their own right: as with coproductions (which so many of them are), their prevalence in Italy and France in the 1960s marks them not as supplementary to the main body of European art cinema of the period but central to it.

A second response concerns availability of filmic materials. The film text has served historically as a crucial primary document in academic film studies and as the basis for course construction as well as the object of much criticism and historical research. It is so pivotal to the canon, the discipline, and the curriculum that the viewing of extant prints or videotape/DVD copies is understood to be an indispensable part of any valid historical study of a film genre or form. But omnibus films produced before 1980 are notoriously difficult to find copies of to view. Out of the main cluster of French and Italian omnibus films produced in the 1960s, I have seen only eighteen. The chances of viewing many more are not encouraging.[42] Since the large number of omnibus films made in France and Italy in the 1960s was the impetus for my interest and the initial focus of my research, the loss or inaccessibility of so many of the films in question would seem to compromise seriously any study of them.

But the issue of extant viewing prints should be neither an incentive for nor a curtailment of studying a particular film type, and textual analysis is only one of many forms historical scholarship can take. The seeming irrefutability of the film text as primary document makes sense only in the context of either a *technological* history concerned centrally with the materiality of the medium itself or an *aesthetic* history whose goals are to establish artists, masterpieces, and the networks of influence for each. Douglas Gomery has put the matter in memorable terms: "Films themselves tell us next to nothing about modes of production, organizational structures, market situations, management decision making, or labor relations, just as close examination of a bar of soap would reveal little data in the study of the personal hygiene industry."[43] Gomery is writing here from the perspective of an economic and industrial historical analysis of cinema, and the kinds of documents necessary to that field of inquiry are in many cases available for omnibus films. National filmographies and indexes, film festival catalogs, press and publicity kits, posters, and other marketing materials have proven invaluable in my research. So have so-called anecdotal forms of history, such as reviews, articles, and ads in trade journals and newspapers.[44] While the loss or relative inaccessibility of so many omnibus films precludes an aesthetic history of the form, it does not preclude others. Given that so much film historical writing on European cinema is concerned with style as it is, the absence of a large research sample of these films obliges one to pursue other avenues of inquiry and study, avenues that may in fact place pressure on the aesthetic discourses that locate the omnibus film outside the category of art cinema.

A third response is that omnibus films indeed constitute an important group of films for study, that the lack of work devoted to them is evidence of one of the many historical gaps in the written history of cinema, and that published research on them would lessen, if not close, the gap.[45] Much important scholarship since the late 1970s has proceeded from the identification of oversights in the discipline's overall historical conceptualization of world cinema, which sacrifices difference and discontinuity in the interest of maintaining narrative coherence and continuity. Certain historical periods, national cinemas, cinematic forms and genres, filmmakers, or some combination thereof formerly absent from the pages of film history, have been made present through such historical gap work. For the amply covered national sound cinemas like those of France and Italy, neorealism and the French New Wave were held up as exemplars of those nations' cinemas to such a degree that the industries, films, and filmmakers that preceded them were long considered aesthetically and/or politically unsophisticated and justly superseded. It was not until the middle 1980s, for example, that film historians began to engage with the Italian film industry under fascism.[46] In this context, might not the omnibus film be a candidate for its own historical study?

It is now a dictum in Anglo-American academic film studies that there is no such thing as one history but many histories, that it is no longer possible or desirable to support one grand narrative that can account for all of the ways we can consider films and film history, that a plurality of approaches to film history and the histories resulting from these approaches are to be understood as evidence of the dynamic and accommodating nature of not only our conceptions of history but also film studies as a discipline.[47] One might even say that film studies has from the beginning been a model of such an inter-disciplinarity.[48] While I agree in principle with these positions, the enabling assumption behind most scholarly writing on film nonetheless concerns the possibility of totality. And the most obvious effect of this will to totality is the macrohistory text, what David Bordwell calls "synoptic history." Bordwell avers that the "last major synoptic history of cinema was offered by Jean Mitry in a series of five volumes published from 1967 through 1980." He goes on to assert that in the 1970s

> younger historians began to doubt that one scholar could write a comprehensive history of style across the world. By concentrating more narrowly on a period, a line of development, or a single stylistic issue, they avoided the peaks-and-valleys overview and began to study continuity and change on a more minute scale. It is probably too soon to identify this revisionist enterprise as a single distinctive program, but we might provisionally call it piecemeal history.[49]

Although piecemeal- or gap-history-making is a consistent feature of Anglo-American academic film studies since its professionalization, there is little to suggest that it has replaced or even seriously challenged what Bordwell elsewhere calls the "Standard Version" of film history. Instead, the two have ridden on parallel tracks and thus largely avoided collisions. I count at least six major "synoptic" histories since 1979: Jack C. Ellis's *A History of Film*, David Cook's *A History of Narrative Film*, David Shipman's *The Story of Cinema*, Douglas Gomery's *Movie History: A Survey*, Robert Sklar's *Film: An International History of the Medium*, and Kristin Thompson and David Bordwell's own *Film History: An Introduction*.[50] Seeing the will to total history as being superseded by more modest piecemeal approaches is to overlook the continuing

presence and currency of the synoptic history in academic film studies today and of the central place it occupies in the curriculum.

For the macrohistory text implies the possibility, the promise,
and the act of writing such a history. And that history is one that has
tended to be written in the same way since the establishment of film
studies' existence in the Anglo-American academic context. It is a
history that welcomes the identification of its own gaps so that these
may be filled and its foundation thereby strengthened. In an interesting application of Derridean theory and method to film studies, Peter
Brunette and David Wills have argued that the "complete" description
of film history "always at least aims to be all inclusive and is under-
written by a teleology providing the completion and closure that
any specific study must always admit to lack in absolute terms."[51] The
macrohistorian's encouragement of piecemeal-history writing is thus
not the overturning of a total film history but its necessary support.
The cumulative, progressive precepts of total history form a closed
circle in which past and present are seamlessly linked in the present—
of the latest edition. If "totalization is . . . only another word for finding an essence, or 'discovering' a truth, through the suppression of elements deemed to be 'inessential' and thus irrelevant to the truth," the
repression of elements that do not fit has as its corollary their eventual
reinstatement, their reintegration into the whole, their realignment
with the totalizing gesture, the truth.[52]

To consider film history as endlessly additive and ultimately inclusive is thus to ignore how the protocols of the discipline itself produce
both historical knowledge and historical gaps, oversights, and invisi-
bilities. Writing a history of omnibus films would buy into the logic
that suspends their value or importance. And yet the research I have
done on omnibus films indicates rich possibilities for their historicization. It is crucial, then, to envision such a historicization in terms
of not only the films themselves but also their long-standing neglect
in film studies. I consider the omnibus film as a potential object of
historical knowledge and as a sign of disciplinary elision, a limit case
because of its particular construction—episodic, multiply authored—
and international prevalence. Gap as symptom, gap *and* symptom: a
rendering historically of the omnibus film must also be accompanied
by a rendering of the organizational categories of film historical writing to which it has remained all but hidden.

Plotting the Paradigms

Revisionist history has made great strides in addressing and redressing many of academic film studies' silences. In 1983 Jeanne Thomas Allen identified three styles of revisionism that pertain to the writing of film history today:

(1) challenging old theses by saying "this, not this";
(2) asking a different question or changing perspective on a familiar topic;
(3) presenting wholly new topics or categories which impel the discovery of new types of documentation and new methods.[53]

Allen goes on to point out that the third style of revisionism, "presenting new categories or topics which motivate the discovery of new types of documentation and methods of scholarship," has been instrumental in establishing the notion of the buried subject: "There is probably no better example of the 'buried subject' of the last couple of decades of historical scholarship than the so-called 'history from below' movement: the foregrounding of segments of society not given the privilege of political power or public voice—women, ethnic groups, racial minorities, labor, children and adolescents."[54] Indeed, the 1990s witnessed an explosion of writing addressing film and other audiovisual media in terms of a broader agenda that examines their roles in producing discourses of gender, sexuality, race, nationalism, colonialism, and identity. The intersections among film and media studies and identity politics have demarcated and drawn attention to "the margins" as political and ideological sites of contestation.[55]

But the center/margin binarism, like the synoptic/piecemeal-history one, carries with it rules of coherence and maintenance. In 1988 Isaac Julien and Kobena Mercer asserted that one issue at stake in the critical examination of ethnicity in the media

is the potential break-up or deconstruction of structures that determine what is regarded as culturally central and what is regarded as culturally marginal. Ethnicity has emerged as a key issue as various "marginal" practices . . . are becoming de-marginalised at a time when "centred" discourses of cultural authority and legitimation are becoming increasingly de-centred and destabilised, called into question from within.[56]

Julien and Mercer indicate that the initial stage of deconstruction "must be to examine and undermine the force of the binary relation that produces the marginal as a consequence of the authority invested in the centre." They also warn of the potential dangers of mere celebration of "marginal" ethnicities: on the one hand, a unitary notion of difference that elides internal differences and diversity; on the other, the desire to correct the omissions of the past that can lead to a one-sided fixation with ethnicity "as something that 'belongs' to the Other alone, thus white ethnicity is not under question and retains its 'centred' position."[57] The struggle to avoid these pitfalls is ongoing.

For academic film studies, from which so much of the writing of history from below and from the margins has proceeded, whatever authority its center might have once wielded should by now be sufficiently contested and thoroughly compromised. Indeed, the call in 1996 for a *re*construction of the field by a group of influential scholars and historians suggests as much.[58] But I do not think this is the case. Attempts at altering the center of the discipline—the canon, the curriculum—have been largely additive rather than reformative. Both Ian Christie and Geoffrey Nowell-Smith have claimed that the canon of film studies has always been a fluid countercanon by dint of the discipline's establishment around May '68.[59] But to posit this canon's formation as countercultural is to overstate the role that post-1968 film theory has played in structuring the discipline. For the development of Anglo-American academic film studies has followed a similar course marked by the emergence of nearly all high art forms.[60] I am in agreement with David Bordwell that "the periods into which we divide history, the kinds of influences and consequences we take for granted, the national schools we routinely name . . . were bequeathed to us by stylistic historians" like Georges Sadoul, Jean Mitry, and André Bazin.[61] Writing at a time when film was declared by its adherents and critics to be an art but was not accepted as such in the houses of culture, these historians borrowed the premises and paradigms of art history to establish "the emergence of the canonical works, the masterpieces that demonstrated the highest possibilities of the medium."[62] These precepts combined easily with those of the first film studies academics trained as philologists and steeped in the New Critical ethos of literary studies in Britain and America in the late 1960s.[63] And the core paradigms and curriculum forged at the meeting of the two—and at the time of European art cinema's apogee—have remained virtually unchanged.

In 1983 Barry Keith Grant edited a collection of essays and film program descriptions that was intended as an "aid in defining the position of film studies in the humanities curriculum."[64] A scansion of the contents of this book reveals a consistent claim for film studies' interdisciplinarity and a likewise consistent roster of courses comprising curricula at a range of universities and colleges in North America. The composite curriculum is structured as follows:

- an introductory course on the principles and terms of film rhetoric and style, an introductory survey of film history, and/or an introduction to the cinema as a social and cultural artifact (two or all three of the above are often combined in a single introductory course);
- film history courses, divided at the introductory level into silent and sound film courses (or pre-1945/post-1945) and that deal largely with American cinema;
- other national cinemas (named as such), especially France, Germany, Italy, Latin America, the Third World, and Japan (combinations of some of these appear in courses like "Foreign Film" or "International Cinema");
- genre courses (again, American cinema is implicit) in especially the musical, the western, the gangster film/film noir, and American film comedy;
- a film theory component, in smaller programs offered as one course, in larger programs as two or more (classical/modern/contemporary);
- a topical course on contemporary Hollywood cinema, courses on documentary cinema, on film and literature, and on film and narrative;
- assorted courses on film and society, women in film, film and the other arts, film and philosophy, film and politics, film and popular culture, et cetera.

Is this not the framework of most academic film studies programs' curricula today, apart from those that include production components? The only really dated aspects of Grant's text are the enrollment figures for the programs listed therein, the reading lists for some of the courses, and the absence of courses on television and/or new media, subjects that have asserted their importance to the degree that they should not be relegated to the trailing "Topics in . . ." category of the curriculum. While there may today be a few deletions and additions to the above outline, the structure of the discipline has remained quite intact.

A plotting of the omnibus film across the disciplinary structure of film studies affords the opportunity for identifying and interrogating film history's organizational categories, its paradigms—and even for offering alternatives to them. That omnibus films are not quite invisible to Western film history is instructive, for this suggests that they are not so much *repressed* as objects of history as they instead resist being channeled or contained. In this sense, I am deploying the omnibus film here as a heuristic device to reveal the operations by which the boundaries that currently organize film historical practice are delineated and maintained. For each paradigm provides a means of access for some aspects of the history and analysis of the omnibus film at the same time as it presents obstacles to its entry.

The paradigmatic analyses that follow advance something different from most contributions to film historiography, which tend to concern themselves with *approaches* to the medium. In 1977 Rick Altman cataloged the kinds of history being practiced in the field of U.S. film history, itemizing thirteen approaches: technology, technique, personality, film and the other arts, chronicle, social, studio, auteur, genre, ritual, legal, industrial, and sociological. Robert C. Allen and Douglas Gomery proposed almost a decade later four traditions of film historical writing: aesthetic, technological, economic, and social. And more recently, Kristin Thompson and David Bordwell have offered five types of explanatory frameworks film historians tend to employ: biographical, industrial or economic, aesthetic, technological, and social/cultural/political.[65] The near identity between Allen/Gomery's and Thompson/Bordwell's list of film historical approaches suggests a certain settling of film historiography. In this respect, the historiographic paradigms I will be dealing with are not hidden or buried but rather quite manifest in the discipline. They are, in fact, the means by which most undergraduate curricula are conceptualized, organized, and managed.

To start, cinema history has over its course been divvied up into *periods.* Certainly one of the most consistent periodizations of film history involves the technological break of sound, and film texts and courses utilize this break to distinguish between films made before 1927 and those made after. "Silent cinema" and "sound cinema" are thus the two most standardized periods of film history. The coming of sound to cinema also prompted a first wave of film histories in Europe and America, including Paul Rotha's *The Film Till Now,* Benjamin Hampton's *History of the American Film Industry,* and Maurice

Bardèche and Robert Brasillach's *Histoire du cinema,* all in the early 1930s.[66] As Bordwell has pointed out, the periodizing of the latter's *Histoire* has been extremely influential in the film historical field.[67] The paradigm of "the period" is so strong it transcends political difference: Georges Sadoul, Surrealist and Marxist, published in the late 1940s through mid-1950s some macrohistories of world cinema that adhere closely to the period scheme of the young fascist Brasillach and his brother-in-law Bardèche[68] as follows:

B&B	Sadoul
1895–1908 ("Film's First Steps")	1897–1909
1908–14 ("prewar")	1909–14
1914–18 (the war years)	1914–18
1919–29 ("silent art")	1919–29

This set of subperiods for pre-sound cinema remains unchanged.

Another common break is World War II, which falls near the midpoint of film history's existence. It functions importantly as both a historical break and a conceptual marker in Gilles Deleuze's film books. Deleuze is clear from the first line of his preface to *Cinema 1* that his purpose is not to produce a history of cinema, and his project has been understood as philosophical and conceptual rather than historical in the strict sense of the term. Deleuze's distinction between two types of images effects a different conception of and operation for cinema—a wide range of popular films in genres of the pre–World War II era for the movement-image, a narrower range of largely European art cinema for the postwar time-image—and to take the distinction as a historical one is to be very frustrated with these books' free play with film history. Nevertheless, one of the aims of Deleuze's cinema books is to argue *through* an analysis of cinema a philosophy of history marked, as D. N. Rodowick has put it, "by confrontations in the postwar *episteme* between existentialism—with its Hegelian conception of history and politics—and the poststructuralism of Deleuze and Foucault, with their Nietzschean and genealogical conceptions of history and thought."[69] In this sense, these cinema books do present many features of a historical work, and they are indisputably "organized across a broad temporal division: an historical break divides the time-image, which appears largely in the period following World War II, from the movement-image that precedes it."[70] Even a philosophical meditation such as Deleuze's cinema books depends upon the paradigm of periodicity for its structure as well as for the crux of its argument.

Deleuze's work aside, the history of cinema tends more often to be apportioned as a series of subperiods, a number of blocks or units of time and their aggregation, all organized linearly as a continuous temporal unfolding with only occasional breaks that serve to provide both academic curricula with their course divisions and macrohistory textbooks with their chapter headings. *The Oxford History of World Cinema* offers two such breaks, so that its three periods for cinema history are articulated in stylistic and cultural terms as silent cinema (1895–1930), classical cinema (1930–60), and, beginning with the new cinemas of France and Italy, modern cinema (1960–present).[71] Within these broad periods smaller units are determined, and it is these smaller units of periodization that serve as the temporal boundaries for upper-level film courses and for most historical research and writing. A glance at the survey histories of film reveals a repetition of the same historical periods and groupings:

> 1880s–1914: Pre- and early cinema (concerned largely with devices, technologies, types of exhibition, the star system, international expansion, et cetera)
>
> 1913–29: Transitional to silent cinema (film grammar; genres; Soviet montage, German Expressionism, French Impressionism, Surrealism; the classical style: Griffith et al.)
>
> 1927–55: Classical sound cinema (the studio system; French poetic realism; World War II, occupation, and propaganda cinema; Italian neorealism; postwar genres)
>
> 1941–75: Modern cinema (Welles/*Citizen Kane;* Italian neorealism, European art cinema, assorted international new waves; the breakdown of the studio system, television; Eastern Central European cinemas, collective and militant filmmaking, some Third Cinema; auteurism, underground/avant garde cinemas, New American cinema)
>
> 1975–present: Contemporary cinema (Third/diasporic/exilic cinema, global/transcultural filmmaking, "world cinema"; big-budget/high concept filmmaking, postclassical cinema, postmodernism, digital/new media)

This recapitulation of world cinema history textbooks demonstrates that the rules of coherence for macrohistories are based on a shared set of assumptions about what the history of the cinema constitutes in the first place, what its temporality "looks" like, and how it is important to divide it into discrete sections. The concept of the historical period is essential to this operation.

Where or how do omnibus films figure according to the paradigm of film historical period? One of the first tasks of the historian is to determine if the body of objects in question conforms to preexistent, standardized historical periods, as that will provide a context and a set of other textual relations to envisage the scope and to shape the contours of the material. Since I have limited my research on omnibus films to the sound era—a periodizing move in itself—I cannot offer evidence as to their prevalence from the 1890s through the 1920s. The consistent clustering of omnibus production that Pierre Leprohon and Peter Bondanella have located squarely in the 1960s at first seems an appropriate periodization; indeed, my interest in omnibus films was initiated precisely by my research into the art cinemas of this period. Of the 747 omnibus films I have identified since 1930, 122 were produced and released in the 1960s, a significant proportion suggesting that their historical time might usefully be confined to that decade. But what about the other five-sixths of world omnibus production that falls outside of this period? A truly global phenomenon, the omnibus film cuts across several of the entrenched periods that currently demarcate the field of film studies. A decade-by-decade breakdown since the coming of sound is revealing: only 8 omnibus films in the 1930s, but 34 in the 1940s, 43 in the 1950s, 122 in the 1960s, 47 in the 1970s, 84 in the 1980s, 178 in the 1990s, and 231 in 2000–07. After a first spike in the 1960s then, omnibus film production reemerged in the 1990s as an increasingly prevalent audiovisual form. The time for this film is now, as well as the 1960s.

Historical periodization stems from a suprahistorical metaphysics whose deployment is based on a tautological search for origins and a teleology of events. So, at least, argues Michel Foucault, whose theorizations of *genealogy* and *archaeology* challenge periodization on a number of fronts, most importantly by deemphasizing the "solemnities of the origin" as a privileged site of truth and by considering change and transformation as motivated discursive constructions rather than as immanent historical effects.[72] A genealogical approach to the history of the omnibus film would not take the current periods of film history as basic units into which chunks of omnibus films may be slotted. Nor would it simply construct new periods to chart the birth, maturation, and decline of the form as a "complete" history of the omnibus film might. Rather, it would demonstrate how historical periods are themselves the result of analysis. In this way, genealogy does not construct periodization anew but calls for a redefinition of its historiographic criteria. The omnibus film, resistant as it is to current film periodization, thus provides an interesting and productive site for genealogical analysis—more interesting and productive, I would claim, than as the subject of a history based upon a traditional conception of the historical period.

Such an analysis would need to take into account as well the historiographic paradigm of *nation,* which is so deeply entrenched in academic film studies that to imagine curricular/course construction and historical writing without it is to conjure forth a field of knowledge production that would barely resemble the discipline. As I have already mentioned, film historical writing absorbed from art and literary history several precepts and organizational categories. One of the most powerful of these is nation. Bordwell relates the matter in these terms:

> Many writers conceived of film history along lines parallel to current conceptions of modern painting. Art historians' rubrics—Parisian Cubism, German Expressionism, Soviet Constructivism, and the like—found their counterparts in film historians' outline of cinema as a succession of national movements. National difference played a large role in the Basic Story; so did differences among individual creators. . . . From nation to creator to individual work: by the end of the silent era, this basic art-historical breakdown had become commonplace in synoptic film histories.[73]

As with all of the paradigms I am considering, nation preexisted film history and film studies and was not a product of it. Some of the more noteworthy critical work on nationalism and nationhood has been and is being pursued outside of the field of film studies, and I am indebted to much of it for my understanding of the subject.[74] Most of it explores the imaginary constructedness and mythical nature of "the nation" through either its emergence as an ideology in the wake of the French Enlightenment and the French Revolution, its confluence with the building of colonial empires in the nineteenth century, or its metamorphoses in the latter half of the twentieth century, when transnationalism and globalization in the economic and cultural spheres presented significant challenges to the sovereignty at the root of the concept.

A number of film scholars have also addressed national cinema as a theoretical construct.[75] Most take as axiomatic that any national cinema is defined in relation to Hollywood, which has dominated world film markets since 1919 and operates as a highly successful, transnational, vertically integrated industrial complex. Hollywood interests have historically taken substantial control of the distribution and exhibition arms of other domestic industries, to the degree that American cinema is rarely spoken of as a national cinema at all, so global is its influence and control—and it is for this reason that courses on one or several aspects of Hollywood cinema are not slotted under the rubric "national cinema." Many have pointed as well to the ways in which nationhood is not a *given* but something to be gained, and how film as a national phenomenon is a *project,* be it cultural, economic, governmental, militaristic, or some combination thereof. In its unproblematized form, the paradigm of a national cinema thus tends to mask the complex interplay of discourses involved in its enunciation that give it voice and shape.

The will to totality underpinning the production of macrohistories of world cinema, and the repression of difference necessary to it, finds a corollary in the production of national histories of film. For what is involved in both is, as Andrew Higson puts it, the specification of "a coherence and a unity" and the proclamation of "a unique identity and a stable set of meanings. The process of identification is thus invariably a hegemonising, mythologising process, involving both the production of and assignation of a particular set of meanings, and the attempt to contain, or prevent the potential proliferation of other meanings."[76] In this respect, no cinema is more a national cinema than that of Hollywood. So complete is its hegemony that it wears both its national interests and its economic enterprise on its sleeve: the rhetoric of democracy and populism is built into the formal organization of the American film, and the guarantors of the truth-value of this rhetoric are the high production values of its surface, the "quality" of entertainment it provides, and the global reach of its popularity.

Despite (or rather because of) the illusory qualities almost all commentators ascribe to the concept of nationhood, the academic publishing field has since the 1990s yielded named series of single-volume histories and studies of various national cinemas—and many of the first to emerge, significantly, were European. Cassell Publications, in conjunction with the British Film Institute, published in 1996 a series of companions to national cinemas, including French, Italian, German, and, in one volume, British and Irish.[77] Wallflower Press's "24 frames" series aims to provide "comprehensive overviews of national and regional cinemas from all over the world. Each volume focuses on 24 key feature films or documentaries that serve as entry-points to the appreciation and study of the history, industry, social and political significance, and key directors and stars of every national cinema around the world."[78] While not always bound to one nation—several titles govern regions or link two or more countries in one volume—this series nonetheless maintains a canon of films and filmmakers for discrete national cinemas, especially for France and Italy, which do receive their own dedicated volumes apiece.[79] Cambridge University Press also has a series, "National Film Traditions," which has so far produced titles on British and Italian cinema.[80] But the longest-running series is Routledge's: launched in 1993, its "National Cinema" series generated studies of the cinemas of France, Italy, Australia, the Nordic countries, and Britain in the 1990s, and in the 2000s eight others.[81] The ease with which these texts lend themselves to courses dedicated to distinct national cinemas works against the challenges that some mount to the idea of the national between their covers. Although much of the theoretical work on national cinemas has become increasingly critical of the concept on both epistemological and geopolitical grounds, considering film history in relation to nation, a mainstay of the discipline, shows no sign of disappearing.

In considering the omnibus film in purely national terms, one finds an occasional correspondence. An extremely interesting spurt of omnibus film production can be found in the USSR in the years 1941–42. Here is Jay Leyda's description of how it all started on 22 June 1941:

> On the day of the [German] invasion [of the Soviet Union] film-makers in every studio had held conferences to determine how best they could help their country fight its war. Without any inter-studio conference, two of the Moscow studios and Lenfilm arrived at the same solution—short, sharply pointed films to be made quickly by any crew that could submit a good idea. Within a week eight different films of various short lengths were in production. . . . As the first shock of attack wore away, the film industry

examined its war-baby, found it worthy, and decided to foster it with an extra production care, a working plan, and an editorial committee. The latter was formed in the first week of July, and included Pudovkin, Donskoy, and Alexandrov. Their job was to organize the spontaneous short productions into regular monthly issues, *Fighting Film Albums.* These were open to short films in any form, any style, so long as they made a useful statement about some phase of the war against fascism.[82]

The first *Fighting Film Album* appeared in movie houses on 2 August 1941, followed by another on 11 August and a third near the end of the month.[83] These omnibus collections consisted of several shorts, as few as two and as many as six. Every month for the next year, a fresh *Fighting Film Album* appeared; in November 1941 the Tbilisi Studio released an album made entirely by Georgian filmmakers. In all, fourteen albums were produced and released in as many months.

Part of what makes the *Fighting Film Album* so interesting as an example of national omnibus cinema production is the evident attention Soviet commentators gave to it and its clear design as an expeditious vehicle for propaganda and national mythmaking. Despite being dismissed by some aesthetic historians as "naive and unrealistic," the collective nature and episodic form of the *Fighting Film Album* provoked considerable discussion among Soviet theorists and filmmakers at the time of its making. Sergei Eisenstein may very well have commented that they were "more passionate than well planned,"[84] but he also led discussions at Mosfilm on the values and problems of the omnibus form, "citing the short-story methods of Robert Louis Stevenson and Ambrose Bierce as useful for study. He read a Russian translation of a Bierce Civil War Story, 'The Affair of Coulter's Notch', as a suggestive model for the short story form."[85] Vsevolod Pudovkin published an analysis of the *Album* form in *Kino.* And at a conference at Lenfilm, every director-writer team from that studio submitted a script for album consideration. As well, the *Fighting Film Albums* appeared to be popular with both home front audiences and soldiers at the front.[86] Although there was no need for them after 1942, at which time the Soviet studios could afford to make wartime propaganda features proper, the omnibus film (and its close relation, the episode film) was to continue sporadically through the mid-1950s in the form of the concert film, the prototype for which, *Kinokontsert (Leningrad Music Hall,* 1941), was made at the time of the first albums.

A more recent example of a national initiative involving omnibus film production was undertaken by Norsk Film of Norway. The goal was to produce, every year from 1996 until the turn of the century, one feature-length omnibus film, each comprising five episodes and each the collaborative effort of five different scriptwriters and directors.[87] Both well-established and lesser known writers were brought together with the country's younger generation of directors for the project, which was budgeted at NOK 10.5 million per film. But only two films were completed: *1996: Pust på meg! (1996: Breath)* and *1997: Tørst—Framtidens forbrytelser (1997: Thirst—Crimes of the Future)*.[88] The plan of one film per year, five writers/directors/episodes per film, was not fulfilled. Nevertheless, the Norsk Film omnibus project, like the Soviet *Fighting Film Albums,* does fit comfortably into the concept of national cinema film production.

But what of the other omnibus films in the filmography? The data bears out the conclusion that omnibus films are cultural products difficult to attribute to specific nations or national cultures. The United States has singly produced the most: 158 or one-fifth of the total. Of these, however, 120 are from 1990 to 2007, and the majority of these did not originate on film but are rather repackages of made-for-network or cable-television anthology series or are straight-to-video products; their status as films is thus not clear-cut. As well, the United States has been a coproducing partner (or, in the case of omnibus films created by distributors through the assembling and packaging of short-film product into a feature-length film/video/DVD, a recipient) of 33 omnibus films, increasingly so since the 1990s. Looking again at French and Italian omnibus production in the 1960s: 28 of France's 34 omnibus films and of Italy's 50 are Italo-French coproductions. Eschewing periodization, the ratios are almost identical: out of Italy's 113 omnibus films, 54 are coproductions; and of France's 90, 63 are so. As well, no fewer than 69 other nations have been involved in omnibus film production or distribution, some in isolation but many through transnational cooperation of one form or another. Omnibus films, especially in their French and Italian contexts but also in their American and other manifestations, present a problematic site for a national study of the form because of their geographic breadth on the one hand and their status as coproductions on the other.

In terms of this study of European art cinema, omnibus film production may thus be sampled as a register of the tensions between nation building and international collaboration that have characterized all of Europe's national cinema industries since the mid-1950s, insofar as so many of them were conceived and marketed as transnational cooperative ventures at this moment in film history. For the omnibus film has often served as a vehicle for showcasing the work of new international directors and, by association, the national cinemas they represented. The *Variety* review of *Love at Twenty*'s premiere at Cannes opens with the statement, "Sketch films are still extremely popular here, but this takes an international stride via five young directors contributing episodes on young love from five different countries."[89] Bosley Crowther's *New York Times* review similarly emphasizes the twin discourses of "youth" and "internationalism" that is so explicitly a part of the film's address.[90] The Exhibitor's Showmanship Manual provided by the American distributor of *Love at Twenty,* Joseph E. Levine, displays a range of iconography germane to the present discussion of nation building via international coproduction.

Ad mat excerpt for *Love at Twenty* (1962), from U.S. Exhibitors' Showmanship Manual. Courtesy of George Eastman House.

Consistent across every ad is the silhouette icon of the young heterosexual couple with joined hands in flight, five two-shots of the five couples who are the subjects of the film's episodes, the flags of the five coproducing nations (France, Poland, Italy, West Germany, Japan), the graphic registration of a wave, and the film's tagline: "The many ways of young love ... the intimate secrets of young lovers ... revealingly treated by five outstanding international directors." In this complex sign system, the dual figures of flag and young couple are rendered graphically interchangeable through the image of the wave. At the extreme right of the ad reproduced here, then, Jean-Pierre Léaud and Marie-France Pisier equal François Truffaut's episode *Antoine et Colette* equals the French flag equals the French New Wave. The young, modern adults in and who have made *Love at Twenty* function here to reproduce their nation through love and, more implicitly, duty. But the structure that enables such reproduction is transnational and cooperative rather than national and isolationist.

In a different way, the concept of nation as imagined community can be *literalized* in omnibus films, in that a country sometimes serves as a site of coherence for, paradoxically, differing versions of it: examples include *It's a Big Country* (United States, 1951), *Cuba '58* (1962), *Brasil verdade* (1968), *La France interdite* (1983), *ID Swiss* (1999), *Costo argentino* (2004), and *Bul-taneun Film-ui Yeondae-ki* (*16 Takes on Korean Society*, South Korea, 2006). A fragmented unity comprised of varied, often competing discourses, the omnibus form mirrors the nation as a tenuous construction that presents itself (at home, abroad) as a stable, univocal entity and identity. Among others, Andrew Higson has argued that one of the functions of national cinemas is "to pull together diverse and contradictory discourses, to articulate a contradictory unity, to play a part in the hegemonic process of achieving consensus, and containing difference and contradiction."[91] And Stephen Crofts emphasizes the need to question the concept of the national in non–First World terms, to recognize how regional and diasporic cinema production and practice challenge the univocality of address so necessary to discourses of nationhood.[92] Omnibus films often participate in that challenge through both their trans- and intranational polyvocality. But it is perhaps when it is so clearly an example of nation as *project* that the omnibus film confounds the national historiographic paradigm, for here it renders too visible the fissures that limn the contours of the modern nation-state.

Along with period and nation, the *film movement* pervades contemporary film studies and film historical writing and thinking. David Bordwell and Kristin Thompson define film movements as consisting of:

1. Films that are produced within a particular period and/or nation and that share significant traits of style and form
2. Filmmakers who operate within a common production structure and who share certain assumptions about filmmaking[93]

The paradigms I am examining are not mutually exclusive categories but paradigms in the semiotic sense, that is, a vertical set of units that entertain relations of similarity and contrast and may be combined with other units. In this respect, the amalgam of period, nation, and movement is without question the most powerful paradigmatic relationship to permeate film historical writing. Pam Cook's *The Cinema Book* is representative of an identifiably British approach to introductory film studies texts, an approach less focused on issues of film form and style and more inclusive of the historical, cultural, and theoretical areas of film study.[94] Some of Cook's cinematic categories—technologies, the star system, developments in theory—little resemble those found in most standard American introductory texts. Part of the explanation for this difference lies in the fact that Cook in particular and the British approach in general tends to be more concerned with *cinema* and the American school with *film,* to use a distinction from the French filmology movement popularized by Christian Metz.[95] Whereas American introductory texts lean toward aspects of film form and style (along with their notable practitioners), British ones deal more inclusively with cinematic production, technology, history, and theory.

That said, Cook's book does replicate some of the historiographic paradigms I am examining: genre, authorship, and to the matter at hand, film movements. In the fourth part, "World Cinemas," the following receive sections or subsections: British social realism, China's Fifth and Sixth Generations, Dogme 95, the French *Nouvelle Vague,* German Expressionism and New German cinema, and Italian neorealism. In *Cinema Studies: The Key Concepts,* Susan Hayward cross-lists at the end of her entry on "European cinema" the following key film movements: German Expressionism, Soviet cinema, French poetic realism, Italian neorealism, British Free Cinema, the French New Wave, the British New Wave, and the New German cinema.[96] Cook's and Hayward's texts establish the touchstones for the Western cinematic tradition (excluding Hollywood). And the terrain that is created in the process is an *even* one—smooth and consistent, equal parts periodization, national cinemas, and the film movements.

Is there room here for the omnibus film? Not if one follows the first definition of a movement as films "produced within a particular period and/or nation and that share significant traits of style and form." For omnibus films, by dint or their fragmented mode of production, rarely share stylistic and formal traits, even in a single film. And they most certainly do not fit into a particular period and/or nation. With the proliferation of paradigms on offer, the omnibus film still proves stubborn to compartmentalize without effecting massive exclusions. Interestingly, omnibus productions can significantly appear at the beginning of film movements, as with *Giorni di gloria* (*Days of Glory,* 1945) for Italian neorealism, *Cinco vezes favela* (*Slum Times Five,* 1962) for Brazil's Cinema Nôvo, *Perličky na dně* (*Pearls of the Deep,* 1965) for the Czechoslovak new wave, *Three to Go* (1972) and *Libido* (1973) for the New Australian cinema, and *Guangyin de gushi* (*In Our Times,* 1982) and *Erh-tzu te ta wan ou* (*The Sandwich Man,* 1983) for the Taiwanese New Wave. But all that can be learned from this is that the omnibus film is amenable to film movements in general but to no one movement in particular.

Closely related to the notion of film movements are styles, modes of film practice, and modes of film production. There is a high degree of slippage among these terms. Bordwell and Thompson define style, for example, as the "repeated and salient uses of film techniques characteristic of a single film or a group of films (for example, a filmmaker's work or a national movement)."[97] In their preface to *The Classical Hollywood Cinema,* Bordwell, Staiger, and Thompson state that a mode of film practice "is not reducible to an *oeuvre* . . . a genre . . . or an economic category. . . . It is an altogether different category, cutting across careers, genres, and studios. It is, most simply, a context. . . . The Hollywood mode of film practice constitutes an integral system, including persons and groups but also rules, films, machinery, documents, institutions, work processes, and theoretical concepts."[98] Elsewhere in the volume, Staiger defines mode of film production as a dynamic relationship involving "1) the labor force, 2) the means of production, and 3) the financing of production."[99]

But in what ways do all of these terms differ, and what is their relation to the idea of film movements? In terms of conceptual breadth, mode of film practice appears to cover the most ground, followed by mode of film production, movement, and lastly style. Yet the matter is complicated by Bordwell, Staiger, and Thompson's master discourse, the classical Hollywood cinema. It is variously a style, a mode of film practice, and a mode of production, as is, say, New German cinema. But whereas New German cinema is also considered a movement, the classical Hollywood cinema is not. Movement thus seems to carry with it limits—of period, of nation—though perhaps also benefits, insofar as movement implies "artistic," the implication being that Hollywood is not. Ultimately, style, mode of film practice, and mode of film production emerge as virtually interchangeable terms that are applicable to all world cinemas. Movement, however, is used for all cinemas except for that of Hollywood.

Rather than taking Hollywood cinema as the dominant mode of production and all others as alternatives, one might instead establish a range of styles, of movements, modes of film practice, what have you. Robert C. Allen and Douglas Gomery, for example, define mode of production as "the overall structure of production organization of a film: the reasons for the making of the film, division of production tasks, technology employed, and [sic] delegation of responsibility and control, and criteria for evaluating the finished film."[100] For Allen and Gomery there are three basic modes of production: individual, especially in avant-garde and experimental filmmaking; collective, as in Argentina's Cine Liberación; and studio, that is, Hollywood (although some, like Jean-Luc Godard, consider all studio systems as part and parcel of the same thing: the "Hollywood-Cinecittà-Mosfilm-Pinewood etc. empire").[101] Is there space *here* for omnibus production?

Although the combined paradigms of period, nation, and movement cannot contain the omnibus film, an adjustment of thinking presents possibilities. It is somewhere in between the collective and the studio modes of production that a whole slew of omnibus production practices may be historically represented. This is, in fact, the space demarcated by Bordwell and Thompson's second definition for film movements: "filmmakers who operate within a common production

structure and who share certain assumptions about filmmaking."
Schools, workshops, units, and generations all have been deployed to
refer to groups of filmmakers working at the same time historically,
in the same place geographically, and with similar methods and goals:
thus, the Brighton school (1900–04); the Kuleshov Workshop (1920–
25); the Empire Marketing Board (1930–33) and General Post Office
(1934–40) units associated with the John Grierson school of documentary; the Polish school at Łódź (1956–63); the National Film Board
of Canada's B (1953–62) and French units (1956–65); the Left Bank
group (1959–) of the French New Wave; the "Prague Group" (1976–
86) of young Yugoslavian filmmakers; China's Fifth Generation, grad-
uates of the Beijing Film Academy (1983–1989), et cetera. Such collective modes of film production and practice appear internationally
throughout the history of cinema. And it is this feature that most generally links them to omnibus film production.

But the omnibus film still falls between the cracks here. Denied the
status of a film movement because of its assumed basis in a European
studio (commercial) mode of production rather than a recognizable
stylistic (artistic) tradition, the omnibus film nevertheless demonstrates
throughout its history a strong connection to collective, often militant
film practice. Pockets of leftist, feminist, and other types of political
collective filmmaking have appeared all over the world throughout
the history of the cinema, and, as I have already suggested in my discussion of the *Fighting Film Albums,* the omnibus form has proven
amenable to the needs of political propaganda or dissent. While the
omnibus projects of the more famous collectives such as France's
Ciné-Liberté *(La Vie est à nous)* and SLON *(Far from Vietnam)* are duly
recognized, the vitality of omnibus production in the collective/mil-
itant mode is striking. Neither a period nor a nation nor a movement,
then, but a collective mode that may be traced through all three is a
direction that might usefully be pursued to render the omnibus film
historically, a route (among others) that I will be mapping in the final
section of this chapter.

Of all the paradigms I am considering, *genre* constitutes the most
deconstructed of the commonly employed methods of identifying
and grouping films—and not simply by academics, archivists, or buffs,
but also by the public and the cinema industries at large.[102] As Edward
Buscombe has noted, genre criticism in literary studies may be traced

to Aristotle, who in his *Poetics* tried to subdivide poetry into various subcategories: tragedy, epic, lyric, et cetera.[103] The introduction of genre into Western film criticism is, of course, more recent. Christine Gledhill has traced the shifts in genre criticism from its initial focus on the western and the gangster film through the theoretical elaborations of Colin McArthur and Tom Ryall in the 1970s to its redirections by Stephen Neale in the 1980s.[104] Germane to the present discussion is the evident theoretical attention granted to genre in light of widespread recognition of its epistemological invalidity as a concept. The reasons for this attention are complex, but one stemmed from the dissatisfaction on the part of many film scholars, critics, and theorists in Britain and in America in the late 1960s through the mid-1970s with the elitism of a film canon based on the legitimizing rhetoric of cinema as Art. While the intent behind genre reassessment was largely to democratize the canon and the emerging field of film studies, the most important effect for this discussion was a discrediting of art cinema and a reappropriation for critical evaluation of a whole range of popular Hollywood films.[105] Film genre study was, and for the most part still is, synonymous with Hollywood cinema.

Peter Brunette and David Wills have noted "that from a deconstructive point of view the concept of genre is, strictly speaking, untenable, relying as it does on exclusions and valorizations that are logically indefensible."[106] Andrew Tudor was one of the first to deconstruct genre, and he did so in clear terms:

> To take a genre such as a western, analyze it, and list its principal characteristics is to beg the question that we must first isolate the body of films that are westerns. But they can only be isolated on the basis of the "principal characteristics," which can only be discovered from the films themselves after they have been isolated. That is, we are caught in a circle that first requires that the films be isolated, for which purposes a criterion is necessary, but the criterion is, in turn, meant to emerge from the empirically established common characteristics of the films.[107]

The democratizing power of genre must seriously be questioned in light of this conundrum, as its study relies from the start on a specific body of films (a generic canon) that is considered (by whom?) most representative of the totality of the genre in question. The earliest studies of American film genres by André Bazin and Robert Warshow were focused on the western and the gangster film, and they laid stress on shared iconography as a determinant for establishing the boundaries and limits of a film genre.[108] These limits are not only spatial but also temporal. Both cause epistemological problems for genre study. In spatial terms, no film can be deemed generically pure, which is not surprising considering cinema's heritage as derivative of other forms of entertainment. Films constantly refer to themselves and to other films as cross-media generic formations.[109] A clear generic definition cannot immediately be imposed on any film, even if the genre to which it purportedly belongs has been defined by a set of codes and conventions. The establishment of certain "core" genres is thus a holding operation, an attempt to fix in visual or narrative terms filmic categories that can never completely contain even one film, let alone the thousands that derive their meaning from generic conventions.

In temporal terms, genres are never static; they change over time, they can disappear or reappear in different guises. Generic conventions, as much as genres themselves, develop and transform through hybridization but more importantly through technological, economic, and ideological change and contradiction. Genres are thus paradoxically placed as simultaneously conservative and innovative, insofar as they respond to expectations and change that are both specific to the entertainment industry and general to culture and politics in the lived world. Bazin and Warshow were aware of this, and they attempted to account for generic change through an evolutionary, teleological model of aesthetic history—the tracing of a given genre from precursors to birth to maturity to decline and decadence. While that model is rarely deployed in genre study today, the drive to contain the aporias of filmic meaning through generic codification, to find a stable place in which to put any type of film on a temporal continuum, remains.

Elsewhere I have posited a taxonomy for the different kinds of collective and/or episodic films, of which the omnibus film is one, to demonstrate how all participate in elements of the others.[110] Episode, omnibus, anthology, compilation, collective, collection: while it is possible to define these as different types or categories, each with its attendant subtypes and subcategories, the relations between them are ultimately more important than their differences. None is "pure" in either conception or product. The same is true of the omnibus film itself, which in its episodic, multicrew, international (co)production is invariably a generic hybrid.

Some omnibus films do fit, and at first glance quite cleanly, into some of the form and genre categories as defined by the most comprehensive list of such terms: *The Moving Image Genre-Form Guide (MIGFG)*, developed by the Motion Picture/Broadcasting/Recorded Sound Division of the Library of Congress.[111] Disney is responsible for a number of cell-animated omnibus films in the 1940s, of which *Fantasia* is the most famous. Other animated subforms, such as Japanese anime (*Manie-Manie Meikyu monogatari* [*Neo-Tokyo*, 1987], *Memories* [1995], and *Genius Party* [2006]) as well as the puppet film (*Fimfárum Jana Wericha* [2002] and *Fimfárum 2* [2006]), are appearing more recently as omnibus films. Certain genres have received considerable omnibus attention too. Chinese, Soviet, Italian, and U.S. omnibus concert films have documented opera, classical, and rock music performances. The horror omnibus has been a popular anglophone film type ever since *Dead of Night,* but there are also manifold examples from other countries, including Poland (*Świat grozy* [*World of Horror,* 1968]), Spain (*Pastel de sangre* [*Cake of Blood,* 1971]), France (*Adrenaline* [1990]), Hong Kong (*Min ching ching yau paai geng* [*Faces of Horror,* 1998], and India (*Darna Zaroori Hai* [*Fear Is Compulsory,* 2006], as well as several American straight-to-video titles since the 1990s and Japanese straight-to-DVD ones in the 2000s. The themes of love and sex are ubiquitous across the corpus of omnibus films I have listed in the appendix. The ones that qualify as melodrama, erotica, and social comedy—many of which are also understood as art films—are too numerous to mention.

High and low genres, popular and specialized forms, radical-political documentaries and commercial entertainments are equally as likely to find representation in a consideration of the compass of omnibus films. Choosing one as typical of the generic diversity of omnibus production would on the one hand misrepresent these films and on the other misrecognize how genre functions in film culture and film studies. This particular critique is in fact implicit in the formulations of the 1960s Italian omnibus/episode film as offered by Pierre Leprohon and Peter Bondanella, for both suggest the multifoliate interconnections among episodic film production. The postneorealist problem film, the sexy documentary, the secret report, the mondo film, erotica, porn: omnibus films are situated among and across all, and these are just the labels Leprohon and Bondanella use. Taking the Library of Congress's *MIGFG* as a guide, the omnibus film finds its way into the following: Adaptation, Ancient world, Biographical, Comedy, Dance, Dark comedy, Erotic, Ethnic, Ethnic (Nonfiction), Experimental [within which: Activist, City symphony, Feminist, Gay/ lesbian, Intermittent animation, Reflexive], Exploitation, Fantasy, Game, Historical, Horror, Jungle, Magazine, Melodrama, Military, Music, Music video, Musical, Mystery, Opera, Political, Prehistoric, Propaganda, Romance, Science fiction, Show business, Sponsored, Sports (Nonfiction), Thriller, Travelogue, Trick, Variety, Women, Youth. Omnibus films conform to no one and often to several genres and forms. In fact, it is more often the case that there are shifts in genre across the episodes of a single omnibus film than that the film will be generically stable—and in so doing it crystallizes the more covert practices of generic mixing that Rick Altman submits as a standard production strategy in mainstream entertainment cinemas like that of classical Hollywood.[112] In this way, the hybridized character of omnibus and other episodic films draws attention to the overlaps and paradoxes of film categorization itself, at the same time as it presents a limit case for the tenets of film genre study.

Before genre, however, the paradigm of film *authorship* in a particular form, auteurism, played a foundational role in establishing the medium as an art and thereby legitimating it as an object of formal and intellectual inquiry. Its basic premise, which is now so much a part of our shared film culture, is that the personal vision, the worldview of certain great directors (or auteurs), is discernible in the particular styles of the films they have made and may be traced across all of their films. Auteurism is thus both a method of organization and an evaluative tool. Initially conceived in the pages of the passionate and polemical Parisian film journal *Cahiers du cinéma* in the mid-1950s, the *politique des auteurs* migrated quickly to Britain and then America, where its chief proponent, Andrew Sarris, rebranding it the auteur theory, deployed it as a means to elevate Hollywood cinema above all others and to establish a hierarchy of American directors, from the pantheon to the also-rans, with only occasional European art films and directors worthy of mention.[113] In Sarris's words: "Film for film, director for director, the American cinema has been consistently superior to that of the rest of the world from 1915 through 1962."[114] That statement is from his influential "Notes on the Auteur Theory in 1962," the penultimate paragraph of which is the following:

Two recent omnibus films—*Boccaccio 70 [sic]* and *The Seven Capital Sins*—
unwittingly reinforced the *auteur* theory by confirming the relative standing of the many directors involved. If I had not seen either film I would
have anticipated that the order of merit in *Boccaccio 70* would be Visconti,
Fellini and De Sica and in *The Seven Capital Sins* Godard, Chabrol, Demy,
Vadim, De Broca, Molinaro. (Dhomme, Ionesco's stage director and an
unknown quantity in advance, turned out to be the worst of the lot.)
There might be some argument about the relative badness of De Broca
and Molinaro, but otherwise the directors ran true to form by almost any
objective criterion of value. However, the main point here is that even in
these frothy, ultracommercial servings of entertainment, the contribution of
each director had less in common stylistically with the work of other
directors on the project than with his own previous work.[115]

By the end of the 1960s, Sarris had little changed his mind about such
matters. "*Spirits of the Dead,*" begins his review of another omnibus
film, "is so much more a producer's package than a director's dream
that the individual ingredients deserve more attention than the total
concoction."[116]

Film authorship as a concept was attacked in the 1970s, particularly in Britain, by leftist film theorists and scholars as romantic and
conservative, and the publication in the 1980s of John Caughie's *Theories of Authorship* and the first edition of Pam Cook's *The Cinema
Book* are indicators of how British film studies looked upon its own
history in relation to film culture. Both consider that relation less in
dialogic than progressive terms, with film culture paving the way for
film studies, which then sped away on its theoretical petrol and left
behind film culture, with its compromised, out-of-date ideas, in the
dust. Caughie declared that the "intervention of semiotics and psychoanalysis into the field has tended to shatter the unity of the author,"
and Cook stated that "the transformation of traditional *auteur* analysis of films since 1968 makes it difficult to take seriously now."[117]
The establishment of a theoretical discourse in Britain at the turn of
the 1960s was understood by the intellectuals circulating around the
journal *Screen* as a definitive break from and an advance over the film
cultural discourses of *Sight and Sound,* which represented an "official film culture and a definite if unexamined critical line" on the
one hand, and of *Movie,* enamored as it was with *Cahiers*-derived
mise-en-scène analysis of largely American directors of the 1950s,
on the other.[118] Auteurism was by the 1980s no longer an issue for a

theoretically inflected film studies led by the British to concern itself much about.

It was, however, an issue that some American film academics would concern themselves with soon enough. In *Making Meaning,* published in 1989, David Bordwell argued convincingly that "the institutional context of academic film studies has been the result of explicatory, chiefly auteur-centered criticism" and that auteurism has lingered, in both disguised and undisguised forms, in later developments such as symptomatic interpretation.[119] Bordwell's analysis signaled how reports of auteurism's death were greatly exaggerated. A special issue of *CineAction!* in 1990 on authorship contained a battery of pieces arguing for its renewed validity as an approach, as did another article of that year by James Naremore.[120] Soon publications on film authorship and the "new auteurism" were flooding the field, its revival cemented in the 2000s with two academic collections dedicated to new or revisited authorship approaches—one of which, the director as brand name and marketing tool, was sounded by Cook at the height of its lowest ebb.[121] In this regard, auteurism is as strong again in Anglo-American film studies as ever. But that strength was always explicitly present throughout the lifespan of academic film studies, as it continues to be now, in the arena of museums, festivals, cinematheques, and repertory cinemas. For these film cultural organs have insistently organized and marketed since the zenith of European art cinema in the 1960s touring series in North America and Europe under and on the names of directors—the most prestigious of which are complete retrospectives, with European art film auteurs topping the list of most desirable subjects. Film authorship thus functions, both inside and outside academic film studies (and the spaces in between), as a crucial paradigm of organization and coherence.

Within this context omnibus films are viewed, as they were decades ago by Sarris, as less than the sum of their parts, a degraded form worthy only of passing attention when an auteur or two is in the mix. Indeed, in the case of the ongoing museum/archive career retrospectives mentioned above, when a featured director has contributed to omnibus films these episodes are either absent or extracted from the omnibus films of their original release and then programmed as shorts preceding other features by the director, or repackaged as short film programs—only occasionally is an entire omnibus film itself shown.[122]

But even passing attention is still attention, and the omnibus film bears the trace of auteurist study through its almost antithetical relation to it. For a staggering number of established auteurs from almost every country of the globe have participated in at least one omnibus project, and art film directors are particularly prominent in the rosters. My research on omnibus films was piqued by my interest in European art cinema, and the core of my omnibus filmography was formed through a typical auteurist activity: the desire to know about, and preferably see, the entirety of a director's oeuvre. And in pursuing the work of the more notable European directors in the field in the 1960s–70s, the contemporary scholar seeking totality on this count would need to ferret out and watch a daunting quantity of omnibus films, one each for:

Ingmar Bergman	Jacques Rivette
Věra Chytilová	Eric Rohmer
Jacques Demy	Jerzy Skolimowski
Rainer Werner Fassbinder	István Szabó
Milos Forman	Andrei Tarkovsky
Louis Malle	François Truffaut
Alain Resnais	

two for:

Theo Angelopoulos	Chris Marker
Marco Bellochio	Ermanno Olmi
Werner Herzog	Roman Polanski
Miklós Jancsó	Nicolas Roeg
Krzysztof Kieslowski	Jan Troell
Alexander Kluge	Agnès Varda
Dušan Makavejev	Krzysztof Zanussi

three:

Costa-Gavras	Jiří Menzel
Vittorio De Sica	Jean Rouch
Federico Fellini	Bertrand Tavernier
Marco Ferreri	Andrzej Wajda

four:

Chantal Akerman	Claude Chabrol
Michelangelo Antonioni	Volker Schlöndorff
Bernardo Bertolucci	

five:

Claude Lelouch	Luchino Visconti
Pier Paolo Pasolini	Wim Wenders
Roberto Rossellini	

six:

    Gillo Pontecorvo

seven:

    Dino Risi   Ettore Scola

twelve:

    Jean-Luc Godard

Ever the exception, Godard's proto-postmodernist cachet and his marketability in the age of cinephilia, equally as much as his prolific-ity, make him king of the omnibuses: seven titles in the 1960s alone. By the time of *Le Plus vieux métier du monde (The Oldest Profession)*, a French–West German–Italian omnibus from 1967, his placement in the directorial lineup and in the order of the episodes bespeaks the degree to which art cinema and its auteurs were embedded in the very discourses—of commerce, of stardom, of hype—that auteurism and art cinema, with their metaphysics and their humanism and their radical formalism (and, in selective cases, their politics) were positioned to resist. *The Oldest Profession* is a typical French/Italian omnibus from the late 1960s: six episodes, six variations on a theme, each directed by a relatively successful but otherwise unremarkable Continental film-maker—save one. The rules of coherence for *The Oldest Profession* are obvious and chronological: prostitution through the ages, from the prehistoric era to the Roman Empire to the French Revolution to the belle epoque to Paris today. In color and dubbed into English for its North American and British releases, this is the kind of commer-cially conceived product maligned by European art film historians: a sex comedy that promises more than it delivers, and in episodes no less. Each historical period is preceded by a title card announcing the name of the episode writ large and of the director responsible for it writ small (except for the first, "The Prehistoric Era," the director for which remains nameless). And then, after the viewer has proceeded through the history of prostitution up to its present incarnations, a drum roll and a soberly scrolling announcement in white text on black background informs the viewer that "the distinguished director Jean-Luc Godard will now show how the oldest profession will con-tinue in the space age, with his sketch . . . *Anticipation*"—the title of which refers not only to its temporality in the history of the film's unifying theme but also to the reason that cinephiles would seek out this film and suffer through the murkiness of the previous episodes' lesser lights in order to be illuminated by the final segment. But herein lies the twist: instead of triumphantly effecting the auteur's assumption over mediocrity, *The Oldest Profession* in fact enables a leveling of high and low taste cultures through its unabashed marketing to two divergent audiences: those who were indeed anticipating Godard's contribution, and those who could not have cared less.

In the grand scheme of things, directorial brands like Godard's are responsible for a very small number of episodes in the omnibus aggregate. The majority of these films, directed as they are by assemblages of no-names, remain obscure and of little interest to film history's entrenched auteurism. Mauro Bolognini has participated in nearly as many omnibus projects as has Godard, with ten in total and one more than Godard during the 1960s. Indeed, Bolognini directed one of the episodes of *The Oldest Profession*. Despite this proximity, the chances of a European film historian being able to name even one Bolognini omnibus contribution are slim. The reasons for this extend beyond the immediate issue of auteurism as a system of judgment, evaluation, and exclusion, which has deemed Bolognini unimportant and uninteresting. Rather, auteurism precludes filmmakers of Bolognini's ilk and the films they have made from being considered *because* they are in such proximity to auteurs in omnibus films. It is not simply that their work pales in comparison to that of the masters among whom they are situated in omnibus films. More to the point, it is this very placement that prevents their work from quite literally being *seen* at all, as all attention is focused on the one or two sections of the film that matter, the one or two directed by auteurs. Within the discourse of authorship and the figure of the auteur, the omnibus film does not open new routes of inquiry but instead leads the historian or the scholar down well-trodden paths.

What occurs in an auteurist study when the object involved is an omnibus film is telling in this respect. In all of the considerable work on European art-film directors, the same protocol is followed when an auteur has contributed an episode to an omnibus film: the episode in question is held apart from the rest of the (always unanalyzed, usually unnamed) segments as particular to its author's oeuvre and so incompatible to a grouping of works by others. In the process, the auteur's episode is shown to fit, if not clearly than arguably, into the evolutionary line of development that is a standard teleology of auteurist studies. Means of coherence and, at times, value are found. Thus Maurizio Viano, writing on two episodes by Pier Paolo Pasolini, posits that, although "they were released one and a half years apart within two different compilation films . . . *La terra vista dalla luna* (The Earth Seen from the Moon) and *Che cosa sono le nuvole?* (What Are the Clouds?) ought to be treated in the same chapter. They were shot one after the other, employed the 'picaresque' couple Totò and Ninetto, and most important of all were part of a unitary project in the wake of the theoretical conclusions reached by *Uccellacci uccellini*."[123] Often as well, the vision of the director is pitted against the wallet of the producer, who is blamed for the failure of an auteur's contribution when it has been haphazardly combined with others. Such was the fate of Pasolini's *La rabbia* (First Part, 1963), what Naomi Greene describes as a "deeply personal and poetic short" that was released by its producer "together with a second short film to be made by a director on the other side of the political spectrum, that is, on the right. The man chosen for this segment was Giovanni Guareschi." Prefaced by a disclaimer about "two ideologies, two opposing doctrines," the omnibus film that resulted was nonetheless unacceptable to Pasolini, who withdrew his name from it.[124] The effect this produces within the discourse of authorship is an increase in value for Pasolini's film, which has provided the proper cue for its excision from the offending project by the author's effacement of his own name on it. Indeed, the particularly high value Pasolini scholars ascribe to his episode films is in this case motivated by the director's own actions and comments about the unassimilability of his work with those of others.[125]

On the one hand antithetical to the discourse of auteurism by dint of its multiple authoring, the omnibus film on the other serves as a remarkable site upon which to gauge auteurism's assumptions and operations. Of all of the paradigms I am reading the omnibus film through and against, authorship is the one most visibly rendered by yet doggedly resistant to it. Part of that resistance stems from the form's often unashamed commerciality, which abuts too uncomfortably with the loftier formal ambitions and/or political concerns that are the art film auteur's stock-in-trade. When the director's name is stitched into the very text of the film itself—as in *RoGoPaG*, named after its four contributing directors (*Ro*ssellini, *Go*dard, *Pa*solini, and *G*regoretti)—the line between the director as visionary, in full control of his film and his work, and the director as marquee value is unquestionably crossed. The omnibus film is thus more of a problem for authorship than authorship is for it. In the historiography of European art cinema especially, the boundary between the omnibus film as gap and as symptom of authorship is at once the most insurmountable and the most transparent.

The final paradigm to consider is *the film text,* a particular conception of which is central to the discipline of film studies and the writing of film history. And the frisson the omnibus film generates through its own internal organization is what places it in excess of this paradigm. The ideology of the feature film is one that both film studies and the commercial film industry share: audiences for both, present either at the weekly required screening or at the movie theater (or positioned in front of the television screen), expect at least eighty-five minutes of visual and aural stimulation. Producers of omnibus films know this—in fact, it serves as the justification for the form itself, a combination of short films into a feature-length package. The tension between the short and the feature that is the structuring principle of the omnibus film, then, presents itself as a problem to the orthodoxy of the complete text, the film as a unified entity whose meaning must be read across the entirety of its duration.

What this means, as was the case for auteur study, is that analysis or historical contextualization of an omnibus film *as a film unto itself* is extremely rare in the discipline and in film historical writing. Rather, omnibus films are dissected and discussed in terms of their "relevant" segments only. Such segmentation of episodic omnibus films is understandable according to the logic of a certain auteuristic film studies tradition. Less understandable is the practice of scholars and historians who apply such a methodology to omnibus films with a concertedly collective or collaborative mode of production. Timothy Corrigan introduces his book *New German Film: The Displaced Image* with the following statements:

> The parameters of this study are two collective statements made by West German filmmakers within a period of fifteen years of each other: the celebrated manifesto issued at Oberhausen in February 1962 and the extraordinary *Germany in Autumn,* a film made by multiple teams of directors and technicians in late 1977. . . . They are both *collective* reactions to an established system, and as such they dramatize an important artistic fact specific to cinema: that artistic change and revolution must be collective if it is to be in any degree effective.[126]

Corrigan considers *Germany in Autumn* to be a dialectical materialist film, one that "makes little attempt to identify the individuals responsible for the separate sections; and it thus willfully dislocates perceptual responsibility from standard aesthetic categories or authorial justifications in order that the spectator accept a new part in that perpetual action." If this is the case, why then does Corrigan proceed to segment the film by director and perform close readings of two episodes rather than read the film dialectically? Why single out Rainer Werner Fassbinder's episode as "crucial" to the film's argument and the Volker Schlöndorff/Heinrich Böll section as "exemplary?"[127]

Corrigan is not alone: every commentator I have read on *Germany in Autumn,* despite recognizing that the film is collective and effectively anti-auteurist, nonetheless fixes either on Fassbinder's autobiographical, confessional episode or on Alexander Kluge's guiding hand in editing the other filmmakers' material as key to the film's meaning. On the side of Fassbinder are the nonspecialists (macrohistorians, prestige reviewers like Vincent Canby and Pauline Kael, et cetera) and, most eloquently, Eric Rentschler, who argues that Fassbinder's contribution "provokes the spectator to try to understand the sequence in inter-textual terms . . . not simply as the vision of an *auteur* who has made a large number of films with their stylistic and thematic continuity, but as one part of a larger vision, as one voice in a more encompassing discussion."[128] For Rentschler, the "more encompassing discussion" is not one that includes any other part of the film *Germany in Autumn* but rather the political and cultural discourses of recent German history—his reading of Fassbinder's episode is not, then, intertextual but extratextual. Opting for Kluge are John Sandford, Anton Kaes, and, most intensively, Miriam Hansen, who argues that the film "does not offer a collection of individual episodes and statements" but instead an open structure, with the "sequences most clearly bearing Kluge's signature . . . spread out over the whole film."[129] Hansen, then, does read *Germany in Autumn* as a textual system rather than as a series of discrete episodes, but only because Kluge oversaw the entire film's editing. The identification of a single auteur is still necessary to provide a stable ground from which to articulate textual meaning for a collective omnibus film.[130]

The explicitly left political import that attends much collective omnibus production, distribution, and exhibition doubly renders such

films' textuality suspect in the eyes of those for whom auteurism remains romantic and humanist. Popular reviewers are perhaps the most
resistant to films being used as partisan political tracts, as this jibes
with neither the aesthetic nor the entertainment poles that are for
them (and, ostensibly, their readers) the cinema's true purpose and
domain. The American reviews for *Far from Vietnam,* for example,
were uniformly scathing.[131] All blamed the film's "anti-Americanism"
and its episodic structure equally for its failure. Bosley Crowther
called it "a frantic and formless compilation," *Variety* "tedious," "a
shrieker," "demagogic while cerebral in its accents, preaching to the
converted."[132] Renata Adler felt that the voice-over narration of the
film was banal and ugly but that if it were cut "the result might
be interesting, a kind of rambling partisan newsreel collage."[133] And
Andrew Sarris had nothing but derision for a film text so clearly
proffered as a collective political statement:

> *Far from Vietnam.* Zero as art. Some polite applause for Jean-Luc Godard,
> Alain Resnais, Joris Ivens. They at least tried to make a personal statement.
> But where was Chris Marker's "unifying" editing? . . . The individual artists
> in *Far from Vietnam* obviously surrendered their consciences for the sake of
> a collective statement. Resnais, Godard, and Ivens even surrendered the
> supposedly sacred right of cutting their own footage. It may be argued that
> the cause was worth the sacrifice. The film certainly wasn't.[134]

Writing in *Movie* in 1968, Richard Winkler is the only writer I
have found to treat *Far from Vietnam* as a readable text tout court and
to perform such a reading. Winkler argues that to "discuss the film as
a series of separate and self-contained episodes (like *Rogopag* or *Paris
Vu Par*) is not merely insensitive: it is a violation of the film's essential
structure. In attempting to isolate the individual parts, such a method
necessarily fragments and distorts the true individuality of the parts."[135]
Winkler attempts in his reading to balance the relations between
episodes with validations of the aesthetic worth of each individual
director's contribution. In other words he tries to have it both ways,
to reveal *Far from Vietnam* as both a dialectical textual system and as a
well wrought urn, as a dialectic built through the "contributions of
several very different directors" and as "a coherent, collective whole."
And to shore up the entropy, Winkler does what every other commentator on the film does: he isolates Godard's *Caméra-oeil* episode
as the film's centerpiece, as "a meditation and a demonstration of the

dialectic, of the relationship between the private and the communal, between the self and others."[136] Whatever the particular merits of *Caméra-oeil,* to turn to it as the linchpin of *Far from Vietnam* is to reinforce a cult of personality that undercuts the possibility of producing a revolutionary reading of the film.

Combined with auteurism, the ideology of the text and its institutional practice, close reading, finds a stubborn adversary in the omnibus film. The relation between textual analysis and the film studies curriculum is a homologous one—every week a screening of a feature film to which the assigned readings and ensuing classroom discussion are directed. This is so entrenched a practice that the editors of a collection of course syllabi can write: "The study of film, of course, has as its primary purpose an active involvement of the viewer's mind, viewing skills, imagination, and sensibility in a close 'reading' of the film text. Out of this close viewing and focused attention to the complex details and patterns of the film text comes an understanding of the film's themes, purpose, implications and extensions beyond the film, along with many other perceptions."[137] While singling out an auteur's episode in an omnibus film may allow for a form of textual analysis, at the same time it violates the text as a whole. Close reading requires the illusion of both a single stable text and a creator for that text. Explicitly fragmented in its construction, clearly outside of the total control of any one given director, the omnibus film provides neither.

Although a reception study of omnibus films is beyond the purview of this study, a brief consideration of omnibus spectatorship is still revealing. For the auteurist excising tendencies of academic critics and historians when confronted with the heterogeneous omnibus film does not necessarily conform to the theatrical exhibition and reception of omnibus films by laypersons and film scholars alike. I cannot imagine anyone attending a screening of an omnibus film only to watch the episode by his or her preferred director, waiting for it to start, and walking out once it has finished. On the other hand, many do seem to watch omnibus films with an eye toward judging the episodes against one another—which was the best, which the worst, which the funniest, which the most boring, et cetera. The omnibus form itself thus produces a kind of spectatorship qualitatively different from that of the narrative feature film.

Constituted as it is on the principle of fragmentation, the omnibus film offers itself as an already segmented feature-length text, and this may go some way toward explaining why it is so rarely analyzed or taught. It ruptures the concept of the formal object of study as a stable text in the first place. At the same time a feature-length film and an amalgam of its opposite, the short, the omnibus film frustrates close formal analysis as *a* text. In other words—and this is something I have been arguing throughout this chapter—the omnibus film, in the very problems it engenders when it is read through the paradigms of film studies, exposes as symptom and as trace the operations of the field itself. The omnibus film thus effects the coordinates of a potential remapping of film historical and analytic concerns. In the case of the paradigm of the film text, the omnibus film exists both within and beyond its current boundaries, and as such illuminates the arbitrary drawing of them.

Remapping the Exquisite Corpse

In the third section of the *Oxford History of World Cinema,* "The Modern Cinema 1960–95," is a subheading titled "Extending the Boundaries" that features entries on what moving-image archives call forms—documentary, avant-garde, animation—on modern film music and on art cinema. Most obviously, these are aspects or modes of film practice that "extend the boundaries" of mainstream cinema in some way, that challenge the conventions of Hollywood filmmaking. They also represent important areas whose inclusion is necessary for a survey film history aiming for comprehensiveness and balance. In this sense, this collection is itself "extending the boundaries" of the standard macrohistory text, which tends to focus on narrative, feature-length film production, and the image. But the residency of the new documentary, of avant-garde and animated cinemas, of modern film music, and of art cinema in this section also speaks toward their existence in film history as outside the boundaries separating center from margins, boundaries that must be "extended" to include them. A trade-off for their inclusion is that they follow the rules that have effected their exclusion, that they historicize their forms according to the paradigms I have plotted in this chapter. And they do: all of these pieces are organized around the principles of national cinemas/movements, subgenres, and especially auteurs—Jean Rouch, Chris Marker, John Cassavetes, Andy Warhol, Michelangelo Antonioni, and Ingmar Bergman are the recipients of sidebars (as is one producer, Anatole Dauman).

The traces are there—of European art cinema in terms of the discipline, of the omnibus film in terms of film historical writing and of art cinema, but also of a potential alternative historiography for both. I have throughout this chapter hinted at the directions such a historiography might take, at once inside and outside film history's organizational structures, at the same time as I have tried to effect some play in the space *between* that inside and outside—a double movement of rule and transgression, accretion and separation, mapping and remapping, departure and return. The history of omnibus production encompasses a set of ongoing responses: to political events, to social and cultural trends, to market forces and audiences, to the changing formats enabling the production and consumption of audiovisual media itself. But that history also traces an underside of European art cinema, already present in its great flowering in the 1960s (and extending beyond) in ways that have not yet been fully explored. By way of a conclusion, then, I will propose three routes for remapping these exquisite corpses.

As the Soviet *Fighting Film Albums* of 1941–42 demonstrate, the omnibus film can serve as an effective vehicle for explicitly partisan message making and national consolidation at times of crisis. But omnibus films have equally as often commented upon occurrences and concerns of international import. The Olympic Games has yielded a reasonably well-known omnibus film, *Visions of Eight* (1973), in which some former new wave directors from Czechoslovakia (Milos Forman), France (Claude Lelouch), the United States (Arthur Penn), and Britain (John Schlesinger) presented, along with four others, their vision of an event or aspect of the 1972 Munich Olympic Games.[138] The legacy of those games was the Black September hostage-taking of eleven Israeli athletes, which led to the killing of two in the Olympic village and the deaths of the other nine during a failed airport rescue; none of the filmmakers chose this drama as a suitable subject upon which to film an essay on the 1972 Olympics, and the exclusion is instructive. For by an inverse operation, *Visions of Eight* is as much a piece of propaganda as any of the *Fighting Film Albums*. As I have argued in previous chapters, the postwar art cinemas of France and Italy can and should be productively read in terms of the broader geopolitical shifts that Europe was undergoing in this period and in which these cinemas were embedded—transnational integration, war, terrorism, decolonization—in ways that have barely been touched on in their cumulative study. Matters of aesthetics and style, then, are inextricable from the sociopolitical contexts that ground and shape them.

Considering these together is not necessarily to locate the geopolitical as a wholly submerged presence, however, as a passive symptom to be prized out of the art-film text through the active force of analysis. Rather, art cinema should be seen as a complex series of responses to, and at times a contestation of, the industrial, economic, cultural, and historical forces of its times and places. And these responses and contestations are clearly visible in the collective modes of politicized film practice in which recognized European art filmmakers of the 1960s and after have participated. *Far from Vietnam, Germany in Autumn,* and *Krieg und Frieden* (*War and Peace,* 1982) are the most well known of the omnibus films of this sort, but there are many others. A DEFA Studios production, *Die Windrose* (*The Wind Rose,* 1957), was commissioned by the International Democratic Women's Federation and made under the supervision of the internationalist filmmakers Alberto Cavalcanti and Joris Ivens. Each episode tells he story of a woman and her role in a different society—Brazil, the Soviet Union, France, Italy, China—and each was directed by a leftist imagemaker of note from each country.[139] Art film directors also participated in *Der Augenblick des Friedens* (*The Moment of Peace,* 1965), a West German–French–Polish cooperative production of episodes that reflected the "moment of peace" in these countries at the end of World War II. The German women's film movement *Frauenfilm,* whose members included most famously Helke Sander, Helma Sanders-Brahms, and Magarethe von Trotta, pursued in the 1980s collective work in films such as *Aus heiterem Himmel* (*Out of the Clear Blue Sky,* 1982), which comprised nine episodes detailing women's reactions to the threat of nuclear war as well as the official and radical power structures in Germany. *Die Erbtöchter* (*The Daughters' Inheritance,* 1983) pursued the theme of chauvinism and repression, drawing connections between patrilineal culture in general and European film culture in particular. *Sieben Frauen—Sieben Sünden* (*Seven Women—Seven Sins,* 1987) and the German-American coproduction *Erotique*

(1993) took up the issues of female desire by refracting the generic conventions of comedy and erotica through the lens of critical work on voyeurism, spectatorship, and visual pleasure.[140]

As I have earlier shown, film history tends to separate art cinema from countercinema, leftist and feminist, via the historical marker of 1968. I am considering them here as overlapping aesthetic, political, and temporal discourses and modes of address in omnibus films not only because art cinema directors often appear in their ranks but also because I recognize political engagement, whether or not it takes the form of outright activism, as a continuing tendency in both art and omnibus film production. Without naming names, European art film practitioners have since the 1990s been active participants in omnibus films that have conferred to celluloid memory thirty individual cases of human rights abuses chronicled by Amnesty International (*Contre l'oubli* [*Against Oblivion,* 1991]), responded on a global scale to the impact of a definitive event of the twenty-first century (*11'09"01 —September 11* [2002]), and portrayed the aspirations of those living within the orbit of the European Union (*Visions of Europe* [2004]). Film history also tends to distinguish art cinema from both the avant-garde proper and documentary, despite their shared exploration and interrogation of film form and realism (as well as, in the case of documentary, the fact that so many art films auteurs made and continue to make them). But the striking proximities—of mode of production, deliberate formal and stylistic inconsistency, critical intent—of the omnibus films noted previously embeds art cinema in a range of aesthetic practices not recognized as such when it is historicized and studied under the paradigms I have plotted in this chapter. The omnibus film allows for a remapping of art cinema in terms of collaborative, international film practices beyond the immediacies of European integration and decolonization in the 1960s.

A genealogy of the omnibus film in relation to political commentary, dissent, or activism, however, must consider the panoply of works that do not perforce contain auteurs within their cohort on subjects that include political revolution (*Osvobozhdennym Kitaj* [*Liberated China,* USSR/China, 1950] and *Histoires de la révolution* [*Stories of the Revolution,* Algeria, 1969]); human rights (the five *If You Were Me* films [2003–07)] made under the auspices of the South Korean National Human Rights Commission); HIV and AIDS (*3,000 scénarios contre un virus* [*3,000 Scenarios to Combat a Virus,* France, 1994] and *AIDS JaaGO,* India/United States, 2007]); immigration and xenophobia (*Filmart Takes Position: ALIEN/NATION* [Austria, 1997] and *Pas d'histoires! 12 regards sur le racisme au quotidien* [France, 2001]); and terrorism (*Underground Zero: Programs 1 & 2* [United States, 2002] and *Madrid 11M: Todos ibamos en ese tren* [*Madrid M11: We Were All on That Train,* Spain 2004]). The omnibus form thus presents itself, in these and other films produced since the 1960s, as a particularly amenable and effective means toward collective commentary on and response to the national, intranational, and global political events and issues of their times. The role that art cinema has played in this regard, both inside and outside of omnibus production, remains to be explored.

Several omnibus films invoke the name and stories of a national literary figure as their organizing principle. Not only do filmed adaptations of a well-known novelist's or playwright's works seem a perfectly natural route for what is sometimes referred to as the novella film to take, they also serve both to pre-sell the film to audiences familiar with the literary sources and potentially to elevate it into the canon of respectability that the writer's fame authorizes. In many instances the literary figure and the omnibus film share a national patrimony: W. Somerset Maugham for Great Britain; O. Henry and Kurt Vonnegut for the United States; Ahsan Abdel-Qadas for Egypt; Anton Chekhov for Russia; Bohumil Hrabal and Josef Škvorecký for Czechoslovakia; Jorge Luis Borges for Argentina; Knut Hamsun for Norway; Natsume Soseki for Japan.[141] But there are some interesting slippages as well. In a few cases, the writer was not part of the literary establishment proper but published in the popular genres of fantasy, horror, science fiction, or crime, such as Rod Serling (*Night Gallery* [1969]), H. P. Lovecraft (*Necronomicon* [1993]), and Edogawa Rampo (*Ranpo jigoku* [*Rampo Noir,* 2005]). And in the cases of Edgar Allan Poe, Comte de Lautréamont, Paul Bowles, and Raymond Queneau, the author's work travels to another country for adaptation.[142]

The overlap here for art cinema in the 1960s is *Spirits of the Dead,* a Franco-Italian production based on Poe stories and the only example of a literary adaptation omnibus undertaken by directors associated with the French New Wave and the new Italian cinema. On the one hand, its singularity suggests the degree to which these particular auteurs, as well as their compatriots, had already achieved the standing of authors in their own right by 1968, the year of the film's release, and hence had no need for a recognized literary figure to confer upon them this status by association. On the other hand, the fact that the literary sources derive from horror fiction creates a frisson regarding the place this film might occupy in the canon of postwar European art cinema—Peter Bondanella rates only the Federico Fellini episode, and Andrew Sarris dismissed it as "so much more a producer's package than a director's dream." As such, *Spirits of the Dead* points to the broader issue of not only the blatantly commercial orientation of much omnibus film production but also the relationship of art cinema to commerce itself, particularly how it often wends its way between high and low culture.

Apart from the collective political statements *Far from Vietnam* and *Germany in Autumn,* the omnibus films noted in the historical writing and scholarship on postwar European cinema almost invariably take this route: *Love at Twenty, Boccaccio '70, RoGoPaG, Paris vu par, Spirits of the Dead.* The only exception here is *Paris vu par,* considered by historians to be not an opening salvo of the French New Wave but its fitting epitaph.[143] And in this sense *Paris vu par* points toward a certain nostalgia for the early 1960s that has characterized an aesthetic line of omnibus film production pursued by art film auteurs of that and later generations since:[144] a literal return to this text in *Paris vu par . . . 20 ans après (Paris Seen By . . . 20 Years Later,* 1984), *Les Français vu par . . .* (1984), and *Paris, je t'aime (I Love Paris,* 2006); a virtual revisiting of film history via its pioneers in *Lumière et compagnie (Lumière and Company)* and *À propos de Nice, la suite* (both 1995, the centenary of cinema). Indeed, the theme of grace in the light of time passing is present in the titles of two recent international auteur-festooned omnibus films, *Ten Minutes Older: The Cello* and *Ten Minutes Older: The Trumpet* (both 2002).

But the more conspicuous course is the one that characterizes the bulk of Italo-French omnibus production during its spike in the 1960s at the same time as it threads its way through the form internationally in the 1970s and 1980s—and from the 1990s has flown flight paths to even farther-flung destinations: erotica, sex, pornography. I have already hinted at how the unabashed commercialism of much omnibus production places in doubt the aesthetic distinction upon which art cinema discourse rests vis-à-vis generic hybridity, stylistic collision, and authorial control. Pierre Leprohon sought to shore up this doubt at an early stage:

> Eroticism is a dominant feature of the modern cinema. But in the episode
> film it ceases to be an ornament or consequence of the plot and becomes
> the sole purpose of the film, and that is doubtless where the problem lies.
> Antonioni and Fellini, and many others, have included in their works
> scenes of greater eroticism than the laborious exhibitionism and smut with
> which some directors waste their time and talents. But what in one case is
> justifiable as being part of a general theme, in another is merely a way of
> making money.[145]

In retrospect, the game was already over when Leprohon wrote this in 1966. The sheer volume of mondo, sexy documentary and love/sex/erotica-inflected omnibus titles, too numerous to mention, is only one indication. A second is the distribution of European art cinema in North America from the 1950s on, which I have argued elsewhere was pitched as an "adult" cinema and marketed throughout the 1960s along similar lines to those of the concurrent independent American exploitation and underground cinemas.[146] And a third is the degree to which the directors Leprohon cites were already or would soon enough be participating in the market lure of sexual display and activity in which art films were then circulating and from which he is at pains to distinguish them.[147] For Fellini had certainly crossed this boundary of taste in his episode for *Boccaccio '70,* and would carry on doing so from *Fellini Satyricon* (1969) through *La città delle donna* (*City of Women,* 1980). Antonioni's *Blow-Up* (1966) and *Zabriskie Point* (1969) marked his entry onto a terrain that has continued to provide even ground for both art cinema and the omnibus film, as his final work—an episode in the indicatively titled *Eros* (2004)—attests.

It is in the interstices among the artistic and the commercial, the artisanal and the mass-produced, the niche and the popular, the high and the low that I am positioning a second alternative historiography for both art cinema and the omnibus film. Remapping art cinema among a network of shifting international interchanges—markets, audiences, industry and community standards—may serve to dismantle once and for all the oppositions that have circumscribed understanding of not only its historical importance but also its aesthetics and content. And these exchanges are ones that the omnibus film, particularly in its ubiquitous erotica and horror manifestations since the

1990s, can illuminate. Both may be traced through previous decades, of course, particularly the 1960s. But the surge in omnibus production in the 1990s and 2000s bears even more concerted analysis. The sheer volume of erotica and horror in this period, often in series, reveals both a particular market need and a generic meeting ground that spans taste cultures through explicitly hybrid forms. The German-produced *Erotic Tales* omnibus series (*I–X,* 1994–2003), for example, has received considerable exposure via major film festivals (usually premiering in Berlin) and features among its directors some notable international art/cult/popular names. Art and hard-core pornography merge in *Destricted* (2006), the seven episodes of which (but one) were conceived, mounted, and executed not by art cinema auteurs but visual artists whose work here extends previous site-specific gallery installations utilizing moving-image technologies such as film and video to the movie theater itself.[148]

At the same time, horror film culture has since at least the 1970s been building a counterpantheon of auteurs (most of whom work in Europe) simultaneously specializing in the genre and pursuing "pure cinema" aesthetics uncannily similar to those of modern art cinema.[149] The international popularity of East Asian horror, in both initial release and Hollywood remake, is echoed in several omnibus series, including *Shake, Rattle & Roll* (1984–2006) from the Philippines and at least three from Japan: *Kaidan shin mimibukuro* (*Tales of Terror from Tokyo and All over Japan,* 2004), *J-Horror Anthology* (2005), and *Kadokawa Mystery & Horror Tales* (2005). And the awarding of the Grand Prix du Jury at the 2004 Cannes International Film Festival to *Oldboy,* a South Korean horror thriller, suggests how artistic innovation and achievement in such films is now perfectly recognizable to festivalgoers and film culture tastemakers alike.[150]

These high/low interchanges of art/erotica/horror production, however, only partially explain the outpouring of omnibus films from the 1990s. With the exception of *Shake, Rattle & Roll,* all of the titles cited above were first broadcast as made-for-network or -cable anthology television programs and made the transition to omnibus films via either subsequent theatrical release, video/DVD (re)packaging, or both. The impact of media technologies such as television, video, and DVD are thus crucial factors in the history of the omnibus film, as indeed they are for European art cinema.

The first repackagings of television series into omnibus films for theatrical release can be traced to the early 1960s, when the Italo-French omnibus was hitting full stride. The two that bracket the decade, *The Devil's Messenger* (1961) and *Night Gallery* (1969), were, significantly, American products, as was the first straight-to-video omnibus, *Tales of the Third Dimension* (1984). While the television-to-theatrical-release and straight-to-video strands played minor roles in this and the next decade, the rise of VCR ownership in the mid-1980s and the introduction of DVD in the late 1990s transformed film consumption in ways that enabled the admixture and dissemination of previously distinct media formats, and the omnibus film was a beneficiary of this development. Indeed, of the 409 omnibus films released since 1990—more than half of the 747 in my filmography—73 were straight-to-video/DVD, 16 were television-to-theatrical-release, and 51 were television-to-video/DVD; of the total, 124 or 30 percent were not shown in theaters, and a great deal more would not have been viewed there either but in the domestic space. The United States was the sole producer/distributor for 120 out of the 409 since 1990, or 29 percent of the total; but of these 120, 47 were straight-to-video/DVD, 2 were television-to-theatrical-release, and 40 were television-to-video/DVD, which means that 87 (72 percent) were not shown in theaters. The data reveals three things: that the repackaging of television series into omnibus films accounts for one-sixth of all of the omnibus films since 1990; that one-third of the omnibus films since then exist solely on video/DVD; and that the basis for the U.S. dominance in that time is due overwhelmingly to straight-to-video/DVD and television-to-video/DVD distribution and consumption. In other words, the Italo-French spike of the 1960s remains the most significant clustering of omnibus *film* production.

That said, it would be a mistake to view these varying media platforms in isolation of one another or to pit film versus video/DVD in the history of European art cinema or of the omnibus film. For it is the consideration of formats and venues of audiovisual consumption in concert that I would propose as a third-alternative historiography for these exquisite corpses. I have posited throughout this book that the 1960s constitutes both a high watermark for European art cinema and a privileged site for the remapping of its discourses in Anglo-American film studies. But what happened to art cinema after that, why, and in what forms does it circulate today, literally and conceptually? The answers to these questions are complex, and I certainly do not have all of them. I do know that the answers need to encompass the roles that media technologies have played alongside geopolitical, aesthetic, cultural, industrial, and institutional forces. And the omnibus film bears with it the trace of these answers.

In omnibus films, the separate sections may or may not carry over characters or cast members from segment to segment, and the dramatic presentations may or may not be connected by a framing or linking device, character, or narrative. As well, the episodes need not be ordered in an integral and contiguous fashion—with each episode presented complete in and unto itself, one at a time—although this is usually the case. The conceit of the omnibus *Amazon Women on the Moon* (1987) is an hour and a half of late-night television viewing, complete with commercials, dead airtime, public service announcements, and channel surfing. Each of the segments was the directorial responsibility of one of five people; some segments are in the film "broadcast" in their entirety, others are attenuated or left and returned to, most relentlessly the splicy feature film that keeps breaking down and provides the title for the entire assemblage. Two Italian films have also used the television broadcast as the structuring model for narrative fragmentation. *Signori e signore, buonanotte (Ladies and Gentlemen, Good Night,* 1976) is a five-director omnibus in which an imaginary TV channel broadcasts a series of programs, each of which highlights a particular Italian cultural stereotype. *Ladri di saponette (The Icicle Thief,* 1989), directed by Maurizio Nichetti, implicates Italian neorealist cinema in the commercialized world of contemporary television and advertising by having the characters of the two occupy each other's programs. All three of these films are considered to be satire, and it is interesting to note that in every case television as technology is responsible for aesthetic visual decline and narrative degradation.

But television cannot be held solely to blame for the waning of European art cinema, although it inadvertently played a contributing role. Susan Hayward indicates how the

> decline in co-productions, coming as it did in the mid 1970s, had little to do with deliberate strategy. France's major co-producing partner was Italy. The two countries had a reciprocal arrangement. . . . This marriage of convenience lasted almost thirty years (1948–75) and its ending, or rather

decline, came as the result of a third party's intrusion on the scene. By the mid 1970s both France and Italy, but particularly Italy, were feeling the full impact of a declining audience seduced away from the large screen by its smaller rival, television.[151]

The ebb in coproductions in the 1970s among the European film industries is paralleled by an ebb in omnibus productions at this time: a further relation between the art and omnibus film, which I have placed side-by-side throughout this chapter. But the rise of television in this regard is not an entirely debilitating force for either.[152] On the one hand, it served as a frequent technological medium for several Italian and French auteurs—Roberto Rossellini entirely from the mid-1960s through to the end of his career, and Jean-Luc Godard sporadically from the mid-1970s on, most notably. And in the case of the New German cinema, it is a key enabling factor in its rise and existence, as Thomas Elsaesser notes:

> A niche opened up between current affairs television and experimental filmmaking. It gave, for instance, many women filmmakers their first opportunity, making the German cinema of the 1970s and 1980s a center of the European women's film. . . . Without television as its partner, the New German Cinema would certainly not have "happened" on the scale that it did. . . . Nothing, in a sense, unites the films made in Germany in the 1970s and early 1980s as much as how films were made in Germany. Typical are not the national character, but the cultural mode of production, not the antagonism with Hollywood or the Romantic legacy of high art, but the Film Funding System and the Television Framework Agreement.[153]

The repackaging of episodes from anthology made-for-network or cable-television series constitutes a prolific strand of omnibus product in the United States from the mid-1980s on. Anthology series yielding such television-to-video/DVD repackages include ones for the National Broadcasting Corporation (*Amazing Stories, Books One–Five* [1986–91]); Home Box Office (*Tales from the Crypt, Vols. 1–3* [1989–90] and *If These Walls Could Talk 1 & 2* [1996, 2000]); Showtime (*Fallen Angels I & II* [1993] and *Red Shoe Diaries 2–17* [1992–2001]); and the Playboy Channel (*Inside Out 1–4* [1992]). Generically, these series/films tend toward fantasy/horror and soft-core pornography on the one hand, and the family and/or historical melodrama dealing with broader social issues (abortion, the Holocaust) on the other. As such, they cover the range of overly proximal or "body genres" as analyzed by Linda Williams.[154] But as I have suggested above, the relations and crossovers among these low generic types and 1960s Italo-French omnibus films need to be mapped in conjunction with the ways in which the media technologies of television, video, and DVD have incorporated and disseminated anew art cinema across new platforms and venues of consumption.[155]

These combinative possibilities are inscribed in the history of both the European art and omnibus film, no more famously than in the case of *The Miracle*. In 1950, the U.S. distributor Joseph Burstyn assembled three short films—Marcel Pagnol's *Jofroi* (1934), Jean Renoir's *Une partie de campagne* (completed 1936, released in France 1946), and Roberto Rossellini's *Il miracolo* from his two-part episode film *L'amore* (1948)—into an omnibus with the new title *Ways of Love*. Its presentation at Pathé's Paris Theatre in New York City beginning 12 December 1950 initiated a string of events that would eventually lead to the landmark U.S. Supreme Court decision on 26 May 1952 that held, for the first time, that films were not merely a business and that they should therefore enjoy the same First Amendment rights of freedom of expression applied to other media.[156] While only *The Miracle* gets talked about today in relation to these developments, *Ways of Love* was conceived of and shown as a three-part omnibus film by its distributor, and many contemporary reviewers had as much and sometimes more praise for the Pagnol and Renoir contributions as they did for the controversial Rossellini one.[157] In fact, *Ways of Love* was, as a whole, voted Best Foreign Film of 1950 by the New York Film Critics. Here, certainly, is a case where the omnibus film does not function simply as the trace of European art cinema but vice versa. More important, it is also a case where the course of film censorship in the United States was affected to such a degree that the consequent challenges to the Production Code over the next decade and a half may not have occurred, or at least would not have occurred with the same force or outcomes. The irony is that *Ways of Love* enabled the eventual establishment of the U.S. rating system in 1968, a key factor in the rise of the New American cinema and of the wane in exhibition of European art cinema in that market.[158]

Rules and transgressions, departures and returns. The omnibus film extends beyond directors' visions and producers' speculations—its format and location of consumption is now more than ever a source of its production. Film festivals have since the 1950s served as crucial venues for establishing and maintaining art cinema's internationalism, even more so today wherein the rubric "world cinema" denotes it on this circuit. Such festivals, annual exhibitions that are also linchpins between production and international distribution, assumed occasionally productive roles themselves in the 1970s, when the art film was waning: *Nedostaje mi Sonja Henie (I Miss Sonia Henie)*, a short collage of three-minute films created by various guests at the Belgrade FEST in 1972, and *Wet Dreams (Dreams of Thirteen,* 1974), an erotica omnibus project initiated by the International Film Festival Rotterdam. More recently, South Korea's Jeonju International Film Festival has from its inception in 2000 sponsored and premiered annually *Digital Short Films by Three Filmmakers,* and the Cannes Film Festival commissioned for its sixtieth anniversary an omnibus film directed by thirty-six previous Palme d'or winners. London-based onedotzero engages in various experimental cross-media production projects as well as touring a festival of the same name internationally, and it distributes DVDs of this material as omnibus packages *(onedotzero_select dvd1-5).* The Parisian independent label lowave promotes international short film and video art via several DVD collections of its creation, aiding such work to reach audiences beyond the film festival circuit.[159] Quickband Networks in the United States has produced an extremely well-reviewed DVD series, *Short* (1997–2001), that has run to fourteen volumes. Finally, three Cinema16 DVDs (2003–6) feature short work by new talent alongside established directors from Britain, continental Europe, and the United States, highlighting how omnibus films have served historically as a training ground for new filmmakers, including many auteurs of European art cinema. These exquisite corpses throw into relief the convergence of film and new media technologies, which has spelled for some the end of cinema as well as of cinema studies.[160] But as with dreams, in ends begin responsibilities.

Appendix
Omnibus Filmography

Film titles are listed chronologically by date and within each year alphabetically by original-language title (where available). Contributing directors are in alphabetical rather than sequential order. Names of individual episodes within each film are not included. Indications appear at the end of entries for films in which episodes were cut or otherwise altered for international release.

†   repackaging of a made-for-network or cable-television anthology series into a feature-length omnibus film

√   straight-to-video, DVD, VCD, or Internet: no theatrical release

‡   omnibus film created by distributors through the assembling and packaging of short-film product into a feature-length film/video/DVD

1930
Elstree Calling [UK] (d. Adrian Brunel, André Charlot, Alfred Hitchcock, Jack Hulbert, Paul Murray)

Paramount on Parade [USA] (d. Dorothy Arzner, Otto Brower, Edmund Goulding, Victor Heerman, Edwin Knopf, Rowland V. Lee, Ernst Lubitsch, Lothar Mendes, Victor Schertzinger, A. Edward Sutherland, Frank Tuttle)‡

1932
If I Had a Million [USA] (d. James Cruze, H. Bruce Humberstone, Ernst Lubitsch, Norman Z. McLeod, Stephen Roberts, William A. Seiter, Norman Taurog)

1933
Geliebe und gelacht [Geleb un gelakht / Live and Laugh] [USA] (d. Sidney M. Goldin, Max Wilner)

1934
Nü'er jing [A Bible for Daughters] [China] (d. Chen Kengran, Cheng Bugao, Li Pingqian, Shen Xiling, Wu Cun, Xu Xinfu, Yao Sufeng, Zhang Shichuan, Zheng Zhengqui)

1936

La Vie est à nous [France] (d. Jacques Becker, Jacques B. Brunius, Jean-Paul Le Chanois, Jean Renoir)

1937

Lianhua jiaoxianqu [Symphony of Lianhua] [China] (d. Cai Chusheng, Fei Mu, He Mengfu, Shen Fu, Situ Huimin, Sun Yu, Tan Youliu, Zhu Shilin)

Yihai fengguang [Vistas of Art] [China] (d. He Mengfu, Situ Huimin, Zhu Shilin)

1940

Fantasia [USA] (d. James Algar, Samuel Armstrong, Norman Ferguson / T. Hee, Wilfred Jackson, Hamilton Luske / Jim Handley / Ford Beebe, Bill Roberts / Paul Satterfield)

1941

Boevoi kinosbornik 1 [Fighting Film Album 1] [USSR] (d. Sergei Gerasimov, Ivan Mutanov / Alexei Olenin, Y. Nekrasov)

Boevoi kinosbornik 2 [Fighting Film Album 2] [USSR] (d. Evgeni Cherviakov, Victor Eisimont, V. Feinberg, Grigori Kozintsev, Herbert Rappaport)

Boevoi kinosbornik 3 [Fighting Film Album 3] [USSR] (d. Boris Barnet, Konstantin Yudin)

Boevoi kinosbornik 4 [Fighting Film Album 4] [USSR] (d. Yakov Aron, Vasili Pronin)

Boevoi kinosbornik 5 [Fighting Film Album 5] [USSR] (d. Mikhail Slutsky, etc.)

Boevoi kinosbornik 6 [Fighting Film Album 6] [USSR] (d. Mikhail Doller, Vsevolod Pudovkin)

Boevoi kinosbornik 7 [Fighting Film Album 7] [USSR] (d. Albert Gendelstein / Aleksandr Rou, Klimenti Mintz, Rafail Perelstein / L. Altsev, Sergei Yutkevich)

Kinokontsert [Kino-kontsert 1941 / Leningrad Music Hall / Russian Salad] [USSR] (d. Isaak Menaker, Adolf Minkin, Herbert Rappaport, Mikhail Shapiro, Sergei Trimoshenko, Mikhail Tsekhanovsky)

1942

Boevoi kinosbornik 8 [Fighting Film Album 8] [USSR] (d. Leonid Lukov, N. Sadkovich)

Boevoi kinosbornik 9 [Fighting Film Album 9] [USSR] (d. Vladimir Braun, Mark Donskoi, Igor Savchenko)

Boevoi kinosbornik 10 [Fighting Film Album 10] [USSR] (d. Yakov Aron, Boris Barnet)

Boevoi kinosbornik 11 [Fighting Film Album 11] [USSR] (d. Vladimir Braun, N. Sadkovich, Ilya Trauberg / I. Zemgano)

Boevoi kinosbornik 12 [Fighting Film Album 12] [USSR] (d. Herbert Rappaport, Vera Stroyeva)

Leningrad v borbe [Leningrad in Combat] [USSR] (d. Roman Karmen, N. Komarevtsev, Valeri Solovtsov, Y. Uchitel)

This Is the Enemy [Counter-Attack] [USSR] (d. Evgeni Cherviakov, Victor Eisimont, Vladimir Feinberg, Grigori Kozintsev, Ivan Mutanov / Alexei Olenin, Herbert

Rappaport, etc.) {USA release combining all of *Fighting Film Album 2, Three in a Shell-Hole* from *Album 1,* and two episodes from other albums}‡

1943

Le Comte de Monte-Cristo [France/Italy] (d. Ferrucio Cerio, Robert Vernay)
Forever and a Day [USA/UK] (d. René Clair, Edmund Goulding, Cedric Hardwicke, Frank Lloyd, Victor Saville, Robert Stevenson, Herbert Wilcox)
Kino-kontsert K25—letiju Krasnoj Armii [Moscow Music Hall] [USSR] (d. Efim Dzigan, Sergei Gerasimov, Mikhail Kalatazov)
Saludos Amigos [USA] (d. Norman Ferguson, Wilfred Jackson, Jack Kinney, Hamilton Luske, Bill Roberts)

1945

Dead of Night [UK] (d. Alberto Cavalcanti, Charles Crichton, Basil Dearden, Robert Hamer)
Giorni di gloria [Days of Glory] [Italy/Switzerland] (d. Giuseppe De Santis, Marcello Pagliero, Mario Serandrei, Luchino Visconti)

1946

Make Mine Music [USA] (d. Bob Cormack, Clyde Geronimi, Joe Grant, Jack Kinney, Hamilton Luske, Josh Meador)
Ziegfeld Follies [USA] (d. Lemuel Ayers, Roy Del Ruth, Robert Lewis, Vincente Minnelli, George Sidney, Norman Taurog, Charles Waters)

1944–47

Dreams That Money Can Buy [USA] (p./d. Hans Richter; d. Alexander Calder, Marcel Duchamp, Max Ernst, Fernand Léger, Man Ray)

1947

Yottsu no koi no monogatari [Four Love Stories] [Japan] (d. Teinosuke Kinugasa, Mikio Naruse, Shiro Toyoda, Kajiro Yamamoto)

1948

Fiacre 13 [France/Italy] (d. Raoul André, Mario Mattoli)
Melody Time [USA] (d. Clyde Geronimi, Wilfred Jackson, Jack Kinney, Hamilton Luske)
On Our Merry Way [USA] (d. Leslie Fenton, King Vidor)
Tri vstrechi [Three Encounters] [USSR] (d. Alexander Ptushko, Vsevolod Pudovkin, Sergei Yutkevich)

1949

The Adventures of Ichabod and Mr. Toad [USA] (d. James Algar, Clyde Geronimi, Jack Kinney)
Quartet [UK] (d. Ken Annakin, Arthur Crabtree, Harold French, Ralph Smart)

Retour à la vie [France] (d. André Cayatte, Henri-Georges Clouzot, Jean Dréville, Georges Lampin)

Train of Events [UK] (d. Sidney Cole, Charles Crichton, Basil Dearden)

1950

Dwie brygady [Two Teams] [Poland] (d. Wadim Berestowski, Janus Nasfeter, Marek T. Nowakowski, Maria Olejniczak, Jerzy Popiołek, Silik Sternfield)

Osvobozhdennym Kitaj [Liberated China] [USSR/China] (d. Ivan Dukinsky, Sergei Gerasimov, Irina Setkina, M. Slavinsky, Elena Svilovoi)

Ren hai wan hua tong [Kaleidoscope] [Hong Kong] (d. Chan Pei, Chiu Shu-sun, Cho Kei, Lee Dut, Lee Ying Yuen, Li Tie, Lo Tun, Ng Wui, Wong Gam Yan, Yue Leung)

Trio [UK] (d. Ken Annakin, Harold French)

Ways of Love [France/Italy] (d. Marcel Pagnol, Jean Renoir, Roberto Rossellini) {USA release combining Pagnol's *Jofroi,* Renoir's *Une partie de campagne,* and Rossellini's *Il miracolo* from his two-part episode film *L'amore*}‡

1951

It's a Big Country [USA] (d. Clarence Brown, Don Hartman, John Sturges, Richard Thorpe, Charles Vidor, Don Weis, William Wellman)‡

Passaporto per l'oriente [Storia di cinque città / A Tale of Five Cities] [Italy/UK] (d. Geza von Cziffra, Romolo Marcellini, Emile Edwin Reinert, Wolfgang Staudte, Montgomery Tully)

1952

El cerco del diablo [Devil's Roundup] [Spain] (d. Antonio del Amo, Enrique Gómez, Edgar Neville, José Antonio Nieves Conde, Arturo Ruiz-Castillo)

Encore [UK] (d. Harold French, Pat Jackson, Anthony Pelissier)

Face to Face [USA] (d. John Brahm, Bretaigne Windust)

Kontsert masterov iskusstov [Concert of Stars] [USSR] (d. Alexander Ivanovsky, Herbert Rappaport)

O. Henry's Full House [USA] (d. Henry Hathaway, Howard Hawks, Henry King, Henry Koster, Jean Negulesco)

Les Sept péchés capitaux [I sette peccati capitali / The Seven Deadly Sins] [France/Italy] (d. Yves Allégret, Claude Autant-Lara, Eduardo De Filippo, Jean Dréville, Georges Lacombe, Carlo Rim, Roberto Rossellini)

1953

L'amore in città [Love in the City / Lo spettatore—Rivista cinematografica, anno 1953, n. 1] [Italy] (p. Cesare Zavattini; d. Michelangelo Antonioni, Federico Fellini, Alberto Lattuada, Carlo Lizzani, Francesco Maselli / Cesare Zavattini, Dino Risi) {USA release excised episode *L'amore che si paga* by Lizzani}

Les Crimes de l'amour [France] (d. Alexandre Astruc, Maurice Barry / Maurice Clavel) {French release of two shorts made independently: Astruc's *Le Rideau cramoisi* and Barry and Clavel's *Mina de Vanghel*}‡

Siamo donne [We, the Women] [Italy] (d. Gianni Franciolini, Alfredo Guarini,
Roberto Rossellini, Luchino Visconti, Luigi Zampa)

The Story of Three Loves [USA] (d. Vincente Minnelli, Gottfried Reinhardt)

Tres citas con el destino [Mexico/Argentina/Spain] (d. Fernando de Fuentes, Léon
Klimovsky, Florián Rey)

Trzy opowieści [Three Stories] [Poland] (d. Konrad Nałęcki, Czesław Petelski, Ewa
Poleska)

1954

Amori di mezzo secolo [Mid-Century Loves] [Italy] (d. Mario Chiari, Pietro Germi,
Glauco Pellegrini, Antonio Pietrangeli, Roberto Rossellini; linking sequences
Vinicio Marinucci)

Continente perduto [Lost Continent] [Italy] (d. Leonardo Bonzi, Mario Craveri, Enrico
Gras, Alberto Francesco Lavagnino, Giorgio Moser)

Destini di donne [Destinées / Daughters of Destiny] [Italy/France] (d. Christian-Jaque,
Jean Delannoy, Marcel[lo] Pagliero)

Pueblo, canto y esperanza [Mexico] (d. Alfredo B. Crevenna, Rogelio A. González,
Julián Soler)

Questa è la vita [Italy] (d. Aldo Fabrizi, Giorgio Pàstina, Mario Soldati, Luigi Zampa)

Se vincessi cento milioni [Italy] (d. Carlo Campogalliani, Carlo Moscovini)

Secrets d'alcôve [Il letto / The Bed] [France/Italy] (d. Henri Decoin, Jean Delannoy,
Gianni Franciolini, Ralph Habib)

A Tale of Three Women [UK] (d. Thelma Connell, Paul Dickson)

1955

Ai, Shangji [Love, Part One] [Hong Kong] (d. Chu Kea, Chun Kim, Lee Sun-fung,
Li Tie, Ng Wui, Wong Hang)

Ai, Xuji [Love, Part Two / Love, The Sequel] [Hong Kong] (d. Chu Kea, Chun Kim,
Li Tie, Ng Wui, Wong Hang)

Aisureba koso [If You Love Me / Because I Love] [Japan] (d. Tadashi Imai, Satsuo
Yamamoto, Kimisaburo Yoshimura)

Kuchizuke [The Kiss] [Japan] (d. Masanori Kakei, Mikio Naruse, Hideo Suzuki)

Three Cases of Murder [UK] (d. David Eady, George More O'Ferrall, Wendy Toye)

Tri zgodbe [Three Stories] [Yugoslavia] (d. Jane Kavcic, France Kosmac, Igor Pretnar)

Trzy starty [Three Starts] [Poland] (d. Stanislaw Lenartowicz, Ewa Petelska, Czesław
Petelski)

1956

Cipelice na asfaltu [Yugoslavia] (d. Zdravko Randić, Boško Vučinić)

Vesenniye golosa [Spring Voices] [USSR] (d. Sergei Gurov, Eldar Ryazonov)

1957

Koniec nocy [End of the Night] [Poland] (d. Julian Dziedzina, Paweł Komorowski,
Walentyna Uszycka)

Of Life and Love [Italy] (d. Aldo Fabrizi, Giorgio Pastina, Mario Soldati, Luchino Visconti) {USA reissue of episodes culled from *Siamo donne* and *Questa è la vita*}‡

Die Windrose [The Wind Rose] [East Germany] (d. Yannick Bellon, Sergei Gerasimov, Gillo Pontecorvo, Alex Viany, Wu Kuo-yin)

1958

O večech nadpřirozených [On Miraculous Happenings] [Czechoslovakia] (d. Jiří Krejčík, Jaroslav Mach, Miloš Makovec)

Power among Men [UK] (p. Thorold Dickinson; d. Alexander Hammid, Gian Luigi Polidoro, V. R. Sarma)

1959

Las canciones unidas [Mexico] (d. Julio Bracho, Tito Davison, Alfonso Patiño Gómez, Chano Urueta)

Vstup zakázán [No Admittance] [Czechoslovakia] (d. Frantisek Vlácil, Milan Vosmik)

1960

Al Banaat wa Al-Saif [Girls and Summer] [Egypt] (d. Fateen Abdel-Wahab, Salah Abou Seif, Ezzeddin Zulfuqar)

La Française et l'amour [Love and the Frenchwoman] [France] (d. Michel Boisrond, Christian-Jaque, René Clair, Jean Delannoy, Jean-Paul Le Chanois, Henri Verneuil)

Gyvieji didvyriai [Living Heroes] [Lithuania] (d. Balys Bratkauskas, Marijonas Giedrys, Vytautas Žalakevičius, Arūnas Žebriūnas)

Három csillag [Three Stars] [Hungary] (d. Miklós Jancsó, Zoltán Várkonyi, Károly Wiedermann)

Jokei [Women's Scroll / A Woman's Testament] [Japan] (d. Kon Ichikawa, Masumura Yasuzo, Kimisaburo Yoshimura)

Yoru no nagare [Evening Stream] [Japan] (d. Yuzo Kawashima, Mikio Naruse)

1961

Attenzione: guerra! [Italy/Czechoslovakia/Belgium] (d. Jiří Brdečka, Alberto Caldana, Břetislav Pojar, Henri Storck)

Cronache del '22 [Italy] (d. Francesco Cinieri, Guidarino Guidi, Giuseppe Orlandini, Moraldo Rossi, Stefano Ubezio)

The Devil's Messenger [Sweden/USA] (d. Curt Siodmak, Herbert L. Strock)†

Le italiane e l'amore [Latin Lovers] [Italy] (d. Gian Vittorio Baldi, Marco Ferreri, Giulio Macchi, Francesco Maselli, Lorenzo Mazzetti, Gianfranco Mingozzi, Carlo Musso, Piero Nelli, Giulio Questi, Nelo Risi, Florestano Vancini)

Les Parisiennes [Tales of Paris] [France/Italy] (d. Marc Allégret, Claude Barma, Michel Boisrond, Jacques Poitrenaud)

Sovershenno seryozno [Absolutely Seriously] [USSR] (d. Leonid Gaidai, Eldar Ryazanov, Vladimir Semakov, Naum Trachtenberg, Eduard Zmojro)

Three Tales of Chekhov [USSR] (d. Marie Andjaparidze, Édouard Botcharov, Irina Poplavskaya)

1962

L'amore difficile [Erotica / Of Wayward Love] [Italy/West Germany] (d. Alberto Bonucci, Luciano Lucignani, Nino Manfredi, Sergio Sollima)

L'Amour à vingt ans [Love at Twenty] [France/Italy/Japan/Poland/West Germany] (d. Shintaro Ishihara, Marcel Ophuls, Renzo Rossellini, François Truffaut, Andrzej Wajda; linking stills Henri Cartier-Bresson)

Boccaccio '70 [Italy/France] (d. Vittorio De Sica, Federico Fellini, Mario Monicelli, Luchino Visconti) {except for Italy and the 1962 Cannes Film Festival, all release prints excised episode *Renzo e Luciana* by Monicelli}

Cinco vezes favela [Slum Times Five] [Brazil] (d. Miguel Borges, Joaquim Pedro de Andrade, Carlos Diegues, Marcos Farias, Leon Hirszman)

Cuba '58 [Cuba] (d. José Miguel Garcia Ascot, Jorge Fraga)

Kapi, vode, ratnici [Raindrops, Water, Warriors] [Yugoslavia] (d. Marko Babac, Živojin Pavlović, Vojislav [Kokan] Rakonjac)

Malenkie mectateli [USSR] (d. O. Greczicho, A. Jastrebow, V. Turow)

RoGoPaG [Laviamoci il cervello] [France/Italy] (d. Jean-Luc Godard, Ugo Gregoretti, Pier Paolo Pasolini, Roberto Rossellini)

Les 7 péchés capitaux [7 Capital Sins / The 7 Deadly Sins] [France/Italy] (d. Claude Chabrol, Philippe de Broca, Jacques Demy, Sylvaine Dhomme, Jean-Luc Godard, Edouard Molinaro, Roger Vadim)

Spóznieni przechodnie [Those Who Are Late / Late Passers-By] [Poland] (d. Jerzy Antczak, Adam Hanuszkiewicz, Gustaw Holoubek, Andrzej Łapicki, Jan Rybowski)

Les Veinards [France] (d. Philippe de Broca, Jean Girault, Jack Pinoteau)

1963

I cuori infranti [Italy] (d. Vittorio Caprioli, Gianni Puccini)

Dva rasskaza [Two Stories] [USSR] (d. Otar Ioseliani, Georgi Shengelaya)

Grad [The City] [Yugoslavia] (d. Marko Babac, Živojin Pavlović, Kokan Rakonjac)

Hlídač dynamitu [The Guard of Dynamite] [Czechoslovakia] (d. Hynek Bočan, Jaromil Jireš, Zdeněk Sirový)

Italia proibita [Italy] (d. Enzo Biagi, Aldo Falivena, Brando Giordani, Sergio Giordani)

I misteri di Roma [Mysteries of Rome] [Italy] (d. Libero Bizzari, Mario Carbone, Angelo D'Alessandro, Lino Del Fra, Luigi Di Gianni, Giuseppe Ferrar, Ansano Giannarelli, Giulio Macchi, Lorenza Mazzetti, Massimo Mida, Enzo Muzii, Piero Nelli, Paolo Nuzzi, Dino B. Partesano, Giovanni Vento)

Les Quatre vérités [Three Fables of Love] [France/Italy/Spain] (d. Luis Garcia Berlanga, Alessandro Blasetti, Hervé Bromberger, René Clair) {USA release excised episode *El Lenador y la Muerte* by Berlanga}

La rabbia [Italy] (d. Giovanni Guareschi, Pier Paolo Pasolini)‡

Weekendy [Weekends] [Poland] (d. Wadim Berestowski / Jozéf Hen, Jan Rutkiewicz)

1964

Alta infedeltà [High Infidelity / Sex in the Afternoon] [Italy/France] (d. Mario Monicelli, Elio Petri, Franco Rossi, Luciano Salce)

Amore in 4 dimensioni [Love in 4 Dimensions] [Italy/France] (d. Mino Guerrini, Massimo Mida, Gianni Puccini, Jacques Romain)

Amori pericolosi [Italy] (d. Alfredo Giannetti, Carlo Lizzani, Giulio Questi)

Les Baisers [France/Italy] (d. Claude Berri, Charles Bitsch, Jean-François Hauduroy, Bertrand Tavernier, Bernard Toublanc-Michel)

La Chance et l'amour [France/Italy] (d. Claude Berri, Charles Bitsch, Eric Schlumberger, Bertrand Tavernier; linking sequences Claude Chabrol)

Controsesso [Countersex] [Italy] (d. Renato Castellani, Marco Ferreri, Franco Rossi)

La donna è una cosa meravigliosa [Italy/France] (d. Mauro Bolognini, Shuntaro Tanigawa, Pino Zac)

Gli eroi di ieri, oggi, domani [I tre magnifici eroi] [Italy] (d. Vincenzo Dell'Aquila / Fernando Di Leo, Sergio Tau, Franz Weisz)

Extraconiugale [Italy] (d. Massimo Franciosa, Mino Guerrini, Giuliano Montaldo)

La Fleur de l'âge, ou les adolescents [The Adolescents / That Tender Age] [Canada/France/Italy/Japan] (d. Gian Vittorio Baldi, Michel Brault, Jean Rouch, Hiroshi Teshigahara)

Go-Go Big Beat [UK] (d. Frank Gilpin, Kenneth Hume)

L'idea fissa [Love and Marriage] [Italy] (d. Mino Guerrini, Gianni Puccini)

La mia signora [Italy] (d. Mauro Bolognini, Tinto Brass, Luigi Comencini)

Místo v houfu [A Place in the Crowd] [Czechoslovakia] (d. Zbyněk Brynych, Václav Gajer, Václav Krška)

Paris vu par [Six in Paris / Paris as Seen by . . .] [France] (d. Claude Chabrol, Jean Douchet, Jean-Luc Godard, Jean-Daniel Pollet, Eric Rohmer, Jean Rouch)

Les Plus belles escroqueries du monde [The Beautiful Swindlers] [France/Italy/Japan/Netherlands] (d. Claude Chabrol, Jean-Luc Godard, Ugo Gregoretti, Hiromichi Horikawa, Roman Polanski) {USA release excised episode *Le Grand escroc* by Godard}

Spots in the Sun [Japan] (d. Kioshi Komori, Nobuo Nakagawa, Tsukasa Takahashi, Kichinosuke Yoshida)

Stranicy proslogo [Pages from History] [USSR] (d. Eldar Shengelaya, Georgi Shengelaya)

Le tardone [Las otoñales] [Italy/Spain] (d. Marino Girolami, Javier Seto)

Tre notti d'amore [Three Nights of Love] [Italy] (d. Renato Castellani, Luigi Comencini, Franco Rossi)

1965

4 X 4 [Sweden/Norway/Denmark/Finland] (d. Rolf Clemens, Palle Kjærulff-Schmidt, Maunu Kurkvaara, Jan Troell)

Amor, amor, amor [Mexico] (d. Benito Alazraki, Juan Jose Gurrola, Jose Luis Ibáñez, Juan Ibáñez, Héctor Mendoza, Miguel Barbachano Ponce)

Der Augenblick des Friedens [Matura / The Moment of Peace] [West Germany/France/ Poland] (d. Georges Franju, Tadeusz Konwicki, Egon Monk)

Le bambole [The Dolls / Four Kinds of Love] [Italy/France] (d. Mauro Bolognini, Luigi Comencini, Dino Risi, Franco Rossi)

Les Bons vivants [France/Italy] (d. Gilles Grangier, Georges Lautner)

I complessi [The Complexes] [Italy/France] (d. Dino Risi, Franco Rossi)

La Guerre secrète [The Dirty Game / La guerra segreta / Spione unter sich] [France/Italy/West Germany] (d. Christian-Jaque, Werner Klingler, Carlo Lizzani, Terence Young)

Ključ [The Key] [Yugoslavia] (d. Vanča Kljaković, Krsto Papić, Antun Vrdoljak)

Das Liebeskarussell [Daisy Chain] [Austria] (d. Axel von Ambesser, Rolf Thiele, Alfred Wiedenman)

Le Lit à deux places [The Double Bed] [France/Italy] (d. Jean Delannoy, François Dupont-Midy, Gianni Puccini, Al World [Alvaro Mancori])

Oggi, domani, dopodomani [Paranoia] [Italy] (d. Eduardo De Filippo, Marco Ferreri, Luciano Salce) {Producer Carlo Ponti later reshot, recut, and redistributed this omnibus film in two other forms. In one, the Ferreri episode (already trimmed down from feature length) was restored to a feature with added new footage and released as *L'uomo dai cinque palloni* (*The Man with the Balloons/Break-Up* in United States, 1968). In the other, *Kiss the Other Sheik* (1968), strictly an export item for the Anglo-American market, Luciano Salce directed (and acted in) a framing story that bound together through the figure of Marcello Mastroianni the two previous Salce and De Filippo epsiodes from *Oggi, domani, dopodomani* into a single narrative feature. Because of its linear narrative and marketing as a showcase of the performer Mastroianni, *Kiss the Other Sheik* is in my typology a compilation film and thus does not appear in this list. See *Variety* (14 August 1968), 6.}

Ot siemi do dwienadcati [From Seven Till Twelve: Three Novellas] [USSR] (d. Chasan Bakajew, Jurij Fridman, Jekaterina Narodicka)

Perličky na dně [Pearls of the Deep / A String of Pearls] [Czechosolvakia] (d. Věra Chytilová, Jaromil Jireš, Jiří Menzel, Jan Němec, Evald Schorm) {Ivan Passer directed an episode that was released separately}

Tagumpay ng Mahirap [Triumph of the Poor] [Philippines] (d. Lamberto V. Avellana, Gerry de Leon, Eddie Romero)

Thrilling [Italy] (d. Carlo Lizzani, Gian Luigi Polidoro, Ettore Scola)

I tre centurioni [Italy/France] (d. Georges Combret, Roberto Mauri)

I tre volti [Italy] (d. Michelangelo Antonioni, Mauro Bolognini, Franco Indovina)

Umorismo nero [La muerte viaja demasiado / Humour noir / Death Travels Too Much] [Italy/Spain/France] (d. Claude Autant-Lara, José María Forqué, Giancarlo Zagni)

Viento distante [The Distant Wind] [Mexico] (d. Salomón Láiter, Manuel Michel, Sergio Véjar)

Zločin v dívčí škole [Crime in the Girls' School] [Czechoslovakia] (d. Jiří Menzel, Ivo Novák, Ladislav Rychmann)

1966

La fabbrica dei soldi [Les Combinards] [Italy/France/Spain] (d. Juan Estelrich, Riccardo Pizzaglia, Jean-Claude Roy)

Le fate [The Queens / The Fairies] [Italy/France] (d. Mauro Bolognini, Mario Monicelli, Antonio Pietrangeli, Luciano Salce)

Gern hab'ich die Frauen gekillt [Spie contro il mondo / Les Carnaval des barbouzes / Killer's Carnival] [Austria/Italy/France] (d. Alberto Cardone, Robert Lynn, Sheldon Reynolds, Louis Soulanès)

I nostri mariti [Our Husbands] [Italy/France] (d. Luigi Filippo D'Amico, Dino Risi, Luigi Zampa)

Le piacevoli notti [Italy] (d. Armando Crispino, Luciano Lucignani)

Puteshestvie [Journey] [USSR] (d. Dzhemma Firsova, Inessa Selezneva, Ina Tumanian)

Las viudas [The Widows] [Spain] (d. Julio Coll, José María Forqué, Pedro Lazaga)

1967

ABC do amor [El ABC del amor / The ABC of Love] [Brazil/Argentina/Chile] (d. Eduardo Coutinho, Rudolfo Kuhn, Helvio Soto)

Aru mittsû [A Certain Adultery] [Japan] (d. Hiroshi Mukai, Kôji Wakamatsu, Shinya Yamamoto)

De trei ori București [Three Times Bucharest] [Romania] (d. Mihai Iacob, Horea Popescu, Ion Popescu-Gopo)

Geschichten jener Nacht [Stories of the Night] [East Germany] (d. Karl-Heinz Carpentier, Gerhard Klein, Ulrich Thein, Frank Vogel)

Lichnaya zhizn Kuzaeva Valentina [The Private Life of Valentin Kuzyayev] [USSR] (d. Ilya Averbakh, Igor Maslennikov)

Loin du Viêt-nam [Far from Vietnam] [France] (d. Jean-Luc Godard, Joris Ivens, William Klein, Claude Lelouch, Chris Marker, Alain Resnais; Agnès Varda segment cut from theatrical release)

Der Paukenspieler [West Germany] (d. Helmut Meewes, Volker Schlöndorff, Franz Seitz, Rolf Thiele, Bernhard Wicki)

Le Plus vieux métier du monde [The Oldest Profession] [France/West Germany/Italy] (d. Claude Autant-Lara, Mauro Bolognini, Philippe de Broca, Jean-Luc Godard, Franco Indovina, Michel Pfleghar)

Quatre d'entre elles [Vier Frauen / Four Women] [Switzerland] (d. Claude Champion, Francis Reusser, Jacques Sandoz, Yves Yersin)

Stimulantia [Sweden] (d. Hans Abramson, Arne Arnbom, Ingmar Bergman, Tage Danielsson / Hans Alfredson, Jörn Donner, Lars Görling, Gustaf Molander, Vilgot Sjöman)

Le streghe [The Witches] [Italy/France] (d. Mauro Bolognini, Vittorio De Sica, Pier Paolo Pasolini, Franco Rossi, Luchino Visconti)

Suaugusių žmonių žaidimai [Grown-Up Games] [Lithuania] (d. Algimantas Kundelis, Ilja Rud-Gercovskis])

Wiener Schnitzel [Austria] (d. Otto Ambros, Hans Herbert, Paul Löwinger)

1968

Armando, belijat kon [Bulgaria] (d. Lyudmil Kirkov, Milen Nikolov)

Brasil verdade [True Brazil] [Brazil] (d. Maurice Capovilla, Manuel Horacio Giminez, Geraldo Sarno, Paulo Gil Soares)

Capriccio all'italiana [The Italian Capriccio] [Italy] (d. Mauro Bolognini, Mario Monicelli, Pier Paolo Pasolini, Steno, Pino Zac)

Diálóg 20-40-60 [Czechoslovakia] (d. Zbyněk Brynych, Jerzy Skolimowski, Peter Solan)

L'Enfer à dix ans [Hell Is Ten Years Old] [Algeria] (d. Youcef Akika, Ghaouti Bendeddouche, Abderrahmane Bouguermouh, Amar Laskri, Sid Ali Mazif)

Faire l'amour: De la pilule à l'ordinateur [Hot Pants] [France/West Germany/Sweden] (d. Jean-Gabriel Albicocco, Thomas Fantl, Sachiko Hidari, Gunnar Hoglund)

Histoires extraordinaires [Tre passi nel delirio / Spirits of the Dead] [France/Italy] (d. Federico Fellini, Louis Malle, Roger Vadim)

Journey into Darkness [UK] (d. James Hill, Peter Sasdy)[†]

Journey into Midnight [UK] (d. Roy Ward Baker, Alan Gibson)[†]

Komedie pomyłek [Comedies of Errors] [Poland] (d. Stanisław Różewicz, Jerzy Zarzycki)

Pražské noci [Prague Nights] [Czechoslovakia] (d. Jiří Brdečka, Miloš Makovec, Evald Schorm)

Sus og dus på by'n [Riot and Revel on Order] [Norway] (d. Knut Andersen, Knut Bohwim, Mattis Mathiesen)

Świat grozy [World of Horror] [Poland] (d. Witold Lesiewicz, Ewa Petelska / Czesław Petelski)

Thalass Kassas [Three Stories] [Egypt] (d. Ibrahim El-Sahn, Mohamed Nabih, Hassan Reda)

Trampas de amor [Mexico] (d. Jorge Fons, Manuel Michel, Tito Novaro)

Trilogia de terror [Trilogy of Terror] [Brazil] (d. Ozualdo Candeias, José Mojica Marins, Luiz Sérgio Person)

Yeo [Woman, Woman, Woman] [South Korea] (d. Jong Jin-u, Kim Ki-young, Yu Hyun-mok)

1969

L'alibi [Italy] (d. Adolfo Celi, Vittorio Gassman, Luciano Lucignani)

Amore e rabbia (Vangelo '70) [Love and Anger] [Italy/France] (d. Marco Bellochio, Bernardo Bertolucci, Jean-Luc Godard, Carlo Lizzani, Pier Paolo Pasolini)

Aus unserer Zeit [Episodes from Our Time] [East Germany] (d. Joachim Kunert, Kurt Maetzig, Helmut Nitzschke, Rainer Simon)

Dager fra 1000 år [Days from a Thousand Years] [Norway] (d. Anja Breien, Egil Kolstø, Espen Thorstenson)

Los desafíos [El Desafío / The Challenges] [Cuba] (d. José Luis Egea, Victor Erice, Claudio Guerín)

Histoires de la revolution [Stories of the Revolution] [Algeria] (d. Ahmed Bedjaoui, Rabah Laradji, Sid Ali Mazif)

Night Gallery [USA] (d. Boris Sagal, Barry Shear, Steven Spielberg)†

Semeynoe schaste [Family Happiness] [USSR] (d. Andrei Ladynin, Aleksandr Shein, Sergei Solovyev)

Siempre hay una primera vez [Mexico] (d. José Estrada, Guillermo Murray, Mauricio Walerstein)

Swiss Made [Switzerland] (d. Fritz Maeder, Fredi M. Murer, Yves Yersin)

Thalath nisa [Three Women] [Egypt] (d. Salah Abou Seif, Henry Bakarat, Mahmoud Zoulficar)

Tres noches de locura [Three Nights of Madness] [Mexico] (d. Rafael Portillo, José María Fernández Unsáin)

1970

Le coppie [The Couples] [Italy] (d. Vittorio De Sica, Mario Monicelli, Alberto Sordi)

Documenti su Giuseppe Pinelli [Ipotesi] [Italy] (d. Elio Petri, Nelo Risi)

Edin mig svoboda [A Moment of Freedom] [Bulgaria] (d. Ivanka Grybcheva, Petar Kaishev)

Hsi, nu, ai, le [Four Moods] [Taiwan] (d. Ching Jui, King Hu, Lee Hsing, Li Han-hsiang)

Three to Go [Australia] (d. Brian Hannant, Oliver Howes, Peter Weir)

Tú, yo, nosotros [Mexico] (d. Jorge Fons, Gonzalo Martínez Ortega, Juan Manuel Torres)

1971

Pastel de sangre [Cake of Blood] [Spain] (d. Francesc Bellmunt, Jaime Chávarri, Emilio Martínez Lázaro, José María Vallés)

1972

Fe, esperanza y caridad [Mexico] (d. Luis Alcoriza, Alberto Bojórquez, Jorge Fons)

Qun ying hui [Trilogy of Swordsmanship] [Hong Kong] (d. Cheng Gang, Yue Feng, Zhang Che)

1973

A qui appartient ce gage? [Canada] (d. Marthe Blackburn, Saia Francine, Susan Gibbard, Jeanne Morazain, Clorinda Warny)

Libido [Australia] (d. David Baker, Tim Burstall, John B. Murray, Fred Schepisi)

Linksmos istorijos [Merry Tales / Funny Stories] [Lithuania] (d. Algimantas Kundelis, Gytis Lukšas, Stasys Motiejūnas)

Visions of Eight [USA] (d. Milos Forman, Kon Ichikawa, Claude Lelouch, Juri Ozerov, Arthur Penn, Michel Pfleghar, John Schlesinger, Mai Zetterling)

1974

Daigdig ng Sindak At Lagim [Philippines] (d. Maria Saret Abelardo, Ruben Arthur Nicdao)

Wet Dreams [Dreams of Thirteen] [Netherlands/West Germany] (d. Max Fischer, Oscar Gigard, Hans Kanters, Geert Koolman, Lee Kraft, Nicholas Ray, Sam Rotterdam [Dušan Makavejev], Falcon Stuart, Jens Joergen Thorsen, Heathcote Williams)

1975

Au-u! [USSR] (d. Gerald Biezanow, Jurij Gorkowienko, Wiktor Kriuczkow)

Collections privées [France/Japan] (d. Walerian Borowczyk, Just Jaeckin, Shuji Terayami)

Fe, Esperanza, Caridad [Philippines] (d. Lamberto V. Avellana, Gerry de Leon, Cirio H. Santiago)

Niezwanyje gosti [USSR] (d. Lewan Chotiwari, Ramaz Chotiwari)

Profesoři za školou [Teacher Is Playing Truant] [Czechoslovakia] (d. Vladimir Blazěk, Zbyněk Brynych, Milan Muchna)

Zwaarmoedige verhalen voor bij de centrale verwarming [Melancholy Tales] [Netherlands] (d. Nouchka van Brakel, Ernie Damen, Bas van de Lecq, Guido Pieters)

1976

Amici più di prima [Italy] (d. Marino Girolami, Gianni Grimaldi, Giorgio C. Simonelli)

Basta che non si sappia in giro! . . . [Italy] (d. Luigi Comencini, Nanni Loy, Luigi Magni)

Ciąg dalszy nastąpi [To Be Continued] [Poland] (d. Paweł Kędzierski, Zbigniew Kamiński)

La goduria [Italy] (d. Luigi Comencini, Nanni Loy, Mario Monicelli)

Obrazki z życia [Pictures from Life] [Poland] (d. Jerzy Domaradzki, Feliks Falk, Krzysztof Gradowski, Agnieszka Holland, Andrzej Kotkowski, Jerzy Obłamski, Barbara Sass)

Quelle strane occasioni [Italy] (d. Anonymous [Nanni Loy], Luigi Comencini, Luigi Magni)

Sana ula hubb [First Year of Love] [Egypt] (d. Salah Abou Seif, Kamal Al Sheikh, Niazi Mustafa, Atef Salem, Hilmi Rafla)

Signori e signore, buonanotte [Italy] (d. Luigi Comencini, Nanni Loy, Luigi Magni, Mario Monicelli, Ettore Scola)

"Sto gramm" dla chrabosti [USSR] (d. Boris Buszmielew, Anatclij Markielow, Gieorgij Szczukin)

Xianggang qi an [The Criminals] [Hong Kong] (d. Cheng Gang, Ho Meng-Hwa, Hua Shan)

1977

Ladies' Rooms [Australia] (d. Pat Fiske, Sarah Gibson, Susan Lambert, Jan MacKay)

I nuovi mostri [The New Monsters / Viva Italia!] [Italy] (d. Mario Monicelli, Dino Risi, Ettore Scola)

Ride bene . . . chi ride ultimo [Italy] (d. Marco Aleandri, Gino Bramieri, Pino Caruso, Walter Chiari)

Three Dangerous Ladies [USA] (d. Robert Fuest, Alvin Rakoff, Don Thompson)

Zdjęcia próbne [Screen Tests] [Poland] (d. Jerzy Domaradzki, Agnieszka Holland, Paweł Kędzierski

1978

Deutschland im Herbst [Germany in Autumn] [West Germany] (d. Heinrich Böll, Alf Brustellin / Bernhard Sinkel, Rainer Werner Fassbinder, Alexander Kluge, Maximiliane Mainka / Peter Schubert, Edgar Reitz, Katja Rupé / Hans Peter Cloos, Volker Schlöndorff)

Dovè vai in vacanza? [Where Are You Going on Holiday?] [Italy] (d. Mauro Bolognini, Luciano Salce, Alberto Sordi)

Ha luo, ye gui ren [Hello, Late Homecomers] [Hong Kong] (d. Karl Maka, Louis Sit, John Woo)

Io tigro, tu tigri, egli tigra [Italy] (d. Giorgio Capitani, Renato Pozzetto)

Rapunzel Let Down Your Hair [UK] (d. Swan Shapiro, Esther Ronay, Francine Winham)

1979

Cuentos éroticos [Erotic Tales] [Spain] (d. Enrique Brasó, Jaime Chávarri, Emma Cohen, Fernando Colomo, Jesús García de Dueñas, Augusto Martínez Torres, Josefina Molina, Juan Tébar, Alfonso Ungría)

Cuentos para una escapada [Tales for a Flight] [Spain] (d. Manuel Gutiérrez Aragón, Jaime Chávarri, Emiliano De Pedraza, Teodoro Escamilla, José Luis García Sánchez, Carles Mira, Miguel Angel Pacheco, Gonzalo Suárez)

I dieci diritti del bambino [Together for Children / Ten for Survival] [Italy] (d. Eugene Fedorenko, Katja Georgi, Klaus Georgi, Johan Hagelback, Roman Kacianoff, Derek Lamb, Kati Macskássy, Manfredo Manfredi, Fernando Ruiz, Seppo Suo-Anttilla)

Sabato domenica e venerdì [Italy/Spain] (d. Pasquale Festa Campanile, Franco Castellano / Pipolo [Giuseppe Moccia], Sergio Martino)

Tre sotto il lenzuolo [Italy] (d. Paolo Dominici [Domenico Paolella], Michele Massimo Tarantini)

Wielki podryw [The Big Kill] [Poland] (d. Jerzy Kołodziejczyk, Jerzy Trojan)

1980

Chto mozhno Kuzenkovu? [USSR] (d. Boris Galkin, Nikolai Lyrchikov, Nikolai Skujbin)

Contos eroticos [Erotic Stories] [Brazil] (d. Joaquim Pedro de Andrade, Eduardo Escorel, Roberto Santos)

Mundo mágico [Mexico] (d. Luis Mandoki, Alejandro Talavera, Raúl Zermeño)

No Nukes [USA] (d. Danny Goldberg, Anthony Potenza, Julian Schlossberg)

Objetivo: Sexo [Objective: Sex] [Spain] (d. Jordi Cadena, Domenec Font, Octavi Martí, Ramón Sala)

Les Séducteurs [Sunday Lovers] [France/Italy] (d. Bryan Forbes, Edouard Molinaro, Dino Risi, Gene Wilder)

Zapowiedź ciszy [Announcement of Silence] [Poland] (d. Lech J. Majewski, Krzysztof Sowiński)

1981

National Lampoon Goes to the Movies [National Lampoon's Movie Madness] [USA] (d. Bob Giraldi, Henry Jaglom)

1982

Aus heiterem Himmel [Out of the Clear Blue Sky] [West Germany] (d. Marie-Susanne Ebert, Monika Funke-Stern, Ebba Jahn, Barbara Kasper, Anke Oehme, Ingrid Oppermann, Renate Sami, Claudia Schilinski, Anqi Welz-Rommel)

Géminis [Gemini] [Spain] (d. Jésus Garay, Manuel Revuelta)

Guangyin de gushi [In Our Times] [Taiwan] (d. Ko I-chen, Tao De-chen, Edward Yang, Zhang Yi)

Krieg und Frieden [War and Peace] [West Germany] (d. Stefan Aust, Axel Engstfeld, Alexander Kluge, Volker Schlöndorff)

Love [Canada] (d. Annette Cohen, Nancy Dowd, Liv Ullmann, Mai Zetterling)

Plaché příběhy [Czechoslovakia] (d. Zdeněk Flídr, Tomáš Tintěra, Dobroslav Zborník)

Progetto Manzù: il vento e l'amore [Italy] (d. Ragnar Löfberg, Aida Mangia, Salvatore Morello, Bruno Roberti, Massimo Russo, Carola Prudencio Soria)

1983

Archipel des amours [France] (d. Jean-Claude Biette, Cécile Clairval, Jacques Davila, Michel Delahaye, Jacques Frenais, Gérard Frot-Coutaz, Jean-Claude Guiguet, Marie-Claude Treilhou, Paul Vecchiali)

Die Erbtöchter [Les Filles héréditaires / The Daughters' Inheritance] [West Germany/France] (d. Vivianne Berthommier, Jutta Brückner, Danièle Dubroux, Marie-Christine Questerbert, Helma Sanders-Brahms, Ula Stöckl)

Erh-tzu te ta wan-ou [The Sandwich Man] [Taiwan] (d. Hou Hsiao-hsien, Tseng Chuang-hsiang, Wan Jen)

La France interdite [France] (d. Gilles Delannoy, Jean-Pierre Garmier, Jean-Pierre Imbrohoris)

Die Gedächtnislücke—Filmminiaturen über den alltäglichen Umgang mit Giften [West Germany] (p. Helke Sander; d. Waldemar Bartens, Lars Becker, Willie Bschorr, Gerd Debler, Gabi Hampl, Maria Hemmleb, Jochen Hick, Anita Horz, Karin Kaufmann, Claudia Ketels, Katrin Klamroth, Ulrike Knolle, Hanne Schmidt, Kerstin Schulte, Angela Tiedt, Vali Valenti)

The Gordimer Stories [USA] (d. Lynton Stephenson, Marie Van Rensburg)

Inflation im Paradies [West Germany] (d. Susanne Blänkner, Nikolai Müllerschön, Wolfgang Rühl, Richard L. Wagner)

Juke Box [Italy] (d. Carlo Carlei, Enzo Civitareale / Antonello Grimaldi / Michele Scura, Sandro De Santis, Valerio Jalongo, Daniele Luchetti)

On, ona, oni [He, She, They] [Poland] (d. Andrzej Mellin, Włodzimierz Szpak, Krzysztof Tchórzewski)

Ripping Yarns [UK] (d. Alan Bell, Jim Franklin, Terry Hughes)[†√]

Ta Lun-hui [The Wheel of Life] [Taiwan] (d. King Hu, Li Hsing, Pai Ching-Jui)

Twilight Zone—The Movie [USA] (d. Joe Dante, John Landis, George Miller, Steven Spielberg)

La vita comincia a . . . [Italy] (d. Meredyth Lucas, Ettore Scola, J. Weinstein, Ante Zaninovic)

1984

L'addio e Enrico Berlinguer [Italy] (d. Ugo Adilardi, Silvano Agosti, Gianni Amico, Alfredo Angeli, Giorgio Arlorio, Gioia Benelli, Roberto Benigni, Bernardo Bertolucci, Giuseppe Bertolucci, Paolo Bianchini, Libero Bizzarri, Carlo Di Palma, Luigi Faccini, Giorgio Ferrara, Nicolò Ferrari, Andrea Frezza, Ansano Giannarelli, Franco Giraldi, Francesco Laudadio, Carlo Lizzani, Luigi Magni, Massimo Manuelli, Francesco Maselli, Giuliano Montaldo, Riccardo Napolitano, Piero Nelli, Renato Parascandolo, Luigi Perelli, Paolo Pietrangeli, Gillo Pontecorvo, Faliero Rosati, Roberto Russo, Massimo Sani, Ettore Scola, Raffaele Siniscalchi, Sergio Spina, Gabriele Tanferna, Anna Tatò, Gianni Toti, Piero Vivarelli)

Paris vu par . . . 20 ans après [Paris Seen By . . . 20 Years Later] [France] (d. Chantal Akerman, Bernard Dubois, Philippe Garrel, Frédéric Mitterrand, Vincent Nordon, Philippe Venault)

Shake, Rattle & Roll [Philippines] (d. Ishmael Bernal, Emmanuel H. Borlaza, Peque Gallaga)

Tales of the Third Dimension [USA] (d. Tom Durham, Worth Keeter, Thom McIntyre, Earl Owensby)[√]

1985

1985—Vad hände katten i råttans år? [Sweden] (d. Gunila Ambjörnsson, Stig Björkman, Staffan Lamm, Lennart Malmer, Solveig Nordlund, Christina Olofson, Göran du Rées, Carl Slättne, Maj Wechselmann, Lars Westman)

Absolutorium [Poland] (d. Slawomir Krynski, Adam Ustynowicz, Filip Zylber)

Address Unknown [USA] (d. Jim Campbell, Luc Courchesne, John Gianvito, Karine Hrechdakian, Cindy Kleine)

Even More Ripping Yarns [UK] (d. Jim Franklin, Terry Hughes)[†√]

Fright Show [USA] (d. Jeffrey Baker / Damon Santostefano, Frank Kerr, Jonathan Mostow, Richard Taylor)

Historias violentas [Mexico] (d. Carlos García Agraz, Daniel González Dueñas, Diego López Rivera, Gerardo Pardo, Víctor Saca)

More Ripping Yarns [UK] (d. Alan J. Bell, Jim Franklin)[†√]

Night Train to Terror [USA] (d. John Carr, Philip Marshak, Tom McGowan, Jay Schlossberg-Cohen, Greg Tallas)

Prima del futuro [Italy] (d. Fabrizio Caleffi / Ettore Pasculli, Gabriella Rosaleva)

Sny i marzenia [Dreams and Day-Dreams] [Poland] (d. Janusz Petelski, Paweł Pitera)

Twisted Illusions [USA] (d. Tim Ritter, Joel D. Wynkoop)

1986

Amazing Stories, Book One [USA] (d. Danny DeVito, Steven Spielberg)†√

Isklyuchenie bez pravil [USSR] (d. Sergei Baranov, Vladimir Bortko, Viktor Buturlin, Valeri Naumov, Aleksandr Rogozhkin)

Halimaw [Philippines] (d. Christopher de Leon, Mario O'Hara)

Jesus—Der Film [West Germany] (d. Michael Brynntrup, Jörg Buttgereit, Chris Dreier, Almut Iser, Konrad Kaufmann, Dietrich Kuhlbrodt, Georg Ladanyi, Giovanni Mimmo, Stiletto, Andreas Wildfang)

Okruchy wojny [Shards of the War] [Poland] (d. Andrzej Barszczyński, Jan Chodkiewicz)

Wang gong pa ba tiao xin [Strange Bedfellows] [Hong Kong] (d. Alfred Cheung, Lo Kin, Eric Tsang)

1987

Amazing Stories, Book Two [USA] (d. Brad Bird, Robert Zemeckis)†√

Amazing Stories, Book Three [USA] (d. Mick Garris, Leslie Linka Glatter, Peter Hyams)†√

Amazon Women on the Moon [USA] (d. Joe Dante, Carl Gottlieb, Peter Horton, John Landis, Robert K. Weiss)

Felix [West Germany] (d. Christel Buschmann, Helke Sander, Helma Sanders-Brahms, Margarethe von Trotta)

Diese Briten, diese Deutschen. Zueinander unterwegs nach Newcastle und Rostock. Zwei Filme—ein Dialog: Von Marx und Engels zu Marks & Spencer [From Marks & Spencer to Marx and Engels] [East Germany/UK] (d. Richard Grassnick / Ellin Hare / Murray Martin / Lorna Powell / Peter Roberts, Barbara Junge / Winfried Junge)

Geisterstunde [West Germany] (d. Susanne Aernicke, Dirk Eickhoff, Pascal Hoffmann, Volker Morlock)√

Manie-Manie Meikyu monogatari [Manie Manie: The Labyrinth Tales / Neo-Tokyo] [Japan] (d. Yoshiaki Kawajiri, Katsuhiro Otomo, Rin Taro)

Nachalo nevedomovo veka [The Beginning of an Unknown Era] [USSR] (d. Larissa Shepitko, Andrei Smirnov) {these two parts of an unrealized four-part omnibus film intended to mark the fiftieth anniversary of the October Revolution were completed in 1967 but shelved for twenty years}

Opera Omnibus [China] (d. Zhuosheng Chen, Feng Feng, Zhigang Feng, Moon Kwan, Yun Ling, Tu Long, Gongling Yang)

Really Weird Tales [USA] (d. John Blanchard, Paul Lynch, Don McBrearty)†√

Robotto kânibaru [Robot Carnival] [Japan] (d. Atsuko Fukushima, Hiroyuki Kitakubo, Hiroyuki Kitazume, Mao Lamdo, Kenji Morimoto, Takashi Nakamura, Hidetoshi Ohmori, Katsuhiro Otomo, Yasuomi Umetsu)

Sieben Frauen—Sieben Sünden [Seven Women—Seven Sins] [West Germany/France/ USA/Austria/Belgium] (d. Chantal Akerman, Maxi Cohen, Valie Export, Laurence Gavron, Bette Gordon, Ulrike Ottinger, Helke Sander)

We Shall Keep Our Love Forever [Kazakhstan/USSR] (d. Murat Alpiyev, Ardak Amirkulov, Serik Aprymov, Abai Karpykov, Rachid Nugmanov)

1988

Aria [Belgium/France/Italy/Austria/UK/USA] (d. Robert Altman, Bruce Beresford, Bill Bryden, Jean-Luc Godard, Derek Jarman, Franc Roddam, Nicolas Roeg, Ken Russell, Charles Sturridge, Julien Temple)

Bakayaro! Watakushi oktte masu [Japan] (d. Takahito Hara, Tetsuya Nakajima, Yukihiko Tsutsumi, Eriko Watanabe)

Brise-glace [Ice-Breaker] [France/Sweden] (d. Jean Rouch, Raúl Ruiz, Titte Törnroth)

Huang-se gushi [The Game They Call Sex] [Hong Kong] (d. Sylvia Chang, Siu-Di Wang)

Les Français vu par . . . [France] (d. Luigi Comencini, Jean-Luc Godard, Werner Herzog, David Lynch, Andrzej Wajda)

Martha, Ruth & Edie [Canada] (d. Norma Bailey, Deepa Mehta, Danièle J. Suissa)

Sposi [Italy] (d. Antonio Avati, Pupi Avati, Cesare Bastelli, Felice Farina, Luciano Manuzzi)

1989

12 registi per 12 città [12 Directors for 12 Cities] [Italy] (d. Michelangelo Antonioni, Bernardo Bertolucci, Giuseppe Bertolucci, Mauro Bolognini, Alberto Lattuada, Carlo Lizzani, Mario Monicelli, Ermanno Olmi, Gillo Pontecorvo, Francesco Rosi, Mario Soldati, Lina Wertmüller, Franco Zeffirelli)

After Midnight [USA] (d. Ken Wheat, Jim Wheat)

Bakayaro! 2: Shiwase ni naritai [Japan] (d. Masahiro Honda, Ryo Iwamatsu, Yusuke Narita, Gen Suzuki)

Brachni shegi [Marital Jokes] [Bulgaria] (d. Ivan Andonov, Docho Bodzhakov, Ivaylo Dzhambazo, Ivanka Grybcheva, Gueorgui Stoyanov)

Cita con la muerte [Mexico] (d. Alfonso Cuarón, Juan Antonio de la Riva, Alfredo Gurrola, Rafael Montero)

Echoes of Conflict [Israel] (d. Amit Goren, Gur Heller, Jorge Johanan Weller)

Kako je propao rokenrol [The Fall of Rock and Roll] [Yugoslavia] (d. Goran Gajic, Zoran Pezo, Vladimir Slavica)

New York Stories [USA] (d. Woody Allen, Francis Ford Coppola, Martin Scorsese)

Night Terror [USA] (d. Paul Howard, Michael Weaver)√

Pieces of Darkness [USA] (d. George Bonilla, J. Johnson Jr. III)√

Razvodi, razvodi [Divorces, Divorces] [Bulgaria] (d. Kosta Bikov, Veselin Branev, Ivaylo Dzhambazov, Ivanka Grybcheva, Georgi Stoev, Rangel Vulchanov)

La Révolution française [France/Italy] (d. Robert Enrico, Richard Heffron)
Tales from the Crypt [USA] (d. Richard Donner, Walter Hill, Robert Zemeckis)[†√]
Terrifying Tales [USA] (d. Paul Bunnell, Armand Garabidian, Ephraim Schwartz)[√]
Terror Eyes [USA] (d. Eric Parkinson, Michael Rissi, Steve Sommers)

1990

Adrénaline [France] (d. Anita Assal, Barthelemy Bompard, Philippe Dorison, John
   Hudson, Jean-Marie Maddeddu, Yann Piquer, Alain Robak)
Bakayaro! 3: Hen na yatsura [Japan] (d. Tsutomu Kashima, Hideki Kuroda, Naoto
   Yamakawa)
Boku ga byôki ni natta wake [The Reason I Got Sick] [Japan] (d. Shoji Kokami,
   Kazuki Omori, Takayoshi Watanabe)
City Life—The International Episode Film [Argentina/Netherlands] (d. Alejandro
   Agresti, Gábor Altorjay, José Luis Guérin, Krzysztof Kieslowski, Clemens
   Kopfenstein, Tato Kotetishvili, Ousmane William M'Bay, Eagle Pennell,
   Carlos Reichenbach, Dick Rijneke / Mildred van Leeuwarden, Mrinal Sen,
   Béla Tarr)
Dark Romances, Vol. 2 [USA] (d. Rodd Matsui, Patricia Miller, Bryan Moore,
   Samuel Oldham, Mark Shepard, John Strysik)[†√]
Due occhi diabolici [Two Evil Eyes] [Italy/USA] (d. Dario Argento, George A.
   Romero)
Five Feminist Minutes [Canada] (d. Christene Browne, Alison Burns, Janis Cole,
   Shawna Dempsey / Tracey Traeger, Ann Marie Flemming, Gwendolyn, Sook-
   Yin Lee, Michelle Mohabeer, Elaine Pain, Cathy Quinn / Francis Leeming)
Mujer transparente [Transparent Woman] [Cuba] (d. Mario Crespo, Ana Rodríguez,
   Mayra Segura, Hector Veitía, Mayra Vilásis)
Red Hot + Blue [USA/UK] (d. Percy Adlon, David Byrne, Alex Cox, Jonathan
   Demme, Philippe Gautier, Jim Jarmusch, Neil Jordan, Ed Lachman, Adelle Lutz
   / Sandy McLeod, Steve McLean, John Maybury, Jean Baptiste Mondino, Zak
   Ove, Mark Pellington, Roger Pomphrey, Matthew Rolston, John Scarlett-Davis,
   Wim Wenders; art breaks Matthew Duntemann; Bill Irwin sequences d. Adelle
   Lutz / Sandy McLeod)[‡]
Les secrets professionnels du Docteur Apfelglück [France] (d. Alessandro Capone,
   Stéphane Clavier, Mathias Ledoux, Thierry Lhermitte, Hervé Palud)
Tales of the Unknown [USA] (d. Greg Beeman, John Kim, Todd A. Marks, Roger
   Nygard)[√]
Tales from the Crypt, Vol. 2 [USA] (d. Howard Deutch, Tom Holland, Mary
   Lambert)[†√]
Tales from the Crypt, Vol. 3 [USA] (d. Howard Deutch, Walter Hill, Arnold
   Schwarzenegger)[†√]
I taràssachi [Italy] (d. Francesco Ranirie Martinotti, Rocco Mortelliti, Fulvio
   Ottaviano)
Women & Men: Stories of Seduction [USA] (d. Frederic Raphael, Tony Richardson,
   Ken Russell)[†√]

1991

Amazing Stories, Book Four [USA] (d. Paul Michael Glaser, Donald Petrie, Martin Scorsese)†√

Amazing Stories, Book Five [USA] (d. Bob Balaban, Leslie Linka Glatter, Norman Reynolds)†√

Contre l'oubli [Écrire contre l'oubli / Against Oblivion / Lest We Forget] [France] (d. Chantal Akerman, René Allio, Denis Amar, Jean Becker, Jane Birkin, Jean-Michel Carré, Patrice Chéreau, Alain Corneau, Costa-Gavras, Dominique Dante, Claire Denis, Raymond Depardon, Jacques Deray, Michel Deville, Jacques Doillon, Martine Francke, Gérard Frot-Coutaz, Francis Girod, Jean-Luc Godard / Anne-Marie Miéville, Romain Goupil, Jean-Loup Hubert, Robert Kramer, Patrice Leconte, Sarah Moon, Philippe Muyl, Michel Piccoli, Alain Resnais, Coline Serreau, Bertrand Tavernier, Nadine Trintignant)

Corsica! [Italy] (d. Nico Cirasola, Gianfrancesco Lazotti, Giorgio Molteni, Italo Spinelli, Pasqaule Squitieri)

Cuentos de Borges I [Borges Tales, Part I] [Argentina] (d. Héctor Olivera, Gerardo Vera)

La domenica specialmente [Especially on Sunday] [Italy/France/Belgium] (d. Francesco Barilli, Giuseppe Bertolucci, Marco Tullio Giordana, Giuseppe Tornatore)

He Said, She Said [USA] (d. Ken Kwapis, Marisa Silver)

Montréal vu par . . . six variations sur un thème [Montreal Sextet] [Canada] (d. Denys Arcand, Michel Brault, Atom Egoyan, Jacques Leduc, Léa Pool, Patricia Rozema)

Visages suisses [Swiss Profiles] [Switzerland] (d. Matteo Bellini, Simon Edlestein, Nicolas Gessner, Kurt Gloor, Claude Goretta, Thomas Koerfer, Pierre Koralnik, Urs Odermatt, Francis Ruesser, François Reichenbach, Hans-Ulrich Schlumpf, Viktor Tognola, Jacqueline Veuve)

With Friends Like These . . . [Canada] (d. Chris Malazdrewicz, Tom Parkinson, Alain Zaloum)

1992

The Dark Dealer [USA] (d. Tom Alexander, Wynn Winberg)

Harb El Khalij . . . wa baad [After the Gulf / Gulf War . . . What Next?] [Tunisia/France/Italy/UK] (d. Borhane Alaouié, Nouri Bouzid, Mostafa Darkaoui, Néjia Ben Mabrouk, Elia Suleiman)

Hotel Room [USA] (d. David Lynch, James Signorelli)†√

Inside Out: Erotic Tales of the Unexpected [USA] (d. Lizzie Borden, Adam Friedman, Linda Hassani, Alexander Payne, Tony Randel, Jeffrey Reiner, Richard Shepard)†√

Inside Out 2 [USA] (d. Nicholas Brandt, Nigel Dick, Martin Donovan, Linda Hassani, Paul Rachman, Tony Randel, Yuri Sivo, John Wentworth)†√

Inside Out 3 [USA] (d. David Bernath / Stuart Cave, Nigel Dick, Martin Donovan, Charles McDougall, Alexander Payne, Paul Rachman, Bernard Rose, Yuri Sivo, John Wentworth)†√

Inside Out 4 [USA] (d. Nigel Dick, Adam Friedman, Antoine Fuqua, Robert

Kubilos, Charles McDougall, Paul Rachman, Bernard Rose, Richard Shepard, John Wentworth)[†√]

Pineapple Tours [Japan] (d. Hayashi Tohma, Tsutomu Makiya, Yuji Nakae)

Prokleta je Amerika [Damned Be America] [Yugoslavia] (d. Ales Kurt, Marko Marinkovic, Slobodan Boban Skerlic)

Red Shoe Diaries 2: Double Dare [USA] (d. Zalman King, Tibor Takacs)[†√]

Southern Winds [Indonesia/Thailand/Philippines/Japan] (d. Mike de Leon, Slamet Rahardjo Djarot, Shoji Kokami, Cherd Songsri)

Strangers [USA] (d. Joan Tewkesbury, Daniel Vigne, Wayne Wang)[†√]

Women & Men: In Love There Are No Rules [USA] (d. Walter Bernstein, Mike Figgis, Kristi Zea)[†√]

1993

80 Mq—Ottantametriquadri [Italy] (d. Ignazio Agosta, Dido Castelli, Cecilia Calvi, Luca D'Ascanio, Luca Manfredi)

Body Bags [USA] (d. John Carpenter, Tobe Hooper)[†]

Erotique [Germany/USA] (d. Lizzie Borden, Clara Law, Monika Treut)

Fallen Angels [USA] (d. Tom Cruise, Alfonso Cuarón, Jonathan Kaplan)[†√]

Fallen Angels II [USA] (d. Tom Hanks, Phil Jouanou, Steven Soderbergh)[†√]

Kekkon [Japan] (d. Jôji Nagao, Hideo Onchi, Seijun Suzuki)

Kurt Vonnegut's Monkey House, Vol. 1 [USA] (d. Allan King, Gilbert Shilton, Paul Shapiro)[†√]

Kurt Vonnegut's Monkey House, Vol. 2 [USA] (d. Stan Daniels, Wayne Tourell)[†√]

Light Grey [Macedonia] (d. Srgjan Janichievich, Darko Mitrevski, Aleksandar Popovski)

Necronomicon [USA] (d. Christophe Gans, Shusuke Kaneko, Brian Yuzna)

Neues Deutschland [Germany] (d. Philip Gröning, Uwe Janson, Gerd Kroske, Dani Levy, Maris Pfeiffer)

Red Shoe Diaries 3: Another Woman's Lipstick [USA] (d. Rafael Eisenman, Zalman King, Ted Kotcheff)[†√]

Red Shoe Diaries 4: Auto Erotica [USA] (d. Michael Karbelnikoff, Zalman King, Alan Smithee)[†√]

Tel Aviv Stories [Israel] (d. Ayelet Menahemi, Nirit Yaron)

Things [USA] (d. Dennis Devine, Jay Woelfel)[√]

Two Mikes Don't Make a Wright [USA/UK] (d. Mike Leigh, Michael Moore, Dean Parisot)[‡]

1994

3,000 scénarios contre un virus [3,000 Scenarios to Combat a Virus] [France] (d. Jean Achache, Philippe Bérenger, Richard Berry, Jane Birkin, Paul Boujenah, Patrice Cazes, Caroline Champetier, Jacky Cukier, Jacques Deray, Xavier Durringer, Sebastien Graal, Laurent Heynemann, Benoit Jacquot, Gerard Jugnot, Cedric Klapisch, Philippe Lioret, Jean Marboeuf, Tonie Marshall, Ivana Massetti, Laetitia Masson, Michel Meyer, Fernand Moskowicz, Jean-Daniel Pillault,

Jacques Renard, Charlotte Silvera, Florence Strauss, Virginie Thévenet, Bernard Verley, Daniel Vigne, Patrick Volson)

Boys' Shorts [USA/Canada] (d. Mark Christopher, Stephen Cummins, Laurie Lynd, Michael Mayson, Marlon Riggs, Christopher Newby)‡

The Cockpit [Japan] (d. Takashi Imanishi, Yoshiaki Kawajiri, Ryôsuke Takahashi)√

Cosmic Slop [USA] (d. Reginald Hudlin, Warrington Hudlin, Kevin Rodney Sullivan)†√

Degenerazione [Degenerates] [Italy] (d. Antonio Antonelli, Asia Argento, Piergiorgio Bellochio, Eleonora Fiorini, Alex Infascelli, Antonio Manetti / Marco Manetti, Andrea Maulà, Andrea Prandstaller, Alberto Taraglio, Alessandro Valori)

Erotic Tales [Tales of Erotica] [Germany] (d. Mani Kaul, Ken Russell, Susan Siedelman)†

Erotic Tales II [Germany] (d. Paul Cox, Melvin van Peebles, Bob Rafelson)†

Les Films sans qualité [France] (d. Claude Bossion / Philippe Stepczak / Christophe Bamy, Denis Chevalier, Pip Chodorov, Laura Friedman, Martine Granier, Henri-François Imbert, Rayonne Lazer / Robert Chaussette, Pierre Merejkowski, Cyril Moulinie / Véronique Schiltz, Arnaud Romet, Ralph Soll, Philippe Stepczak)‡

Future Shock [USA] (d. Eric Parkinson, Matt Reeves, Francis "Oley" Sassone)†

Lian ai de tian kong [Modern Romance] [Hong Kong] (Wai Keung Lau, Lik-Chi Lee, Lun Ah, Jing Wong)

MGM Sarajevo—Covjek, bog, monstrum [MGM Sarajevo—Man, God, Monster] [Bosnia-Herzegovina] (d. Sarajevo Group of Authors [SaGA]: Mirza Idrizović, Ademir Kenović / Ismet Arnautalić, Pjer Žalica)

Parano, n'ayez pas peur d'en rire [France] (d. Anita Assal, John Hudson, Manuel Flèche, Yann Piquer, Alain Robak)

San tung gui shut doi [The New Age of Living Together / In Between] [Hong Kong] (d. Sylvia Chang, Samson Chiu, Yonfan)

Shake, Rattle & Roll V [Philippines] (d. Manny Castañeda, Jose Javier Reyes)

Siren Spirits [UK] (d. Frances Anne-Solomon, Ngozi Onwurah, Pratibha Parmar, Dani Williamson)‡

Three Tales from Senegal [Senegal] (d. Djibril Diop Mambéty, Mansour Sora Wade)‡

Twisted Tales [USA] (d. Rita Klus, Kevin J. Lindenmuth, Mick McCleery)

L'unico paese al mondo [The Only Country in the World] [Italy] (d. Francesca Archibugi, Antonio Capuano, Marco Tullio Giordana, Daniele Luchetti, Mario Martone, Carlo Mazzacurati, Nanni Moretti, Marco Risi, Stefano Rulli)

Vault of Horror 2 [USA] (d. Michael J. Fox, Russel Mulcahy, William Friedkin)†√

Vault of Horror 3 [USA] (d. Steven E. de Souza, Tom Hanks, Stephen Hopkins)†√

1995

À propos de Nice, la suite [France] (d. Catherine Breillat, Costa-Gavras, Claire Denis, Raymond Depardon, Abbas Kiarostami / Parviz Kimiavi, Pavel Lounguine, Raúl Ruiz)

Boys Life [USA] (d. Robert Lee King, Raoul O'Connell, Brian Sloan)‡

Er yue an shi [The Day That Doesn't Exist] [Hong Kong] (d. Wellson Chin, Ko Lam-pau)

Erotic Tales III [Germany] (d. Janus Majewski, Nicolas Roeg, Cinzia Th. Torrini)[†]

Felicidade é . . . [Happiness Is . . .] [Brazil] (d. Jorge Furtado, José Pedro Goulart, Cecílio Neto, José Roberto Torero)

Girlfriends [USA] (d. Barbara Heller, Mitch McCabe, Barbara Rose Michels, Ela Troyano)[‡]

Halbmond [Paul Bowles: Halfmoon] [Germany] (d. Irene von Alberti, Frieder Schlaich)

Historias breves [Argentina] (d. (Adrián Caetano, Gonzalo Suarez Echenique, Jorge Gaggero, Tristán Gicovate, Sandra Gugliota, Lucrecia Martel, Bruno Stagnaro, Andrés Tamborino / Ulises Rosell)

Lumière et compagnie [Lumière and Company] [France/Spain/Sweden] (d. Sarah Moon; "Lumière" films directed by Merzak Allouache, Theo Angelopoulos, Vincente Aranda, Gabriel Axel, John Boorman, Youssef Chahine, Alain Corneau, Costa-Gavras, Raymond Depardon, Francis Girod, Peter Greenaway, Lasse Hallstrom, Michael Haneke, Hugh Hudson, James Ivory / Ismail Merchant, Gaston Kabore, Abbas Kiarostami, Cedric Klapisch, Andrei Konchalovsky, Patrice Leconte, Claude Lelouch, Spike Lee, Bigas Luna, David Lynch, Claude Miller, Idrissa Ouedraogo, Arthur Penn, Lucian Pintilie, Jacques Rivette, Helma Sanders, Jerry Schatzberg, Nadine Trintignant, Fernando Trueba, Liv Ullmann, Jaco Van Dormael, Regis Wargnier, Wim Wenders, Kiju Yoshida, Zhang Yimou)

Memories [Japan] (d. Katsuhiro Otomo, Morimoto Koji, Okamura Tensai)

Paket aranžman [Yugoslavia] (d. Srdan Golubović, Ivan Stefanović, Dejan Zečević)

Picture Windows [USA] (d. Joe Dante, Bob Rafelson, John Boorman)[†√]

Pribytije pojezda [The Arrival of a Train] [Russian Federation] (d. Alexei Balabanov, Vladimir Khotinenko, Aleksandr Khvan, Dmitrii Meshkiev)

Red Shoe Diaries 5: Weekend Pass [USA] (d. Peter Care, Ted Kotcheff, Dominique Othenin-Girard)[†√]

Red Shoe Diaries 6: How I Met My Husband [USA] (d. Phillipe Angers, Bernard Aroux, Anne Goursaud)[†√]

Szeressük egymást gyerekek [Love Each Other] [Hungary] (d. Miklós Jancsó, Károly Makk, Pál Sándor)

Tempo di viaggio [Italy] (d. Andrei Tarkovsky, Tonino Guerra)[‡]

1996

Alien Agenda: Endangered Species [USA] (d. Gabriel Campisi, Ron Ford, Kevin J. Lindenmuth, Tim Ritter)[√]

Alien Agenda: Out of Darkness [USA] (d. Kevin J. Lindenmuth, Mick McCleery)[√]

America's Dream [USA] (d. Paris Barclay, Bill Duke, Kevin Rodney Sullivan)[†√]

Blue Hearts of New York [USA] (d. George Felner, John C. Kelleran, Daniel Maldonado, Nuria Olivé-Bellés, Jennifer Provost, Antonio Siqueira)

Boys in Love [USA] (d. George Camarda, P. David Ebersole, Barry Purves, Terracino)[‡]

Campfire Tales [USA] (d. Matt Cooper, Martin Kunert, David Semel)

Il caricatore [Italy] (d. Eugenio Cappuccio, Massimo Gaudioso, Fabio Nunziata)

Cosmos [Canada] (d. Jennifer Alleyn, Manon Briand, Marie-Julie Dallaire, Arto Paragamian, André Turpin, Denis Villeneuve)

Danske piger viser alt [Danish Girls Show Everything] [Denmark] (d. David Blair, Susanna Edwards, Franz Ernst, Gusztáv Hámos, Marc J. Hawker, Jaime Humberto Hermosillo, Mani Kaul, Mika Kaurismäki, Dušan Makavejev, Lars Norgard, Steen Rasmussen, Ane Mette Ruge, Jacob F. Schokking, Morten Skallerud, Monika Treut, Vibeke Vogel, Anne Regitze Wivel, Krzysztof Zanussi, Zhang Yuan)

Erotic Tales IV [Germany] (d. Detlev Buck, Mika Kaurismäki, Jos Stelling)†

Esercizi di stile [Exercises in Style] [Italy] (d. Sergio Citti, Volfango De Biasi, Maurizio Dell'Orso, Claudio Fragasso, Alex Infascelli, Francesco Laudadio, Luigi Magni, Lorenzo Mieli, Mario Monicelli, Pino Quartullo, Alessandro Piva, Faliero Rosati, Dino Risi, Cinzia Th. Torrini)

Four Rooms [USA] (d. Allison Anders, Alexandre Rockwell, Robert Rodriguez, Quentin Tarantino)

Historias breves II, parte 1 [Argentina] (d. Vicky Biagiola / Liliana Romero, Marcelo Brigante / Fredy Torres, Gregorio Crámer, Maximiliano González, Diego Panich, Gianfranco Quattrini, Diego Sabanés / Dieguillo Fernández, Agustín Torre)

Historias breves II, parte 2 [Argentina] (d. Hernán Belón / Tatiana Mereñuk, Pablo Belzagui, Diego Medina Creimer / Nicolás Theodossiou, Javier Demaría, Gonzalo Suárez Echenique, Rodrigo Grande, Javier Argüello Mora / Araujo, Alberto Ponce)

If These Walls Could Talk [USA] (d. Cher, Nancy Savoca)†√

Maegjuga aeinboda joheun 7gaji iyu [Seven Reasons Why Beer Is Better Than a Lover] [South Korea] (d. Kang Wu-Seok, Kim Yu-Jin, Jang Hyeon-Su, Jang Kil-Su, Jeong Ji-Yeong, Park Cheol-Su, Park Jong-Won)

Rainbow Stories [UK/Germany/Italy/Belgium/Netherlands] (d. Barr / Ferral, Harald Busch, Cane CapoVolto, Nina Danino, Bavo Defurne, Janica Draisma, Marc Geerards, Barbara Hanlo, Tina Keane)

Red Shoe Diaries 8: Night of Abandon [USA] (d. James Gavin Bedford, Rafael Eisenman, Rene Manzor)†√

Red Shoe Diaries 11: The Game [reissued 2000 as *Red Shoe Diaries 18: The Game*] [USA] (d. Philippe Angers, Rafael Esienman, Brian Grant)†√

Red Shoe Diaries 12: Girl on a Bike [USA] (d. Lydie Callier, Stephen Halbert, Tibor Takacs)†√

Red Shoe Diaries 13: Four on the Floor [USA] (d. Rafael Eisenman, Zalman King, David Womark)†√

Si mian xia wa [Four Faces of Eve] [Hong Kong] (d. Kwok-Leung Gan, Eric Kot, Jan Lamb)

Syndig sommer [Norway] (d. Nina F. Grünfeldt, Ellen Lande, Tove Cecilie Sverdrup, Anne Berit Vestby)

Tales till the End [USA] (d. Barry Gaines, Phil Herman, Ben Stanski)√

Twisted Tales [Twisted] [Australia] (d. Christopher Robin Collins, Gregor Jordan, Samantha Lang, Catherine Millar)†√

Virtual Terror [UK] (d. Nigel Barton, Jonathan Glendening, Omid Nooshin, Ian Powell)

Women from Down Under [Australia/USA] (d. Christina Andreef, Christina Parker, Monica Pellizzari, Jane Schneider)‡

1997

1996: Pust på meg! [1996: Breath] [Norway] (d. Eva Dahr, Oddvar Einarson, Mona Hoel, Marius Holst, Eva Isaksen)

Africa Dreaming [South Africa/Namibia/Zimbabwe] (d. Palesaka Letlaka-Nkosi, Richard Pakleppa, Farai Sevenzo)

Alien Agenda: Under the Skin [USA] (d. Ron Ford, Michael Legge, Kevin J. Lindenmuth, Tom Vollmann)√

L'@mour est à réinventer, dix histoires d'amours au temps du sida [Love Reinvented] [France] (d. Merzak Allouache, Françoise Decaux-Thomlet, François Dupeyron, Phillipe Faucon, Anne Fontaine, Jean-Claude Guiguet, Stephen Jones, David Ottenhouse, Pierre Salvadori, Nils Tavernier, Paul Vecchiali, Marion Vernoux)

Boys Life 2 [USA] (d. Mark Christopher, Tom DeCerchio, Nicholas Perry, Peggy Rajski)‡

I corti italiani [Italy] (d. Romeo Conte, Daniele Costantini, Camilla Costanzo / Alessio Cremonini, Raimondo Crociani, Simona Izzo, Mario Monicelli, Gillo Pontecorvo, Federico S. Quadrani, Ettore Scola, Ricky Tognazzi)

Filmart Takes Position: ALIEN/NATION [Austria] (d. Dietmar Brehm, Gustav Deutsche, Paul Divjak, Jochen Ehmann, Hänzel and Gretzel, Michael Domes / Caroline Weihs, Kurt Kren, Marco Lanza, Holger Mader, Shaheen Merali, Kristin Mojsiewicz, Jonas Raeber, Tim Sharp, Sikay Tang)

F.L.A.M.E.S. [Flames—The Movie] [Philippines] (d. Khryss Adalia, Jerry Lopez Sineneng)

Franz Kafka's It's a Wonderful Life and Other Tales [UK/USA] (d. John D. Allen, Peter Capaldi, Richard D'Alessio, Don Scardino)‡

Guilty Pleasures [USA] (d. Joseph Parda, Joseph Zaso)√

The Hunger [Canada/UK] (d. Russell Mulcahy, Jake Scott, Tony Scott)†

Kisses in the Dark [USA] (d. Larry Hankin, Roger Paradiso, Louis Venosta, Sasha Wolf)‡√

Latavio [Life No. 2] [Latvia] (d. Arta Biseniece, Aija Bleja, Viesturs Kairiss, Dzintars Krumins, Mara Linina, Andis Miziss, Igors Verenieks, Ilze Vidauska, Anna Viduleja, Kristine Zelve)

Rescuers: Stories of Courage: "Two Couples" [USA] (d. Tim Hunter, Lynne Littman)†√

Rescuers: Stories of Courage: "Two Families" [USA] (d. Tony Bill, Tim Hunter)†√

Riot [USA] (d. Richard Di Lello, David C. Johnson, Alex Munoz, Galen Yuen)†√

Shake, Rattle & Roll VI [Philippines] (d. Maurice Carvajal, Anton Juan, Frank G. Rivera)

Shopping for Fangs [Canada/USA] (d. Quentin Lee, Justin Lee)

Short Cinema Journal 1:1—Invention [USA] (d. Stephen E. Berkman, Carrie Blank, Eva Ilona Brzeski, Pepe Danquart, Ron Fricke, Mark Gustafson, George Hickenlooper, Daniel Peacock, Albert Watson, Tim Watts / David Stoten)‡√

Short Cinema Journal 1:2—Dreams [USA] (d. Alison De Vere, Carmen Elly, Michael Failla, Mark Gustafson, George Hickenlooper, Guy Maddin, Chris Marker, Joachim Solum / Thomas Lien)‡√

Short Cinema Journal 1:3—Authority [USA] (d. Jane Campion, Bruno de André, Piet Kroon, Alain Resnais, Michael James Rowland, Natasha Uppal, Sasha Wolf)‡√

Sipurim ketzarim Al Ahavah [Short Stories about Love] [Israel] (d. Gil Levenberg, Irit Linur, Oure Rosenwaks)

Subway Stories: Tales from the Underground [USA] (d. Bob Balaban, Patricia Benoit, Julie Dash, Jonathan Demme, Ted Demme, Abel Ferrara, Alison Maclean, Craig McKay, Lucas Platt, Seth Rosenfeld)†√

I vesuviani [Italy] (d. Pappi Corsicato, Antonio Capuano, Antonietta de Lillo, Stefano Incerti, Mario Martone)

Yin yang lu [Troublesome Night] [Hong Kong] (d. Steve Cheng Wai-Man, Victor Tam Long-Cheung, Herman Yau Lai-To)

1998

Creaturerealm: Demons Wake [USA] (d. Michael Legge, Tim Thompson)√

Creaturerealm: From the Dead [USA] (d. Ron Ford, Kevin J. Lindenmuth)√

Crossroads [Raskršće] [Yugoslavia] (d. Tatjana Brzaković, Narcise Darijević, Miloša Petričića)

Enu liezhuan [Bad Girl Trilogy] [Taiwan] (d. Lin Jingjie, Wen Yaoting, Zhan Yingyu)

Evil Streets [USA] (d. Joseph F. Parda, Terry R. Wickham)√

Kawaii hito [Pretty One / Pretty Girl] [Japan] (d. Daishi Muramoto, Shin Togashi, Tetsu Maeda)

Kuldesak [Indonesia] (d. Nan Achnas, Mira Lesmana, Rizal Mantovani, Riri Riza)

Mala época [Bad Times] [Argentina] (d. Mariano De Rosa, Rodrigo Moreno, Salvador Roselli, Nicolás Saad)

Min ching ching yau paai geng [Faces of Horror / Faces of Horrid] [Hong Kong] (d. Lam Jin-wai, Szeto Ying-kit, Yiu Tin-hung)

Slidin'—Alles bunt und wunderbar [Slidin'—Bright and Shiny World] [Austria] (d. Barbara Albert, Michael Grimm, Reinhard Jud)

Things 2 [USA] (d. Mike Bowler, Dennis Devine, Steve Jarvis)√

Three Minutes: A Cineworks Omnibus Compendium [Canada] (d. Jeff Carter, Diarmuid Conway, Mary Daniel, Bonnie Devlin, Bill Evans, Mike Hoolboom, Alex Mackenzie, Claudia Morgado, Sylvie Peltier, Ileana Pietrobruno, Velcrow Ripper, Randy Rotheisier, Mina Shum, Deborah Tabah)

Traição [Treason / Betrayal] [Brazil] (d. José Henrique Fonseca, Arthur Fontes, Cláudio Torres)

Zbogum na dvadesetiot vek [Goodbye 20th Century] [Macedonia] (d. Darko Mitrevski, Aleksandar Popovski)

1999

1997: Tørst—Framtidens forbrytelser [1997: Thirst—Crimes of the Future] [Norway] (d. Karoline Frogner, Nathilde Overrein Rapp, Maria Fuglevaag Warinski)

À vot' service [France] (d. Eric Bartonio, Claude Berne, Myriam Donasis, Laurence Katrian, Gabriel Mamruth, Caroline Sarrion, Alexandre Schmitt, Philippe Vauvillé)

Boys Briefs [USA/France/Germany/Hong Kong] (d. Simon Chung, Pierre Yves Clouin, Luc Feit, David Kittredge, Dean Slotar, Sam Zalutsky)‡

Boys in Love 2 [USA] (d. David Briggs, Todd Downing, Stuart Main, John Scott Matthews, Patrick McGuinn, Joel Moffat, Barry Purves)‡

Erotic Tales V [Germany] (d. Markus Fischer, Rosa Von Praunheim, Georgi Shengelaya)†

Fantasia 2000 [USA] (d. James Algar, Gaetan Brizzi / Paul Brizzi, Hendel Butoy, Francis Glebas, Eric Goldberg, Don Hahn, Pixote Hunt)

Ghessé hayé Kish [Tales of Kish Island] [Iran] (d. Bahram Beyza'i, Abolfazl Jalili, Mohsen Makhmalbaf, Naser Taqva'i)

Historias breves III: "Ojo derecho" [Argentina] (d. Marcelo Del Puerto, Gabriel Lichtmann, Sebastián Rodríguez Lozano, Guido Lublinsky, Fernando Massobrio, Carlos Monroy, Martín Romanella, Roberto Soto)

Historias breves III: "Ojo izquierdo" [Argentina] (d. Gustavo Esteban, Marco Grossi, Santiago Loza, Gustavo Macri, Daniel Mancini, Andrés Muschietti, Liliana Paolinelli, Marcelo Schapces)

ID Swiss [Switzerland] (d. Fulvio Bernasconi, Christian Davi, Nadia Fares, Wageh George, Kamal Musale, Thomas Thümena, Stina Werenfels)

Kass kukub käppadele [Happy Landing] [Estonia] (d. Peeter Herzog, Jaak Kilmi, Rainer Sarnet)

Love Songs [USA] (d. Andre Braugher, Louis Gossett Jr., Robert Townsend)√

Midsommar-Stories [Germany] (d. Elena Álvarez, Michael Chauvistré, Andi Niessner, Livia Vogt, Heike Wasem)

Picture Windows [USA] (d. Peter Bogdanovich, Norman Jewison, Jonathan Kaplan)†√

Praha očima [Prague Stories] [Czech Republic/France/Netherlands] (d. Artemio Benki, Vladimír Michálek, Michaela Pavlátová, Martin Šulík)

Sellised kolm lugu . . . [Tris stasti par . . . / Three Stories About . . .] [Estonia/Latvia] (d. Ervin Õunapuu, Askolds Saulitis, Peeter Simm)

Šest statečných [The Magnificent Six] [Czech Republic] (d. Aurel Klimt, Vladimír Král, Tereza Kučerová, Vojtěch Mašek, Martin Repka, Jaroslav Vojtek)

Short 4: Seduction [USA] (d. Jeremy Boxer, Seth Edelstein, Don Hertzfeldt, Piet Kroon, Don Nichol, Marianne Olsen Ulrichsen, Pedro Serrazina, Masahiro Sugano, Robert Milton Wallace)‡√

Short 5: Diversity [USA] (d. Vin Diesel, Arthur Fiedler, Erik Friedlander, Eileen O'Meara, Jacob Rosenberg, John Schnall)‡√

Short 6: Insanity [USA] (d. Joel Bajrech, Dirk Beiliën, David Birdsell, Everardo Valerio Gout, Don Hertzfeldt, Bob Judd, Brendan Kelly, John McCloskey, Amy Winfrey)‡√

Tube Tales: Stories from the Underground [UK] (d. Gaby Dellal, Stephen Hopkins, Bob Hoskins, Menhaj Huda, Armando Iannucci, Amy Jenkins, Jude Law, Charles McDougall, Ewan McGregor)†√

2000

3 Erotic Tales [Germany] (d. Bernd Heiber, Georgi Shengelaya, Jos Stelling)†

Afrocentricity [USA] (d. Tony Boyd, Jeff Byrd, Lee Davis, Niva Dorrell, Muhammida El Muhajir, Charles Stone III, Chuck Wilson) ‡√

Boys Life 3 [USA/France] (d. Gregory Cooke, David Fourier, Jason Gould, Bradley Rust Gray, Lane Janger)

Erotic Tales VI [Germany] (d. Hal Hartley, Bernd Heiber, Antonis Kokkino)†

Erotic Tales VII [Germany] (d. Fridrik Thor Fridriksson, Amos Kollek, Jos Stelling)†

Erotic Tales VIII [Germany] (d. Eoin Moore, Susan Streitfeld, Petr Zelenka)†

Floating Island [Taiwan] (d. Singing Chen, Chen Wei-ssu, Chou Mei-ling, Chu Hsien-jer, Hsu Juei-lan, Huang Tin-fu, Kuo Chen-ti, MJ Lee, Lee Yung-chuan, Li Chih-chiang, Shen Ko-shang, Jimmy Wu)

If These Walls Could Talk 2 [USA] (d. Jane Anderson, Martha Coolidge, Anne Heche)†√

The Last Five Short Films of the 2nd Millennium [Palestine] (d. Azza Al-Hassan, Rachid Mashharawi, Mai Masri, Elia Suleiman, Subhi Zbeidi)

Maldoror [UK/Germany] (d. Andrew Coram, Steven Eastwood, Filmgruppe Abgedreht, Hant Film, Filmgruppe Chaos, Jenigerfilm, Caroline Kennedy, Duncan Reekie, Colette Rouhier, Kerri Sharp, Paul Tarrago, Jennet Thomas)‡

N [Digital Short Films by Three Filmmakers] [South Korea] (d. Kim Yun-tae, Park Kwang-su, Zhang Yuan)

Red Shoe Diaries 14: Luscious Lola [USA] (d. Rafael Eisenman, Zalman King, Stephen Halbert)†√

Scénarios sur la drogue [France] (d. Alain Beigel, Emmanuelle Bercot, Diane Bertrand, Jean Bocheux, Laurent Bouhnik, Manuel Boursinhac, Guillaume Canet / Jean-Christophe Pagnac, Etienne Chantiliez, Franck Chiche, Antoine De Caunes, Isabelle Dinelli, Jean-Teddy Filippe, Françoise Huguier, Henri-Paul Korchia, Georges Lautner, Lionel Mougin, Guillaume Nicloux, Santiago Otheguy, Vincent Perez, Bernard Schoukroun / Fred Journet, Seb et Simon, Arnaud Sélignac, Jean-Louis Tribes, Marion Vernoux)

Short 7: Utopia [USA] (d. Luc Beauchamp, Frank Chindamo, Sophie Fiennes, Young Man Kang, Mark Osborne, Erik Paesel, Jonathon Stearns, Everardo Valerio / Leopoldo Gout)‡√

Short 8: Vision [USA] (d. Gordon Bijelonic, Alina Hiu-Fan Chau, Leni Reifenstahl, Jonathon Stearns, Charles Stone III, Amy Talkington, Gunnar Vikene, Chi Chi Zhang)‡√

Short 9: Trust [USA] (d. Phil Berger, Olivier Boulanger / Martin Koscielniak, Fatmir Cosi, Nash Edgerton / Kieran Darcy-Smith, Robert Fenz, David R.

Garrett, Michael Horowitz / Colburn Tseng, Hannes Rall, Jonathon Stearns, Tara Veneruso, Pi Ware)‡√

Short 10: Chaos [USA] (d. Gav Barbey, David Birdsell, Paul Bonner, Andrew Busti / Sebastian Castillo, George Lucas, Preston Maigetter, Sienna McLean, Eileen O'Meara, Tahsin Ozgur, Greg Pak, Ferenc Rófusz, Peter Sollett)‡√

Short: International Release [USA] (d. Gav Barbey, Sophie Fiennes / Shari Roman, Young Man Kang, Martin Koscielniak, Muhammida el Muhajir, Hannes Rall, Ferenc Rófusz, Everardo Valerio / Lepoldo Gout, Agnès Varda)‡√

Short: International Release, Vol. 2 [USA] (d. Renaat Coppens, Alina Hu-Fan Chau, Natasha de Betak, Peter Long / Kate Ellis, Gerry McColgan, Peter Rosen, Tara Veneruso)‡√

Stories about Love [Singapore] (d. Cheah Chee Kong, Abdul Nizam, James Toh)

Tabi tabi po [Philippines] (d. Jose Carreon, Tata Esteban, Joven Tan)

Terror Tract [USA] (d. Lance W. Dreesen, Clint Hutchison)

Yo nimo kimyo na monogatari—Eiga no tokubetsuhen [Tales of the Unusual] [Japan] (d. Mamoru Hosi, Masayuki Ochiai, Hisao Ogura, Masayuki Suzuki)†

Začátek světa [The Beginning of the World] [Czech Republic] (d. Vladimír Drha, Pavel Melounek, Dan Svátek)

2001

99euro-films [Germany] (d. Sebastian Beer, Miriam Dehne, Matthias Glasner, Esther Gronenborn, RP Kahl, Michael Klier, Nicolette Krebitz, Peter Lohmeyer, Daniel Petersen, Frieder Schlaich, Mark Schlichter, Martin Walz)

Bangkok Haunted [Thailand] (d. Oxide Pang Chun, Pisut Praesangeam)

Blood of the Werewolf [USA] (d. Joe Bagnardi, Bruce G. Hallenbeck, Kevin Lindenmuth)√

Bogotá 2016 [Colombia] (d. Alessandro Basilel, Ricardo Guerra / Jaime Sánchez, Pablo Mora)

Campfire Stories [USA] (d. Bob Crea, Adrzej Krakowski, Jeff Mazzola)

Dead Room [UK] (p. Seventh Twelfth Collective; d. Julian Boote, Mark Bowden, Gavin Boyd, Ian David Diaz)

Digital Short Films by Three Filmmakers [UK/Taiwan/China] (d. John Akomfrah, Jia Zhangke, Tsai Ming-liang)

Lianai qiyi [Heroes in Love] [Hong Kong] (d. Stephen Fung, GC Goo-bi, Jan Lamb, Nicholas Tse, Wing Shya)

Un mondo diverso è possibile [Another World Is Possible] [Italy] (d. Alfredo Angeli, Giorgio Arlorio, Mario Balsamo, Giuliana Berlinguer, Maurizio Carrassi, Guido Chiesa, Francesca Comencini, Massimo Felisatti, Nicolò Ferrari, Gianfranco Fiore, Massimiliano Franceschini, Andrea Frezza, Giuliana Gamba, Roberto Giannarelli, Franco Giraldi, Wilma Labate, Salvatore Maira, Francesco Maselli, Mario Monicelli, Paolo Pietrangeli, Gillo Pontecorvo, Francesco Ranieri Martinotti, Nino Russo, Gabriele Salvatores, Massimo Sani, Stefano Scialotti, Pasquale Scimeca, Ettore Scola, Daniele Segre, Carola Spadoni, Sergio Spina, Ricky Tognazzi, Fulvio Wetzl)

Pas d'histoires! 12 regards sur le racisme au quotidien [France] (d. Yves Angelo / François
Dupeyron, Yamina Benguigui, Paul Boujenah, Catherine Corsini, Emilie
Deleuze, Xavier Durringer, Philippe Jullien, Philippe Jullien / Jean-Pierre
Lemouland, Philippe Lioret, Vincent Lindon, Fanta Régina Nacro, Christophe
Otzenberger)

Red Shoe Diaries 17: Swimming Naked [USA] (d. Rafael Eisenman, Zalman
King)[†√]

Sei come sei [Italy] (d. Massimo Cappelli, Luca Lucini, Herbert Simone Paragnani,
Guerino Sciulli, Anselmo Talotta, Andrea Zaccariello)

Short 11: Ecstasy [USA] (d. Chris Backhouse, Saul Bass, Drew Daywalt / David
Schneider, Charles and Ray Eames, Fran Krause, Preston Maigetter, Daniel
Peacock, Shawn Scheppes, Jonathon Stearns / Gordon Bijelonic, Andrew
Takeuchi / Rob Schmidt, Alex Turner, Slavko Vorkapich / John Hoffman,
Kirsten Winter)[‡√]

Short: International Release, Vol. 3 [USA] (d. Chris Backhouse, Peter Capaldi, Greg
Durbin, Lotta and Uzi Geffenblad, John Kelly, Preston Maigetter, Daniel
Peacock, Jonathon Stearns, Tara Veneruso)[‡√]

Strange Frequency [USA] (d. Mary Lambert, Bryan Spicer)[†√]

Strange Frequency 2 [USA] (d. Neill Fearnley, Kevin Inch, Jeff Woolnough)[†√]

Tokyo Zance [Japan] (d. Kelly Chan [Wai Lam / Kelly Chen], Katsuhiko Hibino,
Takanori Jinnai, Kazuna Iida, Takashi Matsuo, Naoko Nozawa, Shin
Yamagishi)

2002

11'09"01—September 11 [UK/France] (d. Youssef Chahine, Amos Gitai, Alejandro
González Iñárritu, Shohei Imamura, Claude Lelouch, Ken Loach, Samira
Makhmalbaf, Mira Nair, Idrissa Ouedraogo, Sean Penn, Danis Tanovic)

24 Sata [24 Hours] [Croatia] (d. Goran Kulenović, Kristijan Milić)

Barcelona, Historia de una noche [Barcelona, Story of a Night] [Spain] (d. Jorge Acebo,
Juanma Alonso, Marcelo Bukin, Roberto Castón, Oscar de Gispert, Ramiro
Lapiadra, Gustavo Verástegui)

Belgrade Sound [Serbia] (d. Stefan Arsenijević, Ivana Panić, Jelena Stanković,
Andrijana Stojković)

Fimfárum Jana Wericha [Czech Republic] (d. Aurel Klimt, Vlasta Pospíšilová)

*Folk flest bor i Kina [Utopia—Nobody Is Perfect in the Perfect Country / Most People
Live in China]* [Norway] (d. Martin Asphaug, Arild Fröhlich, Sara Johnsen,
Magnus Martens, Hans Petter Moland, Terje Rangnes, Thomas Robsahm,
Ingeborg Torgerson, Morten Tyldum)

Fragmentos urbanos [Chile] (d. Antonino Ballestrazzi, Sebastián Campos, Claudia
Menéndez, Mauricio Pesutic, Sergio Pineda, Kenji Tanida)

Freitagnacht [Friday Night] [Germany] (d. Franz Müller, Philipp Schäfer, Martin
Scharf, Jens Schillmöller, Tini Tüllmann, Tom Uhlenbruck)

Jam Films [Japan] (d. George Ida, Shunji Iwai, Ryuhei Kitamura, Rokuro
Mochizuk, Tetsuo Shinohara, Yukihoko Tsutsumi, Isao Yukisada)[‡]

Jeon jang keu I hu [After the War / Digital Short Films by Three Filmmakers] [South Korea/Japan/China] (d. Moon Seung-Wook, Nobuhiro Suwa, Wang Xiaoshuai)

Jött egy busz . . . [A Bus Came . . .] [Hungary] (d. Viktor Bodó, Kornél Mundruczó, György Pálfi, Árpád Schilling, Ferenc Török)

Mama Africa [Burkina Faso/France] (d. Fanta Regina Nacro, Zulfar Otto-Sallies, Ingrid Sinclair)‡

Mudjima paemilli [No Comment] [South Korea] (d. Lee Hyun-jong, Park Kwang-hyun, Park Sang-won)

NightThirst [USA] (d. Jon McBride, John Polonia, Mark Polonia)√

Proyect gvul [Border Project] [Israel] (d. Rima Essa, Adi Halfin, Nadav Lapid, Dani Rosenberg, Tamar Singer)

Radhošť [Czech Republic] (d. Tomáš Doruška, Pavel Göbl, Bohdan Sláma)

San geng [Saam gang / Three] [South Korea/Thailand/Hong Kong] (d. Peter Ho-Sun Chan, Kim Jee-Woon, Nonzee Nimibutr)

Six in Austin [USA] (d. Kat Chandler, Gonzo Gonzales, Geoff Marslett, Zack and Wyatt Phillips, Bob Ray, David and Nathan Zellner)

Ten Minutes Older: The Cello [Germany/UK/USA/France] (d. Bernardo Bertolucci, Claire Denis, Mike Figgis, Jean-Luc Godard, Jirí Menzel, Michael Radford, Volker Schlondörff, István Szabó)

Ten Minutes Older: The Trumpet [UK/Germany] (d. Victor Érice, Werner Herzog, Jim Jarmusch, Chen Kaige, Aki Kaurismäki, Spike Lee, Wim Wenders)

Underground Zero: Program 1 [USA] (d. Frazer Bradshaw, Eva Ilona Brzeski, Norman Cowie, David Driver, Robert Edwards, Rob Epstein / Jeffrey Friedman, John Haptas / Kristine Samuelson, Paul Harrill, Laura Plotkin, Jay Rosenblatt, Ira Sachs, Valerie Soe, Caveh Zahedi; curated by Jay Rosenblatt and Caveh Zahedi)

Underground Zero: Program 2 [USA] (d. Bushra Azzouz, Cathy Cook, Cathy Crane / Sarah Lewison, Jeanne C. Finley / John Muse, Martha Gorzycki, Marcia Jarmel, Nancy D. Kates, Barbara Klutinis, Thad Povey / The Scratch Film Junkies, Rock Ross, Lucas Sabean, Abigail Severance / Julia Inez Gandelsonas, Phil Solomon, Mark Street, Greg Watkins, Dan Weir, Chel White, Marina Zurkow)

Urban Visions [Stadtvisionen / Visions urbanes] [Spain/UK/France/Germany/Finland/USA/Italy] (d. Gorka Aguado, Sean Baker, Roger Beebe, Rudolf Buitendach, Stefano Canapa, Pierre-Yves Cruaud, Hilton Earl, Lombardi-Clan, Nosfe, Corrina Schnitt, GG Tarantola)‡

Zur Lage [State of the Nation: Austria in Six Chapters] [Austria] (d. Barbara Albert, Michael Glawogger, Ulrich Seidl, Michael Sturminger)

2003

99euro-films 2 [Germany] (d. Tony Baillargeat, Nacho Cerda, RP Kahl, Harry Kümel, Benjamin Quabeck, Richard Stanley, Ellen ten Damme, Stephan Wagner, Xawery Zulawski)

The Animatrix [USA] (d. Peter Chung, Andy Jones, Kouji Morimoto, Mahiro Maeda, Shinitirô Watanabe, Takeshi Koike, Yoshiaki Kawajiri)

Before I Die [USA] (d. Phil Herman, Dave Castiglione, Joel D. Wynkoop)√

Boys Life 4 [USA] (d. Phillip J. Bartell, Alan Brown, Eric Mueller, Brian Sloan)

Cinema16: British Short Films [UK] (d. Stephen Daldry, Simon Ellis, Jim Gillespie, Peter Greenaway, Tom and Charles Guard, Asif Kapadia, Mike Leigh, Toby MacDonald, Adrian J. McDowell, Morad McKinnon, Christopher Nolan, Martin Parr, Brian Perceval, Lynne Ramsay, Ridley Scott, John Smith)‡√

Digital Short Films by Three Filmmakers [Japan/Iran/South Korea] (d. Aoyama Shinji, Bahman Ghobadi, Park Ki-yong)

Experiments in Terror [USA/Austria] (d. Kerry Laitala, Damon Packard, David Sherman, Peter Tscherkassky, J. X. Williams, Lloyd M. Williams) ‡√

Erotic Tales IX [Germany] (d. Bob Rafelson, Justin Leonard Stauber, Dito Tsintsadze)†

Erotic Tales X [Germany] (d. Bernd Heiber, Amos Kollek, Jos Stelling)†

Firenze, il nostro domani [Italy] (d. Franco Angeli, Franco Bernini, Francesca Comencini, Massimo Felisatti, Nicolò Ferrari, Gianfranco Fiore, Giuliana Gamba, Franco Giraldi, Salvatore Maira, Francesco Maselli, Mario Monicelli, Gillo Pontecorvo, Francesco Ranieri Martinotti, Pasquale Scimeca, Sergio Spina, Fulvio Wetzl)

Ghost Office [Hong Kong] (d. Kuk Kok-leung, Law Wing-cheong, Andy Ng)√

Goregoyles: First Cut [Canada/USA] (d. Augustine Arredondo, Kevin J. Lindenmuth, Alexandre Michaud)√

Horrortales.666 [USA] (d. Ryan Cavalline, Chip Herman, Michael Hoffmann, Gary Whitson)√

Jam Films 2 [Japan] (d. Hide Inoue, Junji Kojima, Eiki Takahashi, Kouki Tange)

Killers [Japan] (d. Hidemichi Okawa, Kazuhiro Kiuchi, Mamoru Oshii, Shuji Kawada, Takanori Tsujimoto)

Monstersdotcom [USA] (d. Andy Kumpon, Kevin J. Lindenmuth, Chris Mack, Wayne Spitzer)√

Next Victim [USA] (d. Michael Chamberlain, Timothy Gates, Jeff Solano)

onedotzero_select dvd1 [UK/France/USA] (d. le cabinet, D-fuse, Richard Fenwick, Tim Hope, Jake Knight, The Light Surgeons, Lynnfox, Andy Martin, mitget, pleix collective, Shynola, Tomato, twenty2product, Unit9, Run Wrake)‡√

The Path [South Korea] (d. Joo Hyun-sook, Kim Yi-chan, Moon Sung-jun, Mixrice)√

Sajang-seongeo [Sex Is . . .] [South Korea] (d. Kim Jeong-gu, Lee Ji-sang, Lee Song Hee-il, Yu Sang-gon)

Senses [UK] (d. Coke Ayala, Naruna Kaplan de Maceno, John I. Marsala, Norma Nebot, Jamie Palmer)

Werewolf Tales [USA] (d. John Bowker, Ron Ford, Joe Sherlock)√

Yeo-seot-gae-ui siseon [If You Were Me] [South Korea] (d. Jeong Jae-eun, Park Chan-wook, Park Jin-pyo, Park Kwang-su, Yeo Kyun-dong, Yim Soon-rey)

2004

1.3.6 [South Korea] (d. Lee Young-jae, Jang Jin, Song Il-gon)

18-J [Argentina] (d. Daniel Burman, Adrián Caetano, Lucía Cedrón, Alejandro Doria, Alberto Lecchi, Marcelo Schapces, Carlos Sorín, Juan Bautista Stagnaro, Adrián Suar, Mauricio Wainrot)

Around Midnight [USA] (d. Laura Giglio, Christopher Kahler, Gary Whitson)$^\surd$

Bem-Vindo a São Paulo [Welcome to São Paulo] [Brazil] (d. Ash, Wolfgang Becker, Renata de Almeida, Maria de Medeiros, Franco de Peña, Hanna Elias, Amos Gitai, Mika Kaurismäki, Max Lemcke, Jim McBride, Mercedes Moncada, Phillip Noyce, Daniela Thomas, Tsai Ming-liang, Andrea Vecchiato, Caetano Veloso, Kiju Yoshida)

The Canterbury Tales [UK] (d. Andy DeEmmony, Julian Jarrold, John McKay, Marc Munden)$^{\dagger\surd}$

Cinema16: European Short Films [European Union] (d. Roy Andersson, Javier Fesser, Jean-Luc Godard, Andres Thomas Jensen, Krzysztof Kieslowski, Jan Kounen, Patrice Leconte, Lukas Moodyson, Nanni Moretti, Chris Morris, Peter Mullan, Juan Solanas, Jan Svankmajer, Lars von Trier, Tom Tykwer, Virgil Wildrich)$^{\ddagger\surd}$

Costo argentino [Argentina] (d. Diego M. Castro / Cristian Arriaga, Mercedes González del Solar, Martín Frías, Julio Gómez, Ricardo Díaz Lacoponi, Gonzalo Pérez / Viviana Hourcade, Hugo Soria, Santiago Villarroel / Hugo Curletto)

CreepTales [USA] (d. Tim Boxell, Stephen Hegyes, Steve Hegyi, Ken Mandel, Greg Middleton, Roger Nygard, James Salisbury, Rod Slane)$^\surd$

Death 4 Told [USA] (d. Bo Buckley, C. Michael Close)

Desperado Tonic [Marmelada] [Slovenia] (d. Varja Močnik, Boris Petkovič, Hanna Antonina Wójcik Slak, Zoran Živulović)

Digital Short Films by Three Filmmakers [South Korea/Japan/Hong Kong] (d. Bong Joon-ho, Ishii Sogo, Yu Lik-wai)

Dong-baek-kkot [Camellia Project: Three Queer Stories at Bogil Island] [South Korea] (d. Choi Jin-sung, Leesong Hee-il, So Joon-moon)

Eros [Italy/Hong Kong/USA] (d. Michelangelo Antonioni, Steven Soderbergh, Wong Kar-wai)

Evil Deeds [USA] (d. Bailee Arnett, Isaak Partlow, Matt Spease)$^\surd$

Hay motivo [There's Good Cause] [Spain] (d. Álvaro del Amo, Vicente Aranda, Mariano Barroso, Antonio José Betancor, Icíar Bollaín, Juan Diego Botto, Daniel Cebrián, Isabel Coixet, Fernando Colomo, José Luis Cuerda, Ana Díez, Miguel Ángel Diez, El Gran Wyoming, Víctor García León, Yolanda García Serrano, José Luis García Sánchez, Chus Gutiérrez, Manuel Gómez Pereira, Mireia Lluch, Víctor Manuel, Julio Medem, Sigfrid Monleón, Pedro Olea, Joaquín Oristrell, Pedro Portabella, Gracia Querejeta, José Ángel Rebolledo, Manuel Rivas, David Trueba, Alfonso Ungría, Imanol Uribe, Pere Joan Ventura)

Historias breves IV [Argentina] (d. Gabriel Dodero, Jonathan Hoffman / Paula Venditti, Daniel Bustamante, Lautaro Núñez de Arco, Martín Mujica, Pablo G. Pérez, Cecilia Urlich, Pablo Pupato, Fernando Tranquilini, Camilo José Gómez)

Kaidan shin mimibukuro 1 [Tales of Terror from Tokyo and All over Japan, Volume One] [Japan] (d. Eiji Arakawa, Hirokatsu Kihara, Ryuta Miyake, Ichiro Nakayama, Ryo Nanba, Shiro Sano, Takashi Shimizu, Keisuke Toyoshima, Norio Tsuruta, Akio Yoshida)$^{\dagger\surd}$

Kaidan shin mimibukuro 2 [Tales of Terror from Tokyo and All over Japan, Volume Two] [Japan] (d. Kei Horie, Ryuta Miyake, Toru Moriyama, Takafumi Ota, Hirohisa Sasaki, Yo Takahashi, Keisuke Toyoshima, Norio Tsuruta, Yudai Yamagudhi, Akio Yoshida)†√

Kaidan shin mimibukuro: Gekijô-ban [Tales of Terror from Tokyo and All over Japan: The Movie] [Japan] (d. Keita Amemiya, Shunichi Hirano, Ryuta Miyake, Hirohisa Sasaki, Kosuke Suzuki, Keisuke Toyoshima, Akio Yoshida)†

Koibumi-biyori [Japan] (d. Kotoe Nagata, Mika Omori, Taikan Suga, Mahoko Takanari)

Lust: 12 Sexy Shorts [France/Germany/Italy/Finland/Japan/Lebanon/Switzerland/ USA] (d. Michael Betancourt, Menotti Bucco, Marco Della Fonte, Natalie Ital, Matto Kämpf, Nosfe, Evelyne and Véronique Pérard / Petit, Bosiljka Simonovic, Takafumi Muranushi, Caroline Tabet, Stefan Weinert, Patrick Volve)‡√

Madrid 11M: Todos ibamos en ese tren [Madrid M11: We Were All on That Train] [Spain] (d. Pedro Barbadillo, Sergio Cabrera, María Campuzano, Carlos Carmona, Jaime Chavarri, Leslie Dann, Alfonso Domingo, José F. Echevarría, Javier Fernández, Ángeles González-Sinde, José Heredia Moreno, Twiggy Hirota, Jorge Iglesias, Estela Ilárraz, Octavio Iturbe, Guido Jiménez, David Lara, Borja Manso, Manuel Martín Cuenca, Nacho Maura, Vicente Mora, Miguel Ángel Nieto, Daniel Quiñones, Miguel Ángel Rolland, Miguel Santesmases, Rocio Sierra, Gonzalo Tapia, Catherine Ulmer, Ángeles Vacas, Óscar Villasante, Ochoa and Gonzalo Visedo)

onedotzero_select dvd2 [UK/Japan/USA/Brazil/Germany/South Africa] (d. Drawing + Manual, Johnny Hardstaff, Ed Holdsworth, Tim Hope, Lobo, MK12, Ne-o, p.i.c.s. [Nakao Hiroyuki], Powergraphixx, Psyop, Alexander Rutterford, Timo Schaedel, Chris Shepherd, Shynola, Tomioka Satoshi, Teevee Graphics [Kojima Junji], Unit9, Xmas)‡√

onedotzero_select dvd3 [UK/USA/Brazil/France/Germany/Japan] (d. Aphex Twin, Dan Chambers, Rex Crowle, Designers Republic, Richard Fenwick, Ruben Fleischer, Logan, Nakd, Neasden Control Centre, Jonas Odell, Plates Animation, pleix collective, Precursor, Psyop, James Reitano, Simon Robson, Timo Schaedel, Tokyo Plastic + The Sancho Plan, Woof Wan Bau, Lester Woog + Cruz)‡√

Queer Boys and Girls on the SHINKANSEN [Queer Boys and Girls on the Bullet Train] [Japan] (d. Akira the Hustler, Hasegawa Kenjiro, Hirai Yuko, Imaizumi Koichi, iri, JohnJ♥, Kang Yen-Nien, Taguchi Hiroki, Takasaki Keiichi, woolala satoko)

Saam gaang yi [Three . . . Extremes / Three, Monster / Three 2] [Hong Kong/Japan/ South Korea] (d. Fruit Chan, Park Chan-wook, Takashi Miike)

Seks, piće i krvoproliće [Sex, Booze, and Short Fuse] [Croatia] (d. Zvonimir Jurić, Boris T. Matić, Antonio Nuić)

Street Tales of Terror [USA] (d. J. D. Hawkins, Frank Corey Shields)√

Tales from the Beyond [USA] (d. Josh Austin, Nate Barlow, Eric Manning, Russell Scott)

Tales from the Crapper [USA] (d. Lloyd Kaufman, Gabriel Friedman, Dave Paiko, Brian Spitz)√

Tokyo Noir [Japan] (d. Masato Ishioka, Naoto Kumazawa)

Tomb of Terror [USA] (d. David DeCoteau, Linda Hassani, C. Courtney Joyner)‡√

Tres veces dos [Three Times Two] [Cuba] (d. Pavel Giroud, Lester Hamlet, Esteban Insausti)

Twentidentity [South Korea] (d. Bong Jun-Ho, Heo Jin-Ho, Hwang Gyu-Deok, Jang Hyeon-Su, Jeong Byeong-Gak, Jo Min-Ho, Kim So-Young, Kim Tae-Gyun, Kim Tae-Yong, Kim Ui-Seok, Kwon Chil-In, Lee Hyeon-Seung, Lee Su-Yeon, Lee Yong-Bae, Lee Young-Jae, Min Gyu-Dong, Oh Byeong-Cheol, Park Gi-Yong, Park Gyeong-Hee, Yu Young-Sik)

Twisted Illusions 2 [USA] (d. John Bowker, Tim Ritter, Joel D. Wynkoop)√

Über die Grenze—Fünf Ansichten von Nachbarn [Across the Border—Five Views from Neighbours] [Austria] (d. Biljana Čakić-Veselič, Jan Gogola, Peter Kerekes, Robert Lakatos, Paweł Lozínski)

Up for Rent [USA] (d. Derek Cole, Shane Cole, Kayla Richardson)√

Visions of Europe [European Union] (d. Fatih Akin, Barbara Albert, Sharunas Bartas, Andy Bausch, Christoffer Boe, Francesca Comencini, Stijn Coninx, Tony Gatlif, Sasa Gedeon, Christos Georgiou, Constantine Giannaris, Theo Van Gogh, Peter Greenaway, Miguel Hermosa, Arvo Iho, Aki Kaurismäki, Damjan Kozole, Laila Pakalnina, Kenneth Scicluna, Martin Šulík, Malgosia Szumowska, Béla Tarr, Jan Troell, Teresa Villaverde, Aisling Walsh)

Visits: Hungry Ghost Anthology [Malaysia] (d. Ho Yuhang, James Lee, Low Ngai Yuen, Ng Tian Hann)

2005

After Midnight [USA] (d. Laura Giglio, Steven A. Grainger, Phil Herman, Isabelle Stephen, Tiffany Warren)√

Allerzielen [All Souls] [The Netherlands] (d. Peter de Baan, Mijke de Jong, Constant Dullaart, Rita Horst, David Lammers, Tim Oliehoek, Rob Schröder / Mariecke van der Linden, Hanro Smitsman, Norbert ter Hall, Eddy Terstall, Maarten Treurniet, Meral Uslu, Marco van Geffen, Michiel van Jaarsveld, Nicole van Kilsdonk, Gerrard Verhage)

Anlat İnstanbul [Istanbul Tales] [Turkey] (d. Ömür Atay, Selim Demirdelen, Kudret Sabanci, Ümit Ünal, Yücel Yolcu)

Byeol-byeol yi-ya-gi [If You Were Me: Anima Vision] [South Korea] (d. 5 Directors Project Team [Chang Hyung-yun, Jung Yeon-joo, Kim Jun, Lee Jin-suk, Park Yun-kyung], Kwon Oh-sung, Lee Amy, Lee Sung-gang, Park Jae-dong, Yoo Jinee)

'Chô' kowai hanashi the movie: yami no eigasai [Japan] (d. Kairakutei Black, Yumeaki Hirayama, Hitoshi Ishikawa, Kanji Tsuda, Miho Yabe)

Cinema different / Different Cinema, Vol. 1 [France/Germany/Taiwan/USA] (d. Richard Beaune, Takahikio Iimura, Maurice Lemaitre, Stephane Marti, Egbert Mittelstadt, Rozenn Nobilet, Colas Ricards / Martin Gracineau, Robert Todd, Hugo Verlinde, Tony Wu / Georges Hsin)‡√

Dark Tales of Japan [Japan] (d. Yoshihiro Nakamura, Masayuki Ochiai, Takashi Shimizu, Koji Shiraishi, Norio Tsuruta)‡√

Da-seot-gae-ui siseon [If You Were Me 2] [South Korea] (d. Kim Dong-won, Jang Jin, Jung Ji-woo, Park Kyung-hee, Ryoo Seung-wan)

Deadroom [USA] (d. James M. Johnston, Nick Prendergast, Yen Tan, David Lowery)

Digital Short Films by Three Filmmakers [Korea/Japan/Thailand] (d. Song Il-gon, Shinya Tsukamoto, Apichatpong Weerasethakul)

Les Européens [France] (d. Sólveig Anspach, Jasmin Dizdar, Emmanuel Finkiel, Saara Saarela, Gerard Stembridge)

Faces of Schlock [USA] (d. Henrique Couto, Chris LaMartina, Andrew N. Shearer)√

Female [Jam Films 3—Female] [Japan] (d. Miwa Nishikawa, Ryuichi Hiroki, Tetsuo Shinohara, Suzuki Matsuo, Shinya Tsukamoto)

Five Worlds [Palestine/Malaysia/Indonesia/Afghanistan/Iran] (d. Sobhi al-Zobaidi, U-Wei bin Hajisaari, Garin Nugroho, Homayoun Paiz, Kamal Tabrizi)

Fucking Different! [Germany] (d. Jürgen Brüning, Michael Brynntrup, Eva Bröckerhoff, Martina Minette Dreier, Juana Dubiel, Undine Frömming, Isabella Gresser, hollyandgolly, Heidi Kull, Markus Ludwig, Peter Oehl, Nathalie Pecillier, Kristian Petersen, Jörg Andreas Polzer, Michael Stock, Graziella Tomasi, Waltraud M. Weiland, Ades Zabel)‡

Guanyu ai [About Love] [Japan/Taiwan/China] (d. Ten Shimoyama, Yee Chin-yee, Zhang Yibai)

Hell Hath No Fury [Canada] (d. Rob Carpenter, Vince d'Amato, Ryan Nicholson, Peter Speers)√

Inu no eiga [All about My Dog] [Japan] (d. Isshin Inudo, Hideki Kuroda, Yoshio Kuroda, Akira Nagai, Tetsuhisa Nezu, Atsushi Sanada, Shinsuke Sato)

J-Horror Anthology: Legends [Japan] (d. Hiroaki Hirakata, Hiroshi Ikezoe, Kiyomi Yada, Naoto Yamakawa)‡√

J-Horror Anthology: Underworld [Japan] (d. Hiroaki Hirakata, Hiroshi Ikezoe, Tatsuro Kashihara, Kazuo Koito, Eiji Satouchi, Tadafumi Tomioka)‡√

Kadokawa Mystery & Horror Tales Vol. 1 [Japan] (d. Tomoyuki Akashi, Kenji Nakanishi)†√

Kadokawa Mystery & Horror Tales Vol. 2 [Japan] (d. Kenji Nakanishi, Takayuki Sato)†√

Kadokawa Mystery & Horror Tales Vol. 3 [Japan] (d. Tomoyuki Akashi, Toshio Oi, Hideaki Yoshida)†√

Lost and Found [Germany/Bosnia-Herzegovina/Bulgaria/Estonia/Romania/Serbia-Montenegro/Hungary] (d. Stefan Arsenijević, Nadejda Koseva, Mait Laas, Kornél Mundruczó, Cristian Mungiu, Jasmila Žbanić)

Mail de todoita story [Stories Sent with e-mails] [Japan] (d. Hiroaki Itou, Hiroshi Shimizu, Suzuki Gen, Kunio Torii)

Naisu no mori—The First Contact [Funky Forest: The First Contact] [Japan] (d. Katsuhito Ishii, Hajime Ishimine, Shunichiro Miki)

Neun [Nine] [Germany] (d. Christian Bach, Janina Dahse, Jakob M. Erwa, Jens Junker, Michaela Kezele, Timo Müller, Sebastian Stern, Pia Strietmann, Carmen Stuellenberg)

Nun-bu-sin ha-ru [One Shining Day] [South Korea] (d. Kim Jong-kwan, Kim Sung-ho, Min Dong-hyun)

Oda do radości [Ode to Joy] [Poland] (d. Anna Kazejak-Dawid, Jan Komasa, Maciej Migas)

onedotzero_select dvd4 [UK/France/Japan/Australia/Austria/Brazil/USA] (d. 12foot6, +Cruz / W&K Tokyo Lab, Airside, Daiki Aizaya, Daniel Askill, Ganzerli Bourdoiseau, Hendrik Dusollier, Dominic Hailstone, Joji Koyama, Lev, Nagi / Uchu Noda / Country, Nakd, Grant Orchard, Pleix, Edouard Salier, Shibashi / Osada Mitsuyuki / Yuko, Kitado Shin, Bernard Stulzaft, Reuben Sutherland, Virgil Widrich)‡√

Ranpo jigoku [Rampo Noir] [Japan] (d. Jissoji Akio, Kaneko Atsushi, Sato Hisayasu, Takeuchi Suguru)

Red Midnight [Italy/USA] (d. Brian Michael Finn, Giovanni Pianigiani, Ray Schwetz)√

Riple Chronicles [Legend of the War City / Tales of a Warring City / Trilogy Narration] [Iran] (d. Rakhshan Bani-Etemad, Abdolhassan Barzideh, Parviz Sheik-Tadi)

Shake, Rattle & Roll 2K5 [Shake, Rattle & Roll V] [Philippines] (d. Uro Q. dela Cruz, Rico Maria Ilarde, Richard Somes)

Solidarność, Solidarność . . . [Solidarity, Solidarity . . . / The Silence] [Poland] (d. Filip Bajon, Jacek Bromski, Ryszard Bugajski, Jerzy Domaradzki, Feliks Falk, Robert Gliński, Andrzej Jakimowski, Jan Jakub Kolski, Juliusz Machulski, Małgorzata Szumowska, Piotr Trzaskalski, Andrzej Wajda, Krzysztof Zanussi)

Speak of the Devil [Denmark] (d. Shaky González, Shaun Rana)√

Stadt als Beute [Berlin Stories] [Germany] (d. Irene von Alberti, Miriam Dehne, Esther Gronenborn)

Stories of Lost Souls [Argentina/Australia/UK/USA] (d. Deborra-Lee Furness, William Garcia, Colin Spector, Toa Stappard, Andrew Upton)√

Street Tales of Terror 2: The Next Chapter [USA] (d. J. D. Hawkins, Frank Corey Shields)√

Tickets [Italy/UK] (d. Abbas Kiarostami, Ken Loach, Ermanno Olmi)

Time to Go John [Australia] (d. Carmela Baranowska, Haavard Berstad, Anna Broinowski, Catfish, Kelly Chapman, Creative Illusions, Daryl Dellora, Catherine Gough-Brady, Nicholas Hansen, Simon Karutz, Kris Keogh, Amanda King / Fabio Cavadini, Jen Hughes, John Hughes, HT Lee, HT Lee / Carmela Baranowska / Cathryn Morgan, Stella Simmering, Pip Starr)

Tsunami Digital Short Films: Program 1 [Thailand] (d. Sompot Chidgasornpongse, Pipope Panitchpakdi, Thunska Pansittivorakul, Pramote Sangsorn, Suchada Sirithanawuddhi, Apichatpong Weerasethakul / Christelle Lheureux)

Tsunami Digital Short Films: Program 2 [Thailand] (d. Margaret Bong Chew Jen, Lek Manont, Folke Ryden, Sonthaya Subyen, Santi Taepanich, Somkid Thamniamdi, Pimpaka Towira)

Unsere zehn Gebote [Germany] (d. Cornelia Grünberg, Karola Hattop, Renata Kaye, Irina Popow, Rüdiger Saß)†√

Zhongguo cunmin yingxiang jihua [China Village Self-Governance Film Project / The Quiet Revolution] [China] (d. Fu Jiachong, Jia Zhitan, Ni Nianghui, Nong Ke, Shao Yuzhen, Tshe Ring Sgrol Ma, Wang Wei, Yi Chujian, Zhang Huancai, Zhou Cengjia)

Zoo [Japan] (d. Masaki Adachi, Hiroshi Andô, Ryû Kaneda, Masatetsu Komiya, Junpei Mizusaki)

2006

3 In 3 Saek [Three People Three Colors: A Love Story] [South Korea] (d. Kim Tae-gyun, Kwak Jae-yong, Jung Yoon-chul)√

09:05 [A-hop-si O-bun] [South Korea] (d. Hwang Byeong-gug, Lee Gae-byok, Park Soo-young / Park Jae-young)

A propósito de Buenos Aires [Regarding Buenos Aries] [Argentina] (d. Manuel Ferrari, Alejo Franzetti, Martín Kalina, Cecilia Libster, Francisco Pedemonte, Clara Picasso, Matías Piñeiro, Juan Ronco, Andrea Santamaría, Malena Solarz, Nicolás Zukerfeld)

All about Love [Philippines] (d. Bb. Joyce Bernal, Don Cuaresma, Jerry Lopez Sineneng)

All the Invisible Children [France/Italy] (d. Mehdi Charef, Emir Kusturica, Spike Lee, Kátia Lund, Jordan Scott / Ridley Scott, Stefano Veneruso, John Woo)

Black Night [Japan/Thailand/Hong Kong] (d. Takahiko Akiyama, Thanit Jitnukul, Patrick Leung)

Bul-taneun Film-ui Yeondae-ki [16 Takes on Korean Society] [South Korea] (d. Cho Dae-hee, Cho Doo-young, Choi Eun-jung, Choi Se-il, Jeong Il-geon, Jun Kyung-jin, Kim Cheun-seok, Kim Hwan-tae, Kwon Woo-jung, Lee Hoon-kyu, Lee Je-soo, Lee Mario, Lee Su-jeong, Naru, Oh Jong-hwan, Park Il-hun, Raul Tae)

Cadavre exquis première édition [Canada] (d. Martin Bourgault, Virginie Brault, Florian Cossen, Brian Desgagné, Stéphan Doe, Diane Gagnon, Jean-François Gros d'Aillon, Michel Lauzon, François Lussier, Jean-Félix Maynard, Philippe Melançon, Antonin Monmart)

Cinema different / Different Cinema, Vol. 2 [France/Argentina/Canada/Japan/Italy] (d. Frédérique Devaux, Olivier Fouchard, Rubén Guzmán, Shiho Kano, Dominik Lange, Valérie Morignat, Solomon Nagler, Mauro Santini)√

Cinema16: American Short Films [USA] (d. Tim Burton, Adam Davidson, Maya Deren, Adam Parrish King, Standish Lawder, George Lucas, Mike Mills, Stefan Nadelman, Joe Nussbaum, Alexander Payne, D. A. Pennebaker, Gus Van Sant, Peter Sollett, Todd Solondz, Rawson Marshall Thurber, Andy Warhol)‡√

City2City [France/Spain/Russian Federation/Germany/Hong Kong/Switzerland/ Finland/UK/Japan] (d. Pablo Altés, Marina Chernikova, Toby Cornish, Nose Chan, Dudouet & Kaplan, Ulrich Fischer, Augustin Gimel, Alli Savolainen, John Smith, Kentaro Taki)‡√

Darna Zaroori Hai [Fear Is Compulsory] [India] (d. J. D. Chakravarthy, Sajid Khan, Jijy Philip, Prawal Raman, Vivek Shah, Ram Gopal Varma; linking sequences Manish Gupta)

Destricted [UK/USA] (d. Marina Abramovic, Matthew Barney, Marco Brambilla, Larry Clark, Gaspar Noé, Richard Prince, Sam Taylor-Wood)

Digital Short Films by Three Filmmakers 2006: Talk to Her [Singapore/Kazakhstan/ Thailand] (d. Eric Khoo, Darezhan Omirbayev, Pen-ek Ratanaruang)

Faces of Schlock 2 [USA] (d. Justin Channell, Henrique Couto, Chris LaMartina, Andrew N. Shearer)√

Fimfárum 2 [Czech Republic] (d. Jan Balej, Aurel Klimt, Břetislav Pojar, Vlasta Pospíšilová)

Genius Party [Japan] (d. Nicolas de Crecy, Atsuko Fukushima, Yuji Fukuyama, Hideki Futamura, Tadashi Hiramatsu, Shoji Kawamori, Koji Morimoto, Kazuto Nakazawa, Shinya Ohira, Tatsuyuki Tanaka, Shinichiro Watanabe, Masaaki Yuasa)

Imahe Nasyon [Philippines] (d. Poklong Anading, Sigfried Barros-Sanchez, Yeye Calderon, Mes de Guzman, Emman Dela Cruz, Neil Daza, Lav Diaz, Dennis Empalmado, Tad Ermitaño, Topel Lee, Milo Paz, Robert Quebral, Ellen Ramos, Raymond Red, R. A. Rivera, Roxlee, Lyle Sacris, EJ Salcedo, Ogi Sugatan, Paolo Villaluna)

Kowai onna [Unholy Women] [Japan] (d. Keita Amemiya, Takuji Suzuki, Keisuke Toyoshima)

LovecraCked! The Movie [USA] (d. Tomas Almgren, Brian Barnes, Brian Bernhard, Elias, Grady Granros, Justin Powers, Jane Rose, Simon Ruben, Doug Sakmann, Ashley Thorpe)

Paris, je t'aime [I Love Paris] [France] (d. Olivier Assayas, Frédéric Auburtin, Gurinder Chadha, Sylvain Chomet, Joel and Ethan Coen, Isabel Coixet, Wes Craven, Alfonso Cuarón, Gérard Depardieu, Christopher Doyle, Richard LaGravenese, Vincenzo Natali, Nobuhiro Suwa, Alexander Payne, Bruno Podalydès, Oliver Schmitz, Walter Salles, Gus Van Sant, Daniela Thomas, Tom Tykwer)

Puso 3 [Philippines] (d. Rahyan Carlos, Peque Gallaga, Soxie Topacio)

Resistance(s) [France/Algeria/Iraq/USA/Palestine/Morocco/United Arab Emirates/ Lebanon/Canada] (d. Usama Alshaibi, Zoulikha Bouabdellah, Taysir Batniji, Frédérique Devaux, Mounir Fatmi, Lamya Gargash, Waël Noureddine, Jayce Salloum)√

Sebeonjjae siseon [If You Were Me 3] [South Korea] (d. Chung Yoon-chul, Hong Ki-seon, Kim Gok / Kim Sun, Kim Hyun-pil, Lee Mi-yeon, Noh Dong-seok)

Shake, Rattle & Roll VIII [Philippines] (d. Rahyan Carlos, Quark Henares, Mike Tuviera)

Shirubâ kamen [Silver Kamen / Silver Mask] [Japan] (d. Mitsunori Hattori, Akio Jissoji, Tsugumi Kitaura)

The Signal [USA] (d. David Bruckner, Dan Bush, Jacob Gentry)

Small Gauge Trauma [UK/Canada/Japan/Spain/Argentina/Belgium/Brazil/ Portugal] (d. Diego Abad, Benoit Boucher, Helene Cattet / Bruno Forzani, Guillaume Fortini, Phillip John, Robert Morgan, Tenkwaku Naniwa, Paco Plaza, Dennison Ramalho, Salvador Sanz, Tomoya Sato, Miguel Ángel Vivas, Sam Walker)‡√

Time Piece [Turkey/USA] (d. Nurdan Arca, Özgür Arik, Edet Belzberg, Linda
Goode Bryant, Alex Gibney, Nathaniel Kahn, Albert Maysles, Ersan Ocak,
Murad Özdemir, Sam Pollard, Şehbal Şenyurt, Mustafa Ünlü)

Trapped Ashes [USA] (d. Sean S. Cunningham, John Gaeta, Monte Hellman, Ken
Russell; linking sequences Joe Dante)

Yume juya [Ten Nights of Dreams] [Japan] (d. Yoshitaka Amano / Shinmei Kawahara,
Kon Ichikawa, Akio Jissoji, Suzuki Matsuo, Miwa Nishikawa, Atsushi Shimizu,
Takashi Shimizu, Keisuke Toyoshima, Yudai Yamaguchi, Nobuhiro Yamashita)

2007

5 Gross [Norway] (d. Susanne Falkum Løvik, Pål Jackman, Therese Jacobsen,
Bobbie Peers, Marius Soma)

AIDS JaaGO [India/USA] (d. Farhan Akhtar, Vishal Bharadwaj, Mira Nair, Santosh
Sivan)

Byeol-byeol yi-ya-gi 2: Yeo-seot-bit-gal mu-ji-gae [If You Were Me: Anima Vision 2]
[South Korea] (d. Ann Dong-hee / Ryu Jung-oo, Gwon Mi-jeong, Hong
Deok-pyo, Lee Hong-soo / Lee Hong-min, Jung Min-young, Park Yong-jae)

*Chacun son cinéma ou Ce petit coup au coeur quand la lumière s'éteint et que le film
commence [To Each His Own Cinema]* [France] (d. Theo Angelopoulos, Olivier
Assayas, Bille August, Jane Campion, Youssef Chahine, Chen Kaige, Michael
Cimino, Joel and Ethan Coen, David Cronenberg, Jean-Pierre and Luc
Dardenne, Manoel De Oliveira, Raymond Depardon, Atom Egoyan, Amos
Gitai, Hou Hsiao-hsien, Alejandro González Iñárritu, Aki Kaurismäki, Abbas
Kiarostami, Takeshi Kitano, Andrei Konchalovsky, Claude Lelouch, Ken Loach,
David Lynch, Nanni Moretti, Roman Polanski, Raul Ruiz, Walter Salles,
Elia Suleiman, Tsai Ming-liang, Gus Van Sant, Lars von Trier, Wim Wenders,
Wong Kar Wai, Zhang Yimou)

Di san zhong wen nuan [3 City Hotshots] [China] (d. Li Xin, Mao Xiaorui, Wu Tiange)

Dus Kahaniyaan [India] (d. Jasmeet Dhodi, Meghna Gulzar, Sanjay Gupta, Apoorva
Lakhia, Hansal Mehta, Rohit Roy)

Enfances [Childhoods] [France] (d. Isild Le Besco, Ismaël Ferroukhi, Yann Le Gal,
Corinne Garfin, Joana Hadjithomas / Khalil Joreige, Safy Nebbou)

Farsh-e Irani [Persian Carpet] [Iran] (d. Behrouz Afkhami, Rakhshan Bani-Etemad,
Bahram Bayzai, Seifollah Daad, Bahman Farmanara, Abbas Kiarostami, Majid
Majidi, Dariush Mehrjui, Reza Mir-Karimi, Jafar Panahi, Mojtaba Raie,
Mohammad Reza Honarmand, Khosro Sinaie, Kamal Tabrizi, Noureddin
Zarrinkelk)

Fucking Different New York [Germany/USA] (d. Dan Borden, Abigail Child, Lala
Endara, Stephen Gallagher, Samara Halperin, Barbara Hammer, Amy von
Harrington, Keith Levy, Hedia Maron, Andre Salas, Todd Verow, Jack Waters)

Geurimja [Resurrection of the Butterfly] [South Korea] (d. Kim Min-sook, Lee
Jung-gook)

GG 19—Eine Reise durch Deutschland in 19 Artikeln [Germany] (d. Ansgar Ahlers,
Marcel Ahrens, Boris Anderson, Sabine Bernardi, Axel Bold, Suzanne von

Borsody, Savas Ceviz, David Dietl, Johannes von Gwinner, Johannes Harth /
  Philipp von Werther, Marion Kracht, André F. Nebe, Carolin Otterbach, Kerstin
  Polte, Christine Repond, Andreas Samland, Harald Siebler, Alan Smithee
  [Nina Franoszek])
Grindhouse [USA] (d. Robert Rodriguez, Quentin Tarantino)
Invisibles [Spain] (d. Mariano Barroso, Isabel Coixet, Javier Corcuera, Fernando
  León de Aranoa, Wim Wenders)
Komšije [Neighbors] [Serbia] (d. Paola Albertini, Dragana Bjelica, Maša Drndić, Bistra
  Georgijeva, Šegor Hadžagić, Frosina Naumovska, Andrea Palašti, Ivan Ramljak,
  Visar Sherifi, Marko Šipka, Ivana Todorović)
Late Fragment—An Interactive Film [Canada] (d. Daryl Cloran, Anita Doron, Mateo
  Guez, Anita Lee, Ana Serrano)
Lost Suburbia [USA] (d. Pete Bune, Sean King, Paul Natale, Elizabeth and Terrence
  Smith)
Memories [Jeonju Digital Project 2007] [Portugal/Germany/France] (d. Pedro Costa,
  Harun Farocki, Eugène Green)
onedotzero_select dvd5 [UK/Brazil/Japan/USA] (d. 12foot6, Duncan Beedie, The
  Blackheart Gang, Alex Chandon, +Cruz / W&K Tokyo Lab, Martin de Thurah,
  Richard Fenwick, Yves Geleyn / Julien Genoulaz, Ian W. Gouldstone,
  Guilherme Marcondes, Takagi Masakatsu, Minivegas, Motomichi Nakamura,
  Nakd, Alessandro Pacciani, Marcin Slawek, Adam Smith, Tokyoplastic, Joel
  Trussell)‡√
Pantaseutik jasal sodong [Fantastic Parasuicides] [South Korea] (d. Cho Chang-ho,
  Kim Sung-ho, Park Soo-young)
Paraiso: Tatlong Kwento ng Pag-asa [Paradise: Three Stories of Hope] [Philippines]
  (d. Ricky Davao, Jun Lana, Joel Ruiz)
Perempuan Punya Cerita [Chants of Lotus / Lotus Requiem] [Indonesia] (d. Nia
  Dinata, Fatimah Tobing Rony, Lasja F. Susatyo, Upi)
Peur(s) du noir [Fear(s) of the Dark] [France] (d. Blutch, Charles Burns, Marie
  Caillou, Pierre di Sciullo, Jerry Kramsky, Lorenzo Mattotti, Richard McGuire,
  Michel Pirus, Romain Slocombe)
Shin onna tachiguishi retsuden [Eat and Run: 6 Beautiful Grifters] [Japan] (d. Kamiya
  Makoto, Kamiyama Kenji, Oshii Mamoru, Tsujimoto Takanori, Yuasa Hiroaki)
The State of the World [O Estado do Mundo] [Portugal] (d. Ayisha Abraham, Chantal
  Akerman, Pedro Costa, Vicente Ferraz, Wang Bing, Apichatpong Weerasethakul)
Tickets [Hong Kong/Singapore/Japan] (d. Kenny Chow, Hermann Ho, Brian
  Hung / Ka Ho Yue, Gavin Lim, Nishio Hiroshi)
Triangle [Hong Kong] (d. Ringo Lam, Johnny To, Tsui Hark)
Vogelfrei [Latvia] (d. Janis Kalejs, Janis Putnins, Gatis Smits, Anna Viduleja)

Notes

1. Recovering European Art Cinema

1. Susan Sontag, "The Decay of Cinema," *New York Times Magazine,* 25 February 1996, 60–61.

2. Sontag, "A Century of Cinema," *Parnassus: Poetry in Review* 22, nos. 1–2 (1997): 23–28, and in *Where the Stress Falls: Essays* (London: Jonathan Cape, 2002), 117–22.

3. See Sontag, "Spiritual Style in the Films of Robert Bresson," "Godard's *Vivre sa vie,*" and "Resnais' *Muriel*" in *Against Interpretation and Other Essays* (New York: Dell, 1966), 181–98, 199–211, 235–44; "Bergman's *Persona*" and "Godard" in *Styles of Radical Will* (New York: Farrar, Straus, and Giroux, 1969), 123–45, 147–89.

4. Jonathan Rosenbaum and Adrian Martin, eds., *Movie Mutations: The Changing Face of World Cinephilia* (London: British Film Institute, 2003); Marijke de Valck and Malte Hagener, eds., *Cinephilia: Movies, Love and Memory* (Amsterdam: Amsterdam University Press, 2005); Christian Keathley, *Cinephilia and History, or The Wind in the Trees* (Bloomington: Indiana University Press, 2006). For other work on cinephilia, see Paul Willemen and Noel King, "Through the Glass Darkly: Cinephilia Reconsidered," in Willemen, *Looks and Frictions: Essays in Cultural Studies and Film Theory* (London/Bloomington and Indianapolis: British Film Institute/Indiana University Press, 1994), 223–57; Laura Mulvey, "Americanitis: European Intellectuals and Hollywood Melodrama," in *Fetishism and Curiosity* (London/Bloomington and Indianapolis: British Film Institute/Indiana University Press, 1996), 19–28; Barbara Klinger, "The Contemporary Cinephile: Film Collecting in the Post-Video Era," in *Hollywood Spectatorship: Changing Perceptions of Cinema Audiences,* ed. Melvyn Stokes and Richard Maltby (London: British Film Institute, 2001), 132–51.

5. Pierre Sorlin, *Italian National Cinema 1896–1996* (London: Routledge, 1996), 131.

6. Gilles Deleuze, *Cinema 2: The Time-Image,* trans. Hugh Tomlinson and Robert Galeta (Minneapolis: University of Minnesota Press, 1989). In elaborating his theory of the time-image, Deleuze relies conspicuously on the corpus of postwar European art cinema, especially films from France and Italy.

7. Penelope Houston, *The Contemporary Cinema* (Harmondsworth, UK: Penguin Books, 1963), 29–31.

8. "For *L'Avventura*: Statement distributed at the 1960s Cannes Film Festival," in *Michelangelo Antonioni: An Introduction,* ed. Pierre Leprohon, trans. Scott Sullivan (New York: Simon and Schuster, 1963), 183–84.

9. Christian Metz, "The Modern Cinema and Narrativity," in *Film Language: A Semiotics of the Cinema,* trans. Michael Taylor (Chicago: University of Chicago Press, 1974), 193–94.

10. John Orr, *Cinema and Modernity* (London: Polity Press, 1993), 24.

11. Dudley Andrew, "French Film at the Mirror: The Cultivation and Deface-ment of the Look," in *Premises: Invested Spaces in Visual Arts, Architecture, and Design in France, 1958–1998* (New York: Guggenheim Museum Publications, 1998), 103.

12. Robert Phillip Kolker, *The Altering Eye: Contemporary International Cinema* (Oxford, UK: Oxford University Press, 1983), 153.

13. Jean-Louis Comolli, Jean Domarchi, Jean-André Fieschi, Pierre Kast, André S. Labarthe, Claude Ollier, Jacques Rivette, and François Weyergans, "The Misfor-tunes of *Muriel,*" trans. Diana Matias, in *Cahiers du Cinéma, 1960–1968: New Wave, New Cinema, Reevaluating Hollywood,* ed. Jim Hillier (Cambridge, Mass.: Harvard University Press, 1986), 69, 70.

14. Ibid., 71; ellipses in original.

15. This economy is by no means limited to the interpretive spectatorship and criticism of the 1960s but continues to this day. An example is Peter Bondanella's second book on Federico Fellini, the introduction to which states: "His films repre-sent a series of complex chapters in the creation of a unique, private, and personal world of poetic, lyrical, visual images. Fellini stands in complete contrast to the pre-vailing conventional wisdom of the academy, for if his cinema represents any ideo-logical stand, it is a courageous defense of the imagination as a valid category of knowing and understanding and a rejection of 'group thought,' political correctness, or sociological explanations of art in favor of the individual imagination and the per-sonal creative act" (Bondanella, *The Films of Federico Fellini* [Cambridge, UK: Cam-bridge University Press, 2002], 2; see also 163–64, n. 1 and 175–76, n. 8).

16. André S. Labarthe, "Marienbad Year Zero," trans. Diana Matias, in Hiller, *Cahiers du Cinéma, 1960–1968,* 55, 58. For examples of this proclivity in the first decade and a half of Anglo-American film criticism, see the following books cover-ing groups of directors: Peter Cowie, *Antonioni, Bergman, Resnais* (London: Tantivy, 1963); John Russell Taylor, *Cinema Eye, Cinema Ear: Some Key Filmmakers of the Six-ties* (New York: Hill and Wang, 1964); Paul Schrader, *Transcendental Style in Film: Ozu, Bresson, Dreyer* (New York: Da Capo Press, 1972); Peter Harcourt, *Six European Direc-tors: Essays on the Meaning of Film Style* (Harmondsworth, UK: Penguin Books, 1974); Bruce F. Kawin, *Mindscreen: Bergman, Godard, and the First-Person Film* (Princeton, N.J.: Princeton University Press, 1978).

17. Haidee Wasson, *Museum Movies: The Museum of Modern Art and the Birth of Art Cinema* (Berkeley: University of California Press, 2005), 26; emphasis in original.

18. David Bordwell, "The Art Cinema as a Mode of Film Practice," *Film Criticism* 4, no. 1 (1979): 56–64; Steve Neale, "Art Cinema as Institution," *Screen* 22, no. 1 (1981): 11–39. The same issue of *Film Criticism* in which Bordwell's article appeared also featured another piece on art cinema, Robert Self's "Systems of Ambiguity in the Art Cinema," 74–79.

19. Geoffrey Nowell-Smith, "Art Cinema," in *The Oxford History of World Cinema,* ed. Nowell-Smith (Oxford, UK: Oxford University Press, 1996), 567–75; Catherine Fowler, ed., *The European Cinema Reader* (London and New York: Routledge, 2002).

20. Bordwell expanded his formal analysis of art cinema as a distinct mode of narration in *Narration in the Fiction Film* (Madison: University of Wisconsin Press, 1985), 205–33. His focus on European cinema of the 1960s here remains the same: his extended example is Alain Resnais's *La Guerre est finie* (1968), and he includes a list of 66 films released between 1957 and 1969 as evidence of the richness of art-cinema narration in this period. Of these, 41 are from four countries in Western Europe—2 for West Germany, 9 for Sweden (8 directed by Ingmar Bergman), and 30 for France and Italy.

21. Bordwell, "The Art Cinema as a Mode of Film Practice," 56, 61.

22. Ibid., 62.

23. Ibid., 57, 58.

24. Ibid., 58.

25. Ibid., 59.

26. Neale, "Art Cinema as Institution," 11.

27. Ibid., 14.

28. Ibid., 15.

29. Ibid., 30.

30. Ibid., 34, 35; emphasis in original.

31. Ibid., 37. For two entertaining characterizations of art film patrons in and around the early 1960s see Arthur Knight, "For Eggheads Only?" in *Film: Book 1—The Audience and the Filmmaker,* ed. Robert Hughes (New York: Grove Press, 1959), 24–32, and Pauline Kael, "Fantasies of the Art House Audience," *Sight and Sound* 31, no. 1 (winter 1961/62): 5–9.

32. "Home" demonstrations are offered at an earlier point of this chapter. For "abroad," see Janet Staiger, "With the Compliments of the Auteur: Art Cinema and the Complexities of Its Reading Strategies," in *Interpreting Films: Studies in the Historical Reception of American Cinema* (Princeton, N.J.: Princeton University Press, 1992), 178–95.

33. Neale, "Art Cinema as Institution," 38–39.

34. Peter Lev, *The Euro-American Cinema* (Austin: University of Texas Press, 1993); Barbara Wilinsky, *Sure Seaters: The Emergence of Art House Cinema* (Minneapolis: University of Minnesota Press, 2001).

35. Other analyses of art cinema audiences and exhibition in the United States include Ronald J. Faber, Thomas C. O'Guinn, and Andrew P. Hardy, "Art Films in the Suburbs: A Comparison of Popular and Art Film Audiences," in *Current Research in Film: Audiences, Economics, and Law,* vol. 4, ed. Bruce A. Austin (Norwood, N.J.: Ablex, 1988), 45–53; Douglas Gomery, "Ethnic Theatres and Art Cinemas," in *Shared Pleasures: A History of Movie Presentation in the United States* (London: British Film Institute, 1992), 180–95; Jim Lane, "Critical and Cultural Reception of the European

Art Film in 1950's America: A Case Study of the Brattle Theatre (Cambridge, Massachusetts)," *Film History* 24 (1994): 49–64; Anthony Henry Guzman, "The Little Theatre Movement: The Institutionalization of the European Art Film in America," *Film History* 17, nos. 2–3 (2005): 261–84.

36. For other work on the institutionalization of the discourse of film art in America, see Michael Budd, "*The Cabinet of Dr. Caligari:* Conditions of Reception," *Ciné-Tracts* 12 (winter 1981): 41–59; "Authorship as Commodity: The Art Cinema of *The Cabinet of Dr. Caligari,*" *Wide Angle* 6 (1984): 12–19; "The National Board of Review and the Early Art Cinema in New York: *The Cabinet of Dr. Caligari* as Affirmative Culture," *Cinema Journal* 26, no. 1 (fall 1986): 3–18. See also Staiger, "With the Compliments of the Auteur."

37. Dudley Andrew, for example, has recently referred to the decades of inspired amateurism preceding the 1970s as "The Stone Age," the period of "theorizing" as "The Imperial Age," and the 1980s on as "The Present Age." See his "The 'Three Ages' of Cinema Studies and the Age to Come," *PMLA* 115, no. 3 (2000): 341–51. In a piece about film studies at his home university written a decade and a half earlier, Andrew was even then nostalgic for what he now calls "The Stone Age": "I believe the greatest eras of film study have already passed us by. When Louis Delluc presided over the film club movement in Paris in the early twenties, scholars and aficionados from all the arts gathered together and, on the basis of a naive interest in film, generated the excitement we call the impressionist movement. What went on then in terms of film discussion, film journals, and actual filmmaking was to me education at its most real and important level. Then again in Paris, right after World War II, André Bazin led a revival of independent filmmaking, all outside the university" ("An Open Approach to Film Study and the Situation at Iowa," in *Film Study in the Undergraduate Curriculum,* ed. Barry Keith Grant [New York: Modern Language Association, 1983], 42).

38. For an overview of this account, peppered with frequent interview statements by the directors involved, see Peter Cowie, *Revolution! The Explosion of World Cinema in the Sixties* (New York: Faber and Faber, 2004).

39. For work on film festivals, see Martin Auty and Gillian Hartnoll, *Water under the Bridge: 25 Years of the London Film Festival,* BFI Dossier 12 (London: British Film Institute, 1981); Julian Stringer, "Global Cities and the International Film Festival Economy," in *Cinema and the City: Film and Urban Societies in a Global Context,* ed. Mark Shiel and Tony Fitzmaurice (London: Blackwell, 2001), 134–44; Janet Harbord, "Film Festivals: Media Events and Spaces of Flow," in *Film Cultures* (London: Sage, 2002); Kenneth Turan, *Sundance to Sarajevo: Film Festivals and the World They Made* (Berkeley: University of California Press, 2002), 59–75; Liz Czach, "Film Festivals, Film Programming, and the Building of a National Cinema," *Moving Image* 4, no. 1 (spring 2004): 76–88; Thomas Elsaesser, "Film Festival Networks: The New Topographies of Cinema in Europe," in *European Cinema: Face to Face with Hollywood,* 82–107; Marijke de Valck, *Film Festivals: From European Geopolitics to Global Cinephilia* (Amsterdam: Amsterdam University Press, 2007). For work on film museums, see Wasson, *Museum Movies.* On the British Film Institute, see Ivan Butler, *"To Encourage the Art*

of the Film": *The Story of the British Film Institute* (London: Robert Hale, 1971), and Colin McArthur, "Two Steps Forward, One Step Back: Cultural Struggle in the British Film Institute," *Journal of Popular British Cinema* no. 4 (2001): 112–27. On archives and preservation, see Anthony Slide, *Nitrate Won't Wait: A History of Film Preservation in the United States* (Jefferson, N.C.: McFarland, 1992); Penelope Houston, *Keepers of the Frame: The Film Archives* (London: British Film Institute, 1994); Tom McGreevey and Joanne Louise Yeck, *Our Movie Heritage* (New Brunswick, N.J.: Rutgers University Press, 1997).

40. Elsewhere I examine the differing histories of development in academic film studies in Britain and America via book publishing; see my "Little Books," in *Inventing Film Studies: Towards a History of a Discipline,* ed. Lee Grieveson and Haidee Wasson (Durham, N.C.: Duke University Press, 2008), 319–49. This collection contains as well several pieces on types and examples of film study occurring before the 1960s inside and outside the academy.

41. Robert C. Allen and Douglas Gomery, *Film History: Theory and Practice* (New York: McGraw-Hill, 1985), 27. For more on film studies' growth in the 1960s and 1970s, see Mitsuhiro Yoshimoto, *Kurosawa: Film Studies and Japanese Cinema* (Durham, N.C.: Duke University Press, 2000), 19, 30, 32, 387, n. 53.

42. For overviews of the political demonstrations and events of 1968, see David Caute, *Sixty-Eight: The Year of the Barricades: A Journey through 1968* (New York: HarperCollins, 1988), and Ronald Fraser, *1968: A Student Generation in Revolt* (London: Chatto and Windus, 1988).

43. For an overview of the student revolutionary movements in France, Italy, and West Germany during this time, see Tony Judt, *Postwar: A History of Europe since 1945* (London: William Heinemann, 2005), 407–21. For more on the "Langlois Affair," see "Editorial: The Langlois Affair," trans. David Wilson, in Hillier, *Cahiers du Cinéma, 1960–1968,* 307–8; Richard Roud, "The Battle for the Cinémathèque," in *A Passion for Films: Henri Langlois and the Cinémathèque Française* (New York: Viking Press, 1983), 148–60; Glenn Myrent and Georges P. Langlois, "You Only Live Twice: The Langlois Affair," in *Henri Langlois: First Citizen of Cinema,* trans. Lisa Nesselson (New York: Twayne, 1995), 236–68. For partisan accounts of May 1968 in France, see Daniel Singer, *Prelude to a Revolution: France in May 1968* (New York: Hill and Wang, 1971), and Richard Johnson, *The French Communist Party versus the Students: Revolutionary Politics in May–June 1968* (New Haven, Conn., and London: Yale University Press, 1972).

44. For accounts of this development in American cinema, see Robert B. Ray, "The 1960s: Frontier Metaphors, Developing Self-Consciousness, and New Waves," in *A Certain Tendency of Hollywood Cinema, 1930–1980* (Princeton, N.J.: Princeton University Press, 1985), 247–95; David E. James, "The American Art Film: Production as Narration," in *Allegories of Cinema: American Film in the Sixties* (Princeton, N.J.: Princeton University Press, 1989), 280–303; David A. Cook, "Auteur Cinema and the 'Film Generation' in 1970s Hollywood," in *The New American Cinema,* ed. Jon Lewis (Durham, N.C.: Duke University Press, 2000), 1–37; Thomas Elsaesser, Alexander Horwath, and Noel King, eds., *The Last Great American Picture Show: New Hollywood*

Cinema in the 1970s (Amsterdam: Amsterdam University Press, 2004). For an engaging introduction based on extensive interviews, see Peter Biskind, *Easy Riders, Raging Bulls: How the Sex–Drugs–and–Rock 'n' Roll Generation Saved Hollywood* (New York: Simon and Schuster, 1998).

45. The decline in European art cinema's fortunes internationally was matched by the New Hollywood cinema's rise, as Jon Lewis reports: "Before 1969, European filmmakers dominated the New York Film Festival program. . . . Beginning in 1969 . . . studio-made American films began to appear with regularity on festival programs not only in New York but worldwide. . . . Beginning in 1970 some familiar new Hollywood directors began to place their films on the festival program. After 1970 new films by Martin Scorsese, Peter Bogdanovich, Robert Altman, Robert Benton, and Bob Rafelson were featured along with work by the usual slate of European cineastes" (Jon Lewis, *Hollywood v. Hardcore: How the Struggle over Censorship Saved the Modern Film Industry* [New York and London: New York University Press, 2000], 163).

46. For coverage of French film culture of the period, including the participation of French audiovisual workers, see Sylvia Harvey, *May '68 and Film Culture* (London: British Film Institute, 1978). See also "Editorial: The Estates General of the French Cinema," trans. David Wilson, in Hillier, *Cahiers du Cinéma, 1960–1968,* 309–10; Richard Porton, "Cinema, May '68, and the Anarchist Imagination," *Spectator* 8, no. 2 (spring 1988): 57–65; Margaret Atack, *May '68 in French Fiction and Film: Rethinking Society, Rethinking Representation* (Oxford, UK: Oxford University Press, 2000).

47. For examinations of the impact of 1968 on intellectual and cultural history and practice, see Colin MacCabe, "Class of '68: Elements of an Intellectual Autobiography 1967–1981," in *Tracking the Signifier: Theoretical Essays: Film, Linguistics, Literature* (Minneapolis: Minnesota University Press, 1985), 1–32; Michele Wallace, "Reading 1968: The Great American Whitewash," in *Invisibility Blues: From Pop to Theory* (London and New York: Verso, 1990), 187–98; Kobena Mercer, "'1968': Periodizing Postmodern Politics and Identity," in *Cultural Studies,* ed. Lawrence Grossberg, Cary Nelson, and Paula Treichler (New York: Routledge, 1992), 424–38; Kristin Ross, *May '68 and Its Afterlives* (Chicago and London: University of Chicago Press, 2000).

48. See, for example, Jim Hillier, "Introduction" to *Cahiers du Cinéma, The 1950s: Neo-Realism, Hollywood, New Wave,* ed. Hillier (Cambridge, Mass.: Harvard University Press, 1985), 1–17.

49. See, for example, John Hess, "La Politique des auteurs, Part One: World View as Aesthetic," *Jump Cut,* no. 1 (1974): 19–22.

50. "Editorial," *Cahiers du cinéma,* no. 203 (August 1968), trans. as "Editorial: Changes in *Cahiers*" by David Wilson in Hillier, *Cahiers du Cinéma, 1960–1968,* 311–12; Jean-Louis Comolli and Jean Narboni, "Cinéma/idéologie/critique," *Cahiers du cinéma,* no. 216 (October–November 1969), trans. as "Cinema/Ideology/Criticism" by Susan Bennett in *Screen* 12, no. 1 (Spring 1971): 27–36. Interestingly, Paul Willemen locates the end of cinephilia in 1968, though he is implicitly speaking of the British scene, which translated political commitment into material action—theory—more quickly than its American counterpart (Willemen and King, "Through the Glass

Darkly," 227). *Pace* Sontag, Thomas Elsaesser recalls the time: "French cinephile disenchantment, of which the same *Cahiers du Cinéma* made themselves the official organ from 1969 onwards, also helped formulate the theoretical-critical agenda that remained in force in Britain for a decade and in the USA for almost two decades. . . . The theological proof that heaven, or cinephilia, does not exist, is what I now tend to think screen theory was partly about" (Elsaesser, "Cinephilia or the Uses of Disenchantment," in de Valck and Hagener, *Cinephilia: Movies, Love and Memory,* 34).

51. Translations of key *Cahiers* articles from this period are collected in Nick Browne, ed., *Cahiers du Cinéma, 1969–1972: The Politics of Representation* (Cambridge, Mass.: Harvard University Press, 1990). See also the chapter titled "Politics" in Robert Lapsley and Michael Westlake, *Film Theory: An Introduction* (Manchester, UK: Manchester University Press, 1988, 2006), esp. 1–8.

52. A useful compendium of *Screen* translations of *Cahiers du cinéma* and *Cinéthique* articles, as well as ones originally published in *Screen* itself, is *Screen Reader 1: Cinema/Ideology/Politics* (London: Society for Education in Film and Television, 1977). For a thorough analysis of the particular directions that avant-garde filmmakers and film journals such as *Cahiers du cinéma* and *Screen* took in their investigation of the intersections between theory, politics, and the avant-garde, see D. N. Rodowick, *The Crisis of Political Modernism: Criticism and Ideology in Contemporary Film Theory* (Urbana: University of Illinois Press, 1988; Berkeley: University of California Press, 1994).

53. As Peter Lev admits, "Only a few attempts have been made to define the art film. . . . The history of the art film has not yet been written" (*The Euro-American Cinema,* 4, 6). David Bordwell concurs: "We still lack a thoroughgoing history of postwar modernism in the European cinema" (Bordwell, *On the History of Film Style* [Cambridge, Mass.: Harvard University Press, 1997], 288). While I am not undertaking a writing of the history of European art cinema—as András Bálint Kovács partially does in the recent *Screening Modernism: European Art Cinema, 1950–1980* (University of Chicago Press, 2007)—I will be analyzing throughout this book film historical writing on art cinema, as well as pressing for what such a history should address and what new knowledges it might generate.

54. In addition to Allen and Gomery's *Film History: Theory and Practice,* there are a handful of book-length studies on film historiography: Paul Smith, ed., *The Historian and Film* (Cambridge, UK: Cambridge University Press, 1976); Roy Armes, ed., *Problems of Film History* (London: British Film Institute, 1981); Marc Ferro, *Cinema and History,* trans. Naomi Greene (Detroit, Mich.: Wayne State University Press, 1988); Robert Sklar and Charles Musser, ed., *Resisting Images: Essays on Cinema and History* (Philadelphia, Pa.: Temple University Press, 1990); Paolo Cherchi Usai, *Burning Passions: An Introduction to the Study of Silent Cinema,* trans. Elizabeth Sansome (London: British Film Institute, 1994); and Bordwell, *On the History of Film Style.* For some notable historical studies of film institutions, see Jan-Christopher Horak, ed., *Lovers of Cinema: The First American Film Avant-Garde, 1915–45* (Madison: University of Wisconsin Press, 1995); Scott MacDonald, ed., *Cinema 16: Documents toward the History of a Film Society* (Philadelphia, Pa.: Temple University Press, 2002); Peter Decherney, *Hollywood and the Culture Elite: How the Movies Became American* (New York:

Columbia University Press, 2005); Wasson, *Museum Movies;* Dana Polan, *Scenes of Instruction: The Beginnings of the U.S. Study of Film* (Berkeley: University of California Press, 2007); Grieveson and Wasson, *Inventing Film Studies.* Key studies of exhibition and reception include Gomery, *Shared Pleasures;* Staiger, *Interpreting Films;* Gregory A. Waller, *Main Street Amusements: Movies and Commercial Entertainment in a Southern City, 1895–1930* (Washington, D.C.: Smithsonian Institution Press, 1995); Melvyn Stokes and Richard Maltby, eds., *American Movie Audiences: From the Turn of the Century to the Early Sound Era* (London: British Film Institute, 1999); Wilinsky, *Sure Seaters;* Mark Jancovich and Lucy Faire with Sarah Stubbings, *The Place of the Audience: Cultural Geographies of Film Consumption* (London British Film Institute, 2003); Charles Acland, *Screen Traffic: Movies, Multiplexes, and Global Culture* (Durham, N.C.: Duke University Press, 2003).

55. Susan Hayward, *Cinema Studies: The Key Concepts,* 3rd ed. (London and New York: Routledge, 2006), 167.

56. Susan Hayward, *French National Cinema,* 2nd ed. (London and New York: Routledge, 2005), 207.

57. A little Praeger Film Library book published in 1970 attests to a consensus that a shift in filmmaking practices was under way and that a second wave of international (that is, non-Hollywood, non–Western European) directors could be identified as constituting a group; see *Second Wave: Newer than New Wave Names in World Cinema* (New York: Praeger, 1970).

58. The third section of Robert Phillip Kolker's *The Altering Eye,* "Politics, Psychology, and Memory," provides a summary of many of these filmmakers and their films. James Roy MacBean's *Film and Revolution* (Bloomington and London: Indiana University Press, 1975) covers some of these as well but favors Godard and Gorin (as did many others), devoting half of the book to their films. Third Cinema provided another form of militant film theory and practice, with two key manifestos from Latin America appearing in translation in 1970–71: Fernando Solanas and Octavio Getino, "Towards a Third Cinema," *Cinéaste* 4, no. 3 (winter 1970–71): 1–14, rpt. in *Twenty-Five Years of the New Latin American Cinema,* ed. Michael Chanan (London: British Film Institute, 1983), 17–27; Julio Garcia Espinosa, "For an Imperfect Cinema," *Afterimage,* no. 3 (summer 1971), rpt. in Chanan, *Twenty-Five Years of the New Latin American Cinema,* 28–33. Finally, the influence of Brecht was important for these formulations; see especially Colin MacCabe, "Realism and the Cinema: Notes on Some Brechtian Theses," *Screen* 15, no. 2 (1974): 7–27; Stephen Heath, "Lessons from Brecht," *Screen* 15, no. 2 (1974): 103–28; Martin Walsh, *The Brechtian Aspect of Radical Cinema,* ed. Keith M. Griffiths (London: British Film Institute, 1981); Sylvia Harvey, "Whose Brecht? Memories for the Eighties," *Screen* 23, no. 1 (May/June 1982): 45–59.

59. Peter Wollen, "The Two Avant-Gardes," *Studio International* 190, no. 978 (November/December 1975), 171–75, rpt. in *Readings and Writings: Semiotic Counter-Strategies* (London: Verso, 1982), 92–104. See also Wollen's influential "Counter Cinema: *Vent d'Est,*" *Afterimage,* no. 4 (1972): 6–17, rpt. as "Godard and Counter-Cinema: *Vent d'Est*" in *Readings and Writings,* 79–91.

60. Paul Willemen, "An Avant Garde for the Eighties," *Framework* 24 (1984), rpt. as "An Avant-Garde for the 90s" in *Looks and Frictions*, 141–61.

61. David Bordwell and Janet Staiger, "Alternative Modes of Film Practice," in *The Classical Hollywood Cinema: Film Style and Mode of Production to 1960* (New York: Columbia University Press, 1985), 381.

62. Bordwell, *Narration in the Fiction Film*, 310.

63. Rodowick, *The Crisis of Political Modernism*, 1–7.

64. See, for example, Ian Aitken, "From Political Modernism to Postmodernism," in *European Film Theory and Cinema: A Critical Introduction* (Edinburgh, UK: Edinburgh University Press, 2001), 132–61.

65. For an overview see Murray Smith, "Modernism and the Avant-Gardes," in *The Oxford Guide to Film Studies*, ed. John Hill and Pamela Church Gibson (Oxford and New York: Oxford University Press, 1998), 395–412.

66. Neale, "Art Cinema as Institution," 12.

67. John Caughie, "Becoming European: Art Cinema, Irony and Identity," in *Screening Europe: Image and Identity in Contemporary European Cinema*, ed. Duncan Petrie (London: British Film Institute, 1992), 33.

68. The abruptness of this transition can be discerned in the differences between the 1969 and 1972 editions of Peter Wollen's *Signs and Meaning in the Cinema* (London: Secker and Warburg), the latter of which contains a new concluding essay that reinterprets the first three in light of the new theoretical developments. It is also quite pointedly evident in a skirmish held in the pages of *Screen* in 1969–70 when Alan Lovell attacked Robin Wood with the stick of auteur-structuralism. The main articles here are Lovell, "Robin Wood: A Dissenting View," *Screen* 10, no. 2 (March–April 1969): 47–55; Wood, "Ghostly Paradigm and HCF: An Answer to Alan Lovell," *Screen* 10, no. 3 (May–June 1969): 35–48; and Lovell, "The Common Pursuit of True Judgement," *Screen* 11, no. 4–5 (August–September 1970): 76–88. Throughout the 1970s, Wood maintained his distance from the *Screen* tendencies in film theory and defended the principles of art, Leavisian New Criticism, and *Cahiers* auteurism—see especially his *Personal Views: Explorations in Film* (London: Gordon Fraser, 1976)—but then came out as a gay critic in 1978 and as an ideological feminist critic in the 1980s.

As for Bergman and Truffaut, they were prime objects of early feminist critique, especially Bergman; see Constance Penley, "*Cries and Whispers*," *Women and Film*, nos. 3–4 (1973), rpt. in *Movies and Methods: An Anthology*, ed. Bill Nichols (Berkeley: University of California Press, 1976), 205–8; Joan Mellen, "Bergman and Women," *Women and Their Sexuality in the New Film* (New York: Horizon Press, 1973), 106–27; and Marsha Kinder and Beverle Houston, "Truffaut's Gorgeous Killers," *Film Quarterly* 27, no. 2 (winter 1973–74): 2–10.

69. David Forgacs, "The Making and Unmaking of Neorealism in Postwar Italy," in *The Culture of Reconstruction: European Literature, Thought, and Film, 1945–50*, ed. Nicholas Hewitt (London: Macmillan, 1989), 53.

70. Ernest Mandel, *Late Capitalism*, trans. Joris de Bres (London: NLB, 1975).

71. Many of Jameson's writings since the mid-1980s address the conjunction of postmodernism and late capitalism. The most important references for this project are

"Postmodernism, or the Cultural Logic of Late Capitalism," *New Left Review* 146 (1984): 53–92, and "The Politics of Theory: Ideological Positions in the Postmodernism Debate," *New German Critique* 33 (1984): 53–65, both rpt. in *Postmodernism, or the Cultural Logic of Late Capitalism* (Durham, N.C.: Duke University Press, 1991), 1–54, 55–66; "Cognitive Mapping," in *Marxism and the Interpretation of Culture,* ed. Cary Nelson and Lawrence Grossberg (Urbana: University of Illinois Press, 1988), 347–57; and *The Geopolitical Aesthetic: Cinema and Space in the World System* (London/Bloomington and Indianapolis: British Film Institute/Indiana University Press, 1992).

72. Charles Jencks, *The Language of Post-Modern Architecture* (New York: Rizzoli, 1976); Jean-François Lyotard, *La Condition postmoderne. Rapport sur le savoir* (Paris: Editions de Minuit, 1979), trans. by Geoff Bennington and Brian Massumi as *The Postmodern Condition: A Report on Knowledge* (Minneapolis: University of Minnesota Press, 1984).

73. For most of these references I have drawn on Ingeborg Hoesterey's introductory essay, "Postmodernism as Discursive Event," to her collection *Zeitgeist in Babel: The Postmodernist Controversy* (Bloomington: Indiana University Press, 1991), xiv, xv. See also Andreas Huyssen, "The Search for Tradition: Avantgarde and Postmodernism in the 1970s" and "Mapping the Postmodern," in *After the Great Divide: Modernism, Mass Culture, Postmodernism* (Bloomington: Indiana University Press, 1986), 160–77, 178–221; David Harvey, *The Condition of Postmodernism* (Cambridge, UK: Basil Blackwell, 1989); John MacGowan, *Postmodernism and Its Critics* (Ithaca, N.Y.: Cornell University Press, 1991); Maureen Turim, "Cinemas of Modernity and Postmodernity," in Hoesterey, *Zeitgeist in Babel,* 177–89.

74. As demarcated, for example, in Nowell-Smith, *The Oxford History of World Cinema.*

75. Colin MacCabe, preface to Jameson, *The Geopolitical Aesthetic,* xiii.

76. Fredric Jameson, "The Existence of Italy," in *Signatures of the Visible* (New York: Routledge, 1992), 156.

77. Hayward, *French National Cinema,* 207.

78. D. N. Rodowick, "A Genealogy of Time: The Nietzschean Dimension of French Cinema, 1958–1998," in *Premises: Invested Spaces in Visual Arts, Architecture, and Design in France, 1958–1998,* 69.

79. Walter Benjamin, "The *Flâneur,*" in *Charles Baudelaire: A Lyric Poet in the Era of High Capitalism* (London: New Left Books, 1973), 59.

80. Wendy Everett, "Re-framing the Fingerprints: A Short Survey of European Film," *European Identity in Cinema,* 2nd ed., ed. Everett (Bristol, UK: Intellect Books, 2005), 19–33.

81. Robert Murphy, *Sixties British Cinema* (London: British Film Institute, 1992), 258.

82. See Judt, *Postwar,* 354–59.

83. On the decline in coproductions in the 1970s as a result of television finance see Hayward, *French National Cinema,* 50. On the importance of television funding for the New German cinema see Thomas Elsaesser, *New German Cinema: A History* (New Brunswick, N.J.: Rutgers University Press, 1989), 32–35, 108–16.

84. Elsaesser, "The New German Cinema," in *European Cinema,* ed. Elizabeth Ezra (Oxford: Oxford University Press, 2004), 200.

85. Nataša Ďurovičová has suggested that the history of sound is both a "test case of historiography in film studies" and a "growth industry" that has developed in three theoretical directions: "economic histories that emphasize the role of determinants like financing, quotas, patents and distribution patterns . . . ; technological histories that consider, for instance, links between broadcast and film sound reproduction in revising the history of miking . . . ; and aesthetic histories, that is, polemics variously engaged with the heritage of Bazinian ontological determinism, and, in particular, with debates over the ideological foundations of the aesthetic ideal of 'realism'" (Ďurovičová, "Translating America: The Hollywood Multilinguals, 1929–1933," in *Sound Theory, Sound Practice,* ed. Rick Altman [New York: Routledge, 1992], 138).

86. Abé Mark Nornes addresses these factors in his recent *Cinema Babel: Translating Global Cinema* (Minneapolis: University of Minnesota Press, 2007).

87. Craig Owens, "The Discourse of Others: Feminists and Postmodernism," in *The Anti-Aesthetic: Essays on Postmodern Culture,* ed. Hal Foster (Seattle, Wash.: Bay Press, 1983), 59. Other texts on feminism and postmodernism that first formed my understanding of their conjuncture include Donna Haraway, "A Manifesto for Cyborgs: Science, Technology, and Socialist Feminism in the 1980s," *Socialist Review* 80 (1985): 65–107; Andreas Huyssen, "Mass Culture as Woman: Modernism's Other," in *After the Great Divide,* 44–62; the essays collected by Linda Nicholson in her anthology *Feminism/Postmodernism* (New York: Routledge, 1990); and Judith Butler, "Contingent Foundations: Feminism and the Question of 'Postmodernism,'" *Praxis International* 11, no. 2 (1991): 150–57.

88. Houston, *The Contemporary Cinema,* 190–91.

89. Andrew Sarris, "Veni, Vidi, Vitti," *Cavalier* (February 1963), rpt. in *Confessions of a Cultist: On the Cinema, 1955/1969* (New York: Simon and Schuster, 1971), 69.

90. Simone de Beauvoir, *Le Deuxième sexe* (Paris: Gallimard, 1949).

91. Jean Domarchi, Jacques Doniol-Valcroze, Jean-Luc Godard, Pierre Kast, Jacques Rivette, and Eric Rohmer, "Hiroshima, notre amour," in Hillier, *Cahiers du Cinéma, The 1950s,* 62–63.

92. Gilles Deleuze, *Cinema 1: The Movement-Image,* trans. Hugh Tomlinson and Barbara Habberjam (Minneapolis: University of Minnesota Press, 1986), 120.

93. Ibid., 121.

94. For an interesting analysis of Deleuze historicization of the time-image that adds "1982, Hong Kong" to the list of breaks, see Ka-Fai Yau, "*Recon-figuration:* Revisiting Modernity and Reality in Deleuze's Taxonomy of Cinema," *Wide Angle* 20, no. 4 (October 1998): 51–74.

95. For a critique of and application of Deleuzean aesthetics to the postwar German *Trümmerfilme,* see Jaimey Fisher, "Deleuze in a Ruinous Context: German Rubble-Film and Italian Neorealism," *Iris* 23 (spring 1997): 53–74.

96. Giuliana Bruno, "Towards a Theorization of Film History," *Iris* 2, no. 2 (1984): 47, 48.

97. Walter Benjamin, "Theses on the Philosophy of History," in *Illuminations,* trans. Harry Zohn (New York: Schocken Books, 1969), 255.

2. The Name above the Subtitle

1. In 1984 Bruce A. Austin published a questionnaire-based reception study of Dryden Theatre patronage titled "Portrait of an Art Film Audience," *Journal of Communication* 34, no. 1 (1984): 74–87. His findings remain pertinent for the filmgoing preferences of Dryden Theatre audiences as discussed here.

2. At the time, I deduced much of this information from contemporary American articles and reviews of the film. Since then, my deductions have been confirmed by Antoine de Baecque and Serge Toubiana, who in their translated biography on François Truffaut note that *Day for Night* was initially pitched at a budget of 3.5 million francs to United Artists, which refused to finance it because UA thought it "too intellectual." Truffaut's longtime producer at Films de la Carosse, Marcel Berbert, then approached Robert Solo, Warner Bros.' London representative, who agreed to co-produce at a meeting in November 1971. The contract was signed in May 1972. See de Baecque and Toubiana, *Truffaut: A Biography,* trans. Catherine Temerson (New York: Knopf, 1999), 295.

3. All three of these reviews are reprinted in *Film 68/69: An Anthology by the National Society of Film Critics,* ed. Hollis Alpert and Andrew Sarris (New York: Simon and Schuster, 1969). The quotations may be found on the following page numbers: Hartung, 217; Kauffmann, 220; Schickel, 221, 221–22, emphasis in original.

4. For an overview of the *New York Times* debates, see Fausto F. Pauluzzi, "Subtitles vs. Dubbing: *The New York Times* Polemic, 1960–1966," in *Holding the Vision: Essays on Film,* proceedings of the First Annual Film Conference of Kent State University, held 21 April 1983, ed. Douglas Radcliff-Umstead (Kent State University, Ohio: International Film Society, 1983), 131–37.

5. John Mowitt's *Retakes: Postcoloniality and Foreign Film Languages* (Minneapolis: University of Minnesota Press, 2005) examines the linguistic basis of foreignness in cinema; *Subtitles: On the Foreignness of Film,* ed. Atom Egoyan and Ian Balfour (Cambridge, Mass.: MIT Press, 2004) presents several scholarly and creative considerations of the figure of the subtitle as a mark of filmic foreignness.

6. David Bordwell and Kristin Thompson, *Film Art: An Introduction,* 7th ed. (New York: McGraw-Hill, 2004), 388. See also Joseph M. Boggs, *The Art of Watching Films: A Guide to Film Analysis,* 4th ed. (Mountain View, Calif.: Mayfield, 1996), 408; Louis Giannetti and Jim Leach, *Understanding Movies,* 2nd Canadian ed. (Toronto: Prentice Hall, 2001), 257. For an early British example, see Ivor Montagu, *Film World: A Guide to Cinema* (Harmondsworth, UK: Penguin Books, 1964), 181–82.

7. Roberto Rossellini, "Ten Years of Cinema," in *Springtime in Italy: A Reader on Neo-Realism,* ed. and trans. David Overbey (Hamden, Conn.: Archon Books, 1978), 96, 111–12 n. 7. I am also thankful to Peter Brunette for pointing out that Rossellini strongly preferred that his late-career history films be dubbed into English for U.S. television broadcast.

8. As quoted in Geoffrey Nowell-Smith, "Italy sotto voce," *Sight and Sound* 37, no. 3 (summer 1968): 145.

9. Jean-Marie Straub and Danièle Huillet, "Direct Sound: An Interview with Jean-Marie Straub and Danièle Huillet," trans. Bill Kavaler, in *Film Sound: Theory and*

Practice, ed. Elisabeth Weis and John Belton (New York: Columbia University Press, 1985), 152.

10. Philip T. Hartung, "The Future of Film: A Symposium," in *Film 67/68: An Anthology by the National Society of Film Critics,* ed. Richard Schickel and John Simon (New York: Simon and Schuster, 1968), 290; Peter Cowie, *1966 International Film Guide* (London: Tantivy, 1966), 7; Penelope Houston, *The Contemporary Cinema* (Harmondsworth, UK: Penguin Books, 1963), 88, 89.

11. Both Tim Bergfelder and Marc Silberman concentrate on the Germanies of the 1950s–1960s. See Bergfelder, "The Nation Vanishes: European Co-productions and Popular Genre Formulae in the 1950s and 1960s," in *Cinema and Nation,* ed. Mette Hjort and Scott MacKenzie (London and New York: Routledge, 2000), 139–52, and *International Adventures: Popular German Cinema and European Co-productions in the 1960s* (Oxford and New York: Berghahn Books, 2005); Silberman, "Learning from the Enemy: DEFA-French Co-productions of the 1950s," *Film History: An International Journal* 18, no. 1 (2006): 21–45.

12. Robin Buss, *Italian Films* (New York: Holmes and Meier, 1989), 9; Susan Hayward, *French National Cinema,* 2nd ed. (London and New York: Routledge, 2005), 11, 50.

13. Peter Lev, *The Euro-American Cinema* (Austin: University of Texas Press, 1993), xii.

14. The other is Bergfelder, *International Adventures.*

15. Thomas H. Guback, *The International Film Industry: Western Europe and America Since 1945* (Bloomington: Indiana University Press, 1969).

16. Geoffrey Nowell-Smith, "Art Cinema," in *The Oxford History of World Cinema,* ed. Nowell-Smith (London: Oxford University Press, 1996), 568.

17. Rick Altman, "Introduction: Sound's Dark Corners," in *Sound Theory, Sound Practice,* ed. Altman (New York: Routledge, 1992), 171–77.

18. See Douglas Gomery, "Economic Struggle and Hollywood Imperialism: Europe Converts to Sound," *Yale French Studies* 60 (1980): 80–93; Dudley Andrew, "Sound in France: The Origins of the Native School," *Yale French Studies* 60 (1980): 94–114; Kristin Thompson, *Exporting Entertainment: America in the World Film Market 1907–34* (London: British Film Institute, 1985); Victoria De Grazia, "Mass Culture and Sovereignty: The American Challenge to European Cinemas, 1920–1960," *Journal of Modern History* 61, no. 1 (March 1989): 53–87; Ian Jarvie, *Hollywood's Overseas Campaign: The North Atlantic Movie Trade, 1920–1950* (Cambridge, UK, and New York: Cambridge University Press, 1992); Thomas J. Saunders, *Hollywood in Berlin: American Cinema and Weimar Germany* (Berkeley: University of California Press, 1994); Ruth Vasey, *The World According to Hollywood, 1918–1939* (Madison: University of Wisconsin Press, 1996); John Trumpbour, *Selling Hollywood to the World: U.S. and European Struggles for Mastery of the Global Film Industry, 1920–1950* (New York: Cambridge University Press, 2002).

19. Kristin Thompson and David Bordwell, *Film History: An Introduction,* 2nd ed. (New York: McGraw-Hill, 2003), 168. Thompson has devoted a considerable amount of scholarly energy to the Film Europe movement; see her "National or

International Films? The European Debate during the 1920s," *Film History* 8, no. 3 (1996): 281–96, and "The Rise and Fall of Film Europe," in *"Film Europe" and "Film America": Cinema, Commerce and Cultural Exchange 1920–1939,* ed. Andrew Higson and Richard Maltby (Exeter, UK: University of Exeter Press, 1999), 56–81.

20. For more on Pommer and Film Europe, see Ursula Hardt, *From Caligari to California: Eric Pommer's Life in the International Film Wars* (Providence, R.I.: Berghahn Books, 1996); Thomas J. Saunders, "Germany and Film Europe," in Higson and Maltby, *"Film Europe" and "Film America,"* 159–61; and Documents 16 and 17 in Higson and Maltby, 392–96.

21. Hardt, *From Caligari to California,* 84–85.

22. As quoted in Thompson and Bordwell, *Film History: An Introduction,* 168.

23. Paul Rotha and Richard Griffith, *The Film Till Now: A Survey of World Cinema,* rev. and enl. ed. (London: Spring Books, 1967), 261; Siegfried Kracauer, *From Caligari to Hitler: A Psychological History of the German Film* (Princeton, N.J.: Princeton University Press, 1947), 131–38; Hardt, *From Caligari to California,* 86.

24. Richard Maltby and Ruth Vasey, "The International Language Problem: European Reactions to Hollywood's Conversion to Sound," in *Hollywood in Europe: Experiences of a Cultural Hegemony,* ed. David W. Ellwood and Rob Kroes (Amsterdam: VU University Press, 1994), 70; André Visson, *As Others See Us* (Garden City, N.J.: Doubleday, 1948), 232–33, as quoted in Maltby and Vasey, 71.

25. Paul Swann, *The Hollywood Feature Film in Postwar Britain* (New York: St. Martin's Press, 1987), 22.

26. See Richard Maltby and Ruth Vasey, "'Temporary American Citizens': Cultural Anxieties and Industrial Strategies in the Americanisation of European Cinema," and Andrew Higson, "Cultural Policy and Industrial Practice: Film Europe and the International Film Congresses of the 1920s," in Higson and Maltby, *"Film Europe" and "Film America,"* 32–55 and 117–31.

27. Thompson and Bordwell, *Film History: An Introduction,* 169; Maltby and Vasey, "The International Language Problem," 85; Karel Dibbets, "The Introduction of Sound," in Nowell-Smith, *The Oxford History of World Cinema,* 213.

28. For more on quotas, see Jens Ulff-Møller, "Hollywood's 'Foreign War': The Effect of National Commercial Policy on the Emergence of the American Film Hegemony in France, 1920–1929," and "Group 2: Kontingents, Quotas and the American Response," in Higson and Maltby, *"Film Europe" and "Film America,"* 189–98 and 361–74.

29. For more on multiple-language versions, see Nataša Ďurovičová, "Translating America: The Hollywood Multilinguals, 1929–1933," in Altman, *Sound Theory, Sound Practice,* 139–53, 261–66; Ginette Vincendeau, "Hollywood Babel: The Coming of Sound and the Multiple Language Version," *Screen* 29, no. 2 (spring 1988): 24–39, rpt. in Higson and Maltby, *"Film Europe" and "Film America,"* 207–24; and Joseph Gancarz, "Made in Germany: Multiple-Language Versions and the Early German Sound Cinema," in Higson and Maltby, 249–73.

30. Andrew, "Sound in France," 98–99, 100.

31. Vincendeau, "Hollywood Babel," 213.

32. Hayward, *French National Cinema*, 22.

33. Andrew, "Sound in France," 101, 103.

34. Vincendeau, "Hollywood Babel," 210–11.

35. Ibid., 211.

36. Robert C. Allen and Douglas Gomery, *Film History: Theory and Practice* (New York: McGraw-Hill, 1985), 136.

37. This is a brief summary of a detailed argument. It is significant that, given my claims regarding European film historiography, Guback's book should be so long out of print.

38. On runaway productions, see Greg Elmer and Mike Gasher, eds., *Contracting Out Hollywood: Runaway Productions and Foreign Location Shooting* (Lanham, Md.: Rowman and Littlefield, 2005).

39. Guback, *The International Film Industry*, 165–66.

40. Ibid., 199.

41. Guback, "Film and Cultural Pluralism," *Journal of Aesthetic Education* 5, no. 2 (1971), rpt. in *Cinéaste* 5, no. 1 (winter 1971–72): 7, and "Cultural Identity and Film in the European Economic Community," *Cinema Journal* 14, no. 1 (fall 1974): 16. See also the following by the same author: "Hollywood's International Market," in *The American Film Industry*, ed. Tino Balio, rev. ed. (Madison: University of Wisconsin Press, 1985), 463–86; "Film as International Business: The Role of American Multinationals," in *The American Movie Industry: The Business of Motion Pictures*, ed. Gorham Kindem (Carbondale: Southern Illinois University Press, 1982), 336–50.

42. ANICA, the Associazione Nazionale Industrie Cinematografiche e Affini, was established in 1945.

43. Made famous by François Truffaut in a polemical article published in the January 1954 issue of *Cahiers du cinéma,* the phrase "Tradition of Quality" could not be uttered by cinephiles since the late 1950s (as with "art cinema" by leftist film critics since the early 1970s) without a shudder of disapproval. The term was coined by Jean-Pierre Barrot in the postwar *L'Écran français* to specify, with marked respect, the kind of French films that made the national film culture proud by their success at film festivals and at the box office. For Truffaut's influential invective, see "Une certaine tendance du cinéma français," *Cahiers du cinéma,* no. 31 (January 1954), rpt. as "A Certain Tendency of the French Cinema" in *Cahiers du Cinéma in English,* no. 1 (1966): 30–41 and in *Movies and Methods: An Anthology,* ed. Bill Nichols (Berkeley: University of California Press, 1976), 224–37.

44. Roy Armes, *French Cinema* (New York: Oxford University Press, 1985), 148. In the case of Italian spaghetti westerns and *pepla,* Marcia Landy has offered potential readings for how we might consider their international casts as registering in more self-conscious ways the pressures placed on national traditions by the internationalization of popular genre filmmaking in this period; see her *Italian Film* (Cambridge, UK: Cambridge University Press, 2000), 19, 185–86. These and other popular European genres have also more generally received increasing scholarly attention since the early 1990s; see, for example, the articles in Richard Dyer and Ginette Vincendeau, eds., *Popular European Cinema* (London and New York: Routledge, 1992);

Christopher Wagstaff, "Italian Genre Films in the World Market," in *Hollywood and Europe: Economics, Culture, National Identity, 1945–95,* ed. Geoffrey Nowell-Smith and Steven Ricci (London: British Film Institute, 1998), 74–85; Christopher Frayling, *Spaghetti Westerns: Cowboys and Europeans from Karl May to Sergio Leone* (London: I. B. Tauris, 1998); Dmitris Eleftheriotis, *Popular Cinemas of Europe: Studies of Texts, Contexts, and Frameworks* (New York and London: Continuum, 2001); Lucy Mazdon, ed., *France on Film: Reflections on Popular French Cinema* (London: Wallflower Press, 2002); Anne Jackel, "*Les Visiteurs:* a popular form of cinema for Europe?" in *European Identity in Cinema,* 2nd ed., ed. Wendy Everett (Bristol, UK: Intellect Books, 2005), 41–49; Rosalind Galt, "The Dialectic of Landscape in Italian Popular Melodrama," in *The New European Cinema: Redrawing the Map* (New York: Columbia University Press, 2006), 26–87.

45. Michel Marie omits from the New Wave several celebrated auteur films produced by Anatole Dauman—*Muriel ou le temps d'un retour* (1963), *Masculin féminin* (1965), *Deux ou trois choses que je sais d'elle* (*Two or Three Things I Know about Her,* 1966), *Mouchette* (1967), and *Au hasard Balthazar* (1966)—for this reason: "The budgets for these 1960s films were considerably higher than the costs of comparable films by [Pierre] Braunberger and Georges de Beauregard. While they all became major works of the modern French cinema, they did not fit the mode of production specific to New Wave projects, since they were expensive and relied heavily upon studios and post-synchronization" (Marie, *The French New Wave: An Artistic School,* trans. Richard Neupert [London: Blackwell Publishing, 2003], 64).

46. Steve Neale, "Art Cinema as Institution," *Screen* 22, no. 1 (1981): 14–15.

47. See, for example, Hayward, *French National Cinema,* 26–29.

48. Neale, "Art Cinema as Institution," 35.

49. Ibid., 34.

50. Lev, *The Euro-American Cinema,* 15–16.

51. Ibid., 31.

52. A French-Italian-American coproduction, *Le Mépris/Contempt* is the only film among Lev's case studies that is not predominantly in English; it is polyglot mix of French, Italian, German, and English, with each character speaking mostly in his or her native tongue. Lev thus remarks, following the lead of the *Variety* reviewer, that the use of multiple languages "makes *Contempt* easy to subtitle but difficult to dub" and that Godard perhaps included the character of the interpreter, played by Georgia Moll, "as a way to maintain his control against dubbing the film" (86). In this he was not entirely successful, and when faced with the eventuality of coproducer Carlo Ponti's dubbing (and cutting) of the Italian-release version, Godard removed his name from Italian prints.

53. See Toby Miller, "The Crime of Monsieur Lang: GATT, the Screen, and the New International Division of Cultural Labour," in *Film Policy: International, National and Regional Perspectives,* ed. Albert Moran (London and New York: Routledge, 1996), 72–84.

54. For an overview of the history of the GATT agreement in relation to French cinematic protectionism from the immediate postwar period, see Jean-Pierre Jeancolas, "From the Blum-Byrnes Agreement to the GATT Affair," in Nowell-Smith and Ricci, *Hollywood and Europe,* 47–60.

55. For an overview of French protectionism regarding audiovisual culture and trade, see Bill Grantham, *"Some Big Bourgeois Brothel": Contexts for France's Culture Wars with Hollywood* (Luton, UK: University of Luton Press, 2000), and Jens Ulff-Møller, *Hollywood's Film Wars with France: Film-Trade Diplomacy and the Emergence of the French Film Quota Policy* (Rochester, N.Y.: University of Rochester Press, 2001).

56. Angus Finney, *The State of European Cinema: A New Dose of Reality* (London: Cassell, 1996), 6.

57. Simon Horrocks, "European Community (Now European Union) and the Cinema," in *Encyclopedia of European Cinema,* ed. Ginette Vincendeau (New York: Facts on File, 1995), 133.

58. For more information on these initiatives, see Paul Hainsworth, "Politics, Culture and Cinema in the New Europe," in *Border Crossing: Film in Ireland, Britain and Europe,* ed. John Hill, Martin McLoone, and Paul Hainsworth (Belfast: Institute of Irish Studies in association with the University of Ulster and the British Film Institute, 1994), 8–33; and Horrocks, "European Community," in Vincendeau, *Encyclopedia of European Cinema,* 133–34. For more on Eurimages, see Finney, *The State of European Cinema,* 108ff. For more on BABEL, see Richard Kilborn, "'Speak My Language': Current Attitudes to Television Subtitling and Dubbing," *Media, Culture and Society* 15, no. 4 (October 1993): 654, and Laurent Creton and Anne Jäckel, "Business 1960–2004: A Certain Idea of the Film Industry," in *The French Cinema Book,* ed. Michael Temple and Michael Witt (London: British Film Institute, 2004), 215. Jäckel has also provided general and detailed overviews of GATT-era French-British coproduction and of contemporary pan-European initiatives respectively in two publications: "European Co-production Strategies: The Case of France and Britain," in Moran, *Film Policy,* 85–97; and *European Film Industries* (London: British Film Institute, 2003), 67–90. See also Catherine Bizern and Anne-Marie Autissier, *Public Aid Mechanisms for the Film and Audiovisual Industry in Europe: Comparative Analysis of National Aid Mechanisms,* vol. 1 (Paris and Strasbourg: Centre National de la Cinematographie/European Audiovisual Observatory, 1998).

59. Finney, *The State of European Cinema,* 5.

60. In addition to the two I deal with here, see also British Screen Advisory Council, *The European Initiative: The Business of Film and Television in the 1990s* (London: BSAC, 1991); Martin Dale, *Europa Europa: Developing the European Film Industry* (Paris: Academie Carat and Media Business School, 1992); and London Economics, *The Competitive Position of the European and U.S. Film Industries* (Madrid: Media Business School, 1993). For an overview of these documents and their relation to film cultural discourses on European coproduction, see John Hill, "The Future of European Cinema: The Economics and Culture of Pan-European Strategies," in Hill et al., *Border Crossing,* 53–80.

61. Terry Ilott, *Budgets and Markets: A Study of the Budgeting of European Film* (London: Routledge, 1996), 15, 108. Ilott's study presents both hard-to-find data on the budgeting of selected coproduced European films and practical assessments of the success of different kinds of European films, "success" meaning a balance between outlay and earnings.

62. Finney, *The State of European Cinema,* 21, 27; see also 30–31. Like Ilott's, Finney's study was EU commissioned, written for the European Film Academy and Screen International in 1993.

63. Ibid., 97–98. Finney traces the idea of eliminating bilateral treaties in favor of a pan-European treaty back to 1981, but such proposals were being put forward more than a decade earlier. In 1970 Eitel Monaco, president of Unitalia and general secretary of ANICA, was already calling for a "radical transformation of European cinematographic laws," including "more decisive and rapid progress in the field of the European integration of film industries and in particular the extension, in each of the six countries, of the system in force for national films to films produced in the other countries of the European Community" ("The Italian Film Industry: Situation and Prospects," *Review of Economic Conditions in Italy* 24, nos. 2–3 [March–May 1970]: 140). See also Monaco's article "The Financing of Film Production in Europe," *Cinema Journal* 14, no. 1 (fall 1974): 18–25.

64. Marsha Kinder, *Blood Cinema: The Reconstruction of National Identity in Spain* (Berkeley: University of California Press, 1993), 441.

65. Duncan Petrie, ed., *Screening Europe: Image and Identity in Contemporary European Cinema* (London: British Film Institute, 1992).

66. Petrie, "Introduction: Change and Cinematic Representation in Modern Europe," in Petrie, *Screening Europe,* 1; Ien Ang, "Hegemony-in-Trouble: Nostalgia and the Ideology of the Impossible in European Cinema," in Petrie, 22.

67. "Discussion," in Petrie, *Screening Europe,* 95.

68. An excellent summary of the current state of play in this regard is Thomas Elsaesser's "European Cinema as World Cinema: A New Beginning?" in *European Cinema: Face to Face with Hollywood* (Amsterdam: Amsterdam University Press, 2003), 485–513.

69. Susan Hayward offers a different set of "typologies of the national" for national cinema in general; see Hayward, *French National Cinema,* 8–16.

70. The reader is encouraged to see Guback, *The International Film Industry,* 181–97, for a much more detailed econoindustrial analysis of European coproduction trends through the 1950s and 1960s than is provided here.

71. Steve Lipkin, "The New Wave and the Post-War Film Economy," in *Current Research in Film: Audiences, Economics, and Law,* vol. 2, ed. Bruce A. Austin (Norwood, N.J.: Ablex, 1986), 173. See also Guback, *The International Film Industry,* 181–97.

72. Colin Crisp is an exception in this regard. Although his study of French cinema from the introduction of sound until the end of the 1950s predates, for the most part, my own concerns here, his work is nevertheless attentive to the political, economic, and industrial considerations of French cinema in the pre– and post–World War II eras until 1960 in ways that I am arguing are necessary for understanding their developments in the full flowering of the French New Wave and after. On the particular issue of coproduction see Crisp, *The Classic French Cinema 1930–1960* (Bloomington and Indianapolis, London and New York: Indiana University Press / I. B. Tauris, 1993), 79–87.

73. Pierre Sorlin, for example, writes: "In a few cases, when the director could control the whole project, the co-operation of two companies helped make difficult

films: Antonioni's *L'avventura* (*The Adventure*, 1960), *La notte* (*The Night*, 1961), and *The Eclipse* (1962) were all co-produced. But, most of the time, greater commercial appeal was the spur, and companies decide to shoot commercial products likely to interest cosmopolitan audiences. Two series of films, the historical or mythological epics and the 'spaghetti westerns,' are the most characteristic products of international collaboration" (Sorlin, *Italian National Cinema 1896–1996* [London: Routledge, 1996], 125).

While Sorlin acknowledges here the existence of coproduced auteur films or art cinema, their existence is nonetheless remarked as exceptional. For if art films are the products of international coproduction deals equally as much as big-budget, historical epics or as commercially oriented popular genres, then they are also the products of larger economic, industrial, and market forces, all of which mounts a rather serious challenge to their celebrated marginality and status as torchbearers of their national cinema cultures.

74. See Geoffrey Nowell-Smith's "Introduction" to Nowell-Smith and Ricci, *Hollywood and Europe*, 8–9.

75. Susan Hayward, *Cinema Studies: The Key Concepts*, 3rd ed. (London and New York: Routledge, 2006), 261.

76. Richard Neupert has pointed out how Godard's privileged status vis-à-vis the matters of international filmmaking and box office viability was not shared by at least one of his New Wave compatriots: "It is interesting to note how little criticism is ever aimed at Godard for failing to make money during this same period. In fact, Godard's failure to attract huge crowds with films such as *A Woman Is a Woman* (1961) and *Les carabiniers* (1963) was used more typically as proof of his radical aesthetic vitality; when Chabrol lost money, he was seen as betraying the spirit of the New Wave. Similarly, when Godard took money from Carlo Ponti to make *Une femme mariée* (*A Married Woman*, 1963) or *Le mépris* (*Contempt*, 1963), he was said to parody the studio system, but when Chabrol shot *A double tour*, a color, international coproduction, his importance for the New Wave was over" (Neupert, *A History of the French New Wave Cinema* [Madison: University of Wisconsin Press, 2002], 129).

77. "French-Italian Film Agreement of August 1, 1966," in Guback, *The International Film Industry*, 210–11.

78. Josephine Dries, *Dubbing and Subtitling: Guidelines for Production and Distribution* (Düsseldorf: European Institute for the Media, 1995), 39.

79. On American remakes of French films, see Carolyn A. Durham, *Double Takes: Culture and Gender in French Films and Their American Remakes* (Hanover, N.H.: University Press of New England, 1998); Lucy Mazdon, *Encore Hollywood: Remaking French Cinema* (London: British Film Institute, 2000); David I. Grossvogel, *Didn't You Used to Be Depardieu? Film as Cultural Marker in France and Hollywood* (New York: Peter Lang, 2002). On remakes generally, see Andrew Horton and Stuart Y. McDougal, eds., *Play It Again Sam: Retakes on Remakes* (Berkeley: University of California Press, 1998); Jennifer Forrest and Leonard R. Koos, eds., *Dead Ringers: The Remake in Theory in Practice* (Albany, N.Y.: SUNY Press, 2002); Constantine Verevis, *Film Remakes* (Edinburgh: Edinburgh University Press, 2006).

80. Dries, *Dubbing and Subtitling,* 41.

81. Thomas Elsaesser, "Hyper-, Retro-, or Counter-Cinema: European Cinema and Third Cinema between Hollywood and Art Cinema," in *Mediating Two Worlds: Cinematic Encounters in the Americas,* ed. John King, Ana M. Lopez, and Manuel Alvarado (London: British Film Institute, 1993), 127.

82. Neale, "Art Cinema as Institution," 35–36.

83. The matter is less clear-cut than this for *The Leopard* than it is for *1900.* In the case of the former, the English-dubbed version is considerably shorter than the Italian one, which raises the whole issue of the "director's cut."

84. Andrew Sarris, review of *The Leopard, Village Voice,* 22 August 1963, rpt. in *Confessions of a Cultist: On the Cinema, 1955/1969* (New York: Simon and Schuster, 1971), 92.

85. Michel Chion, *The Voice in Cinema,* ed. and trans. Claudia Gorbman (New York: Columbia University Press, 1998), 85, 86.

86. Ella Shohat and Robert Stam, "The Cinema after Babel: Language, Difference, Power," *Screen* 26, nos. 3–4 (1985): 41.

87. Thomas L. Rowe, "The English Dubbing Text," *Babel* 6, no. 3 (1960): 117.

88. Rick Altman, "Moving Lips: Cinema as Ventriloquism," *Yale French Studies* 60 (1980): 70.

89. Maltby and Vasey, "The International Language Problem," 78.

90. Ibid., 88.

91. Dries, *Dubbing and Subtitling,* 27–28. The literature on subtitling and dubbing makes for fascinating reading, particularly the industrial analyses. I encourage the reader to seek out the following: Herman G. Weinberg, *Film Subtitling: Art and Business,* interview by Colin D. Edwards, audiocassette (University of California Extension Center, 1969); István Fodor, *Film Dubbing: Phonetic, Semiotic, Esthetic, and Psychological Aspects* (Hamburg: Helmut Buske, 1976); Hans Vöge, "The Translation of Films: Sub-Titling Versus Dubbing," *Babel* 23, no. 3 (1977): 120–25; Virgil Grillo and Bruce Kawin, "Reading the Movies: Subtitles, Silence, and the Structure of the Brain," *Post Script* 1, no. 1 (1981): 25–32; John Minchinton, "Fitting Titles," *Sight and Sound* 56, no. 4 (autumn 1987): 279–82; Dennis Packham, "Euro Titling" [response to Minchinton], *Sight and Sound* 57, no. 1 (winter 1987–88): 73; Georg-Michael Luyken et al., *Overcoming Language Barriers in Television: Dubbing and Subtitling for the European Audience* (Düsseldorf: European Institute for the Media, 1991); Martine Danan, "Dubbing as an Expression of Nationalism," *Meta: Journal des traducteurs/Translator's Journal* 36, no. 4 (1991): 606–14; Candace Whitman-Linsen, *Through the Dubbing Glass: The Synchronization of American Motion Pictures into German, French, and Spanish* (Frankfurt am Main: Peter Lang, 1992); Mikhail Yampolsky, "Voice Devoured: Artaud and Borges on Dubbing," trans. Larry P. Joseph, *October* 64 (spring 1993): 57–77; Antje Ascheid, "Speaking Tongues: Voice Dubbing in the Cinema as Cultural Ventriloquism," *Velvet Light Trap* 40 (fall 1997): 32–41; Jan Ivarsson and Mary Carroll, *Subtitling* (Simrishamn, Sweden: TransEdit, 1998); Abé Mark Nornes, "For an Abusive Subtitling," *Film Quarterly* 52, no. 3 (spring 1999): 17–34; Fotios Karamitroglou, *Towards a Methodology for the Investigation of Norms in Audiovisual Translation* (Amsterdam and Atlanta, Ga.: Rodopi, 2000).

92. Stephen Heath, "Questions of Property: Film and Nationhood," in *Explorations in Film Theory: Selected Essays from Ciné-Tracts,* ed. Ron Burnett (Bloomington: Indiana University Press, 1991), 184.

3. Wandering Women

1. See, for example, Pierre Sorlin, *European Cinemas, European Societies, 1939–1990* (London: Routledge, 1991), 199–205.

2. Robert Phillip Kolker, *The Altering Eye: Contemporary International Cinema* (Oxford, UK: Oxford University Press, 1983), 136.

3. David Bordwell, "The Art Cinema as a Mode of Film Practice," *Film Criticism* 4, no. 1 (1979): 58.

4. Richard Dyer, *White* (London: Routledge, 1997), 184.

5. On Italian colonialism see Robert L. Hess, *Italian Colonialism in Somalia* (Chicago: University of Chicago Press, 1966); Claudio G. Segré, *Fourth Shore: The Italian Colonization of Libya* (Chicago: University of Chicago Press, 1974); Lucio Gambi, "Geography and Imperialism in Italy: From the Unity of the Nation to the 'New' Roman Empire," in *Geography and Empire,* ed. Anne Godlewska and Neil Smith (Oxford, UK: Blackwell, 1994), 74–91; Ruth Ben-Ghiat and Mia Fuller, eds., *Italian Colonialism* (New York: Palgrave Macmillan, 2005); Jacqueline Andal and Derek Duncan, *Italian Colonialism: Legacy and Memory* (Oxford and New York: Peter Lang, 2005).

6. See James Hay, *Popular Film Culture in Fascist Italy: The Passing of the Rex* (Bloomington: Indiana University Press, 1986), esp. 181–200; Angela Dalle Vacche, *The Body in the Mirror: Shapes of History in Italian Cinema* (Princeton, N.J.: Princeton University Press, 1992), 18–56; Maria Wyke, *Projecting the Past: Ancient Rome, Cinema, and History* (New York: Routledge, 1997); Ruth Ben-Ghiat, "The Fascist War Trilogy," in *Roberto Rossellini: Magician of the Real,* ed. David Forgacs, Sarah Lutton, and Geoffrey Nowell-Smith (London: British Film Institute, 2000), 20–35.

7. See Pierre Boulanger, *Le Cinéma colonial: De "L'Atlantide" à "Lawrence d'Arabie"* (Paris: Seghers, 1975); Pierre Sorlin, "The Fanciful Empire: French Feature Films and the Colonies in the 1930s," *French Cultural Studies* 2, part 2, no. 5 (1991): 135–51; Christopher Faulkner, "Affective Identities: French National Cinema and the 1930s," *Canadian Journal of Film Studies* 3, no. 2 (1994): 3–29; Charles O'Brien, "The 'Cinéma Colonial' of 1930s France: Film Narration as Social Practice," in *Visions of the East: Orientalism in Film,* ed. Matthew Bernstein and Gaylyn Studlar (New Brunswick, N.J.: Rutgers University Press, 1997), 207–31; Fatimah Tobing Rony, *The Third Eye: Race, Cinema, and Ethnographic Spectacle* (Durham, N.C.: Duke University Press, 1996), 21–73; David Henry Slavin, "French Cinema's Other First Wave: Political and Racial Economies of *Cinéma Colonial,* 1918 to 1934," *Cinema Journal* 37, no. 1 (fall 1997), 23–46, and *Colonial Cinema and Imperial France, 1919–1939: White Blind Spots, Male Fantasies, Settler Myths* (Baltimore, Md.: Johns Hopkins University Press, 2002).

8. Sorlin, "The Fanciful Empire," 137.

9. For more on France's colonial reforms, decolonization policies, and colonial wars in the postwar era, see John Talbott, *The War without a Name: France in Algeria,*

1954–1962 (London: Faber and Faber, 1981); Miles Kahler, *Decolonization in Britain and France: The Domestic Consequences of International Relations* (Princeton, N.J.: Princeton University Press, 1984); Franz Ansprenger, *The Dissolution of the Colonial Empires* (London: Routledge, 1989), 208–52; Benjamin Stora, *La Gangrène et l'oubli: La mémoire de la Guerre d'Algérie* (Paris: Éditions la Découverte, 1991); Maurice Larkin, *France since the Popular Front: Government and People, 1936–1996,* 2nd ed. (Oxford, UK: Clarendon Press, 1997), 223–37, 254–60, 272–79.

10. For more on Rouch's films and film practice, see Mick Eaton, ed., *Anthropology-Reality-Cinema: The Films of Jean Rouch* (London: British Film Institute, 1979); Paul Stoller, *The Cinematic Griot: The Ethnography of Jean Rouch* (Chicago: University of Chicago Press, 1992); Jean Rouch, *Ciné-Ethnography,* ed. and trans. Steven Feld (Minneapolis: University of Minnesota Press, 2003); "Visual Anthropology—Cine-Trance: A Tribute to Jean Rouch (1917–2004)," special issue, *American Anthropologist* 107, no. 1 (2005). On Marker see Susan Howe, "Sorting Facts, or Nineteen Ways of Looking at Marker," in *Beyond Document: Essays on Nonfiction Film,* ed. Charles Warren (Hanover, N.H.: University Press of New England, for Wesleyan University Press, 1996), 295–343; Geneviève Van Cauwenberge, "Le point de vue documentaire dans *Le Joli mai,*" in *Théorème 6: Recherches sur Chris Marker,* ed. Philippe Dubois (Paris: Presses Sorbonne Nouvelle, 2002), 83–99; Catherine Lupton, *Chris Marker* (London: Reaktion Books, 2005); Nora M. Alter, *Chris Marker* (Urbana: University of Illinois Press, 2006).

11. Dina Sherzer, introduction to *Cinema, Colonialism, Postcolonialism: Perspectives from the French and Francophone Worlds,* ed. Sherzer (Austin: University of Texas Press, 1996), 6, 7; Martine Astier Loutfi, "Imperial Frame: Film Industry and Colonial Representation," in Sherzer, *Cinema, Colonialism, Postcolonialism,* 25; Susan Hayward, *French National Cinema,* 2nd ed. (London and New York: Routledge, 2005), 32–33.

12. The quoted phrase is from Larkin, *France since the Popular Front,* 223.

13. Roy Armes, *French Cinema* (New York: Oxford University Press, 1985), 166; Alan Williams, *Republic of Images: A History of French Filmmaking* (Cambridge, Mass.: Harvard University Press, 1992), 336.

14. Loutfi, "Imperial Frame," 20–29.

15. On René Vautier see Nicole Brenez, "Forms 1960–2004: 'For It Is the Critical Faculty That Invents Fresh Forms' (Oscar Wilde)," in *The French Cinema Book,* ed. Michael Temple and Michael Witt (London: British Film Institute, 2004), 231–33.

16. Philip Dine, *Images of the Algerian War: French Fiction and Film, 1954–1990* (New York: Oxford University Press, 1994), 218–19. See also Leslie Hill, "Filming Ghosts: French Cinema and the Algerian War," *Modern Fiction Studies* 38, no. 3 (1992): 787–804.

17. A postwar leftist French film culture was slow to emerge compared to an equivalent literary and print culture, which in the pages of newspapers, magazines, and journals like *Combat, Esprit, France-Observateur,* and *Les Temps Modernes* argued consistently throughout the 1950s for the end of French imperialism. Of the original 121 signers of the "Declaration of the Right of Draft Evasion in the Algerian War" (initiated by Dionys Mascolo, Marguerite Duras, and Maurice Blanchot, circulated

illegally throughout the summer and fall of 1960, and more commonly known as the "Manifesto of the 121"), only a very few film personnel are in evidence: Alain Cuny, Danièle Delorme, Alain Resnais, Claude Sautet, Simone Signoret. For more on French anticolonial intellectual culture see Paul Clay Sorum, *Intellectuals and Decolonization in France* (Chapel Hill: University of North Carolina Press, 1977) and Ian H. Birchall, "Imperialism and Class: The French War in Algeria," in *Europe and Its Others,* vol. 2, ed. Francis Barker, Peter Hulme, Margaret Iverson, and Diana Loxley (Colchester, UK: University of Essex, 1985), 162–74. For a detailed assessment of government control of information and tallies of the staggering number of press seizures during the Algerian war, see Martin Harrison, "Government and Press in France during the Algerian War," *The American Political Science Review* 58, no. 2 (1964): 273–85.

18. Michel Marie makes a case for Jacques Rivette's *Paris nous appartient (Paris Belongs to Us,* 1961) as well. See Marie, *The French New Wave: An Artistic School,* trans. Richard Neupert (London: Blackwell Publishing, 2003), 83–84.

19. Unnamed critic quoted in Loutfi, "Imperial Frame," 26. On the banning of the film, see Richard Neupert, *A History of the French New Wave Cinema* (Madison: University of Wisconsin Press, 2002), 221.

20. "Interview with Jean-Luc Godard," in *Godard on Godard,* ed. and trans. Tom Milne (New York: Da Capo Press, 1972), 178.

21. "Interview with Jean-Luc Godard," in *Le Petit Soldat: A Film by Jean-Luc Godard* (New York: Simon and Schuster, 1967), 11.

22. Dine, *Images of the Algerian War,* 223–24.

23. Gilles Deleuze, *Cinema 2: The Time-Image,* trans. Hugh Tomlinson and Roberta Galeta (Minneapolis: University of Minnesota Press, 1989), 118.

24. Naomi Greene places *Muriel* in the context of other Resnais films—*Hiroshima mon amour, Stavisky* (1974), and *Providence* (1976)—to examine the director's concerns with memory, mourning, and trauma, individual and collective. See Greene, "Alain Resnais: The Ghosts of History," in *Landscapes of Loss: The National Past in Postwar French Cinema* (Princeton, N.J.: Princeton University Press, 1999), 31–63.

25. Dine, *Images of the Algerian War,* 228.

26. See Joan Mellen, *Filmguide to the Battle of Algiers* (Bloomington: Indiana University Press, 1975); Robert Stam, *The Battle of Algiers: Three Women, Three Bombs* (New York: Macmillan Films Study Extract, 1975); Murray Smith, "*The Battle of Algiers:* Colonial Struggle and Collective Allegiance," *Iris* 24 (autumn 1997): 105–22.

27. Ella Shohat and Robert Stam, *Unthinking Eurocentrism: Multiculturalism and the Media* (New York: Routledge, 1994), 254.

28. Ibid., 220, 221.

29. Ibid., 245 n. 2. The other European art films cited in *Unthinking Eurocentrism* are *8½* (175 n. 74), *Orfeu negro* (187, 305), *Les Carabiniers* (266), and *The Battle of Algiers.*

30. For a comparative analysis of filmgoing and film culture in France and Italy in this period, see Pierre Sorlin, "Tradition and Social Change in the French and Italian Cinemas of the Reconstruction," in *The Culture of Reconstruction: European Literature, Thought, and Film, 1945–1952,* ed. Nicholas Hewitt (New York: St. Martin's Press, 1989), 88–102.

31. See Paul Ginsborg, *A History of Contemporary Italy: Society and Politics, 1943–1988* (London: Penguin, 1990), 214. The quotation is from Ginsborg's article "Family, Culture and Politics in Contemporary Italy," in *Culture and Conflict in Postwar Italy,* ed. Zygmunt G. Baranski and Robert Lumley (New York: St. Martin's Press, 1990), 33.

32. David Forgacs, *Italian Culture in the Industrial Era, 1880–1980: Cultural Industries, Politics, and the Public* (Manchester, UK: Manchester University Press, 1990), 104.

33. Ibid., 105.

34. Geoffrey Nowell-Smith, with James Hay and Gianni Volpi, *The Companion to Italian Cinema* (London: Cassell/British Film Institute, 1996), 161.

35. Larkin, *France since the Popular Front,* 117–18, 186; Michael Kelly, Tony Jones, and Jill Forbes, "Modernization and Avant-Gardes (1945–1967)," in *French Cultural Studies: An Introduction,* ed. Jill Forbes and Michael Kelly (Oxford, UK: Oxford University Press, 1995), 143.

36. Angelo Restivo notes that, in Italy between 1950 and 1970, "car ownership jumped from eight cars per thousand Italians to two-hundred cars per thousand" (Restivo, *The Cinema of Economic Miracles: Visuality and Modernization in the Italian Art Film* [Durham, N.C., and London: Duke University Press, 2002], 45). For an extended discussion of car culture in France in the 1950s and 1960s, see Kristin Ross, *Fast Cars, Clean Bodies: Decolonization and the Reordering of French Culture* (Cambridge, Mass.: MIT Press, 1995), 15–54.

37. See Richard F. Kuisel, *Seducing the French: The Dilemma of Americanization* (Berkeley: University of California Press, 1993), 104–5.

38. The international trade fair of domestic goods that provides the locale for the first half of Jacques Tati's *Playtime* (1967) is a parody of the Salon des Arts Ménagers.

39. David Forgacs, "Culture and Consumption, 1940s to 1990s," in *Italian Cultural Studies: An Introduction,* ed. David Forgacs and Robert Lumley (Oxford, UK: Oxford University Press, 1996), 275.

40. Ginsborg, "Family, Culture, and Politics in Contemporary Italy," 34.

41. Ross, *Fast Cars, Clean Bodies,* 11.

42. Hayward, *French National Cinema,* 166. For an analysis of Gabin as star text, see Ginette Vincendeau, "Jean Gabin: From Working-class Hero to Godfather," in *Stars and Stardom in French Cinema* (London and New York: Continuum, 2000), 59–81.

43. On the Tradition of Quality see Armes, *French Cinema,* 146–68; Williams, *Republic of Images,* 277–98; Colin Crisp, *The Classic French Cinema, 1930–1960* (Bloomington: Indiana University Press, 1993); Rémi Fournier Lanzoni, *French Cinema: From Its Beginnings to the Present* (New York: Continuum, 2002), 157–67.

44. Noël Burch and Geneviève Sellier identify the dominant female figure in French cinema of the period, accounting for one-quarter of the films released between 1945 and 1955, as "a *sale garce* or 'evil bitch', who uses her powers of seduction to exploit, enslave and/or destroy men. Opposite her is a helpless victim—a young man old enough to have been mobilized in 1939, . . . 1950 marked the turning point, with the huge success of *Caroline chérie* (Richard Poitier) making Martine

Carol *the* female star of the French screen" (Burch and Sellier, "Evil Women in the Post-war French Cinema," in *Heroines without Heroes: Reconstructing Female Identities in European Cinema, 1945–51,* ed. Ulrike Sieglohr [London and New York: Cassell, 2000], 47–48). See also Burch and Sellier's *La Drôle de geurre des sexes du cinema français, 1930–1956* (Paris: Nathan, 1996).

45. See Sarah Leahy and Susan Hayward, "The Tainted Woman: Simone Signoret, Site of Pathology or Agent of Retribution?" in Sieglohr, *Heroines without Heroes,* 77–88; and Hayward, "Setting the Agenders: Simone Signoret—The Pre-Feminist Star Body," in *Gender and French Cinema,* ed. Alex Hughes and James S. Williams (Oxford, UK: Berg, 2001), 107–23.

46. Forgacs, "Culture and Consumption, 1940s to 1990s," 278.

47. See Luisa Cicognetti and Lorenza Servetti, "'On Her Side': Female Images in Italian Cinema and the Popular Press, 1945–1955," *Historical Journal of Film, Radio and Television* 16, no. 4 (1996): 555–63.

48. Giuliana Bruno, *Streetwalking on a Ruined Map: Cultural Theory and the City Films of Elvira Notari* (Princeton, N.J.: Princeton University Press, 1993), 51.

49. Pierre Sorlin, *Italian National Cinema, 1896–1996* (London: Routledge, 1996), 109. See also Cicognetti and Servetti, "'On Her Side,'" 557, 562–63.

50. For an examination of Magnani's roles and image, see Tony Mitchell, "The Construction and Reception of Anna Magnani in Italy and the English-Speaking World, 1945–1988," *Film Criticism* 24, no. 1 (1989): 2–21. See also Marcia Landy, *Italian Film* (Cambridge, UK: Cambridge University Press, 2000), 279–83.

51. Michael Silverman has noted that not simply Mangano's tight and spartan attire but also the manner in which her action is choreographed and photographed in *Bitter Rice* reveals the influence of American capital investment in the Italian film industry and of American culture on the nation's screens: 1948 was the peak for American imports in Italy, with Hollywood product accounting for three-quarters of all new films shown publicly. Implicit in Silverman's analysis of America capital incursion are several binarisms—America/Italy, sensationalism/neorealism, wealth/poverty, exploiter/exploited—the locus for and registration of which is the body of Sylvana Mangano. Michael Silverman, "Italian Film and American Capital, 1947–1951," in *Cinema Histories, Cinema Practices,* ed. Patricia Mellencamp and Philip Rosen (Los Angeles: University Publications of America, 1984), 35–46. See also Landy, *Italian Film,* 283–84.

52. From Morando Morandini's entry on Sylvana Pampanini in Nowell-Smith, *The Companion to Italian Cinema,* 91–92.

53. Mira Liehm, *Passion and Defiance: Film in Italy from 1942 to the Present* (Berkeley: University of California Press, 1984), 142.

54. For an overview of postwar Italian female stars, particularly for a history of the "buxom school," see Stefano Masi and Enrico Lancia, *Italian Movie Goddesses: Over 80 of the Greatest Women in Italian Cinema* (Rome: Gremese, 1972).

55. Millicent Marcus, from the entry on Gina Lollobrigida in Nowell-Smith, *The Companion to Italian Cinema,* 72. Mary P. Wood makes a similar case: "Lollobrigida and Loren represented an innocent sensuality, free from any suggestion of vice or

transgression, and their performances emphasized both their physical attributes (plump breasts, stomachs and hips) and their 'southernness'. These stars epitomize physically the class which has left poverty behind, and as long as it knows its place it can enjoy the fat of the land" (Wood, "Woman of Rome: Anna Magnani," in Sieglohr, *Heroines without Heroes,* 157). See also Réka Buckley, "National Body: Gina Lollo-brigida and the Cult of the Star in the 1950s," *Historical Journal of Film, Radio, and Tele-vision* 20, no. 4 (October 2000): 527–47.

56. In *Bitter Rice* the character played by Mangano is conferred the title Miss Rice Worker.

57. Giovanna Grignaffini, "Female Identity and Italian Cinema of the 1950s," in *Off Screen: Women and Film in Italy,* ed. Giuliana Bruno and Maria Nadotti (London: Routledge, 1988), 121; emphases in original.

58. Ibid., 123.

59. Many of the established actresses of the Tradition of Quality made a name for themselves through nude scenes—Martine Carol most obviously, but even the grande dame of classical French cinema, Edwige Feuillère, made the transition from a cele-brated stage career to screen icon by generating a frisson with her bath scene in Abel Gance's *Lucrèce Borgia* (1935), the 1953 remake of which displayed Carol *au bain* as well.

60. Ginette Vincendeau, "The Old and the New: Brigitte Bardot in 1950s France," *Paragraph* 15, no. 1 (1992): 77–79, 81. A version of the article appears as a chapter in Vincendeau's *Stars and Stardom in French Cinema,* 82–109.

61. See Alastair Phillips, "La séductrice française No. 1: Le cas de 'Martine Chérie,'" *Iris,* no. 26 (autumn 1998).

62. As quoted in Georges Sadoul, *Dictionary of Films,* trans. and ed. Peter Morris (Berkeley: University of California Press, 1972), 196; ellipses in original.

63. As quoted in Vincendeau, "The Old and the New," 76; ellipses in original.

64. See Truffaut's "B. B. Is the Victim of a Plot," in Wheeler Winston Dixon, *The Early Film Criticism of François Truffaut* (Bloomington: Indiana University Press, 1993), 71–75, and Jean-Luc Godard's review of *Sait-on-jamais?* in Milne, *Godard on Godard,* 55–57.

65. Edgar Morin, *The Stars,* trans. Richard Howard (New York: Grove Press, 1960), 30–31.

66. Simone de Beauvoir, *Brigitte Bardot and the Lolita Syndrome,* trans. Bernard Fretchman (London: André Deutsch / Weidenfeld and Nicolson, 1960), 30.

67. Vincendeau, "The Old and the New," 86.

68. Ibid., 89.

69. Larkin, *France since the Popular Front,* 55, 58, 254.

70. Kelly, Jones, and Forbes, "Modernization and Avant-Gardes," 150.

71. Such dynamics extend back at least twenty years in French cinema; see Ginette Vincendeau, "Daddy's Girl: Oedipal Narratives in 1930s French Films of the 1930s," *Iris* 8 (January 1989): 70–81.

72. Vincendeau, "The Old and the New," 90. The linkage of Bardot with "the primitive" is also made by Jean-Luc Godard in a one-paragraph article titled "B. B.

of the Rhine" and published in *Arts* in December 1958; see Milne, *Godard on Godard*, 101.

73. I am implicitly arguing here against Sarah Leahy's reading of Bardot as a corrective to anxieties provoked by decolonization and colonial war: "Just like the saluting black soldier on the cover of *Paris-Match* described by Barthes, . . . Bardot came to embody a certain unproblematic image of France at this time of decolonization. . . . Bardot's image in the 1950s . . . unites youth, beauty, prosperity, femininity, fashion and sex appeal; she promotes the idea of a France not in the process of losing her colonies in a very bloody way, but of a country embarking on a sustained period of economic growth and modernization" (Leahy, "The Matter of Myth: Brigitte Bardot, Stardom and Sex," *Studies in French Cinema* 3, no. 2 [2003]: 75). Leahy does, however, present the possibility for Bardot to be considered as a figure of recolonization; see page 77.

74. Baudelaire was a persistent proponent of the notion of the modern self and the modern environment in the nineteenth century. His statements on the matter are collected in his 1863 book *The Painter of Modern Life*, trans. and ed. Jonathan Mayne (Oxford, UK: Phaidon Press, 1964). Baudelaire's collection of poems *Les Fleurs du mal* (Boston: Godine, 1983) is the benchmark for many of Benjamin's writings, including his Arcades Project, later published in two volumes as *Das Passagen-Werk*, ed. Rolf Tiedenmann (Frankfurt am Main: Suhrkamp Verlag, 1982) and in one volume as *The Arcades Project*, trans. Howard Eiland and Kevin McLaughlin (Cambridge, Mass.: Belknap Press / Harvard University Press, 1999). Susan Buck-Morss has published an authoritative study of this aspect of Benjamin's work in her book *The Dialectics of Seeing: Walter Benjamin and the Arcades Project* (Cambridge, Mass.: MIT Press, 1989). Georg Simmel discusses the flâneur in two pieces on the social psychology of city life, "The Stranger" and "The Metropolis and Mental Life," both in *The Sociology of Georg Simmel*, ed. and trans. Kurt Wolff (Glencoe, Ill.: Free Press, 1950). Siegfried Kracauer wrote some formative pieces on cinema, mass culture, and modernity for the daily newspaper *Die Frankfurter Zeitung* between 1921 and 1930. Several of these pieces were edited by Kracauer himself in 1963 under the title *Das Ornament der Masse*, translated and edited by Thomas Y. Levin as *The Mass Ornament: Weimar Essays* (Cambridge, Mass.: Harvard University Press, 1995). For more on the writings of these German theorists of modernity, see David Frisby's *Fragments of Modernity: Theories of Modernity in the Work of Simmel, Kracauer, and Benjamin* (Cambridge, UK: Polity Press, 1985).

75. See Anke Gleber, *The Art of Taking a Walk: Flanerie, Literature, and Film in Weimar Culture* (Princeton, N.J.: Princeton University Press, 1998), 25–26, 39, 49–50. The title of Gleber's work is a phrase from Franz Hessel's own writings on flanerie, the most important of which are *Ermunterung zum Genuß: Kleine Prosa*, ed. Karin Grund and Bernd Witte (Berlin: Brinkman and Bose, 1981), and *Ein Flaneur in Berlin* (1929), rpt. as *Spazieren in Berlin* (Berlin: Das Arsenal, 1984).

76. For Benjamin, the petit bourgeoisie "had to enjoy this identification with all the pleasure and uneasiness which derived from a presentiment of its own destiny as a class. Finally, it had to approach this destiny with a sensitivity that perceives charm

even in damaged and decaying goods" (Benjamin, "The *Flâneur,*" in *Charles Baude-laire: A Lyric Poet in the Era of High Capitalism* [London: New Left Books, 1973], 59).

77. As quoted in Gleber, *The Art of Taking a Walk,* 46.

78. Janet Wolff, "The Invisible *Flâneuse:* Women and the Literature of Modernity," in *Feminine Sentences: Essays on Women and Culture* (Cambridge, UK: Polity Press, 1990), 47. The contemporary works on modernity in Wolff's discussion are Marshall Berman's *All That Is Solid Melts into Air: The Experience of Modernity* (London: Verso, 1983) and Richard Sennett's *The Fall of Public Man* (Cambridge, UK: Cambridge University Press, 1974).

79. Buck-Morss, "The Flaneur, the Sandwichman, and the Whore: The Politics of Loitering," *New German Critique* 39 (1986): 120.

80. Aristide Boucicaut's Au bon marché opened in Paris in 1852, Macy's in New York in 1857. The *grand magasin* was immortalized in Emile Zola's 1883 novel *Au bonheur des dames (The Ladies' Paradise)* and sixty years later in André Cayatte's film of the same name, as well as in Mario Camerini's *Grandi magazzini (Department Stores,* 1938).

81. Anne Friedberg, *"Les Flâneurs du Mal(l):* Cinema and the Postmodern Condition," *PMLA* 106, no. 3 (1991): 421.

82. See Friedberg's *"Les Flâneurs du Mal(l)"* and her book *Window Shopping: Cinema and the Postmodern* (Berkeley: University of California Press, 1993); Elizabeth Wilson, *The Sphinx in the City: Urban Life, the Control of Disorder, and Women* (Berkeley: University of California Press, 1991), 58–60; Erika D. Rappaport, "'A New Era of Shopping': The Promotion of Women's Pleasure in London's West End, 1909–1914," in *Cinema and the Invention of Modern Life,* ed. Leo Charney and Vanessa R. Schwartz (Berkeley: University of California Press, 1995), 130–55; Miriam Hansen, *Babel in Babylon: Spectatorship in American Silent Film* (Cambridge, Mass.: Harvard University Press, 1991), and "Early Cinema, Late Cinema: Transformations of the Public Sphere," in *Viewing Positions: Ways of Seeing Film,* ed. Linda Williams (New Brunswick, N.J.: Rutgers University Press, 1994), 134–52; Giuliana Bruno, *Streetwalking on a Ruined Map.* Bruno has extended her conception of film as "modern cartography" across some European art films in *Atlas of Emotion: Journeys in Art, Architecture, and Film* (New York: Verso, 2002); see especially 31–33, 36–39, 96–99.

83. Anke Gleber, "Women on the Screens and Streets of Modernity: In Search of the Female Flâneur," in *The Image in Dispute: Art and Cinema in the Age of Photography,* ed. Dudley Andrew (Austin: University of Texas Press, 1997), 55–85. See also Catherine Russell, "Parallax Historiography: The Flâneuse as Cyberfeminist," *Scope: an online journal of film studies* (July 2000), http://www.nottingham.ac.uk/film/journal/articles/parallax-historiography.htm.

84. Gleber, *The Art of Taking a Walk,* 31. See also Siegfried Kracauer, "The Little Shopgirls Go to the Movies," "Film 1928," and "Cult of Distraction," in *The Mass Ornament,* 291–328.

85. Moya Luckett has published an article on female flanerie in "swinging London" films of the mid-1960s; see Luckett, "Travel and Mobility: Femininity and National Identity in Swinging London Films," in *British Cinema, Past and Present,* eds. Justine Ashby and Andrew Higson (London: Routledge, 2000), 233–45.

86. Sandy Flitterman-Lewis, *To Desire Differently: Feminism and French Cinema* (Champaign/Urbana: University of Illinois Press, 1990), 218, 264. See also Janice Mouton, "From Feminine Masquerade to Flâneuse: Agnés Varda's Cléo in the City," *Cinema Journal* 40, no. 2 (winter 2001): 3–16.

87. Flitterman-Lewis, *To Desire Differently,* 268. Jill Forbes subsequently challenged Flitterman-Lewis's reading by drawing on details and features of the film that are at times similar to my own; see Forbes, "Gender and Space in *Cléo de 5 à 7,*" *Studies in French Cinema* 2, no. 2 (2002): 83–89.

88. The radio news is at the top of the program and is translated in the subtitles as follows: "Today brought more rioting in Algeria. The latest casualty figures: twenty dead and sixty wounded. In Paris before a military tribunal, Commander Robin, a rebel in the Algerian uprising, was sentenced to six years in prison."

89. For some comparisons of the Algerian references in *Cléo de 5 à 7, Chronique d'un été,* and *Le Joli mai,* see Naomi Greene, "Representations 1960–2004: Parisian Images and National Transformations," in Temple and Witt, *The French Cinema Book,* 249.

90. Flitterman-Lewis, *To Desire Differently,* 274.

91. In episode X, Cléo and her friend, Dorothée, stop by the projection booth of a movie theater to visit briefly Dorothée's lover, Raoul. He invites the two to watch from the booth a comic short he has just threaded up to run. The film is an homage to silent comedy and the Lumière *actualité Arroseur et arrosé* (1896) and stars Jean-Luc Godard and Anna Karina as a happy young couple parting on a bridge over the Seine. Godard, donning his trademark tortoise-shell sunglasses, gets turned around and witnesses an Anna in blackface and a black dress descend the stairs to the riverbank, trip on a man's watering hose, receive an accidental blast from the hoser, and, presumably dead, get taken away by a man in funeral clothes and his hearse. A dejected Godard removes his glasses to wipe his tears, then sees in the other direction the real, white Anna in a similar situation on the other bank but with not nearly as dire consequences. Two intertitles—"Ah! je voyais tout en noir à cause de mes lunettes!" and "Maudite lunettes noires!"—reinforce the degree to which the film is a wry joke about the famously glum Godard, surely, but it is also clearly meant to apply to Cléo's situation and as an encouragement to look without hiding behind her own dark shades. Here as elsewhere, the Godard/Karina intertext is based on a conception of woman as duplicitous and is manifested in a racialized moment of female masquerade.

92. Flitterman-Lewis reads the ring as "an excellent emblematic formulation of the association of vision and motivation underlying the feminist problematic in Varda's film. Early on, Cleo's lover José had referred to her . . . as 'my pearl': Cleo objectified in traditional definitions of feminine beauty. Then once her sudden awareness of life is triggered by the song, Cleo observes a street performer swallowing frogs: Cleo 'sees' reality. But it is ultimately Antoine who condenses these two meanings in his interpretation of the ring's significance. . . . He thus makes of this ring a symbol of their rapport, giving the ring a new meaning that combines Cleo's former identity as beautiful object with her new vision of the social world" (Flitterman-Lewis, *To Desire Differently,* 283).

93. Jean-Pierre Jeancolas, *Le Cinéma des Français: La Ve République (1958–1978)* (Paris: Stock, 1979), 137, as referenced by David Nicholls in "Louis Malle's *Ascenseur pour l'échafaud* and the Presence of the Colonial Wars in French Cinema," *French Cultural Studies* 7, part 3, no. 21 (October 1996): 272.

94. Like Ross, Lynn Higgins examines these relations in her book *New Novel, New Wave, New Politics: Fiction and the Representation of History in Postwar France* (Lincoln: University of Nebraska Press, 1996). Higgins considers the nouveau roman and the nouvelle vague, like history and aesthetics, as enfolded movements, and provides a remarkable reading of Robbe-Grillet's and Resnais's *L'Année dernière à Marienbad* (*Last Year at Marienbad,* 1961) as a colonial allegory; see pages 104–8.

95. Ross, *Fast Cars, Clean Bodies,* 77.

96. Ibid., 7.

97. Ibid., 123, 124.

98. Roberto Rossellini and Ingmar Bergman were accorded by *Cahiers du cinéma* the distinction of being the creators of the protomodern woman in their films of the 1950s starring Ingrid Bergman and Harriet Andersson, particularly *Viaggio in Italia* (*Voyage in Italy,* 1953) and *Sommaren med Monika* (*Summer with Monika,* 1953). Rossellini had been a favored director of the journal from its inception, largely via the neorealist championing of one of its cofounders, André Bazin. Throughout the 1950s, Rossellini was frequently interviewed and extolled in the pages of *Cahiers.* Ingmar Bergman was the subject of a Cinémathèque Française retrospective in 1958, after which followed the release in France of almost all of his films. In 1958–59, there were few issues of *Cahiers* that did not contain at least one piece on Bergman; he was a particularly hot director for French cinéphiles. See especially Godard's "Bergman-orama" and his review of *Summer with Monika,* both in Milne, *Godard on Godard,* 75–80, 84–85, which are notable for their reassessment of Vadim's modernity through the revelation of Bergman's films of the early 1950s.

99. Upon the release of *Breathless,* Godard's *Cahiers* colleague Luc Moullet was already defending him from the charge of misogyny by pointing out that the "misogyny is external, confined to the subject matter" of the film and not to the man himself, and similar accusations and defenses of varying degrees of sophistication have characterized the critical writings on the director's sexual politics to the present (Luc Moullet, "Jean-Luc Godard," in *Cahiers du Cinéma, 1960–1968: New Wave, New Cinema, Reevaluating Hollywood,* ed. Jim Hillier [Cambridge, Mass.: Harvard University Press, 1986], 42). The most notable feminist writers who have been critical of Godard's representation of women are Molly Haskell, *From Reverence to Rape: The Treatment of Women in the Movies* (New York: Penguin, 1973), 299–302, and Yosefa Loshitzky, whose chapter "From Metapornography to Meta-heresy: Godard's Images of Sexuality" in *The Radical Faces of Godard and Bertolucci* (Detroit: Wayne State University Press, 1994), 135–73, is devoted to the breadth of Godard's career. Haskell's and Loshitzky's critiques bookend a burst of affirmative psychoanalytic feminist attention to the filmmaker's representations of sexuality. See especially Laura Mulvey's and Colin MacCabe's cowritten piece "Images of Women, Images of Sexuality" in *Godard: Images, Sounds, Politics,* ed. MacCabe et al. (London: British Film Institute,

1980), 79–101; most of the articles in the special triple issue of *Camera Obscura* 8-9-10 (fall 1982) devoted to Godard; and the catalog of the fall 1992 retrospective of the Miéville years, *Jean-Luc Godard: Son + Image, 1974–1991*, ed. Raymond Bellour and Mary Lea Bandy (New York: Museum of Modern Art / Harry N. Abrams, 1992), which includes an important new essay by Laura Mulvey, "The Hole and the Zero: The Janus Face of the Feminine in Godard," 75–88.

100. Through the mid-1960s, lead actresses in Godard's films who were not Karina nonetheless often resemble her in looks and disposition: Marina Mase in *Les Carabiniers* (1963); Brigitte Bardot when in a black bob wig in *Le Mépris;* Macha Méril in *Une femme mariée* (1964); Chantal Goya in *Masculin féminin* (1966).

101. As I argue in chapter 4, the privileging of the feature over the short in auteurist-led criticism is ubiquitous. It therefore comes as no surprise that Karina's final role in a Godard film—as a prostitute in *L'An 2000 (Anticipation)*, the concluding episode of the omnibus film *The Oldest Profession*—is frequently ignored in discussions of Godard's Karina years and that the director's filmic concern with prostitution in the 1960s is regarded as a trilogy and not a tetralogy.

102. Godard's updating of this heroine of a famous nineteenth-century French novel finds an instructive echo in the figure of Camille, after Alexandre Dumas's *La Dame aux camélias*, as portrayed by Brigitte Bardot in *Le Mépris*. Though her performance and characterization are more dignified, Bardot/Camille's end is effectively the same as Karina/Nana's in both versions; as such, they point to a certain faithfulness in Godard's refigurations of nineteenth-century female characters with respect to their originals—Zola's naturalism, Dumas's romanticism—that calls into question the degree to which they are updates at all.

103. Richard Neupert notes that Roger Vadim too stated in interviews around *And God Created Woman* "that he was a sort of ethnographer, documenting a new sort of woman" (Neupert, *A History of the French New Wave Cinema*, 80).

104. Kaja Silverman and Harun Farocki, *Speaking about Godard* (New York: New York University Press, 1998), 2, 13.

105. The separation of Karina and Nana here is reinforced by their differing connections to the film she watches and cries at as Nana, and stars and cries in as Karina: like Dreyer of *La Passion de Jeanne d'Arc*, Karina is a Dane making films in France; like the actress Maria Falconetti after *Jeanne d'Arc*, Nana will become a prostitute. See Siew Hwa Beh, "*Vivre Sa Vie*," *Women and Film*, no. 1 [1972], rpt. in *Movies and Methods: An Anthology*, ed. Bill Nichols (Berkeley: University of California Press, 1976), 181.

106. Silverman, in conversation with Farocki, *Speaking about Godard*, 28.

107. Susan Sontag, "Godard's *Vivre Sa Vie*," *Against Interpretation and Other Essays* (New York: Dell, 1966), 209.

108. Haskell, *From Reverence to Rape*, 299–300. Interestingly, Haskell organizes her chapter on European women/actresses, "The Europeans," by directors.

109. Brigitte Bardot and Catherine Deneuve are much more stable (though differing) national embodiments, each having served as models for the plaster bust of Marianne, the symbol of the French Republic that graces every city and town hall in

France. See Ginette Vincendeau, "Catherine Deneuve and French Womanhood," *Sight and Sound* 3, no. 4 (April 1993), rpt. in *Women and Film: A Sight and Sound Reader*, ed. Pam Cook and Philip Dodd (Philadelphia, Pa.: Temple University Press, 1993), 41–49.

110. Seberg appears briefly in *Pierrot le fou* late in the film. Ferdinand has become separated from Marianne, who has just telephoned him to help her deal with some agents/gangsters threatening her in an apartment; when he arrives on the scene she has fled after dispatching one of her captors, leaving Ferdinand to face bathtub torture, Algerian war–style. He tells his interrogators what they want to know and starts searching for Marianne, ending up in a run-down movie theater screening newsreels of American atrocities in Vietnam. He pays little attention to the screen until he hears Seberg's voice and watches snippets of her pointing and shooting a movie camera in *Le Grand escroc*, an episode Godard had shot for the omnibus film *Les Plus belles escroqueries du monde* (*The Beautiful Swindlers*, 1964) and the only other film he made starring Seberg. By the time of *Pierrot le fou*, then, Seberg had become a thoroughly compromised representation of America in Godard's cinema: her presence on the screen reminds Belmondo and the viewer of more innocent times at the same time as she stands in for both Marianne and Vietnam atrocity footage. Guy Austin has examined Seberg's ambivalent status as a white Nordic American in relation to her domestic activism for black causes (as well as the de/racination of the 1980s star Isabelle Adjani's mixed ethnic identity—her father was Algerian) in "Foreign bodies: Jean Seberg and Isabelle Adjani," in *Stars in Modern French Film* (London: Arnold, 2003), 92–106.

111. The phrase is from Mulvey and MacCabe, "Images of Women, Images of Sexuality," 95.

112. Stephen Snyder offers a full set of oppositions for the two characters in *The Transparent I: Self/Subject in European Cinema* (New York: Peter Lang, 1994), 85–86.

113. Nicholls, "Louis Malle's *Ascenseur pour l'échafaud*," 273.

114. For an intertextual reading of the film's complex mapping of female sexuality and space, see T. Jefferson Kline, "Remapping Tenderness: Louis Malle's *The Lovers with No Tomorrow*," in *Screening the Text: Intertextuality in New Wave Cinema* (Baltimore, Md.: Johns Hopkins University Press, 1992), 24–53. See also Guy Austin, "Red Woman/White Woman: Jeanne Moreau and Catherine Deneuve," in *Stars in Modern French Film*, 36–39.

115. See Vincendeau, *Stars and Stardom in French Cinema*, 122–28.

116. A fine description of Lidia's flanerie in this sequence can be found in Sitney, *Vital Crises in Italian Cinema*, 150.

117. Guido Aristarco, "Literary Cinema," in *Michelangelo Antonioni: An Introduction*, ed. Pierre Leprohon, trans. Scott Sullivan (New York: Simon and Schuster, 1963), 160–62. Peter Brunette spends a considerable amount of space in *The Films of Michelangelo Antonioni* (Cambridge, UK: Cambridge University Press, 1998) on the sequence of Lidia's flanerie to counter the many symbolic readings that have been derived from it; see pages 57–62.

118. Lidia's diminished, intermittent presence among the brutalist architecture of modern Milan has led some to read the film as a critique of bourgeois European

alienation resulting from capitalist modernization. Such a reading generalizes the conditions of character in a way that I am resisting in this chapter. See Brunette's *The Films of Michelangelo Antonioni* for an attempt to get beyond the "alienation" thesis so as to analyze the films' more specific sociopolitical and feminist critiques of Italian society at the height of the economic boom.

119. Ian Cameron and Robin Wood's description of the nightclub scene as "another piece of modern grotesqueness" that adds to the film's theme of decadent, repressed eroticism is a representative critical response; Cameron and Wood, *Antonioni,* rev. ed. (New York: Praeger, 1971), 82.

120. Pascal Bonitzer has suggested that "*La notte* is not only a film in black and white, but a film *about* black and white, a giant chessboard on which the characters move by themselves or are moved by chance, to which they have offered up a desire gone dead" (Bonitzer, "The Disappearance [on Antonioni]," in *L'avventura,* ed. Seymour Chatman and Guido Fink [New Brunswick, N.J.: Rutgers University Press, 1989], 215). The chessboard-as-floor makes an appearance in *La notte*—in the shuffle-board/compact game Valentina invents with Giovanni, which soon becomes a hit with the other guests at the Gherardinis' party—as it did in the mambo scene of *And God Created Woman;* I would press for a reading of its presence beyond the symbolic/architectural.

121. See, for example, Dominique Fernandez, "Antonioni, poète du matriarcat," *La Nouvelle revue française,* 1 November 1960, rpt. as "The Poet of Matriarchy" in Leprohon, *Michelangelo Antonioni,* 158–60; Andrew Sarris, "Veni, Vidi, Vitti," *Cavalier* (February 1963), rpt. in *Confessions of a Cultist: On the Cinema, 1955/1969* (New York: Simon and Schuster, 1971), 69–73.

122. Seymour Chatman, *Antonioni, or The Surface of the World* (Berkeley: University of California Press, 1985), 83.

123. See Clara Orban, "Antonioni's Women: Lost in the City," *Modern Language Studies* 31, no. 2 (fall 2001): 11–28.

124. See Frank P. Tomasulo, "The Architectonics of Alienation: Antonioni's Edifice Complex," *Wide Angle* (July 1993): 10; Sitney, *Vital Crises in Italian Cinema,* 160.

125. Commentators on *The Eclipse* tend to explain this scene symbolically in terms of Vittoria's mental state and desire for escape. See, for example, Joan Esposito, "Antonioni and Benjamin: Dialectical Imagery in *Eclipse,*" *Film Criticism* 9, no. 1 (fall 1984): 30; Chatman, *Antonioni,* 61; Dalle Vacche, *The Body in the Mirror,* 7; Kevin Z. Moore, "Eclipsing the Commonplace: The Logic of Alienation in Antonioni," *Film Quarterly* 48, no. 4 (1995): 28, 29; Restivo, *The Cinema of Economic Miracles,* 121. For a brief reading of the scene that places it within the context of colonialism, see Brunette, *The Films of Michelangelo Antonioni,* 84–85.

126. Vanessa Maher, "Immigration and Social Identities," in Forgacs and Lumley, *Italian Cultural Studies,* 160. See also Donald Martin Carter, *States of Grace: Senegalese in Italy and the New European Immigration* (Minneapolis: University of Minnesota Press, 1997).

127. Maher, "Immigration and Social Identities," 162. The continuities of these categories extend from the Risorgimento to the present. See Paul M. Sniderman et

al., *The Outsider: Prejudice and Politics in Italy* (Princeton, N.J.: Princeton University Press, 2002), and John Dickie, "Imagined Italies," in Forgacs and Lumley, *Italian Cultural Studies,* 28.

128. For a reading of *Two Women* in the context of Loren's performance and star textuality, see Landy, *Italian Film,* 289–92.

129. In a discussion of Rossellini's *Voyage in Italy,* Giuliana Bruno comments on the exotic character Naples holds for North European travelers in ways that dovetail with the argument I am making here; see Bruno, *Atlas of Emotion,* 369–73.

130. Early in *Rocco and his Brothers,* as the southern Parondi family arrives on a cold, wet morning with their belongings heaped on a hand-drawn cart to occupy a basement council flat in Milan, two women neighbors who spy them have a brief exchange that begins as follows: "Hello, Signora Maria." "Heavens! Did you see that?" "Africa."

131. Esposito, "Antonioni and Benjamin," 32. See also David Forgacs, "Antonioni: Space, Place, Sexuality," in *Spaces in European Cinema,* ed. Myrto Konstantarakos (Exeter, UK: Intellect Books, 2000), 103.

132. Sitney, *Vital Crises in Italian Cinema,* 159. Brunette notes that Antonioni actually worked on the construction of EUR when he would have been in his late twenties (*The Films of Michelangelo Antonioni,* 15, 77). In *L'avventura,* after the Messina episode with which I opened this chapter, Claudia and Sandro stop in the Sicilian ghost town of Caltanisetta (mistaking it for Noto)—another of Mussolini's building projects, this one an experiment in fascist rationalist architecture. See Mitchell Schwarzer, "The Consuming Landscape: Architecture in the Films of Michelangelo Antonioni," in *Architecture and Film,* ed. Mark Lamster (New York: Princeton Architectural Press, 2000), 201; Tomasulo, "The Architectonics of Alienation," 6.

133. Although it is beyond the scope of this book, an examination of the discourses of popular European cinemas during the economic miracle and beyond in relation to modernization and colonialism dovetails in interesting ways with my arguments about gender and art cinema. In a chapter titled "The White Man's Muscles," Richard Dyer offers an analysis of the Italian *peplum* cycle of 1957–65, which starred American bodybuilders in whose "spirit-perfected body" resided the "capacity to sort out the problems of lesser beings, in a context of a damaged identity: Italian working-class masculinity at a moment of rapid industrialisation and in the wake of a period of nationalist, incipiently imperialist and racist politics, fascism, that had promised working-class men so much . . . . The period of the peplum is . . . a period of mass internal migration in Italy, from the rural South to the industrial North, from labour based on strength to one based on skill with machines. . . . The peplum celebrates a type of male body for an audience to whom it had until now been a source of economic self-worth" (*White,* 165, 169). Angela Dalle Vacche too hints at a recolonizing project underpinning male popular Italian cinema: "From the mid-1950s to the mid-1960s, in the 'peplum' film, the body-documents of neorealistic comedic microhistory revert to the body-monuments of operatic macrohistory. . . . In the 1960s the fixed scripts of the peplum and the spectacle of the male body lose their energy. The industry, then, recycles the well-known parameters—body, history, spectacle,

allegory—into the Spaghetti Western" (*The Body in the Mirror,* 52, 56). One can see, then, a two-pronged effort by two very different types of national cinema discourses to recolonize certain sectors of the nation by representing and appealing to working-class masculinity through *pepla* and spaghetti westerns, and to middle-class femininity through modern art cinema. Different trajectories, similar destinations, and sometimes—as in Pasolini's "myth" films of the late 1960s (*Edipo re* [1967], *Appunti di viaggio per un film sull'India* [1968], *Porcile* [1969], *Appunti per un'Orestiade africana* [1970], and *Medea* [1970]), in which primitivist and orientalist regress downward (to the peasantry and subproletariat), backward (to the Middle Ages or preclassical Greece), or outward (to southern Italy, Africa, India, the Arab world) are offered as utopic alternatives to modern, bourgeois capitalist reality—they intersect. While the connections between postwar modernity, decolonization, inter- and intranational migration, nation building, and popular and art cinema are extremely complex, their examination is a necessary part of the kind of remapping of the discipline and its paradigms that I am calling for in this book.

4. Exquisite Corpses

1. A woman's body fragmented as a means of celebrating it as art occurs in the famous second shot of Jean-Luc Godard's *Le Mépris* (1963), in which a naked Brigitte Bardot/Camille verbally reduces herself to body parts and asks her lover, Paul, played by Michel Piccoli, if these different components are as pretty as her eyes. When Paul answers positively to every item of Camille's litany, she asserts, "Then you love me totally." In this and other scenes, *Le Mépris* has been interpreted as implicitly criticizing and subverting the requirements of big-budget commercial filmmaking, in this case the filmic inclusion of Bardot's nude body. But as Harun Farocki notes, "Camille's body connotes 'art' more than 'sexuality'; the camera transforms it into a reclining structure, and the red and blue light in which the first and last parts of this scene are shot locate Camille in a world apart from our own" (Farocki, in conversation with Kaja Silverman, *Speaking about Godard* [New York: New York University Press, 1998], 34).

2. I have relied for this account on a portion of Paul Schimmel's essay "Leap into the Void: Performance and the Object," in *Out of Actions: Between Performance and the Object, 1949–1979,* ed. Russell Ferguson (Los Angeles: Museum of Contemporary Art, Los Angeles, 1998), 31–36.

3. On the mondo film, see Mikita Brottman, "Carnivalising the Taboo: The Mondo Film and the Opened Body," *Cineaction* 38 (1995): 25–37; Amy Staples, "An Interview with Dr. Mondo," *American Anthropologist* 97, no. 1 (March 1995): 110–25; Stuart Swezey, "Gualtiero Jacopetti," in *Amok Journal, Sensurround Edition: A Compendium of Psycho-Physiological Investigations,* ed. Stuart Swezey (Los Angeles: Amok, 1995), 132–39; Charles Kilgore, "Mondo Movies," *Ecco: The World of Bizarre Video,* no. 22 (1997): 28–44; Mark Goodall, "Shockumentary Evidence: The Perverse Politics of the Mondo Film," in *Remapping World Cinema: Identity, Culture, and Politics in Film,* ed. Stephanie Dennison and Song Hwee Lim (London and New York: Wallflower Press, 2006), 118–26.

4. James Clifford, "On Ethnographic Surrealism," in *The Predicament of Culture: Twentieth-Century Ethnography, Literature, and Art* (Cambridge, Mass.: Harvard University Press, 1988), 120.

5. Ibid., 136.

6. Ibid., 140. See also C. W. Thompson, ed., *L'Autre et le sacré: Surréalism, cinéma, ethnographie* (Paris: Éditions L'Harmattan, 1995).

7. Ibid., 147.

8. David Kerekes and David Slater, *Killing for Culture: An Illustrated History of Death Film from Mondo to Snuff* (London: Creation Books, 1994), 110.

9. Michael Scriven et al., "Wars and Class Wars (1914–1944)," in *French Cultural Studies: An Introduction,* ed. Jill Forbes and Michael Kelly (Oxford, UK: Oxford University Press, 1995), 63.

10. See as examples Salvador Dalí, "The Object as Revealed in Surrealist Experiment," in *Theories of Modern Art: A Source Book by Artists and Critics,* ed. Herschel B. Chipp (Berkeley: University of California Press, 1968), 417–27; William S. Rubin, *Dada and Surrealist Art* (New York: Abrams, 1968), 278; Alastair Brotchie and Mel Gooding, *Surrealist Games* (London: Redstone Press, 1991), 143–44.

11. Elza Adamowicz, *Surrealist Collage in Text and Image* (Cambridge, UK: Cambridge University Press, 1998), 55.

12. Ibid., 80, 82.

13. I locate the rise and consolidation of film studies in North America and Britain in the decade 1965–75 because it was during this period that the discipline took the shape it continues to assume today. See my "Little Books," in *Inventing Film Studies: Towards a History of a Discipline,* ed. Lee Grieveson and Haidee Wasson (Durham, N.C.: Duke University Press, 2008), 319–49.

14. Both David Bordwell and Robert B. Ray have assessed, albeit from differing positions, the inertia of Anglo-American film studies resulting from, as Mitsuhiro Yoshimoto describes it, "the hegemonic status of theory-inspired film criticism in the discipline": "From Bordwell's standpoint, poststructuralist film criticism's emergence in the 1970s and its dominance in the 1980s did not introduce anything particularly new to film studies; on the contrary, its proliferation ensured the continuation of routine interpretive practices to such an extent that film criticism has become totally repetitive and uninteresting. . . . According to Ray, the impasse of film studies is created not by poststructuralist theory's inherent flaws but by the discrepancy between the radical potential of theory as practice and the sterile thematization of theory in routine, streamlined interpretation" (Yoshimoto, *Kurosawa: Film Studies and Japanese Cinema* [Durham, N.C.: Duke University Press, 2000], 33, 34).

See David Bordwell, *Making Meaning: Inference and Rhetoric in the Interpretation of Cinema* (Cambridge, Mass.: Harvard University Press, 1989); Robert B. Ray, "Introduction: Reinventing Film Studies," *The Avant-Garde Finds Andy Hardy* (Cambridge, Mass.: Harvard University Press, 1995), 1–23.

15. "Canons and Metonymies: An Interview with Jacques Derrida," in *Logomachia: The Conflict of the Faculties,* ed. Richard Rand (Lincoln: University of Nebraska Press, 1992), 198–99.

16. Robert B. Ray has pressed for the avant-garde arts and the surrealist tradition as alternative models for thinking and writing about films. Although I do not share the same enthusiasms as Ray for surrealism as a teaching tool, I support his challenge to some of the long-standing catechisms of contemporary film studies. See Ray, "Invention Finds a Method: Surrealist Research and Games," in *The Avant-Garde Finds Andy Hardy*, 40–73.

17. Susan Rubin Suleiman, *Subversive Intent: Gender, Politics, and the Avant-Garde* (Cambridge, Mass.: Harvard University Press, 1990), 12. I will note here that while the Surrealists considered themselves resisters to dominant French colonial ideology and supporters of decolonization, their particular investments in colonial *objets* as fetishes points to some of the problems with their particular mode of celebration/exoticization of the Other. For an in-depth critique of Surrealist colonial counter-strategies, see Panivong Norindr, *Phantasmatic Indochina: French Colonial Ideology in Architecture, Film, and Literature* (Durham, N.C.: Duke University Press, 1996), 52–71. And for an interesting chastisement of "a congenitally self-righteous left wing," see Dudley Andrew, "Praying Mantis: Enchantment and Violence in French Cinema of the Exotic," in *Visions of the East: Orientalism in Film*, ed. Matthew Bernstein and Gaylyn Studlar (New Brunswick, N.J.: Rutgers University Press, 1997), 232–52. Additionally, Surrealist visual practice has undergone considerable analysis concerning its imaging of the female body. See Hal Foster, *Compulsive Beauty* (Cambridge, Mass.: MIT Press, 1991); Mary Ann Caws, *The Surrealist Look: An Erotics of Encounter* (Cambridge, Mass.: MIT Press, 1997); Johanna Malt, *Obscure Objects of Desire: Surrealism, Fetishism, and Politics* (Oxford, UK: Oxford University Press, 2004).

18. One Surrealist's particular game obsession, Marcel Duchamp's beloved chess, found filmic expression through the collective efforts of aging members of the Parisian avant-garde in *Acht mal Acht (8 X 8: A Chess Sonata in 8 Movements)*. Directed by Hans Richter, this eight-part episode film was made in Switzerland in 1957 and featured Jean Arp, Duchamp, Man Ray, Jacqueline Matisse, Yves Tanguy, Alexander Calder, Willem de Vogel, Dorothea Tanning, Max Ernst, Jean Cocteau, and Paul Bowles. Seeing this film now, one is struck by its quaint reliance on trick visual effects (reverse motion, pixillation, et cetera), which were explored quite fully in the Surrealist and Dada films of the late 1920s and 1930s. What holds the film together is the shared commitment the artists in it demonstrate to the principles of play and playing with the film medium. It is in that spirit that I would like to situate the work in this chapter.

19. For a discussion of the canon in general and the *Sight and Sound* lists in particular, see Peter Wollen, "The Canon," in *Paris Hollywood: Writings on Film* (London and New York: Verso, 2002), 216–32.

20. David Bordwell, *Narration in the Fiction Film* (Madison: University of Wisconsin Press, 1985), 39.

21. Peter Bondanella, *The Cinema of Federico Fellini* (Princeton, N.J.: Princeton University Press, 1992), 165. See also Bondanella, "*8½*: The Celebration of Artistic Creativity," in *The Films of Federico Fellini* (Cambridge, UK: Cambridge University Press, 2002), 93–115.

22. Christian Metz remarked that the "character of the director, Guido, Fellini's representative in the film, resembles his creator like a twin, with his narcissistic complacency, his immense sincerity, his disorderly existence, . . . his open desire to 'put everything' into the film (just as Fellini puts all of himself into his films, and especially into *8½*, which is like a pause in his career, a general viewing of the past, an aesthetic and effective summing up). . . . The title *8½* designates the film less in terms of its own characteristics than in terms of a sort of retrospective reference to all of Fellini's previous work" (Metz, "Mirror Construction in Fellini's *8½*," in *Film Language: A Semiotics of the Cinema*, trans. Michael Taylor [Chicago: University of Chicago Press, 1974], 229).

23. The names of the other episodes are, in alphabetical order: *L'amore che si paga* (*Paid Love*, d. Carlo Lizzani); *Gli italiani si voltano* (*Italians Turn Around*, d. Alberto Lattuada); *Paradiso per tre ore* (*Paradise Four Hours*, d. Dino Risi); *La storia di Caterina* (*Story of Caterina/The Love of a Mother*, d. Francesco Maselli and Cesare Zavattini); *Tentato suicidio* (*Attempted Suicide*, d. Michelangelo Antonioni).

24. The other episodes are *Il lavoro* (*The Job*, d. Luchino Visconti), *Renzo e Luciana* (d. Mario Monicelli), and *La riffa* (*The Raffle*, d. Vittorio de Sica).

25. According to Peter Bondanella, the Lizzani episode "was censored from the original American version by the Italian government because of its shocking revelation that prostitution existed in Italy!" (*Italian Cinema: From Neorealism to the Present*, 3rd ed. [New York and London: Continuum, 2001], 101). The *Variety* reviewer, upon seeing the six-episode version of *L'amore in città*, described *L'amore che si paga* as "an unsensational inspection of prostitution, which stresses the human side and tragic precedents of the nightwalkers, with camera lensing actual prosties" (*Variety*, 10 March 1954, 6).

26. *Variety*, 16 April 1962, 6. This explanation is not unreasonable, given conventions regarding running times for feature films, particularly a bouncy sex comedy like *Boccaccio '70*. With the addition of Monicelli's episode, *Renzo e Luciana*, the four-part film runs 210 minutes; it included an intermission when it was shown in its entirety at the National Film Theatre in London in August 2004 as part of a Fellini retrospective. As a three-parter, *Boccaccio '70* is still well over two hours long. But the decision to delete Monicelli's film as opposed to one of the others begs the question of the directorial star system. A perusal of the posters, ad slicks, and other publicity materials for *Boccaccio '70* circulated by American distributor Joseph E. Levine reveals the degree to which the abutment of internationally famous Italian director and female star was key to the film's marketing. I address the marketing in the United States of *Boccaccio '70* in "Art, exploitation, underground," in *Defining Cult Movies: The Cultural Politics of Oppositional Taste*, ed. Mark Jancovich et al. (Manchester, UK: Manchester University Press, 2003), 209–11.

27. Kevin Jackson, *The Language of Cinema* (New York: Routledge, 1998), 55.

28. Ibid., 84.

29. Overlapping categories and nonstandardized terminology are consistent across the several dictionaries of film language. See, for example, *The Oxford Companion to Film*, ed. Liz-Ann Bawden (London: Oxford University Press, 1976), 231; Frank

Beaver, *Dictionary of Film Terms: The Aesthetic Companion to Film Analysis,* rev. and exp. ed. (New York: Twayne, 1994), 71; Ira Konigsberg, *The Complete Film Dictionary,* 2nd ed. (New York: Penguin Reference, 1997), 70, 121. For an examination of terminology for omnibus and related films, see my "Film History, Film Genre, and Their Discontents: The Case of the Omnibus Film," *The Moving Image* 1, no. 2 (fall 2001): 56–87.

My reasons for choosing the terms "episode" and "omnibus" over the others have to do with frequency and potential connotative meanings. "Compendium," "novella," and "story" appear relatively infrequently as terms. "Portmanteau" tends to be used by British writers only and "sketch films," or *films à sketches,* by French ones or by those specializing in French or Italian cinema. "Anthology," "collective," and "compilation" are related to but not synonymous with the categories of the episode and the omnibus film. I have chosen the term "episode" to refer to the single-director version because it suggests that the film is composed of discrete parts or episodes but does not imply more than one "creator." That leaves "composite" and "omnibus" as possibilities for the multidirector type. Both are used often and interchangeably, and both denote a structure composed of different parts or elements. But omnibus carries with it other traces of meaning that composite does not—connotations of transport, of travel, of boundary crossing, of permeability—that are for me central to the use to which I put these films in this chapter.

30. Mira Liehm calls them composite films but the references are scattered; see *Passion and Defiance: Film in Italy from 1942 to the Present* (Berkeley: University of California Press, 1984), 62, 98–99, 232, 244–45. In addition, P. Adams Sitney's *Vital Crises in Italian Cinema: Iconography, Stylistics, Politics* (Austin: University of Texas Press, 1995), Angela Dalle Vacche's *The Body in the Mirror: Shapes of History in Italian Cinema* (Princeton, N.J.: Princeton University Press, 1992), and Marcia Landy's *Italian Film* (Cambridge, UK: Cambridge University Press, 2000) contain few to no references.

31. Pierre Leprohon, *The Italian Cinema,* trans. Roger Greaves and Oliver Stallybrass (New York: Praeger, 1972), 179, 180.

32. Ibid., 183. Leprohon's examples of topical/sensationalist problem films include both omnibus and episode films. Eleven directors contributed episodes to *Le italiane e l'amore (Latin Lovers,* 1961), for example, while *I nuovi angeli (The New Angels,* 1962) was directed by Ugo Gregoretti and *Comizi d'amore* (1964) by Pier Paolo Pasolini.

33. Ibid.

34. Bondanella, *Italian Cinema: From Neorealism to the Present,* 159.

35. Ibid., 157.

36. Leprohon begins his section on the omnibus film with the justification that to "ignore it would be to ignore works by some of the best directors" of Italy and France (179). Bondanella endnotes the few works one need concern oneself with: "Pasolini's *Ricotta (La ricotta)* from *Rogopag (Rogopag,* 1962); Visconti's *The Job (Il lavoro)* and Fellini's *The Temptations of Doctor Antonio (Le tentazioni del dottor Antonio),* both from *Boccaccio '70* (1962); and Fellini's *Toby Dammit (Toby Dammit),* from *Tales of Mystery (Histoires Extraordinaires,* 1968)" (471 n. 11).

37. One collection of essays in French deals with the production contexts of omnibus films in France of the 1950s and 1960s: Dominique Bluher and François Thomas, eds., *Le Court Métrage français de 1945 à 1968: De l'âge d'or aux contrebandiers* (Rennes: Presses universitaires de Rennes, 2005).

38. Ella Shohat and Robert Stam, *Unthinking Eurocentrism: Multiculturalism and the Media* (New York: Routledge, 1994), 29. The text the authors are referring to in this quotation is David Bordwell, Janet Staiger, and Kristin Thompson's *The Classical Hollywood Cinema: Film Style and Mode of Production to 1960* (New York: Columbia University Press, 1985).

39. A partial exception in this regard is Nowell-Smith, *The Oxford History of World Cinema,* which, especially in its second and third sections, considers several international cinemas in relation to one another and not simply Hollywood—though Hollywood cinema is not deemed in this text a national cinema as are the others. On the other hand, Louis Giannetti's and Scott Eyman's *Flashback: A Brief History of Film,* 4th ed. (Englewood Cliffs, N.J.: Prentice-Hall, 2001) is notable for its alternation of chapters, decade by decade, between "American Cinema" and "European Cinema" through the 1940s and "International Cinema" since the 1950s.

40. See Paul Willemen, "The National," in *Looks and Frictions: Essays in Cultural Studies and Film Theory* (London/Bloomington and Indianapolis: British Film Institute/ Indiana University Press, 1994), 211.

41. In "Alternative Modes of Film Practice," the final chapter of *The Classical Hollywood Cinema,* David Bordwell and Janet Staiger write that one of the effects of "Hollywood's international dominance" was that "it spurred Europeans to imitation. French Westerns, pseudo-DeMille sex comedies, and *King Kong Made in Japan* (1933) are only the most striking symptoms of a much deeper commitment to the classical mode. It is evident that the 'ordinary film' of France, Germany, and even Japan and Russia constructed causality, time, and space in ways characteristic of the normal Hollywood film. The accessibility of Hollywood cinema to audiences of different cultures made it a transnational standard. This trend has, of course, continued to the present" (379). The matter-of-factness of this passage is predicated on an assumption of Hollywood's colonization of foreign screens in particular and capitalism in general as historical inevitability. The result is the reduction of a concerted economic and political program of international expansion and incursion on the part of the American film industry since World War I to free-market cant: accessibility.

42. Film archivists can attest to the speed with which film prints become damaged by projection, shipment, or chemical deterioration due to improper storage and care. Little can be done once a print is damaged, and most archives focus their attention on adequately conserving what they have and preserving the occasional film deemed historically important for one reason or another. The prognosis for omnibus films on this front is at the moment bleak unless initiatives are made, first and foremost, to distinguish them as a specific film type worthy of scholarly and archival attention. A large proportion of these films were made in an era of notoriously unstable color film stock prone to fading, and as they are not considered to be historically important little is being done to preserve the few already on deposit in archives.

43. Douglas Gomery, "Researching Film History," in *Film History: Theory and Practice,* ed. Robert C. Allen and Douglas Gomery (New York: McGraw-Hill, 1985), 39.

44. For a discussion of the issues of historical sources and documentation in contemporary film studies, particularly as they pertain to revisionist film history, see Barbara Klinger, "Film History Terminable and Interminable: Recovering the Past in Reception Studies," *Screen* 38, no. 2 (summer 1997): 107–28, and *Looking Past the Screen: Case Studies in American Film History and Method,* ed. Jon Lewis and Eric Smoodin (Durham, N.C.: Duke University Press, 2007).

45. I have borrowed the notion of the historical gap from Jan-Christopher Horak, whose work on American avant-garde cinema between the World Wars offers a corrective to a long-held position within film studies, perpetuated most obviously by P. Adams Sitney's seminal book *Visionary Film: The American Avant-Garde* (Oxford, UK: Oxford University Press, 1974), that the American avant-garde tradition begins in 1943 with the first films of Maya Deren. See Horak's "Introduction: History in the Gaps" in *Lovers of the Cinema: The First American Film Avant-Garde 1919–1945,* ed. Horak (Madison: University of Wisconsin Press, 1995), 3–13. For an early example of gap identification, see Jay Leyda's "Waiting Jobs," *Film Quarterly* 16, no. 2 (winter 1962–63): 29–33.

46. Namely Elaine Mancini, *Struggles of the Italian Film Industry during Fascism, 1930–1935* (Ann Arbor, Mich.: UMI Research Press, 1985); James Hay, *Popular Film Culture in Fascist Italy: The Passing of the Rex* (Bloomington: Indiana University Press, 1987); and Marcia Landy, *Fascism in Film: The Italian Commercial Cinema, 1931–1943* (Princeton, N.J.: Princeton University Press, 1986).

47. Nowell-Smith's *The Oxford History of World Cinema,* a wide-ranging collection of articles that covers the first one hundred years of world cinema, is evidence of both the highly specialized and professionalized nature of the field and the increasing prevalence of the edited anthology as a teaching tool. In his introduction to the Oxford collection, Nowell-Smith puts the matter in practical terms: "The sheer diversity of world cinema, the number of films made (many of which do not circulate outside national borders), and the variety of cultural and political contexts in which the world's cinemas have emerged, means that it would be foolish or arrogant, or both, for any one person to attempt to encompass the entire history of cinema single-handed. This is not just a question of knowledge but also of perspective" (xx).

48. Erik S. Lunde and Douglas A. Noverr make this point in their introduction to *Film Studies* (New York: Marcus Wiener, 1989). Indeed, they title the final section of their collection of syllabi and course materials "Interdisciplinary and Cultural Approaches to Film."

49. David Bordwell, *On the History of Film Style* (Cambridge, Mass.: Harvard University Press, 1997), 118.

50. Jack C. Ellis, *A History of Film,* 6 eds. (the last two with Virginia Wright Wexman) (Englewood Cliffs, N.J.: Prentice-Hall, 1979, 1985, 1990, 1995; Boston: Allyn and Bacon, 2002, 2006); David A. Cook, *A History of Narrative Film,* 4 eds. (New York: Norton, 1982, 1992, 1996, 2004); David Shipman, *The Story of Cinema,* 2 vols. (London: Hodder and Stoughton, 1982); Douglas Gomery, *Movie History: A Survey*

(Belmont, Calif.: Wadsworth, 1991); Robert Sklar, *Film: An International History of the Medium,* 2 eds. (Englewood Cliffs, N.J.: Prentice Hall, 1993, 2001); Kristin Thompson and David Bordwell, *Film History: An Introduction,* 2 eds. (New York: McGraw-Hill, 1994, 2003).

51. Peter Brunette and David Wills, *Screen/Play: Derrida and Film Theory* (Princeton, N.J.: Princeton University Press, 1989), 33.

52. Ibid., 34.

53. Jeanne Thomas Allen, "Film History: A Revisionist Perspective," *Journal of University Film and Video Association* 35, no. 4 (1983): 5.

54. Ibid., 6.

55. See, as overviews, Shohat and Stam, *Unthinking Eurocentrism,* and *Multiculturalism, Postcoloniality, and Transnational Media* (New Brunswick, N.J.: Rutgers University Press, 2003).

56. Isaac Julien and Kobena Mercer, "Introduction: De Margin and De Centre," *Screen* 29, no. 4 (autumn 1988): 2.

57. Ibid., 3, 6.

58. David Bordwell and Noël Carroll, eds., *Post-Theory: Reconstructing Film Studies* (Madison: University of Wisconsin Press, 1996).

59. Ian Christie, "Canon Fodder," *Sight and Sound* 2, no. 8 (1992): 31–33; Geoffrey Nowell-Smith, "New Concepts of Cinema," in *The Oxford History of World Cinema,* 758–59.

60. Here is Stanley Aronowitz's version of that process: "Products of a culture industry are appropriated by an emerging critical group, the members of which have 'discovered' among the welter of film commodities a few nuggets that qualify as Art. A few directors and their films are anointed with the status of canonical works, about which issue a plethora of studies, commentaries, and theoretical writings which, together, elaborate the aesthetic criteria that mark status in an otherwise banal field that may be called mass-audience culture. Gradually, there are enough critical works about Great Films, their directors and their styles, to develop a canonical bibliography, enough to constitute reading lists from which to transmit a *tradition.* Gradually, the members of the academy, rather than the newspaper and magazine critics, are the official arbiters of taste. In the case of film . . . some of the academics are recruited from among journalists. However, a fairly large cohort hold degrees in English or other language disciplines. Others hold degrees from the subdiscipline of American Studies. . . . Typically, they bring with them the methodological precepts of their 'native' discipline and impose it on film" (Aronowitz, *Roll Over Beethoven: The Return of Cultural Strife* [Hanover, N.H.: Wesleyan University Press, 1993], 172–73).

For other accounts of the development of academic film studies, see Dudley Andrew, "The 'Three Ages' of Cinema Studies and the Age to Come," *PMLA* 115, no. 3 (2000): 341–51; David Bordwell, *Making Meaning,* 19–29; and Robert B. Ray, "The Bordwell Regime and the Stakes of Knowledge," in *How a Film Theory Got Lost and Other Mysteries in Cultural Studies* (Bloomington and Indianapolis: Indiana University Press, 2001), 57–58.

61. Bordwell, *On the History of Film Style,* 6–7.

62. Ibid., 9.

63. Eric de Kuyper argues a similar point: "For the segmentation and categorization of their objective(s) film historians work with notions such as: 'nationality', 'year of production', 'director' (with that special category or niche: the 'author') and 'actors'. Then come notions of 'style', 'genre', 'school', or 'studio'. All these notions, which enable the film historian to set the film in an aesthetic frame (with perhaps the exception of 'studio') come from the history of art or the history of literature" (de Kuyper, "Anyone for an Aesthetic of Film History?" *Film History* 6, no. 1 [spring 1994]: 104).

64. Barry Keith Grant, introduction to *Film Study in the Undergraduate Curriculum,* ed. Grant (New York: Modern Language Association, 1983), x.

65. Charles F. [Rick] Altman, "Towards a Historiography of American Film," *Cinema Journal* 16, no. 2 (spring 1977): 1–25; Allen and Gomery, *Film History: Theory and Practice,* passim; Thompson and Bordwell, "Introduction: Film History and How It Is Done," in *Film History: An Introduction,* 5.

66. Paul Rotha, *The Film till Now: A Survey of World Cinema* (London: Jonathan Cape, 1930); Benjamin Hampton, *History of the American Film Industry* (New York: Covici, Friede, 1931); Maurice Bardèche and Robert Brasillach, *Histoire du cinéma* (Paris: Denoël and Steele, 1935), trans. and ed. by Iris Barry as *The History of Motion Pictures* (New York: Norton / MoMA, 1938).

67. Bordwell, *On the History of Film Style,* 40–41, 281 n. 94.

68. See Mary Jane Green, "Fascists on Film: The Brasillach and Bardèche *Histoire du cinéma,*" in *Fascism, Aesthetics, and Culture,* ed. Richard J. Golsan (Hanover, N.H.: University Press of New England, 1992), 164–78.

69. D. N. Rodowick, "A Genealogy of Time: The Nietzschean Dimension of French Cinema, 1958–1998," in *Premises: Invested Spaces in Visual Arts, Architecture, and Design in France, 1958–1998* (New York: Guggenheim Museum Publications, 1998), 68; emphasis in original.

70. Ibid.

71. This tripartite periodization is not new. Lewis Jacobs's edited collection *The Emergence of Film Art* (New York: Hopkinson and Blake, 1969) relied on it as well, although for Jacobs modern cinema (which he refers to in his heading as "The Creative Present") begins in 1950 rather than 1960. Periodization may thus rely on sliding historical criteria; technological and sociohistorical shifts are much more stable markers than stylistic ones.

72. The concepts of genealogy and archaeology appear throughout Foucault's writings, but the most important theoretical statements on their strategic deployment are to be found in his *The Archaeology of Knowledge,* trans. A. M. Sheridan Smith (New York: Pantheon, 1972), and the essay "Nietzsche, Genealogy, History," in *Language, Counter-Memory, Practice: Selected Essays and Interviews,* ed. Donald F. Bouchard, trans. Donald F. Bouchard and Sherry Simon (Ithaca, N.Y.: Cornell University Press, 1977), 139–64. Foucault's critique of the "solemnities of the origin" may be found in "Nietzsche, Genealogy, History," 142–45.

73. Bordwell, *On the History of Film Style,* 20.

74. I have drawn upon the significant literature on nationalism throughout this book. The most influential works have been Hugh Seton-Watson, *Nations and States:*

An Enquiry into the Origins of Nations and the Politics of Nationalism (London: Methuen, 1977); Benedict Anderson, *Imagined Communities: Reflections on the Origin and Spread of Nationalism* (London: Verso, 1983); Ernest Gellner, *Nations and Nationalism* (Ithaca, N.Y.: Cornell University Press, 1983); John Breuilly, *Nationalism and the State* (Chicago: University of Chicago Press, 1985); and Homi K. Bhabha, ed., *Nation and Narration* (London: Routledge, 1990).

75. See the following: Philip Rosen, "History, Textuality, Nation: Kracauer, Burch, and Some Problems in the Study of National Cinemas," *Iris* 2, no. 2 (1984): 69–84, and "Nation and Anti-Nation: Concepts of National Cinema in the 'New' Media Era," *Disapora* 5, no. 3 (1996): 375–402; Andrew Higson, "The Concept of National Cinema," *Screen* 30, no. 4 (1989): 36–46; Stephen Crofts, "Reconceptualizing National Cinema/s," *Quarterly Review of Film and Video* 14, no. 3 (1993): 49–67; Thomas Elsaesser, "ImpersoNations: National Cinema, Historical Imaginaries," in *European Cinema: Face to Face with Hollywood* (Amsterdam: Amsterdam University Press, 2003), 57–81. Several of these, alongside other important analyses of the nation in relation to cinema, appear in three collections: *Cinema and Nation,* ed. Mette Hjort and Scott MacKenzie (London and New York: Routledge, 2000); *Film and Nationalism,* ed. Alan Williams (New Brunswick, N.J.: Rutgers University Press, 2001); and *Theorizing National Cinema,* ed. Valentina Vitali and Paul Willemen (London: British Film Institute, 2006).

76. Higson, "The Concept of National Cinema," 37. Higson extends this line, arguing that "the concept of the 'transnational' may be a subtler means of describing cultural and economic formations that are rarely contained by national borders," in "The Limiting Imagination of National Cinema," in Hjort and MacKenzie, *Cinema and Nation,* 64.

77. The authors and titles are as follows: John Caughie, with Kevin Rockett, *The Companion to British and Irish Cinema;* Thomas Elsaesser, *The Companion to German Cinema;* Geoffrey Nowell-Smith, with James Hay and Gianni Volpi, ed., *The Companion to Italian Cinema;* Ginette Vincendeau, *The Companion to French Cinema.* The British Film Institute has also published complete histories of three national cinemas in the form of edited collections: *The British Cinema Book,* ed. Robert Murphy (1997, 2001); *The German Cinema Book,* ed. Tim Bergfelder and Erica Carter (2002); *The French Cinema Book,* ed. Michael Temple and Michael Witt (2004).

78. http://www.wallflowerpress.co.uk/.

79. *The Cinema of Italy,* ed. Giorgio Bertellini (London and New York: Wallflower Press, 2004); *The Cinema of France,* ed. Phil Powrie (2006).

80. Marcia Landy, *Italian Film* (Cambridge, UK: Cambridge University Press, 2000); Jim Leach, *British Film* (Cambridge, UK: Cambridge University Press, 2004).

81. Susan Hayward, *French National Cinema* (1993, 2005); Pierre Sorlin, *Italian National Cinema 1896–1996* (1996); Tim O'Regan, *Australian National Cinema* (1997); Sarah Street, *British National Cinema* (1997); Tytti Soila, Astrid Söderbergh Widding, and Gunnar Iversen, *Nordic National Cinemas* (1998).

82. Jay Leyda, *Kino: A History of the Russian and Soviet Film,* 3rd ed. (Princeton, N.J.: Princeton University Press, 1983), 366.

83. Leyda claims that the second album was exhibited in North and South America as *This Is the Enemy*. Based on the 15 July 1942 *Variety* review for *This Is the Enemy*, which was shown in early July 1942 at the Stanley in New York City, this is partially the case. The review describes *This Is the Enemy* as comprising eight episodes, including all of *Album 2*, one from *Album 1 (Three in a Shell-Hole)*, and two other episodes from other albums.

84. Neya Zorkaya, *The Illustrated History of the Soviet Cinema* (New York: Hippocrene Books, 1989), 174–75.

85. Leyda, *Kino*, 366. Eisenstein's interest in Bierce as a model would be realized two decades later in Robert Enrico's *Au coeur de la vie*, a 1962 episode film of three adaptations of Bierce stories, one of which—*An Occurrence at Owl Creek Bridge*—won an award at Cannes and an Oscar in Hollywood and would become a mainstay of "Introduction to the Art of Film" courses for the next two decades.

86. See Peter Kenez, *Cinema and Soviet Society, 1917–1953* (Cambridge, UK: Cambridge University Press, 1992), 193–94.

87. "Five Films—40 Directors and Scriptwriters," in *Films from Norway 2/96* (Oslo: Norwegian Film Institute, 1996), n.p.

88. *Norwegian Feature Films 1998* (Oslo: Norwegian Film Institute, 1998), 2, 44.

89. *Variety*, 30 May 1962, 6.

90. Bosley Crowther, review of *Love at Twenty, New York Times,* 7 February 1963, 6(5).

91. Higson, "The Concept of National Cinema," 44.

92. Crofts, "Reconceptualizing National Cinema/s," 60–64.

93. David Bordwell and Kristin Thompson, *Film Art: An Introduction,* 7th ed. (New York: McGraw-Hill, 2004), 464.

94. Pam Cook, ed., *The Cinema Book,* 3rd ed. (London: British Film Institute, 2007). See also Jill Nelmes, ed., *An Introduction to Film Studies,* 4 eds. (London: Routledge, 1996, 1999, 2003, 2007), and John Hill and Pamela Church Gibson, eds., *The Oxford Guide to Film Studies* (New York: Oxford University Press, 1998).

95. See Metz, *Language and Cinema,* trans. Donna Jean Umiker Sebeok (The Hague: Mouton, 1974), 12. Metz attributes Gilbert Cohen-Séat as the originator of this distinction in 1946; see Cohen Séat, *Essais sur les principes d'une philosophie du cinéma,* new ed. (Paris: Presses Universitaires de France, 1958), 53 ff.

96. Susan Hayward, *Cinema Studies: The Key Concepts,* 3rd ed. (London and New York: Routledge, 2006), 122–23.

97. Bordwell and Thompson, *Film Art: An Introduction,* 505.

98. Bordwell, Staiger, and Thompson, *The Classical Hollywood Cinema,* xiii.

99. Staiger, "The Hollywood Mode of Production: Its Conditions of Existence," in *The Classical Hollywood Cinema,* 89.

100. Allen and Gomery, *Film History: Theory and Practice,* 86.

101. The quoted phrase is from a news release for *La Chinoise* (1967) penned by Godard and reprinted as "Manifesto" in *Godard on Godard: Critical Writings by Jean-Luc Godard,* ed. and trans. Tom Milne (New York: Da Capo Press, 1972), 243.

102. See Rick Altman, *Film/Genre* (London: British Film Institute, 1999).

103. Edward Buscombe, "The Idea of Genre in the American Cinema," *Screen* 11, no. 2 (1970), rpt. in *Film Genre Reader II,* ed. Barry Keith Grant (Austin: University of Texas Press, 1986), 11.

104. Christine Gledhill, "Introduction" to "History of Genre Criticism," in Cook, *The Cinema Book,* 252–59. Gledhill's brief yet useful historical narrative refers to a number of key texts in genre study. See especially Robert Warshow, "The Gangster as Tragic Hero," *Partisan Review* (1948), rpt. in *The Immediate Experience* (New York: Atheneum, 1970), 127–33, and "Movie Chronicle: The Westerner," also in *The Immediate Experience,* 35–54; André Bazin, "The Western: Or the American Film Par Excellence," in *What Is Cinema? vol. 2,* ed. and trans. Hugh Gray (Berkeley: University of California Press, 1971), 140–48, and "The Evolution of the Western," also in *What Is Cinema? vol. 2:* 149–57; Tom Ryall, "The Notion of Genre," *Screen* 11, no. 2 (1970): 22–32; Stephen Neale, *Genre* (London: British Film Institute, 1980).

105. See especially Jim Kitses, *Horizon's West* (London: Thames and Hudson / British Film Institute, 1969); Colin McArthur, *Underworld USA* (London: Secker and Warburg / British Film Institute, 1972); Jean-Loup Bourget, "Social Implications of the Hollywood Genres," *Journal of Modern Literature* 3, no. 2 (April 1973): 191–200; Barbara Klinger, "'Cinema/Ideology/Criticism'—The Progressive Text," *Screen* 25, no. 1 (January–February 1984): 30–44.

106. Brunette and Wills, *Screen/Play,* 45. See also Jacques Derrida, "The Law of Genre," *Glyph* 7 (1980): 202–32.

107. Andrew Tudor, "Genre," in *Theories of Film* (New York: Viking, 1973), rpt. in Grant, *Film Genre Reader II,* 5.

108. Rick Altman complicated this model in "A Semantic/Syntactic Approach to Film Genre," *Cinema Journal* 23, no. 3 (spring 1984): 6–18, rpt. in Grant, *Film Genre Reader II,* 26–40.

109. See Altman, "Are Genres Stable?" and "Why Are Genres Sometimes Mixed?" in *Film/Genre,* 49–68, 123–43.

110. Betz, "Film History, Film Genre, and Their Discontents," 73–82.

111. http://www.loc.gov/rr/mopic/migintro.html. See also Brian Taves, "Toward a Comprehensive Genre Taxonomy," *Moving Image* 1, no. 1 (spring 2001): 131–50.

112. Altman, *Film/Genre,* 123–43.

113. For other overviews see the pieces collected by and the editorial commentary of John Caughie in *Theories of Authorship: A Reader* (London: Routledge, 1981); Robert Lapsley and Michael Westlake, "Authorship," in *Film Theory: An Introduction* (Manchester, UK: Manchester University Press, 1988), 105–28; Pam Cook, "Authorship and Cinema," in Cook, *The Cinema Book,* 387–483; and Mitsuhiro Yoshimoto, *Kurosawa: Film Studies and Japanese Cinema,* 29–37.

Andrew Sarris's *The American Cinema: Directors and Directions, 1929–1968* (New York: Dutton, 1968) expanded on his pro-American version of auteurism and proved as influential as *Cahiers' politique des auteurs* for the course of Anglo-American film studies, its entries and filmographies of American directors serving as a checklist for the first generation of academically trained film students. European auteurs are relegated in this book to a category titled "Fringe Benefits."

114. Andrew Sarris, "Notes on the Auteur Theory in 1962," *Film Culture,* no. 27 (winter 1962–63): 5. For an early, scathing critique of Sarris, see Pauline Kael, "Circles and Squares," *Film Quarterly* 16, no. 3 (spring 1963): 12–26.

115. Sarris, "Notes on the Auteur Theory in 1962," 8.

116. Sarris, review of *Spirits of the Dead, Village Voice,* 11 September 1969, rpt. in *Confessions of a Cultist: On the Cinema, 1955/1969* (New York: Simon and Schuster, 1971), 459.

117. Caughie, *Theories of Authorship,* 200; Pam Cook, "Authorship," in *The Cinema Book,* ed. Cook (London and New York: British Film Institute / Pantheon Books, 1985), 116.

118. "Editorial," *Screen* 12, no. 3 (1971): 11.

119. Bordwell, *Making Meaning,* 53, 97–104.

120. Florence Jacobowitz and Richard Lippe, eds., "Rethinking Authorship," *CineAction!* (summer–fall 1990): 21–22; James Naremore, "Authorship and the Cultural Politics of Film Criticism," *Film Quarterly* 44, no. 1 (fall 1990): 14–22.

121. See especially Timothy Corrigan, "The Commerce of Auteurism: Coppola, Kluge, Ruiz," in *A Cinema without Walls: Movies and Culture after Vietnam* (New Brunswick, N.J.: Rutgers University Press, 1991), 101–36, and his "Auteurs and the New Hollywood," in *The New American Cinema,* ed. Jon Lewis (Durham, N.C.: Duke University Press, 1998), 38–63; Dudley Andrew, "The Unauthorized Auteur Today," in *Film Theory Goes to the Movies,* ed. Jim Collins, Hilary Radner, and Ava Preacher Collins (New York: Routledge, 1993), 77–85; Stephen Crofts, "Authorship and Hollywood," in Hill and Church Gibson, *The Oxford Guide to Film Studies,* 310–24; Dana Polan, "Auteur Desire," *Screening the Past,* no. 12, http://www.latrobe.edu.au/www/ screeningthepast/firstrelease/fr0301/dpfr12a.htm; Virginia Wright Wexman, ed. *Film and Authorship* (New Brunswick, N.J.: Rutgers University Press, 2003); David A. Gerstner and Janet Staiger, eds., *Authorship and Film* (New York and London: Routledge, 2003); Thomas Elsaesser, "European Culture, National Cinema, the Auteur, and Hollywood," in *European Cinema: Face to Face with Hollywood,* 35–56.

122. Having lived in London since summer 2001, I will use the programming of the National Film Theatre (NFT) as an example. From June 2001 to December 2006, the NFT offered seasons organized under several rubrics, though none appearing with anything like the frequency and volume of seasons dedicated to individual directors, of which there were 72—fully one-third of the aggregate. Of these, the ones on Michelangelo Antonioni, Valie Export, Jean-Luc Godard, Werner Herzog, Krzysztof Kieslowski, Marcel Ophuls, and Roman Polanski did not screen their contributions from some eight omnibus films. Episodes programmed as shorts preceding other of the directors' feature films include Godard's from *RoGoPaG, Paris vu par, Far from Vietnam,* and *Aria* (1988); Eric Rohmer's from *Paris vu par;* Ingmar Bergman's from *Stimulantia* (1967); Henri-Georges Clouzot's from *Retour à la vie;* and Victor Erice's from *Los desafios* (1969). There were three special short programs: "Visconti—on Work, Witches and Women," featuring his contributions to *Siamo donne, Boccaccio '70,* and *Le streghe;* "Antonioni Shorts (1943–1953)," which included *Attempted Suicide* from *Love in the City;* and "Compilation Short Films" in the Godard retrospective,

culling episodes from *Les 7 péchés capitaux* (*7 Capital Sins*, 1962), *Les Plus belles escroqueries du monde* (*The Beautiful Swindlers*, 1964), *Le Plus vieux métier du monde* (*The Oldest Profession*, 1967), and *Amore e rabbia*. Only five omnibus films were shown in their entirety: *Days of Glory* in the Visconti retrospective; *Love in the City* (all six episodes), *Boccaccio '70* (all four episodes), and *Spirits of the Dead* in the Federico Fellini; and *La Vie est à nous* in the Jean Renoir.

123. Maurizio Viano, *A Certain Realism: Making Use of Pasolini's Film Theory and Practice* (Berkeley: University of California Press, 1993), 162.

124. Naomi Greene, *Pier Paolo Pasolini: Cinema as Heresy* (Princeton, N.J.: Princeton University Press, 1990), 67.

125. See Pasolini's own comments in this regard in *Pasolini on Pasolini*, ed. and trans. Oswald Stack (Bloomington: Indiana University Press, 1970), 59, 111–12.

126. Corrigan, "Introduction" to *New German Film: The Displaced Image* (Austin: University of Texas Press, 1983), xi; emphasis in original.

127. Ibid., 18, 20.

128. Eric Rentschler, "Life with Fassbinder: The Politics of Fear and Pain," *Discourse* 5 (1983): 75–90.

129. John Sandford, *The New German Cinema* (New York: Da Capo Press, 1980), 147–48; Anton Kaes, *From Hitler to Heimat: The Return of History as Film* (Cambridge, Mass.: Harvard University Press, 1989), 25–27; Miriam Hansen, "Cooperative Auteur Cinema and Oppositional Public Sphere: Alexander Kluge's Contribution to *Germany in Autumn*," *New German Critique* 24–25 (fall–winter 1981–82): 46, 47.

130. It is interesting in this regard to note the difficulty that has existed in pinning down the directorial credits for collectively produced political omnibus films like *La Vie est à nous* and *Germany in Autumn*, which vary from scholar to scholar. Thompson and Bordwell, for example, reckon as fourteen the number of directors involved in making *Germany in Autumn* (*Film History: An Introduction*, 576). Hansen lists nine ("Cooperative Auteur Cinema and Oppositional Public Sphere," 45). The critical consensus seems to be with Corrigan, who states that the film features "the work of eleven German directors" (*New German Film*, 17; see also Robert Fischer and Joe Hembus, *Der neue deutsche Film: 1960–1980* [Munich: Goldmann Verlag, 1981], 144). The variations are more extensive for *La Vie est à nous;* see Betz, "Film History, Film Genre, and Their Discontents," 83, n. 10.

131. For a positive personal recollection of the film's premiere at the 1967 New York Film Festival, see Jonathan Rosenbaum, "Is the Cinema Really Dead?" in *Movie Wars: How Hollywood and the Media Limit What Movies We Can See* (Chicago: A Cappella Books, 2000), 33–35.

132. Bosley Crowther, review of *Far from Vietnam*, *New York Times*, 2 October 1967, 58(1); review of *Far from Vietnam*, *Variety*, 4 October 1967, 12.

133. Renata Adler, review of *Far from Vietnam*, *New York Times*, 11 June 1968, 54(4).

134. Sarris, review of *Far from Vietnam*, *Village Voice*, 12 October 1967, rpt. in *Confessions of a Cultist*, 317, 318.

135. Richard Winkler, review of *Far from Vietnam*, *Movie* 15 (1968): 34.

136. Ibid., 35.

137. Lunde and Noverr, *Film Studies,* 4.

138. See David Scott Diffrient, "An Olympic Omnibus: International Competition, Cooperation, and Politics in *Visions of Eight,*" *Film and History* 35, no. 2 (2005): 19–28.

139. See Joris Ivens, *The Camera and I* (New York: International Publishers, 1969), 272–73.

140. Women's collective filmmaking in the omnibus mode is notable as well from the 1970s in Australia (*Ladies' Rooms* [1977], *Women from Down Under* [1998]) and especially in Canada: *A qui appartient ce gage?* (1973), *Love* (1982), *Martha, Ruth & Edie* (1988), *Five Feminist Minutes* (1990). The last of these was created to celebrate the fifteenth anniversary of the National Film Board of Canada's women's unit, Studio D. Of the 240 submissions, sixteen proposals by as many women filmmakers were selected, each of whom was given $10,000 and 600 feet of 16mm film to make a five-minute film.

141. The films in question are, for Maughan, *Quartet* (1949), *Trio* (1950), and *Encore* (1952); *O. Henry's Full House* (1952); *Kurt Vonnegut's Monkey House, Vols. 1 & 2* (1993); for Abdel-Qadas, *Al Banaat wa Al-Saif* (Girls and Summer, 1960); *Three Tales of Chekhov* (1961); for Hrabal, *Pearls of the Deep;* for Škvorecký, *Zločin v dívčí škole* (*Crime in the Girls' School,* 1965); *Cuentos de Borges I* (*Borges Tales, Part I,* 1991); for Hamsun, *1997: Thirst—Crimes of the Future;* and for Soseki, *Yume juya* (*Ten Nights of Dreams,* 2006).

142. Respectively, *Due occhi diabolici* (*Two Evil Eyes,* Italy/United States, 1990); *Maldoror* (UK/Germany, 2000); *Halbmond* (*Paul Bowles: Halfmoon,* Germany, 1995); *Esercizi di stile* (*Exercises in Style,* Italy, 1996).

143. See Michel Marie, *The French New Wave: An Artistic School,* trans. Richard Neupert (London: Blackwell Publishing, 2003), 84; Richard Neupert, *A History of the French New Wave Cinema* (Madison: University of Wisconsin Press, 2002), 267.

144. This nostalgia for *Paris vu par* has been picked up elsewhere by filmmakers who have since the late 1980s mined its concept to pay homage to other cities in their countries; examples include *New York Stories* (1989), *Montréal vu par . . . six variations sur un thème* (*Montreal Sextet,* 1991), *Tel Aviv Stories* (1993), *Praha očima* (*Prague Stories,* 1999), *Six in Austin* (2002), and *Amlat İnstanbul* (*Istanbul Tales,* 2005).

145. Leprohon, *The Italian Cinema,* 182–83.

146. Betz, "Art, exploitation, underground," passim.

147. For an early critique of this tendency, see Pauline Kael, "Fantasies of the Art House Audience," *Sight and Sound* 31, no. 1 (winter 1961/62): 5–9.

148. On the intersections between art cinema and sexploitation, see Eric Schaefer, "Conclusion: The End of Classical Exploitation," in *"Bold! Daring! Shocking! True!": A History of Exploitation Films, 1919–1959* (Durham, N.C.: Duke University Press, 1999), 32–42; Joan Hawkins, "Sleaze-mania, Euro-trash, and High Art: The Place of European Art Films in American Low Culture," in *Cutting Edge: Art-Horror and the Horrific Avant-Garde* (Minneapolis: University of Minnesota Press, 2000), 3–32; Jack Stevenson, "And God Created Europe: How the European Sexual Myth Was Created

and Sold to Post-war American Movie Audiences," in *Fleshpot: Cinema's Sexual Myth Makers and Taboo Breakers,* ed. Jack Stevenson (Manchester, UK: Critical Mission, 2002), 17–48; Elena Gorfinkel, "Radley Metzger's 'Elegant Arousal': Taste, Aesthetic Distinction, and Sexploitation," in *Underground U.S.A.: Filmmaking beyond the Hollywood Canon,* ed. Xavier Mendik and Steven Jay Schneider (London and New York: Wallflower Press, 2002), 26–39. On pornography, see Linda Williams, *Hard Core: Power, Pleasure, and the "Frenzy of the Visible"* (Berkeley and Los Angeles: University of California Press, 1989); Laurence O'Toole, *Pornocopia: Porn, Sex, Technology and Desire* (London: Serpent's Tail, 1998); Linda Williams, ed., *Porn Studies* (Durham, N.C.: Duke University Press, 2004).

149. This counterpantheon would include Dario Argento, Mario Bava, Coffin Joe (José Mojica Marins), David Cronenberg, Lucio Fulci, Jess Franco, Jean Rollin, and George A. Romero. For studies of European art/horror interchanges, see Leon Hunt, "A (Sadistic) Night at the Opera: Notes on the Italian Horror Film," *Velvet Light Trap,* no. 30 (fall 1992): 65–75; Carol Jenks, "*Daughters of Darkness:* A Lesbian Vampire Art Film," *Necronomicon, Book One,* ed. Andy Black (London: Creation Books, 1996), 22–34; Hawkins, *Cutting Edge,* passim; Andy Willis, "Spanish Horror and the Flight from 'Art' Cinema, 1967–73," in Jancovich et al., *Defining Cult Movies,* 71–83, and "Italian Horror Cinema: Between Art and Exploitation," in *Italian Cinema: New Directions,* ed. William Hope (Oxford, UK: Peter Lang, 2005), 109–30; Peter Hutchings, "The Argento Effect," in *Defining Cult Movies,* 127–41; Ernest Mathijs and Xavier Mendik, eds., *Alternative Europe: Eurotrash and Exploitation Cinema since 1945* (London and New York: Wallflower Press, 2004).

150. *Oldboy's* director, Park Chan-wook, subsequently contributed to a pan-Asian horror omnibus that enjoyed widespread consumption in its DVD form, *Saam gaang yi* (*Three . . . Extremes,* 2004).

151. Hayward, *French National Cinema,* 50.

152. See Sorlin, "Fifth Generation: The World in a Box," in *Italian National Cinema, 1896–1996,* 144–64, and Dorota Ostrowska and Graham Roberts, eds., *European Cinemas in the Television Age* (Edinburgh, UK: Edinburgh University Press, 2007).

153. Thomas Elsaesser, "The New German Cinema," in *European Cinema,* ed. Elizabeth Ezra (Oxford, UK: Oxford University Press, 2004), 202, 210. See also Elsaesser, *New German Cinema: A History* (New Brunswick, N.J.: Rutgers University Press, 1989), 32–35, 108–16.

154. Linda Williams, "Film Bodies: Gender, Genre, and Excess," *Film Quarterly* 44, no. 4 (summer 1991): 2–13, rpt. in Grant, *Film Genre Reader II,* 140–58.

155. For examinations of new media technologies and spectatorship/consumption, see Thomas Elsaesser and Kay Hoffmann, eds., *Cinema Futures: Cain, Abel or Cable* (Amsterdam: Amsterdam University Press, 1998), 9–26; Frederick Wasser, *Veni, Vidi, Video: The Hollywood Empire and the VCR* (Austin: University of Texas Press, 2001); Mark Jancovich and Lucy Faire with Sarah Stubbings, *The Place of the Audience: Cultural Geographies of Film Consumption* (London: British Film Institute, 2003), 154–250; Barbara Klinger, *Beyond the Multiplex: Cinema, New Technologies, and the Home* (Berkeley: University of California Press, 2006); Henry Jenkins, *Convergence Culture:*

Where Old and New Media Collide (New York and London: New York University Press, 2006).

156. U.S. Supreme Court, Joseph Burstyn, Inc. v. Wilson, 343 U.S. 495 (1952). For more on *The Miracle* case and its effects, see Richard S. Randall, "Censorship: From *The Miracle* to *Deep Throat,*" in *The American Film Industry,* ed. Tino Balio, rev. ed. (Madison: University of Wisconsin Press, 1985), 510–36; Garth Jowett, "'A Significant Medium for the Communication of Ideas': The *Miracle* Decision and the Decline of Motion Picture Censorship, 1952–1968," in *Movie Censorship and American Culture,* ed. Francis G. Couvares (Washington, D.C.: Smithsonian Institution Press, 1996), 258–76; Jon Lewis, *Hollywood v. Hardcore: How the Struggle over Censorship Saved the Modern Film Industry* (New York and London: New York University Press, 2000), 97–105.

157. See, for example, review of *Ways of Love, Variety,* 12 December 1950; Bosley Crowther, review of *Ways of Love, New York Times,* 13 December 1950, 50(2), and "Short-Story Movie," *New York Times,* 17 December 1950; Wanda Hale, "The Paris Presents Rare Movie Program," *New York Daily News,* 13 December 1950, 82.

158. See Lewis, *Hollywood v. Hardcore,* 135–229.

159. These DVDs include *Urban Visions* (*Stadtvisionen/Visions urbanes,* 2002), *Cinema different/Different Cinema, Vols. 1 & 2* (2005–06), and *City2City* and *Resistance(s)* (both 2006).

160. See, for example, Anne Friedberg, "The End of Cinema: Multi-media and Technological Change," in *Reinventing Film Studies,* ed. Christine Gledhill and Linda Williams (London: Arnold, 2000), 438–52.

Index

MARK BETZ is senior lecturer in film studies at King's College, University of London.